# Month-By-Month
# GARDENING IN NEW YORK

Cataloging in Publication Data is available
ISBN: 1-59186-111-X

Published by Cool Springs Press, a Division of Thomas Nelson, Inc.,
P.O. Box 141000, Nashville, Tennessee 37214

First printing 2005

Printed in the United States of America
10 9 8 7 6 5 4 3 2 1

Managing Editor: Cindy Kershner
Designer: James Duncan Creative
Horticulture Editor: Troy Marden
Illustrator: Bill Kersey, Kersey Graphics
Production Artist: S.E. Anderson

On the cover: *Paeonia lobata* (peregrina) 'Claire Viette', photo by André Viette

Cool Springs Press books may be purchased in bulk for educational, business, fundraising, or
sales promotional use. For information, please email **SpecialMarkets@ThomasNelson.com.**

Visit the Thomas Nelson website at **www.ThomasNelson.com** and the Cool Springs Press
website at **www.coolspringspress.net**

# Month-By-Month
# GARDENING IN NEW YORK

### ANDRÉ & MARK VIETTE
#### WITH JACQUELINE HÉRITEAU

COOL SPRINGS PRESS
A Division of Thomas Nelson Publishers
*Since 1798*

# Dedication

I dedicate this book to my mother and father, Jessie and Martin Viette, who instilled in me strong family values, a good work ethic, and a deep love of plants.

# Acknowledgements

I want to thank the many people who have touched my life and made me a better person. Especially my wife, Claire, who has been by my side throughout my career and has given me such wonderful children—Mark, Scott, Holly, and Heather. And my son Mark, who works with me daily in the nursery, shares teaching duties with me at Blue Ridge Community College, and has been such an important part of the "In the Garden" radio programs. It has been a wonderful partnership. And my father, a great plantsman, who passed on to me his keen knowledge of plants and their culture. I also wish to thank the many fine professors at Cornell University who helped mold my scientific mind. Rachel Carson changed my approach to the way we use our planet when I met her when I was just 24 years old. And I wish to recognize all my fellow members, past and present, of the New York Hortus Club, members who through the years have represented the finest in horticulture from New York City, New York, Connecticut, and New Jersey. And finally, my very good friend and fellow author, Jacqueline Hériteau. Jacqui is a knowledgeable gardener and author of many distinguished books in the field of gardening. She is fabulous to work with and has the organization and work ethic to get things done.

André Viette
Fishersville, Virginia

# Contents

# Contents

# Introduction

## *The Benefits of a Month-By-Month Gardening Schedule*

You are not alone when you garden. Mother Nature is your partner, a very senior partner, and a record of how, when, and what she does will help answer questions you will ask yourself in the years ahead. The eleven month-by-month plant chapters that follow cover a year in the life of each type of garden plant, starting with Annuals and ending with Water Gardening. It's based on our own garden logs, and we hope you will make it the basis for yours by writing all over it, tucking in catalog pages, and attaching memos, plant names, nursery receipts, and how-to articles.

If you make it your own personal gardening guide, here's how it will help. A record of the microclimates in your garden teaches lessons you can use year after year. Your record of when you divide a perennial is a better guide than memory when slow flower production is suggesting it may be time to divide again. A reliable record of where you placed what plants answers questions that come up the next year and years later. It helps locate the name of a species or variety you can't remember. Last year's notes also can tell you where to look for the tulips you planted 10 to 12 inches deep to outwit the voles.

To get you thinking about memos to make to yourself, we've included garden log prompts in the Planning sections of Chapter 1, Annuals.

## GOOD GARDENING PRACTICES

For new gardeners and for gardeners new to the long, cold winters in Zones 3, 4, and 5, we have good news . . . in spite of our short growing season, we grow all the best-loved temperate zone plants, indoors if need be.

In Zone 7, at the Viette Nursery on the north shore of Long Island (where, when he was five years old, André already was beginning to realize how plants flourish in the uniquely fertile soil there), spring comes two or three weeks earlier than it does just a few miles inland, on the mainland, or next to the Great Lakes, which are all Zone 6. But in the cool upstate zones you can have **hyacinths, daffodils,** and **forsythia** blooming in February and March by forcing them indoors. They won't bloom outdoors until April or May, and gardeners have to wait until May and early June to set out **petunias, basil, tomatoes,** and other cold-tender plants. Even so, by planting varieties that mature early, you can have sun-ripened **tomatoes** by mid-July—just as gardeners do on Long Island.

In other words, you can grow almost anything here really worth having by:

- Planting cold-hardy species and varieties;

- Providing winter protection for **roses** and **shrubs** whose hardiness is iffy in your zone;

- Lengthening the growing season by setting out plants started early in a nursery or by you;

- Treating cold-tender plants such as **geraniums** and **canna** and tropical **water lilies** as annuals, or wintering them in a frost-free location;

- Making room indoors to winter over cold-tender perennials, and forcing the blooming of spring-flowering bulbs and branches;

# Introduction

## Did You Know?

### What Plant Names Can Tell You

Botanical plant names, which are in Latin—the language of science when the first herbals were written—tell you a lot about a plant.

A plant tag that reads *Picea abies* forma *pendula* is saying this is a **Weeping Norway Spruce**. *Picea*, means spruce, the genus, or overall group; *abies* means a species or category of spruce that came from Norway*; pendula* says this variety is pendulous or weeping. Names between single quotes, like *Spiraea japonica* 'Anthony Waterer' indicate the plant is a named, or cultivated, variety, a "cultivar (cvs.)."

• Taking advantage of microclimates to outwit your climate's limitations.

## CLIMATES AND MICROCLIMATES

Choosing plants that do well in New York is the first step to a fulfilling gardening experience. The USDA 1990 climate zone map at the end of this Introduction classifies regions according to their average lowest winter temperature. Zone 1 has the coldest climate; Zone 11 the warmest. New York is classed Zones 3 to 7. The plant hardiness information provided by garden literature, nurserymen, and plant tags is keyed to these zones.

**Outwitting your climate.** However, your zone classification isn't the final word on what you can grow.

Cities are 5 to 10 degrees warmer than the 'burbs and the country, making them an entire climate zone warmer. High, windy hills can be a zone colder. Slopes facing north are colder than those facing south. Cold also sinks, so low valleys and even low spots in your garden are cooler than higher ground—there'll be frost there before it lands elsewhere.

The Viette Nursery stood on high ground in East Norwich, Long Island. Not even five minutes away, just down Wolver Hollow Road, the glacier had left a deep valley with very high, straight sides that prevented the air from circulating. The frost could be wicked on Wolver Road on an early spring evening, but it wouldn't even have touched the Viette nursery. André could plant annuals as much as ten days earlier than gardeners on Wolver Hollow Road.

Being near water moderates your climate. In winter the shore stays warmer than ten to twenty miles inland, so you can risk some plants that might not survive winters inland. But spring weather is colder by 10 degrees or more than inland because the ocean keeps winter cold—you'll have to wait a bit to plant. Inland temperatures have greater fluctuations in early fall and late spring and harder freezes—wrap those **roses** for winter! In summer, the shore is cooler because the ocean takes time to warm up. These same modifications of climate occur around coastal bays, rivers, lakes, Lake Erie, and Lake Ontario, as well as Long Island Sound and the Atlantic.

In addition, you can take advantage of the microclimates in your garden—spots that are warmer or cooler. Shade cools; a south-facing wall warms; white and reflective surfaces increase light and heat. An evergreen windbreak, a vine-covered pergola, a large tree, a high hedge all moderate drying summer winds and winter chill.

Yet another way to offset climate limitations is to choose varieties that peak "early," "mid-season," or "late." If your growing season is short, plant early varieties. If you are subject to late frosts, avoid flower bud damage by planting late varieties. To enjoy a long season, plant all three varieties.

Another way to outwit a short growing season is to start seeds indoors early—in late winter (see starting seeds indoors in the January pages of

# Introduction

Annuals) for spring crops and in late summer for fall crops. You can also start seeds for hardy annuals early outdoors in a cold frame or a hot bed (see September, Chapter 3, Herbs & Vegetables), or try them in the open garden under "hot caps," cloches, tenting, or walls of water. These plant protectors also keep insects and small pests away in the early stages of plant growth.

## LIGHT

Plant tags and garden literature indicate a plant's light needs.

- Full sun means at least six hours of direct, full sun.

- Part sun calls for four to six hours of direct sun or dappled light all day.

- Shade can be two to three hours of direct sun a day or bright dappled shade all day (for example, the shade from a tall tree).

The farther north you are, the more direct sun plants need. Plants that do best in partial sun or shade, **New Guinea impatiens** and **hostas,** for example, can take more sun in the cool north than in Zone 7. Plants receiving full sunlight are often the most cold-hardy.

When a flowering species fails to flower, it may well be short of light. Plants that flop forward are usually telling you they need more light. Proximity to a wall painted white or a reflective surface increases the amount of light a plant receives.

## SOIL PREPARATION AND IMPROVEMENT

Soil is your plant's support system—literally—and its drinking fountain and larder. You can help soil do all it can do for your plants by supplying and replenishing the elements that maintain the structure we call "good garden loam," the pH (acidity versus alkalinity) suitable for the plants you are growing, and its fertility. It sounds much more complicated than it is.

**Soil structure.** Most garden plants need well-drained soil, and New York soils are generally well-drained. We're forever digging up rocks left behind when the ice sheet that came down from Canada and covered the area 20,000 to 25,000 years ago melted. Close to the coast, the soil becomes sandy, sometimes a little too well-drained in some areas because overly sandy soil doesn't retain water or the nutrients dissolved in it. That can be a problem. When short of moisture, plants desiccate and starve, and, we now believe, change some starches into sugars that insects find tasty. A different problem occurs in housing developments, where thin soil on an underlayer of impenetrable hardpan stunts plant growth. The solution to these and most other soil problems is to dig in humusy organic materials such as compost, leafmold (rotted leaves), or peat.

Humus, which is the spongy residue of various forms of organic material, holds moisture and nutrients. They are the great modifiers of rocky, sandy, and hardpan soils, but they're not a permanent fix. As plants grow, they deplete the soil's organic content and the organics lose their capacity to hold moisture and nutrients. A simple solution is to maintain a two- or three-inch topcoat of mulch, and dig it in annually.

**Soil pH.** A plant's access to nutrients also depends on the soil's pH—its relative acidity or alkalinity. Soil with a pH of 7.0 is neutral; pH 4 is very acid; pH 8 is alkaline. Most garden plants do best in soil with a pH between 5.5 and 6.5. Most herbaceous flowers and vegetables do well when the pH is between 6.0 and 7.0. A few plants wander outside these generalizations—**rhododendrons,** for example, do best in soil pH between 4.5 and 6.0, and **lilacs** with a pH near 7.5, a figure attainable by digging into the soil a biannual dusting of ground limestone.

Soils in Long Island and some other areas are quite acid. To find the pH of your soil, test it with one of the soil

# Introduction

testing kits sold at garden centers and by mail-order suppliers. They also sell the products used to adjust soil pH.

• To raise the pH of soils whose pH is too low, mix in 5 to 10 pounds of limestone per 100 square feet of garden bed to raise the pH 1 point. But first, if you have a fireplace, try dusting wood ashes, which contain lime (as well as potassium, often lacking in our soils), over the soil to raise the pH.

• To lower pH 1 point in soil, apply elemental fertilizer sulfur (water-soluble garden sulfur) at the rate of 5 to 10 pounds per 100 square feet. Other acidifiers are aluminum sulfate and iron sulfate; they act faster but do not last as long in the soil.

**Fertilizing.** You must fertilize annually. How often depends on the type of fertilizer you use and the plants. **Roses** are the piggiest of the lot. The fertilizers we recommend are organic and release their nutrients slowly during the season, so we get solid stocky plants with loads of gorgeous foliage and flowers.

A sound annual soil maintenance program for an established garden includes:

• Checking and adjusting the soil pH in late winter.

• Fertilizing (see Understanding Fertilizers) and adding soil supplements when the ground can be worked.

## Did You Know?

### Easy Ways to Conserve Water

• Water early in the morning, not when the sun is blazing because then you lose water to evaporation. Watering during the day reduces water loss by the plant due to transpiration, and that can be a good thing when the weather is very hot and plants are wilting.

• Mulch your gardens.

• Shut the hose off when moving between gardens.

• Turn the hose off at the faucet when you finish watering.

• Water deeply; when the water has penetrated to a depth of 6 to 8 inches, that's enough.

• Install rain barrels under drain pipes, and cover them with mosquito netting.

• Watering slowly and deeply.

• Maintaining the mulch cover.

• Every three to five years adding the supplements recommended under Supplemental Organic Fertilization.

## STARTING A RAISED BED

A raised bed is the best start a plant can have and the solution to a site with poor drainage. Good drainage is essential for most plants. When you start building a raised bed governs when you can plant because it takes three to four weeks to get ready. Starting in late summer or around Labor Day has obvious advantages.

*1* Outline the bed with a garden hose or marking paint. An island bed is ideal since you can get at the middle from either side. Long, slow, gentle curves are easy to maintain and pleasant to look at.

*2* Thoroughly water the turf covering the area to get the grass roots activated.

*3* Spray the entire area with RoundUp® Weed and Grass Killer, following the instructions on the label. It takes about two weeks for the turf to completely die. As an alternative, you can remove the turf—the top layer of growth and its roots—but it's hard work.

*4* Cover the area with enough weed-free garden soil you buy or dig up to raise the soil level about 12 to 16 inches above ground.

# Introduction

**5** Determine the soil pH and amend it to reach a pH between 6.0 and 7.0, following the procedures described earlier.

**6** Cover the bed with 3 inches of humus, or so that 1/4 of the content of the topsoil is organic matter. Decomposed bark, compost, partially decomposed leaves or seaweed, sphagnum peat moss, black peat humus, and decomposed animal manures are all okay.

**7** For each 10-foot by 10-foot area (100 square feet), add the following—available at most garden centers.

### • A new garden in full sun

> Plant-tone—5 to 10 pounds
> Rock phosphate—5 to
>   10 pounds
> Green sand—5 to 10 pounds
> Clay soils only—gypsum 5 to
>   10 pounds
> Osmocote eight-month—
>   2 pounds (apply shortly
>   before planting)

### • A new garden in shade

> Holly-tone—4 to 7 pounds
> Superphosphate—3 to 5 pounds
> Green sand—5 to 10 pounds
> Clay soils only—gypsum 5 to
>   10 pounds
> Osmocote eight-month—
>   2 pounds (apply shortly
>   before planting)

### • A new bed for bulbs

> Bulb-tone—5 to 10 pounds
> Rock phosphate—5 to 10 pounds
> Green sand—5 to 10 pounds
> Clay soils—gypsum 5 to
>   10 pounds
> Osmocote eight-month—
>   2 pounds (apply shortly
>   before planting)

### • A new bed for roses

> Rose-tone or Plant-tone—5 to
>   10 pounds
> Rock phosphate—5 to
>   10 pounds
> Green sand—5 to 10 pounds
> Clay soils—gypsum 5 to
>   10 pounds
> Osmocote eight-month—
>   2 pounds (apply shortly
>   before planting)

*Note: If the area you are planting measures only 10 square feet, combine 1/10 of the amount of each supplement given for a raised bed of 100 square feet. If you have leftovers, they keep.*

**8** Rent or borrow a rear-tine rototiller, and mix all this deeply and thoroughly. The bed should now be so soft you can dig in it with your bare hands.

**9** When you are ready to plant, rake the bed smooth and discard rocks, lumps, and bumps.

**10** Finally, pack and tamp the edge of the bed into a long, gradual slope, and cover it with mulch to keep the soil from eroding. Or, frame the bed with low retaining walls of stone, painted cement blocks, 2×2 red cedar, pressure-treated wood, or railroad ties.

*Note: Before planting in a new flower bed, or even a planting hole, that is not a raised bed, mix into the existing soil the same proportion of supplements excepting for the garden soil, and follow the same procedures as for a raised bed.*

## UNDERSTANDING FERTILIZERS

When to fertilize depends on the type of fertilizer you are using. The first annual application is made before growth begins in spring, and the last annual application is made as growth slows toward the end of the growing season.

- In Zones 3 and 4, about August 15.
- In Zone 5, about September 1.
- In Zones 6 and 7, early September to early October.

**Organic fertilizers.** Natural organic fertilizers have a positive effect on soil microorganisms and beneficial earthworms. In their presence, soil

# Introduction

structure and aeration are improved. The organics break down gradually, depending on the amount of moisture in the soil, on the temperature, and on the microbial activity. Nutrients are continually released over a three- to four-month period or longer.

Each organic fertilizer has its own rate of application. Fairly typical are the **granular** products Holly-tone (for acid-lovers) and Plant-tone (for all others). They are sprinkled over and mixed into the soil surface four to six weeks before growth begins in spring and, for perennials, again toward the end of the growing season. It's easy to apply; you can use your fingers to scratch hand-fuls of it about a quarter inch deep into the soil surface.

For Holly-tone, in a new bed for acid-loving plants like **azaleas** and **rhododendrons,** we apply 10 pounds per 100 square feet; for an established bed—we apply 5 pounds per 100 square feet. For Plant-tone, which is used for all other plants, for a new bed we apply 10 pounds per 100 square feet and for an established bed we apply 5 pounds per 100 square feet.

**Water-soluble organic fertilizers** that are immediately available to plants can be found as starter solutions, as well as in products for foliar feeding to off-set signs of nutrient deficiencies. Garden centers carry soluble organics such as fish emulsion, liquid seaweed, and the products to make "compost tea." Manure teas are made by steep-ing dehydrated manure.

**Lynette Courtney's worm compost tea.** Combine $1/2$ cup worm compost and castings with $1/2$ gallon water, and steep two days. Worm guru Lynette Courtney conducted trials of worm compost tea as a spray-on fungicide that suggest it's worth trying. Strain worm compost tea through a coffee filter to avoid clogging the spray mech-anism, and spray on.

**Supplemental organic fertilization.** In addition to the annual applications of fertilizers, we recommend applica-tions every three to five years of rock phosphate and green sand, the soil additives we use when preparing a planting bed. If your soil is clay, also add gypsum.

**Chemical fertilizers. Granular chemi-cal fertilizers,** known as "complete fertilizers," are made up of the three essential plant nutrients—nitrogen (N), phosphorous (P), and potassium (K) in balanced proportions. Numerals on the bags, like 5-10-5, 10-10-10, and their variations, refer to the propor-tions of each essential element present in that mix. If you use only this type of fertilizer, make the year's first applica-tion just before the plants begin to grow in spring, and continue every four to six weeks until the growing sea-son ends in your area.

If you use **water-soluble chemical fer-tilizers,** they must be applied every two weeks, beginning two weeks before growth starts in spring and ending two weeks before the growing season is over. You should also add it to the water used as a starter solution at planting time, and for foliar feeding for plants showing signs of nutrient deficiency.

**Slow-, controlled-, or time-release chemical fertilizers.** The complete chemical fertilizers have been pack-aged by scientists, so they act like tiny time pills releasing their nutrients over a specified period. Examples are Osmocote and Sierra controlled-release fertilizers, which come in three- to four-month, eight- to nine-month, and twelve- to fourteen-month formu-lations. A similar product is Scott's controlled-release Agriform fertilizer tablets which can last up to two years.

**Fertilizer contents.** To be all they can be, plants need the three primary plant nutrients—nitrogen for foliar growth, phosphorous for healthy roots and flower development, and potassium to maintain vigor—as well as a number of secondary and trace elements.

Fertilizers are formulated for plants that do best in either a low pH or a normal pH. Where soils are acid and the pH recommended for the plants is between 6.0 and 7.0, we recommend balancing the acidity by using a non-

# Introduction

acid slow-release fertilizer blend such as Plant-tone. In soils whose pH is above 7.0, up in the alkaline range, we suggest balancing the alkalinity by using Holly-tone or another fertilizer formulated for acid-loving plants.

## PLANTING SEASONS

The **spring planting** months in most of New York are April and May. Gardeners in Zone 5 and colder usually wait until after Memorial Day to set out cold-tender plants. We start to prepare the garden for planting after the soil dries. Make a "snowball" of soil—if it is so wet it won't easily crumble, the soil is still too wet for planting. Keep track in your garden log of the first and last frosts in your yard—that will be a better guide than any generalization experts offer.

**Summer** is okay for planting container-grown plants.

Labor Day is the start of the important **fall planting** season. The soil will remain warm for many weeks, and the plants will be putting out roots rather than putting effort into top growth and flowers.

We have given detailed planting instructions for each category of plant in the eleven plant chapters.

## WATERING

From early spring onward, there's usually enough rain to keep gardens growing through early June. Our driest months are July and August, and you will probably need to water two or three times before the weather starts to cool toward late August. One of the most important preparations for winter is a deep and thorough watering before the soil freezes.

**Always water slowly, gently, deeply.** The ideal is to put down 1½ inches of water at each session. To measure, set an empty 1-pound coffee can or other container to catch the water; record in your garden log the time it takes your sprinkler to deliver 1½ inches. Overhead watering is fine as long as you water deeply.

There's less waste if you water before the sun reaches the garden in the early morning or in late afternoon or evening. Evening watering is okay since dew naturally wets foliage every clear night anyway.

Electrically-timed mechanical watering systems tend to ignore the weather and water too often and shallowly; however, they can do a good job if they are set up with the correct low-gallon nozzles and timed to run long enough to water gently and deeply every week or ten days.

## MULCH

We recommend applying and maintaining a mulch cover 2 to 3 inches deep around annuals and perennials, and 3 inches deep around trees and shrubs. Cover an area that is wider than the plant's diameter, and start the mulch 2 to 3 inches from the plant's central stem because piling mulch right up against the plant can rot it. Mulch keeps weeds down, minimizes moisture loss, and maintains soil temperatures. Mulch that's deeper than

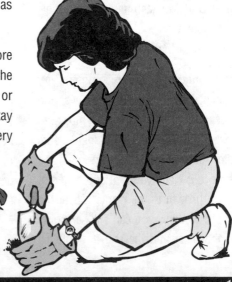

Transplanting
Seedlings

# Introduction

our recommendation keeps the ground so wet that the roots lack oxygen, and it keeps the soil frozen late into spring. Deep mulch also makes a cozy home for field mice.

Organic mulch is best. As it decomposes on the underside, organic mulch replenishes the soil's supply of humus. You can mulch with almost any healthy organic material available—seaweed or chopped leaves for example—as long as it is at least partially decomposed. The commercial mulches we recommend include cypress mulch, pine needles, fir, hardwood, and shredded pine bark.

As mulch decomposes—whether it's spread over or mixed into the soil—it has only a very slight effect on pH.

**Mulch maintenance.** Top off the mulch cover before the dandelions start to go to seed. Replenish your mulch in fall to delay the freezing of the ground and to keep moisture available for roots that will continue to grow until the earth grows cold.

As a **winter mulch** we recommend airy organics like straw, pine needles, and pine boughs. Apply winter mulch to roses and other cold-tender plants after the ground has frozen hard, and remove it when you first spot signs of active growth in the plants. Cover the plants so thinly you can still see some of the plant and the soil through the

mulch. For coastal dwellers, marsh hay and salt hay from the shore are excellent winter mulches as they are weed-free, and they can be saved, covered, in a pile from year to year. A burlap windbreak is helpful to young shrubs and trees for their first winter.

## STAKING

**Flowers.** Growing in the right light, given improved soil, and fertilized with organic fertilizers, only a few of the tallest flowers should need staking. Tall, weak growth can be caused by lack of light, force-feeding with non-organic fertilizers, and over-fertilization.

How to stake **tomatoes,** taller houseplants, and newly-planted trees, and the training of **peas, beans,** and other vining vegetables and ornamentals to stakes and other forms of support, are discussed in the appropriate chapter.

## WEEDING

Remove weeds to eliminate competition, to improve air circulation, and to avoid the pests and diseases inherent to some. A radical approach is to put down a weed barrier such as a landscape fabric; it lets in water and air but inhibits weeds. Hide it under a layer of mulch.

Even with a weed barrier you'll likely have some of the little pests to deal with. Weeds start up in spring and come into their own in mid-summer, along with drought and high heat. Before renewing or applying a summer mulch, rake them up. If you get the little green heads before they're an inch high, you won't have to hoe them when they are 8 inches high. Don't pull big weeds from bone-dry soil in a drought; water the garden first, and then gently free the weeds and their roots. If you let weeds flourish and go to seed, they'll haunt you for years. Start weed-free and stay weed-free.

## KEEPING YOUR GARDEN HEALTHY

The first defense against plant problems is to follow healthy garden practices. There's a huge bonus . . . lower maintenance. Here are some approaches that prevent difficulties—

- Introduce plant diversity into your garden and your neighborhood.

- Give cultivars of native plants a place in your design.

- Buy only healthy plants that are pest- and disease-resistant.

- Limit your choices to plants that thrive in your climate and your soil; these best withstand insect attacks and diseases to which the species

# Introduction

may be susceptible, and they survive the normal droughts.

- Rotate crops of annual flowers, vegetables, and herbs.

- Clear out and destroy infested and diseased plants.

- Keep the garden free of weeds that are carriers of insects and diseases.

- When you can, buy from the nearest reliable full-service garden center or nursery, and ask for field-grown or container stock that has proven successful in your area.

- Avoid plants identified as invasive.

- Keep growth unchecked by watering during dry periods.

- Fertilize and replenish the soil's organic content.

**Give back to the earth.** Nourish the earth—and the earth will nourish your garden. Compost amends and replenishes the soil. Many towns give away wood chip mulches, and some market composted leaves, but your own compost is easy and satisfying to make. Instructions appear in the October section of Chapter 9, Trees, the month we have lots of dry brown leaves, an important ingredient in compost.

Healthy leaves, weeds, grass clippings, vegetable garden debris, and vegetable or fruit peels are the other compost ingredients. Don't compost fruit in bear country because it attracts them. Don't compost fish or meat, which attracts neighborhood pets. Don't compost garden debris that is diseased or harbors insects.

**Pests and diseases.** In the Appendix, under Pests, Diseases, and Controls, you will find information about coping with mammal and insect pests, the diseases that can afflict your garden, and how integrated pest management (IPM) can help.

## Pruning and Grooming

Pruning keeps plants groomed, shapely, healthy, and productive. We prune shrubs and trees before growth begins to shape them, to repair winter damage, and to encourage new growth. We prune shrubs that bloom in summer and fall on new wood to encourage new growth, and we prune shrubs that bloom in spring on old wood as soon as they have finished blooming.

In summer, we thin seedlings and pinch out—deadhead—all plants to keep flowers coming. Learning how to prune well takes time and patience; the upside is that the need to prune gives you an excuse to poke around in the garden every day.

## Gardening in New York

Our state is a great place to be a gardener. Ithaca is, after all, home to the Cornell University Extension Service whose horticultural research facilities, alumni, and Liberty Hyde Bailey Hortorium are legendary. The Public Gardens and the Resources sections in the Appendix provide addresses for outstanding sources of plant materials and public gardens.

But your garden's greatest asset is still you. Once a month, starting in June, André goes through his six-acre garden with hand-held shears. It takes him about an hour to deadhead spent flowers and groom the plants. During dry spells, he waters twice a month with hose-fed brass impulse sprinklers that deliver two gallons a minute. They run for twelve hours in each spot.

André says, "I like to go to the garden at the end of the day. The land cools at sunset and often a mist comes up. There's a strong scent of the earth, and the flower colors seem more intense. Working my way through the beds, I see the plants from different perspectives and I get fresh ideas. This part of gardening isn't work. It's my time to be with the flowers."

*André and Mark Viette with*
*Jacqueline Hériteau*

# USDA Cold Hardiness Zones

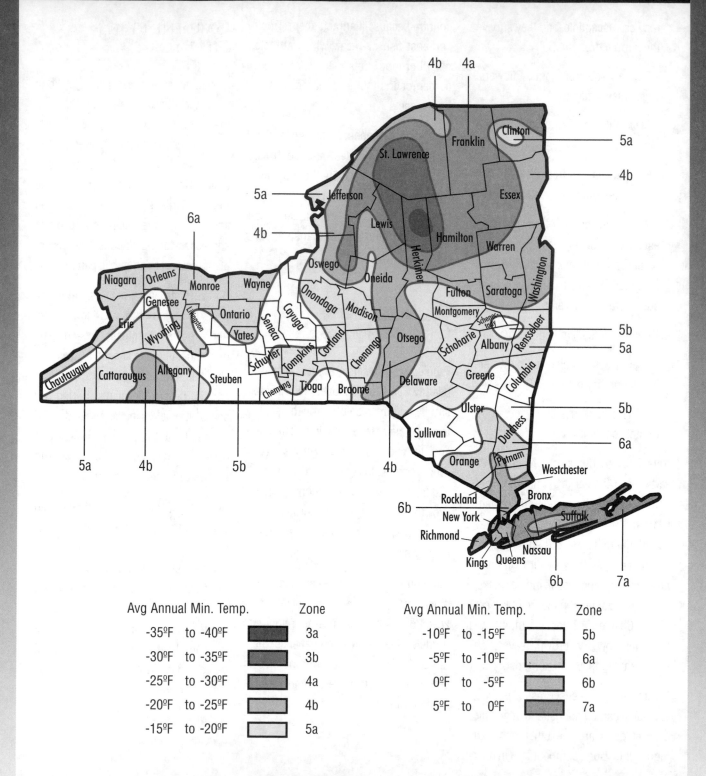

| Avg Annual Min. Temp. | Zone | | Avg Annual Min. Temp. | Zone |
|---|---|---|---|---|
| -35ºF to -40ºF | 3a | | -10ºF to -15ºF | 5b |
| -30ºF to -35ºF | 3b | | -5ºF to -10ºF | 6a |
| -25ºF to -30ºF | 4a | | 0ºF to -5ºF | 6b |
| -20ºF to -25ºF | 4b | | 5ºF to 0ºF | 7a |
| -15ºF to -20ºF | 5a | | | |

# CHAPTER ONE

# Annuals & Biennials

*The flowers with lavish bloom that we count on to keep our gardens filled with color all summer long are grown as annuals.*

They must be replanted every year. But a garden without annuals, like summer without butterflies, is underprivileged. The group includes true annuals, biennials, short-lived perennials, and a few cold-tender perennials and tropicals that don't survive our winters outdoors. Seed packets and plant tags say which is which.

Here's an overview:

**True annuals.** The botanist's "true" annual develops from seed, grows up and blooms, sets seed, and dies in one year. **Zinnias, sunflowers,** and **marigolds** are "true" annuals. Some reseed themselves and come back year after year, like **love-in-a-mist** (*Nigella*), **larkspur,** and **four-o'clocks.**

**Biennials.** Seeds of "true" biennials bloom the second year after sowing, but they don't come back again unless they are self-sowers. Most **verbascum** (*Mullein*) species are true biennials. Common **foxglove** may behave like a biennial or a perennial. Fragrant **sweet William** and furry-leaved **silver sage,** which raises superb flower spikes in late spring, are short-lived perennials grown as biennials. To keep a biennial or a short-lived perennial blooming in your garden every year, set out one-year-old seedlings every year or sow seeds every year for next year's bloom.

**Cold-tender perennials. Geraniums, coleus, pentas, impatiens,** and **lantana** are among the perennials grown as annuals in New York because they cannot survive our winters. Several do well wintered indoors. (See September, Care.)

**Tropicals and semi-tropicals. Glory bush** (*Tibouchina urvilleana*) and lovely **mandevilla** vines are perennial in very warm climates. They winter well in a greenhouse—are so-so as houseplants.

## USES OF ANNUALS

**Colorful fillers.** Summer-flowering annuals—**sweet William, pinks, rocket larkspur,** and **garden balsam,** for example— are your best bet for filling gaps in perennial beds to mask the oh-so-slow ripening of spring-flowering bulbs. Low-growing annuals are perfect fillers for empty spaces in new beds of perennials and shrubs. Annuals that are good cutting flowers are a kitchen garden's best friends.

**Hedges and screening.** Some annuals grow big enough that you can use them to plant a temporary hedge—**giant marigolds** ('Climax' marigolds) and **burning bush** (*Scoparia forma* (sic) *trichophylla*), for example. **Annual vines** grow like weeds, making them perfect screening while a slow-growing vine gets going (see Chapter 10, Vines, Ground Covers, and Ornamental Grasses). They'll cover poles, tree stumps, and other garden eyesores in a matter of weeks.

**Bedding plants.** Long-blooming annuals (and flowering bulbs) are used for "bedding out," a practice used by municipalities to create flower beds that bloom all season. A typical sequence is a spring display of **pansies,** replaced when they fade by **marigolds,** replaced for fall by **ornamental cabbages.** Bedding out is a good way to deal with an area regularly scalped during winter snow removal. **Ageratum, wax begonias,** and **sweet alyssum** are also used to create ribbons of color to spell out municipal and business names and logos, a fun garden project to mark a very special anniversary.

**Baskets and planters.** Annuals have modest root system so lots can be fitted into a relatively small container. Cascade-type **petunias** are the stars, along with tiny, bright-as-sunshine creeping **zinnias** (*Sanvitalia procumbens*, a true annual), and the tender perennials *Scaevola aemula*, *Sutura cordata* 'Snowflake', and s**weet potato vine.** Spills of **ivy** and **balcon geraniums, helichrysum,** and **variegated vinca** lend grace to flowery compositions.

**Cutting flowers.** Cut-and-come-again annuals are among the best cutting flowers. To have masses of blooms for bouquets, plant **zinnias, snapdragons, cosmos,** and **China asters.** Give them a bed of their own in an out-of-the-way place. Or plant them in your kitchen garden—they'll make it beautiful!

**Children's gardens.** Annuals are a child's best garden friend. Quick popper-uppers, like **zinnias, marigolds,** and **sunflowers,** satisfy a youngster's need for early results. Seeing buried seeds grow, watching butterflies and bees seeking nectar, and sharing flowers and a garden's endless surprises give children proud stories to tell.

## SEQUENCE OF BLOOM

Keeping color in the garden all season long requires that you know the sequence in which plants in the annuals group bloom. Garden literature, seed packets, and our annuals list tell you when each species peaks—spring, summer, or fall. Some species come in varieties that bloom either early, mid-season, or late. Where the growing season is very short, plant early-blooming varieties. To enjoy a long season, plant all three varieties, or sow seeds every two weeks until July.

If you want to have annuals in bloom in mid- to late spring, set out seedlings of those that peak in cool weather, like **pansies** and **pot marigolds.** To keep the summer garden blooming, sow a series of seeds of heat-tolerant annuals like **marigolds** and **zinnias.** For late summer color in semi-shade, plant **impatiens** seedlings. To have loads of flowers in summer and until frosts, sow seeds or plant seedlings of **cosmos** (we love 'Sonata White'), **China asters,** and especially **snapdragons.** To keep your garden going into late fall, as space becomes available set out **pansy** seedlings and **ornamental cabbages** and **kale.** In our gardens, the pansies are still good to go in spring.

To have a garden that's interesting in and out of bloom, include annuals with colorful foliage—they're the long-distance runners. **Dusty miller** (*Senecio cineraria*) in cultivars 'Silver Dust' and 'Cirrus' stay silver. **Variegated geraniums** and kaleidoscopic **coleus** grow and glow until the frosts begin.

## STARTING ANNUALS AND BIENNIALS FROM SEED

For mass "bedding" displays and effective garden design, you will need enough seeds or seedlings of annuals to plant them in groups of five, seven, ten, or more; the smaller the plant, the more you will need. Garden centers and mail-order catalogs sell seedlings of annuals, but growing your own saves money and provides a more interesting plant selection. Save even more—and avoid leftover seeds—by buying seeds with friends.

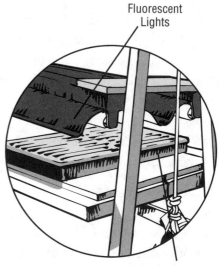

Fluorescent Lights

Seed-Starter Tray in 10x20" Flat Tray

You'll find annuals and biennials are easy to grow outdoors from seed. To get a head start, you can sow seeds indoors in late March or in April. (See starting seeds indoors under Planting in January.)

# Annuals & Biennials

When to sow seeds indoors depends on how long the seeds take to germinate, how quickly the plants grow, and how soon they can be moved to your garden (which depends on how much cold they can stand). Seed packets label the seeds "hardy," "half-hardy," or "tender," and most packets suggest when and where to sow the seeds in the garden and whether and when they can be started indoors.

**Hardy.** The seedlings of hardy annuals and biennials can take some frost. These can be started outdoors in early spring, even before the last frost. Seed packets indicate that some can even be sown in fall after freezing temperatures have come.

**Half-hardy.** These seedlings are harmed by frost, but they tolerate cool, wet weather and cold soil. You can sow these seeds outdoors a couple of weeks after the last frost.

**Tender.** These seeds grow fastest and do best when they are sown outdoors only after both the air and the soil have warmed. Indoors you can start these in late March or in April, depending on your zone.

**Sowing the seeds.** The planting depth for seeds is usually given on the seed packet. The rule of thumb is to sow seeds at a depth about three times the seed's diameter, not its length.

**Always sow seeds in moist soil, and always water them well after planting. If you can plant shortly after a rain or before, you won't have so much watering to do.**

Larger seeds are sown in "hills," groups of four to six, or three to five, equidistant from each other. Flowers for edging are usually sown in "drills," dribbled at spaced intervals along a shallow furrow created by dragging the edge of a rake or a hoe handle along the planting line.

**Preparing the soil.** Annuals and biennials depend on modest root systems to produce masses of flowers and foliage. So they need soil that is well supplied every year with nutrients as well as sustained moisture, especially the first several weeks in the garden.

In the general Introduction to our book, we've described the step-by-step preparation needed for a new garden bed. For annuals, that's a requirement every year, and it applies to the preparation of planting holes as well as beds. It includes checking and adjusting the soil pH every year as well.

**Transplanting seedlings.** The seedlings of hardy annuals will grow fastest transplanted after the air temperature has reached 55 degrees Fahrenheit during the day. The others will do best planted after the soil has warmed. Transplanting too early just leaves seedlings sulking and yellowing. But you can give seedlings of hardy annuals an early start under a cold frame or hot bed (see September, Chapter 3, Herbs & Vegetables), or in the open garden under "hot caps," cloches, tenting, and other solar heat collectors. Before planting seedlings—your own or seedlings from the garden center—it's a good idea to let them "harden-off" or acclimate a bit either in a sheltered location protected from direct sun and wind or in a cold frame. Apply a 2-inch layer of mulch after planting.

## CARE

Annuals do their best when they have a good headstart and are deadheaded. Here's how:

*1* Thin seedlings to space the plants as recommended on the seed packet.

*2* Shortly after seedlings reach a height of 2 or 3 inches, pinch out the tips of cascading plants, like **petunias,** and branching annuals that have one, two, or three central stems, like **cleome** and **snapdragons.** Repeat during the growing season.

*3* "Deadhead" (remove) fading blooms or harvest flowers to prevent the formation of seedheads. Plants developing seeds generally stop or are slow blooming.

*4* Snip off stems of plants crowding others in a container or a bed, as **nasturtiums** often will.

*5* Remove weeds as they appear. Some self-sowers are so productive they become weeds—**love-in-a-mist** comes to mind—so root them out as you would weeds.

## WATERING

Seeds and seedlings need rain or watering not only before and right after planting, they also need enough water, especially the early weeks, to maintain soil moisture so they can maintain constant growth. In periods of drought and any time you see signs of wilting, water deeply. Soil that has been plentifully supplied with humus and that has a 2- to 3-inch mulch cover will need less watering.

Specific directions for slow, deep watering are given in the general Introduction to the book.

## FERTILIZING

In the Introduction to the book, under Soil Preparation and Improvement, we explain how to prepare and fertilize soil for a new bed, including checking and adjusting the pH. To keep an established bed for annuals productive, it really is important to **check and amend the pH every year.**

If you are using an organic fertilizer such as Plant-tone, mix it into the top 3 inches of the soil at the rate of 5 pounds per 100 square feet, four to six weeks before planting. If you are using a chemical fertilizer, either granular or slow-release like Osmocote, apply it just before planting. Annuals that slow after a first flush of bloom may benefit from a modest extra fertilization with a water-soluble fertilizer, either organic or chemical.

In addition, throughout the season, maintain a 2- to 3-inch mulch cover because as the underside decomposes it adds to the organic content of the soil. Every three to five years, mix in applications of rock phosphate, green sand, and gypsum, the soil additives recommended when preparing a planting bed. (See Understanding Fertilizers in the Introduction to this book.)

## PESTS

Annuals suffer from the pests and diseases common to other flowers. Aphids jam **petunia** tips, small green caterpillars bug **geraniums,** whiteflies love **lantana,** and spider mites spin tiny traps in **marigolds** and **verbena.** The plants withstand minor invasions when you prepare the soil well and fertilize annually. Space and prune the plants so that air keeps flowing through, and there will be fewer problems.

For specific controls for common pests and diseases, turn to the section on Pests, Diseases, and Controls in the Appendix of the book.

# Annuals & Biennials

| Common Name (*Botanical Name*) | Type | Height (Inches) | Bloom Time | Light | Description |
|---|---|---|---|---|---|
| **Ageratum, Flossflower** (*Ageratum houstonianum*) | Annual | 6 to 12 | Late spring to frost | Sun, part sun | Flowering edger—blue, violet-blue, pink, or white. |
| **Alyssum, Sweet** (*Lobularia maritima*) | Annual | 4 to 8 | Summer to fall | Sun, part sun | Scented edger—dainty white, mauve, lavender florets. Try 'Blue Danube'. |
| **Bachelor's-button** (*Centaurea cyanus*) | Annual | 12 to 30 | Summer | Sun, part sun | Fluffy flower heads in blue, purple, pink, white. |
| **Begonia, Wax/ Fibrous Begonia** (*Begonia semperflorens-cultorum* cvs.) | Tender perennial | 6 to 12 | Late spring to early fall | Part sun, part shade | White, pale pink, rose, coral, deep pink, red, and bicolors. |
| **Black-eyed Susan** (*Rudbeckia hirta*) | Short-lived perennial | 24 to 30 | Summer | Sun | Yellow daisies with dark centers. |
| **Blanket Flower** (*Gaillardia pulchella*) | Annual | 24 to 30 | Summer | Sun | Showy yellow/red daisy-faced flowers. |
| **Busy Lizzie, Impatiens** (*Impatiens* cvs.) | Tender perennial | 8 to 24 | Late spring to fall | Part shade, shade | Best flowering plant for shade with many colors. |
| **Celosia** (*Celosia argentea* var. *cristata*, Plumosa Group) | Annual | 12 to 24 | Summer to frost | Sun, part sun | Feathered plumes in intense colors top green or bronze foliage. 'Fireglow' in deep red. |
| **Cockscomb** (*Celosia argentea* var. *cristata*, Cristata Group) | Tender perennial | 6 to 12 | Summer through fall | Sun | Velvety flowers in dazzling primary colors. |
| **Coleus** (*Solenostemon scutellarioides* cvs.) | Tender perennial | 12 to 18 | Late spring to early fall | Part shade | Variegated foliage plant in dazzling color combinations; new varieties can take sun. |
| **Corn Poppy** (*Papaver rhoeas*) | Annual | 18 | Summer | Sun | Modern strains come in a wide range of colors. |
| **Cosmos** (*Cosmos bipinnatus*) | Annual | 36 to 48 | Summer until frost | Sun | Open-faced flowers on graceful branches with fern-like foliage. White, pastels, and wine-red. |
| **Dianthus Heddewiggii Pinks** (*Dianthus chinenesis*) | Annual/ biennial | 6 to 12 | Mid-summer to fall | Sun | Grassy foliage and clove-scented flowers; various shades. Blooms first season. |
| **Dusty Miller** (*Senecio cineraria*) | Annual | 12 | Spring, summer, fall | Sun | Silver-gray foliage plant for edging. |
| **Edging Lobelia** (*Lobelia erinus*) | Short-lived perennial | 6 to 8 | Spring | Part sun, part shade | Cascading; clouds of flowers in shades of blue, violet, wine red, white. |

# Annuals & Biennials

| Common Name (Botanical Name) | Type | Height (Inches) | Bloom Time | Light | Description |
|---|---|---|---|---|---|
| Flowering Tobacco (*Nicotiana alata*) | Tender perennial | 15 to 24 | Summer into fall | Part sun, part shade | The species whites are fragrant, but most hybrids are not. Woodland tobacco (*N. sylvestris*) is tall and handles cold. |
| Forget-me-not (*Myosotis sylvatica*) | Biennial or short-lived perennial | 7 to 12 | Spring | Sun | Dainty florets in appealing gentian blue. |
| Four-o'clocks (*Mirabilis jalapa*) | Tender perennial | 10 to 18 | Mid-summer to fall | Sun, part shade | Late season fragrant, petunia-like flowers in many colors. |
| Foxglove (*Digitalis* spp. and cvs.) | Biennial | 30-plus | Mid-spring to early summer | Sun, part shade | Straight stately flowering spikes hung with thimble-shaped blooms. |
| Geranium (*Pelargonium* x *hortorum*) | Tender perennial | 8 to 14 | All summer | Sun, part shade | Flowers are shades of red, salmon, fuchsia, pink, white, and bicolors. |
| Gerbera, African Daisy (*Gerbera jamesonii*) | Tender perennial | 12 to 18 | Summer | Sun | Big, daisy-faced flowers in brilliant shades. |
| Globe Amaranth (*Gomphrena globosa*) | Annual | 8 to 30 | Late spring to early fall | Sun | Sweet little round flowers in shades of lavender, orange, pink, purple, red, and white. |
| Heliotrope (*Heliotropium arborescens*) | Tender perennial | 15 (dwarf) to 48 | Summer to fall | Sun, part shade | Sweetly scented flat flowerheads in deep purple, lavender, or white. |
| Larkspur (*Consolida ambigua*) | Self-sowing annual | 18 to 36 | Spring | Sun, part shade | Open-faced; blue, pale pink, lavender, white; look for 'Evening Fragrance'. |
| Licorice Plant (*Helichrysum petiolare*) | Tender perennial | 16 to 18 | Spring through fall | Sun | Silvery foliage; trailing stems for baskets and planters; 'Limelight' is one of several appealing shades. |
| Love-in-a-mist (*Nigella damascena*) | Annual | 12 to 18 | Spring | Sun | Spurred, spidery flowers in blue and other shades; look for 'Miss Jekyll' in rose/white. |
| Marigold (*Tagetes* spp. and cvs.) | Annual | 8 to 36 | Summer and fall | Sun | Fluffy; from dwarf to giant in gold, orange, yellow, mahogany, and bicolors; pungent; handles drought and neglect. |
| Mexican Sunflower (*Tithonia rotundifolia*) | Annual | 36 to 60 | Summer to fall | Sun | Spectacular, indestructible; branching; masses of showy flowers in sunny shades. |
| Nasturtium (*Tropaeolum majus*) | Annual | 8 to 12 | Summer and fall | Sun | Showy edible foliage and flowers in vivid colors. Use vining 'Whirlybird' varieties for baskets; bushy 'Alaska Mixed' has variegated foliage. |

# Annuals & Biennials

| Common Name (Botanical Name) | Type | Height (Inches) | Bloom Time | Light | Description |
|---|---|---|---|---|---|
| New Guinea Impatiens (*Impatiens* cvs.) | Tender perennial | 12 to 24 | Summer | Part sun | Colorful foliage and big, open-faced bicolor flowers in brilliant shades. |
| Ornamental Cabbage and Kale (*Brassica oleracea*) | Biennial grown as an annual | 8 to 14 | Fall to spring | Sun | Cabbage and kale with beautiful, colorful foliage; lasts fall through winter. |
| Pansy (*Viola* x *wittrockiana*) | Annual/ tender perennial | 4 to 8 | Spring, fall, winter | Sun, part shade | Solid colors or combinations; the 'Atlas' and 'Icicle' series withstand moderate winters. |
| Petunia (*Petunia* x *hybrida*) | Tender perennial | 6 to 18 | Spring through summer | Sun | Cascading and upright forms; colors are white, yellow, orange, pink, red, blue, lavender, magenta, and showy bicolors. |
| Portulaca, Moss Rose (*Portulaca grandiflora*) | Annual; reseeds | 4 to 8 | June to frost | Sun | Sprawling succulent stems and foliage; big open-faced flowers in bright shades. Thrives in sandy soil. |
| Pot Marigold (*Calendula officinalis*) | Annual | 18 to 25; dwarf, 12 | Spring | Sun, part shade | Pungent cool-season daisy-like flower in shades of orange, gold, lemon, apricot, and white. |
| Red Salvia (*Salvia splendens*) | Tender perennial | 7 to 24 | Summer to early fall | Sun | Delicate cut-and-come-again flowers; modern varieties in white, pink, salmon, purple, and bicolors. |
| Snapdragon (*Antirrhinum majus*) | Tender perennial | 8 to 36 | Spring to late fall | Sun, part shade | Upright flowering spires clustered with pea-like blooms, dark red to rose, yellow, white, and bicolors; stands early frosts. |
| Spider Flower (*Cleome hasslerana*) | Annual | 36 to 48 | Summer through fall | Sun, part sun | Airy, spidery flowers in white and shades of pink, rose, lilac, and purple; some varieties self-sow abundantly. |
| Sunflower (*Helianthus annuus*) | Annual | 2 to 12 feet | Summer | Sun | Huge central disc surrounded by ray petals; new varieties in exotic color combinations. |
| Verbena (*Verbena* x *hybrida*) | Tender perennial | 10 to 20 | Summer | Sun | Free-flowering creeper-trailer with small flowers in white, red, pink, yellow, purple. |
| Vinca, Pink/ Madagascar Periwinkle (*Catharanthus roseus*) | Tender perennial | 4 to 18 | Summer | Sun, part shade | Open, flat flowers in colorful shades with a contrasting eye. |
| Wishbone Flower (*Torenia fournieri*) | Annual | 8 | Summer through fall | Part shade, shade | Bushy, small, for window boxes and planters; masses of bicolor blooms. |
| Zinnia, Tall (*Zinnia elegans*) | Annual | Dwarf to 36 | Summer to fall | Sun | Cut-and-come-again ray flowers in every size and many vivid colors. |

 PLANNING

January is for dreaming. Use pages torn from garden catalogs to create your own album of annuals. It is a real help in planning your garden. Put a sticky note by each plant to remind yourself where it would fit in your garden and why you pulled the page. Organize the pages according to their season of bloom. When considering flowers prone to powdery mildew, such as **zinnias, verbena,** and **annual phlox,** choose disease-resistant varieties.

Another useful reference is an album made up of catalog pages showing garden equipment and accessories you like; it also helps locate better pricing for expensive items.

**Garden log.** Make a record of the catalogs that provide the most useful information.

 PLANTING

**Starting seeds indoors.** Starting seeds indoors can save you money, and it's also fun during the dreary days of winter.

**Equipment.** Seed starting kits include strips of planting pockets, watertight flats, plastic covers to keep the soil moist during germination, and plant labels. But you can improvise with baking tins or egg cartons for planting, popsicle sticks for labels, and dry cleaner's plastic to tent them. It's best to disinfect used equipment with a solution that is 1 part bleach to 9 parts water.

Seed packets tell you whether or not the seeds can be started early indoors; for plants quick to start, start them four to six weeks before they go outdoors, and eight to ten or twelve weeks for slowpokes. **Plant together in the same container only the seeds that germinate at about the same speed.**

Use a sterile seed-starting mix for plants that will be moved outdoors after four to six weeks. Use a commercial potting mix for plants that will be indoors longer. Thoroughly soak pots made of clay or peat before filling them so they won't soak up water meant for your seedlings. Start in individual peat pots seeds that transplant with difficulty or grow quickly, like **vines, beans, peas,** and **melons.**

**Sowing the seeds.** Dampen the planting medium in its bag, and scoop it into the containers. Seeds that need light to germinate should be sprinkled over the growing medium. Seeds that germinate in the dark, sow in planting holes made with a pencil or a pointed stick—¼ inch deep for medium-sized seeds and 1 inch deep for large seeds—then cover them with soil.

Seeds are usually good for five years. Germination rates slow with age, so when the seeds are older, sow two in each planting pocket and discard the weakest seedling.

To plant a flat, make shallow furrows, drop in the seeds, and top with soil. Mix very fine seeds half and half with sand, sprinkle them from a saltshaker, and dust starter mix over them.

Label each planting pocket.

**Germination.** Cover the containers during germination. Moderate (ambient) light is enough at this stage. Hardy annuals do not need bottom heat and do best in a cool room or basement. For others, provide bottom heat and air temperatures of 65 to 70 degrees Fahrenheit. Heat mats are available, but a waterproof heating pad on Low will do.

When the seeds have germinated, remove the cover and move the flat to good light **where the temperature is between 55 and 65 degrees Fahrenheit.** Water flats of seedlings from the bottom, or mist the seedlings. Open windows or doors to air the room often. Rotate flats in a window often to keep the seedlings growing straight.

When seedlings become crowded, transplant each to an individual 3- to 4-inch pot filled with potting mix.

*Seedlings that will be indoors for six weeks need good light.*
*An installation of two or three 4-foot fluorescent lights*
*burning sixteen hours a day is helpful.*

Seedlings that will be indoors for six weeks need good light. An installation of two or three 4-foot fluorescent lights burning sixteen hours a day is helpful. Set the seedlings about 3 inches below the lights. As the seedlings grow, raise the light to 4 to 6 inches, and when the seedlings show strong growth, reduce the lights to fourteen hours a day.

Damping off is a fungal disease that rots stems, causing the plants to fall over. Thinning the seedlings, airing, a sterile growing medium and equipment, and good drainage help. Spraying with the fungicide Thiram (Arasan) is a good preventative.

## Did You Know?

### These Annuals Are Easy to Start Indoors Early

- **Ageratum,** 8 to 10 weeks
- **Cosmos,** 4 to 6 weeks
- **Celosia,** 5 to 6 weeks
- **China Aster,** 6 to 10 weeks
- **Cleome,** 6 to 10 weeks
- **Flowering Tobacco,** 9 to 11 weeks
- **Mallow** (*Lavatera trimestris*), 6 to 8 weeks
- **Marigolds,** dwarf, 8 to 10 weeks
- **Marigolds,** tall, 5 to 6 weeks
- **Petunia,** 11 to 15 weeks
- **Portulaca,** 10 to 12 weeks
- **Salvia,** 8 to 10 weeks
- **Snapdragon,** dwarf, 12 to 14 weeks
- **Snapdragon,** tall, 6 to 10 weeks
- **Verbena,** 8 to 10 weeks
- **Zinnias,** dwarf, 6 to 8 weeks
- **Zinnias,** tall, 4 to 6 weeks

Start these seeds the designated number of weeks before planting season, and the seedlings will be ready to plant when the weather breaks.

## CARE

Change the water in which cuttings taken last fall are rooting, and add charcoal, the kind that keeps the water in fish tanks clear.

In Zones 6 and 7, during the January thaw there's enough warmth in the sun to heat up the interior of a south-facing cold frame (see September, Herbs & Vegetables chapter). If you are over wintering cold-tender flowers there—**geraniums,** for example—monitor the interior temperature on sunny days and ventilate. In warm Zone 7 if the year is mild, you can also try starting seeds for hardy annuals that self sow in a cold frame—**spider flower** and **larkspur,** for example.

## PRUNING

Pinch back leggy cuttings and plants.

## WATERING

Maintain moderate moisture in pots of annuals and tropicals wintering indoors.

## FERTILIZING

We gain almost a whole hour of extra daylight this month, so indoor plants are starting to grow again. Add a half-strength dose of houseplant fertilizer to the water for cuttings, plants, and tropicals stored indoors for winter that are showing new growth.

## PESTS

Keep an eye out for aphids, mites, and whiteflies on plants growing indoors; spray infected plants with insecticidal soap for houseplants.

## PLANNING

Plan to attend one or more of the spring flower and garden shows for inspiration.

Before finalizing catalog orders and your buying plans, make sure there is a suitable place and space for each plant chosen. When the snow is gone but before the soil is ready to be worked, go out to your garden and reserve the space meant for the plants you are planning to order. Take along a set of row markers on which you have written the names of the plants you will be setting out. You'll find the heights and widths of the plants in the pages of your catalog album, on seed packets, and in our charts. Keep tall plants to the back, mid-height in the middle, and shorties up front.

Then:

- **In gardens of perennials and shrubs,** outline each bay meant for annuals with a stick, and in the center place a row marker indicating the flower that goes there.

- **In cutting and kitchen gardens,** plant a row marker at the end of each row indicating the vegetables or flowers you plan to plant there.

- **In a garden for annuals,** outline the bays intended for each annual and press a row marker into the ground to designate which plant belongs where.

**Ordering seeds.** Check your buying plans against your inventory of seeds that were left over or saved from last year, and take a look at the cuttings and potted plants brought indoors last fall. List what you have, will order by mail, will buy at a garden center, and what you will have to go looking for. Seeds of the most fragrant **petunias,** 'Celebrity White', 'Ultra White', and 'Apollo', for example, may take time to locate.

When you are sure you have space for everything you plan to order, write up and mail your orders for the catalogs, and prepare shopping lists for later purchases at garden centers. Many mail order houses now offer seedlings as well as seeds.

**Garden log.** Note design ideas picked up at flower shows and in visits to other gardens. Record the dates if and when you start seeds indoors.

## PLANTING

**Indoors.** In warm Zones 6 and 7, between the end of this month and mid-March you can start seeds indoors or in a cold frame for hardy annuals like **ageratum, alyssum, balsam, cleome, geraniums, pansies, annual phlox, stock, snapdragons,** and slow-growers like **petunias.** (See starting seeds indoors under Planting and the list of annuals that are easy to start indoors in January of this chapter.)

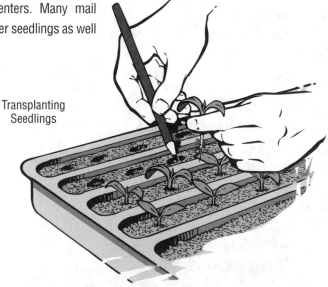

Transplanting
Seedlings

*Before finalizing catalog orders and your buying plans, make sure there is a suitable place and space for each plant chosen.*

 ## CARE

Begin repotting plants brought indoors last fall, and pot up the strongest cuttings. (See March, How to Make New Plants from Stem Cuttings.) Continue to fertilize them.

If you planted a cover crop in your garden in the fall (see Planting in October), turn it under when winter moisture is gone and the ground becomes workable this month or next.

## PRUNING

Thin seedlings in the flats of seeds started indoors when they become crowded. Use fine-pointed nail or embroidery scissors to cut the stems off at the base; pulling them up is very likely to disturb the roots of those nearby. In pockets where two seeds were sown, when the second set of leaves opens, remove the weakest seedling.

 ## WATERING

Maintain the soil moisture for seeds started indoors.

## Did You Know?

### These Annuals (and Tender Perennials) Have Colorful Foliage

- **Alternanthera** (*Alternanthera* cvs.)
- **Beefsteak Plant, Jacob's Coat** (*Acalypha wilkesiana* cvs.)
- **Burning Bush** (*Bassia scoparia* forma(sic) *trichophylla*)
- **Coleus** (*Coleus* x *hybridus*)
- **Coppertone Mallow** (*Hibiscus acetosella*)
- **Dusty Miller** (*Senecio cineraria*) 'Silver Dust' and 'Cirrus'
- **Joseph's Coat** (*Amaranthus tricolor*) 'Joseph's coat'
- **New Guinea Impatiens** (*Impatiens hawkeri* cvs.)
- **Polka Dot Plant** (*Hypoestes phyllostachya*)
- **Snow on the Mountain** (*Euphorbia marginata*)
- **Variegated Impatiens** (*Impatiens wallerana* cvs.)
- **Variegated Wax Begonia** (*Begonia semperflorens* Cultorum cvs.)
- **Variegated Zonal Geranium** (*Pelargonium*) 'Ben Franklin'

 ## FERTILIZING

Every other time you water plants wintering indoors, include fertilizer at half strength.

 ## PESTS

Seedlings started indoors suffering from poor drainage, lack of air, and crowding are vulnerable to the fungal disease called "damping off," which rots stems near the soil surface. If the problem appears, discard the affected plants, reduce watering, and increase light and fresh air. If the problem persists, mist the seedlings with a fungicide such as Thiram (Arasan).

# MARCH

##  PLANNING

The saying is that if March comes in like a lion, it will go out like a lamb. Most often it comes in the opposite way—all sun and blue skies, then roars out in snow and sleet. Don't let the days of the lamb fool you! Revel in the first **snowdrops,** in the satiny gold of **winter aconite** and early **daffodils** inching their way toward the sun. But save your urge to plant hardy annuals outdoors until the soil has drained enough to be workable. The earth is ready to work when a ball of earth packed between your hands crumbles easily; if it sticks together, the soil is still too wet.

**Garden log.** Chronicle the progress of seeds started indoors and outdoors.

## PLANTING

**Indoors.** In Zones 3 to 5—towards the middle of the month you can start seeds indoors for slow-growing and hardy annuals. (See the January pages of this chapter for Starting Seeds Indoors under Planting and the list of annuals that are easy to start indoors.)

After a seedling opens its second set of leaves, you can transplant the ones outgrowing their planting pockets to individual pots filled with potting soil.

In warm Zone 7—late this month on a mild year you may be able to start some hardy seeds outdoors.

**Sowing annuals outdoors.** Most annuals sown outdoors come into bloom soonest when the seeds are sown where they are to flower. Plant in well-worked, moist soil, be sure to water gently but thoroughly after planting, and ensure unchecked growth by maintaining the soil moisture as the young plants grow. When the seedlings are growing well, cover the bed with a 2- to 3-inch mulch cover, keeping it 2 to 3 inches away from the stems of the seedlings.

**Planting depth.** The planting depth for seeds appears on seed packets. The rule of thumb is to sow seeds at a depth about three times the seed's diameter, not its length.

To sow **fine seeds** evenly, "broadcast" them, that is, sprinkle them over well-worked soil, then cover them with a thin layer of seed starter mix or soil. When the seedlings are up, thin them to the distance suggested on the seed packet, or at least 3 to 5 inches apart.

**Larger seeds** are sown in "hills," groups of four to six, or three to five, equidistant from each other. Flowers for edging paths or the front of a flowerbed are usually sown in "drills," dropped at spaced intervals along a shallow furrow. To make the furrow, drag the edge of a rake or a hoe handle along the planting line.

**Preparing the beds.** As soon as the snow is gone and winter moisture has left the soil, you can begin readying beds for planting. A new bed needs the careful preparation described under Soil Preparation and Improvement in the Introduction to the book. Established beds for annuals and areas reserved for annuals in gardens of perennials and shrubs must be refurbished every year.

• Clear away last year's plantings.

• Check the soil pH and adjust it, if needed, to between 6.0 and 7.0. If you need to raise the pH, try dusting wood ashes over the beds to add calcium, which sweetens the soil, and potash (potassium), which strengthens stems and keeps growth healthy. Retest, and if the pH is still too low, follow the instructions for adjusting pH in Soil Preparation and Improvement in the Introduction to the book.

*As soon as the snow is gone and winter moisture has left the soil, you can begin readying beds for planting.*

• Work fertilizer into the top 3 to 6 inches of the soil (except for **nasturtiums**). If you are using an organic fertilizer, apply it four to six weeks before planting begins. If you are using a chemical fertilizer—granular or coated for slow release—apply it just before planting.

 ## CARE

**Indoors.** Transplant seedlings as they outgrow their planting pockets. Pinch out the growing tips of seedlings that are becoming leggy.

Repot **geraniums, lantana,** and **mandevilla** and other tender perennials saved from last year and discard poor performers.

 ## PRUNING

Clear the ground of last year's annuals, including **ornamental cabbages** and **kale** planted last fall.

 ## WATERING

Maintain the soil moisture for seeds and seedlings started indoors.

## Did You Know?

### How to Make New Plants from Stem Cuttings

Cuttings and potted-up plants brought indoors last fall can provide you with new plants for this year's garden. Here's how you can multiply your holdings:

**Geraniums.** Cut off the top 4 inches of a sturdy, healthy stem just below a leaf node. Remove the leaves from the bottom 2 inches of the stem. Let the cuttings dry for a few hours or overnight. Then put the bottom half of the cutting in a solution that is a gallon of water with $1/2$ to 1 teaspoon of bleach, and set them in a bright window. When they have grown a full set of roots— usually three or four weeks—transplant your cuttings to 3- to 4-inch pots filled with a gritty potting mix or non-clumping kitty litter. Or, root the cuttings in a rooting mixture. Grow your cuttings in a south-facing window.

You can also get cuttings to root by dipping the ends lightly in a rooting hormone and standing them in damp vermiculite or sand tented with plastic film. When the cuttings have developed enough roots to resist a slight tug, they're ready to transplant.

**Coleus and wax begonias.** Cut off the top 6 inches of a leafy stem just below a leaf node. Remove the leaves from the bottom 3 inches, then place the bottom of the cutting in water containing a few drops of bleach, and set it in a semi-sunny window to root. When it has grown roots, transplant it into an all-purpose potting mix. Grow it in an east- or west-facing sunny window.

 ## FERTILIZING

You can start fertilizing transplanted seedlings started indoors when the appearance of two or three new pairs of leaves indicates the root system is growing again. Every two weeks, fertilize all the seedlings that will remain indoors another six weeks or more with a houseplant fertilizer at half strength.

 ## PESTS

If seedlings started indoors are toppling, see Pests, February.

Spider mites can be a problem with indoor seedlings. For controls, see Pests, Diseases, and Controls in the Appendix.

# APRIL
## Annuals & Biennials

## PLANNING

Find time to prepare containers for the growing season ahead. Before filling moss-lined baskets with soil, patch or replace the moss so the earth won't dribble out. You'll find bags of moss at garden centers and florist shops. Fill your pots, window boxes, and planters with fresh, commercially bagged potting mix that includes slow-release fertilizers and moisturizing polymers that will save you time watering.

Prepare containers for planting—even if they're too big to empty—by mixing a slow-release fertilizer and 2 inches of compost into the top 6 inches of the soil.

When seedlings for baskets and window boxes first appear at garden centers, they are in top condition. This is a good time to acquire and plant annuals if you have a cool, sunny place to keep them until the weather is warm enough for them to go into your garden.

Plan to include in your containers the annuals with a graceful drooping habit, like **variegated vinca, sweet potato vine,** and **cascade petunias.** Leave space in the hanging baskets for second and third plantings of cascade petunias. Petunias tend to play out in August, even when deadheaded regularly; adding petunia seedlings at three-to-four week

intervals will keep the containers in full flower until September. The 'Surfinia' and 'Wave' petunias have more staying power than others.

**Garden log.** Record the date of the last frost, when you planted what in your garden, and how the plants fared.

## PLANTING

Sow seeds indoors of annuals that need four to six weeks to mature before going outdoors. (See January.)

Where the date of the last anticipated frost is in April, get ready to plant seeds and seedlings of hardy annuals outdoors a little before the date of the last frost, and of semi-hardy annuals a little after it.

Wait until night temperatures are steady at or above 55 degrees Fahrenheit to put seeds and seedlings of tender annuals and perennials outdoors.

If the **icicle pansies** planted last fall look meager, give them a few weeks of warm weather to grow full, and then fill in around them with fresh **pansy** seedlings.

To hide the yellowing leaves of the early spring-flowering bulbs, plant or set out pots of big container-grown **sweet william, pot marigolds,** and tall **snapdragons.**

## CARE

**Indoors.** Transplant seedlings outgrowing their containers to larger pots.

Easy transplanting instructions:

*1* Prepare and fertilize the beds for planting as explained in March. The soil should still have enough moisture to make watering before planting unnecessary.

*2* To prepare seedlings for life outdoors, harden them off for five or six days in a sheltered spot out of the wind and direct sun. The soil they are growing in will dry more quickly outdoors, so water as needed. Seedlings fresh from a greenhouse also benefit from a few days in a sheltered spot before being planted in the open garden.

*3* Check the soil moisture daily, especially flats whose soil is hidden by foliage. A six-pack's tiny planting pockets can dry out in just hours on a windy day, and you won't know it until the leaves collapse.

*4* When it is time to plant, in addition to the seedlings, take to the garden a pail of water to which you have added starter solution or a dose of manure tea or liquid seaweed.

*5* Make planting holes with the end of your trowel for as many seedlings as you will be putting in the area. Remove an equal number of seedlings from their containers; use a sharp knife to separate any that are entangled.

**6** Before setting a seedling in its hole, gently unwind roots circling the rootball and cut off those matted at the bottom. Set the seedlings upright in their planting holes, starting with the hole farthest from you. Add 1/2 cupful of starter solution to each planting hole.

**7** When the water has drained, fill the holes with soil, and firm the soil. The seedlings should be set in tightly enough that they resist a gentle tug. Pinch out the central stem and branch tips of the seedlings that branch to encourage early branching, which will produce more surfaces for flowers.

**8** Water the area with a sprinkler for half an hour or so.

**9** Spread a 2-inch mulch over the bed, but try to keep it two inches or so away from the stems of the seedlings.

**10** Maintain the soil moisture to assure unchecked plant growth.

## Did You Know?

### These Annuals Are Best for Baskets

- **Bacopa** (*Sutera cordata* 'Snowflake')
- **Basket Begonia** (*Begonia* x *tuberhybrida* Pendula Group)
- **Black-eyed Susan Vine** (*Thunbergia alata*)
- **Cascade Petunia** (*Petunia* x *hybrida*)
- **Cigar Flower** (*Cuphea ignea*)
- **Creeping Zinnia** (*Sanvitalia procumbens*)
- **Edging Lobelia** (*Lobelia erinus*)
- **Fanflower** (*Scaevola aemula*)
- **Impatiens, Busy Lizzy** (*Impatiens wallerana*)
- **Ivy-leaf and Balcon Geraniums** (*Pelargonium peltatum*)
- **Lady's-eardrops** (*Fuchsia* x *hybrida*)
- **Nasturtium** (*Tropaeolum majus*)
- **Painted Nettle** (*Coleus blumei*)
- **Rose Moss** (*Portulaca grandiflora*)
- **Sapphire Flower** (*Browallia speciosa*)
- **Tall Nasturtium** (*Tropaeolum majus*)
- **Trailing Coleus** (*Coleus rehnelthianus* 'Trailing Rose')
- **Verbena** (*Verbena* x *hybrida*)
- **Water Hyssop** (*Bacopa caroliniana*)
- **Yellow Sage** (*Lantana camara*)

## WATERING

Seeds and seedlings in the garden need rain often enough to maintain soil moisture. If the weather turns dry towards the end of the month, water your seedlings deeply. Specific directions of deep watering are given in the general Introduction.

## PRUNING

Deadhead early-spring annuals—**pansies, sweet william, wallflowers.**

## FERTILIZING

**Indoors.** Continue to fertilize seedlings of the annuals and tender perennials that will remain indoors until the air temperature reaches 55 degrees Fahrenheit at night.

If you are using chemical fertilizers, you will need to fertilize according to the formulation inscribed on the fertilizer container.

## PESTS

Spider mites can be a problem for seedlings indoors. See Pests, Diseases, and Controls in the Appendix.

## PLANNING

In zones where the last frost may come in mid-May, plan to plant seeds and seedlings of hardy annuals outdoors a little before that date, and of semi-hardy annuals a little after it.

Cruise the garden centers searching for seedlings to fill gaps left by **spring-flowering bulbs,** and look for annuals for late summer bloom—**cosmos,** for example, and **China asters**. Buy a few annuals that are fragrant at night and flowers that will reflect moonlight—white, pale yellow, or pink. Seedlings of white **annual stock** are very fragrant late in the day; it may slow with mid-summer heat but revives when mid-August cools.

**Garden log.** As spring gardens begin to peak, visit public and private gardens and record the plant combinations you wish were blooming in your own garden right now.

Take note when night temperatures reached a steady 55 degrees Fahrenheit, what you planted when, and what is blooming.

Evaluate your spring garden and your responses to it.

## PLANTING

This month is a big planting season. When night temperatures are 55 to 60 degrees Fahrenheit, you can sow seeds of tender annuals outdoors and set out seedlings of tender perennials grown as annuals. Most **tropicals** can safely be moved back outdoors at that temperature, too.

Where spring bulbs leave gaps, make successive sowings of **zinnias** and **annual phlox.** Make second and third plantings of **petunia** seedlings in window boxes and hanging baskets.

Sow late-blooming biennials for next year's display—either indoors, outdoors in a well-ventilated cold frame (see September, Herbs & Vegetables), or in an out-of-the-way place in the garden.

As the **pansies** die, where summers are cool replace them with **edging lobelia.** Where heat comes in May, replace them with heat-tolerant **impatiens, New Guinea impatiens, wax begonias, dwarf snapdragons, dwarf marigolds, dwarf zinnias,** or **sweet alyssum** (a fragrant edger that will perfume evenings in late summer).

## CARE

Thin seedlings to 2 to 3 inches apart.

If plants in hanging baskets and containers become crowded, remove the least vigorous seedlings.

## PRUNING

Deadhead **pansies** and shear **lobelia** to prolong the flowering cycle.

Monitor and pinch out the tips of branching and vining annuals that develop one or more strong central stems. Continue to pinch them back until the stems are 6 inches long. Tall **snapdragons, salvia, stock, petunias,** and other cascading plants are among those that benefit from persistent pinching.

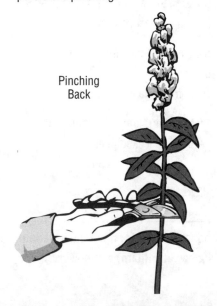

Pinching Back

*Unless the garden is moist from recent rain, before every planting gently and slowly water long enough to lay down 1 to 1½ inches.*

**Weeding.** Weeds aren't always ugly, but they always take up water and soil nutrients. They appear plentifully now, and by mid-summer the big roots are hard to pull. A permanent mulch, close planting, and planting through a porous black fabric keep them down.

If they're less than 1 inch high, you can rake weeds up. When they're 6 inches high, you'll need a hoe to cut them down. After that—well, the worst thing for a newly established garden is to have weeds go to seed there or nearby. They'll haunt you for years to come.

Don't pull big weeds from bone-dry soil—they're more tenacious than they are in moist soil, and the upheaval of the soil can cost moisture. Water the garden first, then tug the weeds out gently but firmly to get the roots up. Shake the soil back into the garden, and compost the weeds.

 WATERING

Unless the garden is moist from recent rain, before every planting gently and slowly water long enough to lay down 1 inch. Use an empty can to measure the water. Let soil dry slightly. After planting, water the area for half an hour more.

Maintain the moisture in beds of newly planted seeds and seedlings. Unchecked growth is essential to the development of root systems strong enough to bloom and withstand summer heat and dry spells. If you do not have a good soaking rain every week to ten days, water planted beds gently and slowly long enough to lay down 1 or 1½ inches.

This month begin biweekly checks of the moisture in big plant containers; check the moisture level in small pots and hanging baskets every day or two.

 FERTILIZING

Begin a regular fertilizing program for hanging baskets and container plants.

They'll benefit from biweekly applications of a soluble fertilizer or manure tea at half strength.

If you are using chemical fertilizers in the garden, you will need to repeat according to the formulation inscribed on the fertilizer container.

 PESTS

Be on guard against aphids, spider mites, whiteflies, and, in rainy weather, snails and slugs. See Pests, Diseases, and Controls in the Appendix for more information.

# JUNE
## Annuals & Biennials

 PLANNING

Visit public gardens and study what they have used as follow-on plants for spring bulbs.

**Garden log.** Record the dates and locations of especially worthwhile late spring plant sales.

Continue to record and date the development of this year's plantings.

It is far enough into the season now to evaluate the performance of transplants of rooted cuttings and plants saved from last year—**geraniums, coleus, impatiens, wax begonias,** and others—and decide whether this is something you want to do again in the fall.

### PLANTING

Remove hardy spring flowers that have gone by, like **larkspur, nigella,** and **pot marigold,** to make space for seedlings of annuals that will bloom in summer and fall—**snapdragons, blue** and **white salvia, China asters, cosmos, nasturtiums,** for example. Try 'Silver Cup' **mallow** (*Lavatera trimestris*), whose showy pink blooms light up the late garden.

Make space in baskets and containers for fresh petunia seedlings. They'll keep color there after earlier plantings play out.

Use seedlings of annuals to fill gaps opening up in perennial beds as the remnants of the spring-flowering bulbs disappear.

Volunteers of self-sown **snapdragons, French marigolds, cosmos,** and other annuals pop up every year, and they make good fillers even if they don't have a long blooming season ahead.

### CARE

Maintain a 2-inch mulch around your annuals, but try to keep it 2 to 3 inches away from the crowns of the plants. Fine grade hammermill bark, pine and hardwood bark, west coast fir bark, cedar bark, and cypress are excellent. Cocoa hulls are pretty, but they aren't best where mold or varmints are problems. Compost and ground leaves (saved in bags last October) can also be used but tend to get weedy.

The tallest flowers may benefit from staking—tall **snapdragons** and **zinnias,** 'Climax' **marigolds** and **woodland tobacco.** Set the stakes within 2 to 3 inches of the stems. Choose stakes as tall as the plants are likely to grow. Tie the main stems loosely to the stakes with soft green wool, raffia, or cotton string. Keep track of the upward growth of the tall plants, and tie them higher up as they soar.

### PRUNING

Be ruthless with weeds. Root out prolific self-sowing annuals like **love-in-a-mist** just as you would weeds. To kill a large weed or several at one time without harming neighboring plants, remove the top and bottom of a plastic gallon jug, set it over the group or plant, and spray the plants inside with herbicide.

Continue to pinch out the tips of the **petunias** and other cascading plants and branching annuals.

Controlling Weeds

Snip off at ground level the stems of plants crowding others, as **nasturtiums** often will, and cut back the outer stems of perennials that are crowding annuals planted among them.

# WATERING

Check the moisture in plant containers, hanging baskets, and window boxes daily or every other day. On hot, windy days even large containers may need frequent watering. Terracotta containers dry out especially quickly.

Maintain moisture in new plantings of seeds and seedlings. Annuals have shallow roots and need sustained moisture. Gently water plants that show signs of wilting at noon or in late afternoon.

# FERTILIZING

Check and, if needed, add enough more compost or fertile potting soil to plant containers to maintain the soil level where it was when you first planted them. Continue to fertilize with a half dose of houseplant fertilizer or weak manure tea every two weeks.

If you are using chemical fertilizers in the garden, you will need to repeat according to the formulation inscribed on the fertilizer container.

## Did You Know?

### The Importance of Deadheading/Harvesting

Removing fading blooms stops plants from developing seeds and stimulates the production of flowers. It's called "deadheading." If your garden is small, you can pinch out dying blossoms while you drink your morning cuppa. If the area is big, go to the garden in late afternoon and enjoy the sunset while you search out and remove spent blooms.

"Pinching out" is the quick and easy way to deadhead large flowers on slender stems. Place your thumbnail and forefinger behind the bracts—the small scale-like leaves behind the petals—and squeeze the flower head off. To deadhead stems too thick to pinch out, use small pointed pruning shears made especially for the purpose; they're as fine as embroidery scissors.

Shearing with hand-held shears is the easy way to deadhead plants that cover themselves with tiny florets, **sweet alyssum,** for example.

Shearing may help plants attacked by mildew; cut them down to the ground. Diseased foliage goes into the garbage—not into the compost pile. Then apply sulfur, ultrafine horticultural oil, copper fungicide, Immunox, or Bayleton. Plant mildew-resistant varieties next year.

Harvesting most annuals has the same effect as deadheading. Cut the stems of **zinnias** and **cosmos** just above a pair of leaves, which is where the next set of flowering stems will develop.

Annuals that have been blooming lavishly benefit from a sidedressing of compost, or a foliar feeding of liquid fish emulsion, liquid seaweed, manure, or compost tea.

 PESTS

Avoid overwatering in hot muggy weather because it encourages mildew. If powdery mildew appears, as it often does on **nonresistant** varieties of **zinnias** and **annual phlox,** remove severely infected plants, and thin the bed to allow air all around. Check the plantings often, and take spent flowers, fallen petals, and leaves to the trash. Don't compost them. Spray the planting with a combination of 1 tablespoon of baking soda and 1 tablespoon of ultrafine horticultural oil in a gallon of water. See Pests, Diseases, and Controls in the Appendix for stronger measures.

PLANNING

Before your vacation, arrange to have the container plantings watered, and group the containers in a semi-shaded spot.

**Garden log.** Note when summer dry spells begin and how long they last.

Weary of deadheading? Make a note to try annuals that self-clean next year—**narrowleaf zinnias, wax begonias, impatiens, ageratum, pentas, New Guinea impatiens,** and **spider flower.**

When you sow biennials, note their location so you will know to leave the soil undisturbed when preparing the garden beds this fall and early next spring.

 PLANTING

Early this month you can start seeds of hardy fall-flowering annuals—**pansies, calendula** (try the newcomer 'Pink Surprise'), **ornamental cabbage,** and **kale.** Biennials for next year's bloom to start now include **foxglove, money plant,** and **sweet william.**

 CARE

Remove crowded plants and poor performers from baskets and window boxes. If there is space, available seedlings, and six to eight weeks of growing weather ahead, replant with fresh seedlings.

Monitor staked annuals, and tie the main stems and branches higher up.

 PRUNING

Continue to deadhead. Hoe out unwanted self-sowers. Cut back by half the **petunia** stems with only a few buds remaining at the tips. Pinch off spiky **coleus** flowers and ungainly stems. Shear **ageratum, dwarf zinnias, marigolds,** and **cosmos,** to encourage a new round of flowers.

 WATERING

Check the moisture in large plant containers every three to four days; check small pots and hanging baskets every day or two.

Don't try to stimulate bloom in **ageratum** and other annuals that brown out in high heat by watering or fertilizing. Water lightly only when needed. They'll recover when the weather cools.

When there's no rain for eight to ten days, water the gardens slowly and deeply. Overhead watering should not cause problems as long as you water deeply and the foliage dries between sessions. Watering early in the morning saves water loss to evaporation. Daytime watering lowers leaf temperatures and reduces stress, but evening watering is all right. Where mildew is a problem, avoid wetting the foliage.

 FERTILIZING

Plants that are blooming vigorously may benefit from a sidedressing of a handful of compost. Or, with a hose sprayer, apply diluted solutions of fish emulsion, liquid seaweed, manure, or compost tea to the foliage.

If you are using chemical fertilizers in the garden, you will need to repeat according to the formulation inscribed on the fertilizer container.

Continue to fertilize container plants every two weeks with a half-strength dose of liquid fertilizer.

Top containers—where the soil has shrunk—with a layer of compost.

 PESTS

In hot, airless corners, aphids, spider mites, and whiteflies are a threat. Spray with a Neem-based product to help.

Japanese beetles emerge this month. Spraying now with a Neem product may help. Plan to treat the garden and the lawn

*Remove crowded plants and poor performers from baskets and window boxes. If there is space, available seedlings, and six to eight weeks of growing weather ahead, replant with fresh seedlings.*

## Did You Know?

### How to Dry Flowers for Potpourris and Winter Bouquets

As flowers used in potpourris and dried bouquets come into bloom, harvest the best specimens. Summer's dry heat is a good time for drying flowers.

When harvesting for **potpourris**, pick the flower heads in a dry, hot moment of the day. Spread the petals over paper towels on screens. Set the screens to dry in a warm, airy, dry place—a high-ceilinged attic, for example, or a garage.

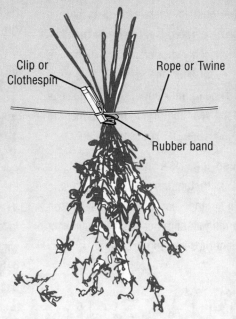

Clip or Clothespin

Rope or Twine

Rubber band

For **dried bouquets,** harvest large, moist flowers like **zinnias** when the blooms are fully open. Single varieties are better for drying than doubles. Harvest dryish flowers like the **everlastings** and **salvia** just before the buds open. Cut fresh, healthy stems 12 to 14 inches long, and strip away all the lower leaves to prepare them for drying.

**Air drying.** Tie the stems together in small, loose bunches, then enclose the heads in paper bags as they shed. Label the bags. Hang the bunches upside down for two to ten days, or until very dry, in a warm, airy, dark place. Direct sunlight fades the colors.

**Silica gel.** Use this light, grainy gel to dry delicate, moist flowers like **cosmos.** Spread 2 or 3 inches of gel in a large box. Wire the flower stems, lay them on the gel, and cover them with more silica gel. In twenty-four hours check a flower; if it is dry, remove the others from the gel, and leave them on top of it for another day. Then store them layered in tissue in air-tight, labeled boxes to which you have added a few tablespoons of silica gel. If gel clings to the petals, pour a little clean sand over them to remove them. With use, the gel's blue crystals turn pink. To restore it for later use, spread the gel over cookie sheets covered with paper towels and heat in a conventional oven on low, thirty minutes for a 1-pound can. The gel turns light blue when it is ready to use again. The gel gets hot, so let it cool it in the oven five to ten minutes and then store it in air-tight containers.

**Oven-drying.** Dryish flowers dry well in a conventional oven on a low setting, and a microwave oven at half-power can dry flowers in minutes. Dry a test flower for each batch to learn the length of time the others will need. Support the flower with paper towels before drying it. The outside petals dry sooner than those inside. To avoid over-drying in either type of oven, check progress often through the oven window.

for Milky Spore in late summer. It begins to be effective next year. The common recommendation for treatment is to apply according to the instructions on the container or three times per year for two years; it is said that once the population of spores in the soil is built up, they will remain active for up to twenty years.

If you face powdery mildew, remove the infected plants and thin the bed to provide more air. Remove spent flowers, fallen petals, and leaves, and take them to the trash. Then apply sulfur, ultrafine horticultural oil, copper fungicide, Immunox, or Bayleton. Plant mildew-resistant varieties next year. For other controls, see the section on Pests, Diseases, and Controls in the Appendix of the book.

PLANNING

The way summer shuts down toward mid-August in upstate gardens always takes us by surprise. Suddenly the days are noticeably shorter, and the nights are cool even when the sun is hot at midday. Time to think about gathering seeds for next year and drying flowers that are peaking. (See Did You Know in July.)

**Garden log.** Note the annuals that are best withstanding August heat and drought and record those that go on blooming as summer cools. You'll want to plant those again next year.

 PLANTING

Toward the end of the month replace spent annuals with seedlings of **pansies, calendula, flowering cabbage, kale,** and other fall annuals. If you didn't start them yourself earlier, you'll find seedlings at garden centers.

 CARE

Check, and if needed, replenish the mulch. It decomposes in summer heat.

Check the annuals you have staked. If needed, install taller stakes.

During the hottest part of summer, many annuals stall—**ageratum** and **French marigolds,** for example. They slow or stop blooming. Don't try to force them to grow by watering or fertilizing. This is the plant's way of protecting itself. When the weather cools they'll come back.

 PRUNING

Late summer annuals provide some of the year's loveliest bouquets, so harvest as the summer flowers peak!! Our favorite bouquets include airy **cosmos** with spikes of blue **salvia,** mid-sized **dahlias, snapdragons,** and stems of **basil** and **mint** for their sweet spicy aroma.

Attics and garages are hot and dry in August, perfect for air-drying (see July) **statice, blue salvia,** and other flowers. They make beautiful winter bouquets.

About mid-month, cut the remaining **petunia** stems back by two-thirds and sprinkle the foliage with a manure tea or liquid fertilizer; they'll bloom into September.

 WATERING

Continue to check the moisture in big plant containers every four days; check small pots and hanging baskets every day or two. Containers will have filled up with roots by now—so they need more frequent watering than earlier when plenty of moist soil surrounded the roots.

You will probably have to water the gardens twice this month. If you can, water in the early morning. Water gently and deeply, as described in July. In extreme heat, shower the garden at noon to lower the temperature and provide the plants with immediate relief. Where mildew is a threat, water the soil rather than the plants.

Water your compost pile when you water the garden. Turn it often.

 FERTILIZING

If you are using chemical fertilizers in the garden, you will need to repeat according to the formulation inscribed on the fertilizer container.

The mulch you applied is decomposing and providing fresh organic elements, and the organic fertilizers added to the soil last spring are still making nutrients available.

But the self-sowing annuals that will give you next year's crop can use a little help—**alyssum, larkspur,** and **nigella,** for example. Push the remaining mulch away and rake compost or a four-month slow-release fertilizer into the soil under the parent plants. The seeds will do best if they fall into a 1- or 2-inch layer of damp, humusy soil. When the seedheads are dry and the seeds are loose inside, then shake the flower heads vigorously over the soil. Let the plants stand into fall to drop their remaining seeds.

 PESTS

Do not let weeds get a headstart!! They're drifting into your garden right now, looking for a place to live.

Vary deer deterrents; they'll be coming for your **impatiens** by the end of the month.

Aphids, thrips, and spider mites love warm weather. Plants infested by spider mites have a faded, stippled look. Blow them away with a strong spray from the hose; rogue out badly infested plants. If the damage is considerable, consider a non-toxic spray.

## Did You Know?

### How to Harvest, Dry, and Store Seeds

Harvesting seeds can give you great pleasure. To be sure you get the plant you expect from the seeds collected, harvest only seeds of species plants. Seeds of cultivars do not reliably repeat the qualities that are special; some or all may revert to the original species.

**Harvesting.** Harvest seeds that are ripe but not so ripe that the seedheads drop or spew seeds to the ground. Ripe seeds are usually dark. When the vegetative envelopes swelling at the base of spent flowers begin to yellow and dry up, you can begin to harvest. Place the open end of a paper bag under a seedhead, and snip it into the bag.

**Drying seeds.** Spread seedheads and seeds on screens (try second-hand shops) lined with newspaper, and set them to dry in a warm, dry room until the seed envelopes are crackling dry, about five days. Separate the seeds from the chaff by rubbing the seedheads between your palms over a bowl. Gently blow away the chaff. Spread the seeds out to dry for another ten days.

**Storing seeds.** Pour the seeds into glass jars, and cap them tightly. In a few days, if moisture has appeared inside the glass, air dry the seeds another few days. Store them in jars or small freezer bags. Label and date each one. Put a small mesh bag filled with flour into each container to absorb moisture. Some gardeners prefer to store seeds in the fridge.

Japanese beetles are completing their above-ground feeding and dropping into the soil to lay their eggs. Spraying with a Neem product may help now, and for the future, treat the garden and the lawn around with Milky Spore in late summer. It begins to be effective the following year. (See July, Pests.)

If mildew persists despite July treatments, clear the bed, rake out the remains of the plants, and dispose of them in the trash—do not compost. Apply to the soil the controls recommended under Pests in July.

## PLANNING

As you begin to plant the flowering bulbs for next spring, look through your catalogs for appealing annuals that will come up early enough to screen the ripening bulb foliage after the flowers fade.

**Garden log.** Visit public and neighboring gardens, and keep notes on attractive combinations of fall bedding plants.

Note the date of the first light frost, the one that blackens the tips of the **impatiens,** and report how each of the annuals withstood it and how window box and basket plants fared as summer ended.

Note where the self-sowers are likely to have dropped seed and where you have sown biennials so you will know to leave the soil undisturbed when preparing the garden beds next spring.

## PLANTING

Where frosts come early, begin to clear away played-out annuals. *Petunia integrifolia* and "supertunias" in the Wave series withstand some frost, so let them bloom on, along with the **snapdragons, variegated myrtle,** and **geraniums,** which can take a lot of cold. If you expect a long warm Indian summer ahead, replant the beds and planters in protected spots with seedlings of **pansies, violas, calendula, flowering cabbages, kale,** and other hardy annuals. Replace the soil in window boxes and containers before replanting them. The growing medium needn't include water-holding polymers.

## CARE

When nighttime temperatures plunge towards 55 degrees Fahrenheit, get ready to move **tender perennials** and **tropicals** indoors. A week before the move, rinse the plants and clean the exterior of the containers, and when the plants are dry spray them with an insecticide to protect them from whiteflies and spider mites.

Tropicals like **mandevilla** and **bougainvillea** thrive in a greenhouse and indoors in a sunny place. Growing in big tubs, they may survive in a semi-dormant state in a frost-free garage, garden shed, or basement if you keep the soil damp. To spare your back, move them when the soil is almost dry.

Several tender perennials make happy houseplants if you transplant them to fresh potting soil. **Impatiens** (African violet potting mix; semi-sun), **pentas,** and **browallia** do well indoors.

We keep the most striking **coleus** by growing bouquets of cuttings in water. Here's how:

- Cut a dozen or more stems 12 to 14 inches long. Make the cut just below a node.

- Strip the leaves from the bottom 6 inches, and arrange the stems in a big glass bowl in clean water containing 6 drops of a liquid fertilizer.

- Keep the cuttings in a cool room in good light.

- Change the water every month, and add a few drops of liquid fertilizer. Pinch out flower spikes as they appear.

**Geraniums** can come indoors, too, and succeed in a cool room with lots of sun. Repot them in clean clay pots filled with slightly gritty potting soil. Or, water them; place roots, dirt, and all in individual plastic bags; tie them just below the foliage; and store in a cool, dark room for winter.

Another way to keep **geraniums** is by rooting cuttings. Cut 4-inch stems just below a node, and let them dry for a few hours. Then, dip the cut ends lightly in rooting hormone, and stand them in damp vermiculite or sand. Tent them with plastic film, and keep the film in place until the stems have developed enough roots to resist a slight tug. Then transplant the rooted cuttings to individual pots.

**Wax begonias** and **impatiens** make excellent houseplants and bloom all winter. Select healthy plants, cut the tops back by a third, dig them, transplant them to potting soil, water, and place them in a sunny window.

# PRUNING

Harvest **impatiens** stems with half-opened buds for fillers for bouquets. A branch of one of the giant **marigolds** makes a bouquet all by itself and lasts a week or so.

Continue to deadhead and harvest late-summer bloomers. Deadhead the **pansies.**

# WATERING

If you encounter dry spells, maintain soil moisture where you have sown seeds for biennials and where there are self-sowers.

## Did You Know?

### How to Create a Geranium Tree Standard

A **geranium** (or a **lantana** or **rosemary** for that matter) with a strong central stem is easy to train as a tree standard. Repot it in gritty potting soil. Tie the central stem firmly to a straight, sturdy stake. Bring the plant indoors to a sunny window in a cool room. Turn it at least once a month so all sides get equal sun.

• In January or February when new growth begins, remove all the branches and leaves except those growing at the top of the central stem. Pinch out the tips of those branches to begin to shape the top into a globe.

• In May, repot the plant, and move it outdoors for the summer. Continue pruning.

• When the central stem reaches 4 feet, allow the plant to bush out at the top. Continue to pinch the branch tips to encourage it to bush out in the shape of a globe.

• In coming years continue to prune, shape, repot, and stake the plant. Winter it indoors, and summer it outdoors.

 FERTILIZING

Apply a light foliar feeding to snapdragons, stock, and other annuals that bloom until frosts.

# PESTS

Deer are becoming very active; here they mow down the tops of **impatiens** right by the front door. So as the month begins, re-establish your protection by exchanging all the deer deterrents you set out earlier for new or different deterrents.

Weed seeds are maturing. Rake up seedlings. Water mature weeds, then tug on them gently but firmly so as to get all of the roots up. Shake the soil clinging to the roots back into the garden. If you can't pull them without disturbing a nearby plant, chop the weeds back to the crown with a hoe and put the seedheads in the trash.

# OCTOBER
## Annuals & Biennials

## PLANNING

This is an especially good time to start—or to change—the shape or size of a flower bed. Use a garden hose to outline potential changes, and live with them a few days before you start to dig.

Early fall is ideal for dividing and moving most perennials. If you'd like to make more space for annuals next year in perennial beds, make the moves now.

**Garden log.** Record the date of the first hard frost, the one that hits the **salvias** and **snapdragons.**

Note the bedding plants used in public gardens to replace faded summer annuals.

Note the planting of a cover crop and its progress.

## PLANTING

**Cover crop.** A cover crop is a planting of a fast-growing grass or legume sown in an empty bed or row to prevent the soil from eroding, to keep weeds from getting started, and sometimes as a way to overgrow and choke out a die-hard weed. Turned under after it has grown up, this "green manure" provides the soil with organic matter that enhances soil structure, adds nutrients, increases microbial activity, and helps to break up compacted areas.

In our area **winter rye** and **winter wheat** are the most popular cover crops. Sometimes combined with **hairy vetch** (*Trifolium pratense*), a nitrogen-capturing legume, they are usually sown in early fall and decompose underground over the winter.

Planting a cover crop is simple enough. Till a quick-acting fertilizer into the soil, then broadcast the seeds over the bed. Keep the soil moist until the seeds have sprouted. Dig and turn under your cover crop before the plants go to seed, at least ten days before planting the garden. Where soils are too wet to dig in early spring, a cover crop is turned under before the ground freezes in late fall or early winter.

## CARE

Pull up and compost frost-blackened **marigolds, impatiens,** and the tender annuals still out in the garden and in containers.

Turn the compost pile.

Clear away the remains of annuals planted over spring-flowering bulbs.

## PRUNING

Continue to deadhead the **pansies, calendula,** and any other flowers still blooming.

## WATERING

If the weather turns dry, water the **pansies,** the areas around the self-sowing annuals, and the cover crop if you planted one.

## FERTILIZING

Get a head start on spring by checking the pH of your soil now.

## PESTS

Watch out for whiteflies and spider mites on the plants brought indoors for winter. If occasional showers and applications of insecticidal soap don't keep them away, apply an insecticide. See Pests, Diseases, and Controls in the Appendix for more information.

PLANNING

From the public library, borrow garden books, such as Graham Rice's books, *Discovering Annuals* and *The Sweet Pea Book* (Timber Press), and videos that can teach you more about using annuals in garden design.

**Garden log.** Do you use a computer or paper diary? A computer log is easy to adjust, change, improve, and has a "find" button. If you are computer literate with a digital camera or photography software, you could include images. Writing in a diary takes time, but you may be more open to inspiration and pleasant memories. Holding a written diary in your hand can be a richer experience than looking something up on the computer.

 PLANTING

The annuals are all done for now. Focus on spring-flowering bulbs!

 CARE

Empty, clean, and store hanging baskets, window boxes, and other containers.

Stack wire baskets, and hang them from a rafter in a garage or basement. Scrub plastic and terracotta containers with a scrub pad. Then dip them in a solution of

## Did You Know?

### About Growing Scent-Leaf Geraniums

**Scent-leaf geraniums** are aromatic tender perennials that are happy indoors in the winter and outdoors in the summer. The blooms are modest, but brush against the foliage and the room fills with potent scents of nutmeg, mint, rose, or lemon.

**Lemon geranium** (*Pelargonium crispum*) is so fragrant its leaves are used in finger bowls. The flowers are two-toned pink. Recommended are 'Prince Rupert', 'Mable Grey', and 'Lemon Fancy'.

**Rose geranium** (*P. graveolens*) has the sweetest scent. It has green-gray foliage and rose-lavender flowers with a dark purple blotch.

**Apple geranium** (*P. odoratissimum* 'Gray Lady Plymouth') has beautiful variegated foliage. The leaves are ruffled and the flowers white.

**Peppermint geranium, woolly geranium** (*P. tomentosum*) smells of peppermint. It has large, soft, fuzzy, grape-like leaves and bears tiny purple-veined white flowers.

$1/2$ cup bleach to 3 gallons of water. Rinse and store upside down out of the weather; they tend to crack if left outside. If not using your window boxes, turn them upside down.

Spread the soil from hanging baskets, small and medium pots, planters, and window boxes over your compost pile.

 PRUNING

Deadhead your indoor plants.

 WATERING

Maintain soil moisture in plants you brought indoors for the winter.

 FERTILIZING

Do not fertilize the plants you brought indoors until they show signs of new growth in January.

 PESTS

Watch out for whiteflies and spider mites on plants indoors. If occasional showers and applications of insecticidal soap don't keep them away, apply an insecticide.

See Pests, Diseases, and Controls in the Appendix for more information.

# DECEMBER

## PLANNING

Go back to the album of catalog pages of garden accessories prepared last January to look for gifts for gardeners on your holiday list. And do family and friends a favor by telling them about tools and accessories you'd enjoy receiving.

Evaluate the progress of the tender perennials you brought indoors in the fall. Presented in an attractive cache pot or a vase, some might make holiday gifts. If the plants lack light, consider investing in a garden under grow lights. Cuttings root well there, and in late winter and early spring a light garden promotes growth in seeds started indoors.

If you know now which seeds you intend to start indoors, use spare moments to make row markers for them.

**Organize a seed-saver file.** Organize your supply of seeds—those purchased that weren't used and the seeds gathered in your garden. Nicely packaged, they make nifty stocking stuffers.

One of the most convenient ways I have found to file and store seeds is in a spiral binder equipped with clear plastic sleeves. Place each variety of seed in its own small freezer bag. Mark the date on the bag, and store each bag inside its own sleeve in the binder. Slide a catalog image of the seed, and any comments you have, into each sleeve.

André Viette stores seeds in small plastic bags, which he keeps in the crisper in a refrigerator. Seeds are generally considered viable for three to five years after they have been gathered, though it may be that with each passing year fewer seeds will germinate.

**Garden log.** Record the progress of the cuttings of, or potted, **tender perennials** you brought in earlier in the fall. Note especially whether there's enough light indoors for all you brought in—sunny sills, a picture window, or a Florida room—and whether you are enjoying them or finding they take too much space and are too much work.

## PLANTING

Transplant well-rooted cuttings of the plants you brought in the fall.

## CARE

**Indoors.** Cuttings of **geraniums, coleus, impatiens,** and **wax begonias** growing in water should have masses of hair-like rootlets by now. Discard any that aren't rooting. If the water is growing murky, change it and add a few small pieces of charcoal to keep it pure. We recommend adding $1/2$ teaspoon of bleach per gallon of water.

## PRUNING

**Indoors.** Pinch out the tips of the **wax begonias** and **geraniums** you brought indoors as they get leggy.

**Outdoors.** After several heavy frosts, check the **pansies,** flowering **cabbages,** and **kales**—and discard those that are dead.

## WATERING

Maintain the soil moisture in pots of tender perennials wintering indoors.

## FERTILIZING

There is no fertilizing at this time.

## PESTS

Continue to check for whiteflies and spider mites on the plants wintering indoors. Misting, fresh air, occasional showers, and applications of insecticidal soap should keep them healthy.

# CHAPTER TWO

# Bulbs, Corms, Rhizomes, & Tubers

*Spring's earliest, brightest colors, summer's most extraordinary perfumes, fall's sweetest little blossoms develop from bulbs, corms, rhizomes, and tubers, a different category of perennial. Easy to start and a snap to maintain, most multiply rapidly on their own.*

Professionals have agreed that the technical name for bulbs, corms, rhizomes, and tubers is "ornamental geophyte." But we are saved from having to remember that by Dr. August A. de Hertog, horticulturist with the University of North Carolina famed for his work with **tulips.** Dr. de Hertog assured us that, "Plants with underground storage organs can all correctly be called 'bulbs' rather than 'ornamental geophytes.'"

The term, coined by Danish plant geographer Christian Raunkiaer in 1933, has been shortened to 'geophytes.' What geophytes have in common is that they are all large storage organs ready to produce a plant—like seeds, but on a much larger scale.

Dr. de Hertogh predicts geophytes will be the name our children and our children's children will know. For now, we refer to the group as bulbs; our children can take it from there.

## PLANNING

You can count on bulb flowers to bloom the first year planted. Under the right circumstances, you can expect many species and varieties, but not all, to come back year after year. To have the large bulb flowers perennialize, you must allow the foliage to ripen at least six weeks before removing it.

There are bulb flowers that bloom in every season. In spring **daffodils** and **bluebells** spread carpets of color in our woodlands. Summer gardens are sweet with the perfume of the majestic **lilies.** Autumn **crocus** come up when the trees start to shed, and fragrant **paperwhite narcissus** and **hyacinths,** golden **daffodils,** cheery **amaryllis,** and a host of others can create a sequence of bloom in your home all winter long.

**Spring-flowering bulbs.** The year's first flowers, these bulbs are planted the preceding fall. They all tolerate our winters. All but the **narcissus/daffodil/hyacinth** group need protection from creatures that think of them as food. If you plant **tulips,** which are favorites of the squirrels, 8 inches down, it's a safeguard. Where snow cover is not certain, covering bulb plantings with a winter mulch will limit the depth of the freeze line and protect the bulbs beneath.

Mulch just before or right after the ground starts to harden, not earlier.

We mentioned the group's only drawback before: the foliage must be allowed to "ripen" (patience is a virtue; possess it if you can!) for many weeks after the blooms fade. The larger bulbs, like **tulips** and **daffodils,** take forever, so plan to place them where the growth of summer-flowering bulbs like the big **lilies,** perennials, or annuals will screen the fading leaves. Another option is to have a garden of flowering bulbs interplanted with annuals.

**Summer-flowering bulbs.** The **lilies** start up as the **daffodils** fade. Others begin to grow when the weather becomes milder. Early and late varieties bring color to mixed borders and container gardens when they need it most, mid- and late summer. The summer-flowering bulbs whose winter hardiness rating is north of Zone 6 may be planted in mid-fall (or mid-spring) without special protection for winter. Those that are at the upper edge of their cold tolerance in Zone 6 are safest in a protected spot and provided with a winter mulch. Examples are **crocosmia** and **wood sorrel** (*Oxalis adenophylla*).

## Did You Know?

### Which Is What?

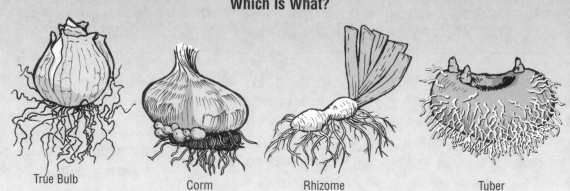

True Bulb     Corm     Rhizome     Tuber

• **"True" bulbs** are onion-like and have pointed tops, compressed scales, and flattish bottoms that develop roots quite modest compared to the system of the same size perennial. Examples are **daffodils, tulips,** and **hyacinths.** Stored within the bulb are the stem, the flower bud, and layers that are compressed leaves. Plant bulbs flat end down.

Some bulbs, like onions, are protected by a papery cover called a "tunic." **Lilies** and some other true bulbs have no protective cover; they are easily damaged and dry out quickly, so handle with care!

• **Corms** are round, fleshy, thick storage units that have flattish bottoms and a top that has one or more growing tips. This group includes **crocus, gladiolus, crocosmia,** and **freesia.** Plant these with the flattish part down.

• **Rhizomes** are fleshy lengths of thick, modified stem. They have lumpy tops and flattish bottoms from which the roots emerge. Examples are **cannas** and **bearded irises.** Lay rhizomes horizontally on the soil with the bottom down and the top even with the soil surface.

• **Tubers** are swollen rounded stems with "eyes," or growth buds, here and there. Think old potato. The eyes will grow roots or shoots, depending on their position in the soil. Examples are **dahlias, caladiums,** and **lotus.** Lay these horizontally under 2 or 3 inches of soil, or at whatever depth the supplier recommends.

Summer-flowering bulbs rated as "tender" in our area, **canna, caladiums, colocasia, dahlias, gladiolus,** and the perfumed **tuberose,** for example, must be lifted in fall, dried, and stored for winter indoors in a cool, dry place. Most need cool storage temperatures—between 35 to 50 degrees for bulbs such as **canna, dahlias, tigridia.** Others can be stored at room temperatures—**caladiums** and **calo-**casia, for example. Except for Zones 6 and 7, these tender bulbs are best started indoors early and set out in the garden when it's warm enough to plant tomato seedlings.

**Fall-flowering bulbs.** These bulbs usually are planted in summer for fall blooming. If you haven't grown the lovely late bloomers, try a few this fall. **Colchicum, fall crocus,** and **winter daffodil** open showy blooms just above ground in early September; in spring large glossy leaves rise and, after many weeks, disappear for the summer. The beautiful **resurrection lily** (*Lycoris squamigera*) produces exotic, fragrant, trumpet-shaped blooms from bulbs planted in mid-summer; north of Zone 5 it must be brought in to winter in a frost-free place.

**Bulbs for winter.** In New York, these bulbs bloom indoors. In early fall, plan to pot up spring-flowering bulbs—we especially recommend **tulips, daffodils,** and perfumed **hyacinths**—for forcing into bloom indoors in winter (see September). A few cold-tender bulb flowers can also be forced into bloom indoors in winter, notably **amaryllis** (*Hippeastrum*) and perfumed **paperwhites** (see November).

## PLANTING

**Light. Crocus, daffodils, bluebells** (*Squill, Scilla*), and the lovely **wood hyacinth** bloom in partial shade, as do some of the smaller bulbs. But most big bulb flowers do their best in full sun and need at least six hours of sun daily to come into flower a second year. That said, **daffodils** and other early flowering spring bulbs growing under deciduous trees bloom well because the trees don't leaf out until the bulb foliage has ripened.

**Soil for bulbs.** The garden and container soil in which bulbs do best is light and very well drained. Repeat, **very well drained.** Ideally, a raised bed on a slope. There are always exceptions to the rule; a few summer-bloomers tolerate moist spots—**canna, bog iris, summer snowflake, crinum, rain lily,** and **spider lily.**

The pH range most bulbs prefer is 6.0 to 7.0. There are exceptions to that rule, too. The most popular **lilies** prefer a somewhat acidic soil (see About Lilies, February). For step-by-step instructions on creating a raised bed and adjusting soil pH, turn to the section on Soil Preparation and Improvement in the Introduction to the book.

When you are planting bulbs in an existing bed, the soil needs the same careful preparation as for a raised bed for bulbs. (See Soil Preparation and Improvement in the Introduction to the book.) Outline the area, then cover it with 3 to 4 inches of humus, enough so that one quarter of the content of the soil from the hole will be organic matter. The humus can be decomposed bark, compost, partially decomposed leaves or seaweed, sphagnum peat moss, black peat humus, decomposed animal manures, or other decomposed organic material. Adding humus is particularly important if your soil has high clay content. Add the organic fertilizer Bulb-tone. Mix the humus and fertilizer into the soil as you dig it out of the hole along with the amendments for a raised bed.

**Planting.** About bulb planters—these tools work well only if the soil has been well prepared. We recommend the Dutch method of planting bulbs, which is to use a spading fork to dig a generous hole or a bed, remove the soil, and mix it thoroughly with the soil amendments mentioned above. Then, return 2 or 3 inches of improved soil to the hole, tamp it down, and plant the bulbs on top at the depth recommended.

We've explained the planting depth and spacing for the various bulb sizes in the Planting section of the October pages later. When you aren't sure of the planting depth, set the base of the bulbs at a depth that is about four times the diameter of the bulb itself.

Set true bulbs so the pointed tips are upright; set corms and tubers with the roots facing down. Set rhizomes horizontally in the soil with the roots down.

If voles, chipmunks, and squirrels hang around, plant all but the **daffodils** with a deterrent such as VoleBloc™ or PermaTill, small sharp chips of expanded natural slate. Using it is easy. Line the planting hole or bed with 2 inches of either product. Set the bulbs on top, and fill in around them with VoleBloc or PermaTill leaving just the bulb's tip exposed. Cover with an inch of VoleBloc or PermaTill, then fill the rest of the hole with a mixture of 30 percent VoleBloc or PermaTill and improved soil from the hole. Mulch with 2 inches of pine needles, oak leaves, composted wood chips, or shredded bark.

## CARE AND MULCHING

**Fall care.** Clear away dead leaves and the remains of annuals and perennials over bulb areas to prevent raking over tender new bulb foliage in spring. A light winter mulch of pine boughs helps keep leaves off.

**Mulch.** Most bulbs do not tolerate wet feet, especially when their blooming period is over. Two or 3 inches of a light mulch is all you need to give the garden a nice finish, keep weeds down, retain soil moisture, and moderate soil temperature. Never cover bulbs with more than 2 or 3 inches of mulch.

## PERENNIALIZING AND MULTIPLYING YOUR BULBS

Most hardy bulbs planted in the garden will perennialize. **Tulips** are iffy. Growers identify those likely to come back year after year. **Darwin hybrids** and the little **species tulips** almost always return. Fertilize tulips generously after they finish blooming, and you have a better chance of having them repeat and even multiply.

Smaller bulbs and naturalized **daffodils** don't need deadheading, but deadheading the larger bulbs helps them to store up the energy needed for a fine flower show the following year. Even more important than deadheading is that you allow the foliage of the large bulb flowers six to seven weeks to ripen (yellow) before removing it. **Tulip** foliage may be cut when it is yellow halfway down. The leaves of the smaller bulbs tend to disappear on their own.

Once small bulb flowers are established in a garden, they send up clumps of grass-like foliage—in spring for bulbs that flower in fall, and in late summer for bulbs that bloom in spring. Those grassy clumps aren't weeds! If you happen to dig up small bulbs when you are planting in the area, just push them back into the soil, and they likely will survive.

**Dividing bulbs, rhizomes, and tubers.** You can multiply your holdings and, in some species, improve their performance by periodically dividing your bulbs. True bulbs growing well produce offsets that in three to four years may crowd the planting and cause the flowers to be smaller and diminish.

The best time to divide bulbs is after the foliage has withered, and it's easy to do. Use a spading fork to dig and lift the bulb clump. Then you can either pull the bulbs gently apart or halve the clump, and replant. Bulblets (baby bulbs) need years to become mature enough to bloom, so plant these in an out-of-the-way place. You don't have to divide naturalized **daffodil** bulbs to keep them gorgeous . . . just fertilize them. **Lilies,** on the other hand, do best when the big bulbs are moved or divided every four years.

You may divide rhizomes and tubers either before the growing cycle begins (easier since there is no foliage to contend with) or when it is over. Dig the rhizomes or tubers, and cut them into sections that each contain at least one growth bud or eye.

Tuberous roots, such as **dahlias,** do best when they are separated shortly before growth begins.

**Transplanting.** It once was the custom to lift bulbs intended for transplanting after they had bloomed in spring, store them for the summer, and replant in the fall. But now Dutch growers assure us the best place for winter-hardy bulbs at every season is in the ground. Lifted and stored they are susceptible to fungus and disease. But growers do recommend lifting and storing bulbs that can't survive winters in your garden.

Spring-flowering bulbs can be transplanted successfully in spring, summer, or fall. You can move **daffodils** in bloom. Or wait until the flowers have faded, then cut off the flower heads, leaving the green leaves. Dig the plants with care so as not to damage the roots, and move the whole clump to the desired location. Allow the foliage to ripen naturally, just as it would have in its original spot. You can also dig the bulbs in summer or very early fall. However, after the foliage dies they're not easy to locate, and digging blind may damage the bulbs; so before the foliage fades, mark the positions of bulbs you want to move.

# Bulbs, Corms, Rhizomes, & Tubers

Summer-flowering bulbs that are hardy enough to be left in the ground in New York's warm coastal regions, Zone 6 (-10° F winter lows) or Zone 7 (0° F winter lows), may be transplanted either in fall after the foliage has yellowed or in spring just as growth begins.

Fall-flowering bulbs may be moved after the blooms fade. Those with foliage that comes up in spring, like the fall-blooming **crocus,** can be moved then.

Winter-flowering bulbs that have been forced into bloom indoors are weakened. They won't be good for forcing a second year. **Tulips** and the smaller bulb flowers are best discarded. Some other spring-flowering bulbs, notably **daffodils,** and often **hyacinths,** forced into bloom indoors and then replanted out in the garden, sometimes come back the next year. If you plan to try them out in the garden, keep forced **daffodils** and **hyacinths** in a sunny window and continue to water and fertilize them while the foliage ripens and dies down. Keep them in a cool spot during the summer, then plant them in the garden in early fall. Many will eventually bloom in their outdoor locations.

**Watering.** It's not necessary to water the soil after planting bulbs. But you do have to keep the soil moderately damp for bulbs growing in containers.

On the rare occasion when spring runs dry, provide spring-flowering bulbs with ample moisture from the moment the tips first break ground and during the season of active growth. Once the foliage disappears, the bulbs are dormant and excess watering can be detrimental. Underground automatic sprinkling systems spell death to most bulbs unless adjusted to water deeply and only when moisture is needed—not every day, not every other day, not even every third day.

Summer-flowering bulbs need moderate moisture all during their growing and blooming season, just as perennials do. Water deeply every week to ten days unless you have a soaking rain.

**Fertilizing.** All bulbs need continuing fertilization if they are to thrive and multiply.

There are two schools of thought on fertilizing spring-flowering bulbs.

In their book *Daffodils*, daffodil gurus Brent and Becky Heath recommend applying a diluted organic fertilizer to spring-flowering bulb plantings from the time the tips show in spring until the bulbs bloom. They suggest fertilizing again in early fall with a slow-release product (5-10-12 or 5-12-20) such as Bulb Mate.

André recommends fertilizing spring-flowering bulbs as soon as they finish blooming with Bulb-tone at the rate of 4 to 6 pounds to every 100 square feet, and again in early September. André

also recommends fertilizing established summer-flowering bulbs in early spring before growth begins and again in mid-fall.

**Pests.** Squirrels, chipmunks, and voles truly believe you plant all bulbs except **daffodils** (which are toxic) just for their delight, in the ground, planters, window boxes, and hanging baskets. The solution is to plant bulbs in VoleBloc or PermaTill, as recommended in Planting, earlier. Deer love **tulips, crocus, lilies,** too! Spraying is not always a deterrent, but a temporary chicken wire enclosure (see Pests, Diseases, and Controls in the Appendix) or bird netting may save them.

## Did You Know?

### Favorite Cutting Tulips

These tulips together make beautiful bouquets and are all readily available. Use this list as you plan your garden.

- 'Duke of Wellington', big, pure white
- 'Temple of Beauty', lily-shaped pink/orange
- 'Marilyn', white with rose-red streaks
- 'Ballerina', fragrant yellow/red/orange
- 'Fancy Frills', fringed rose/white
- 'Queen of the Night', deep purple-maroon
- 'Aleppo', fringed raspberry/rose/apricot

# Bulbs, Corms, Rhizomes, & Tubers

| Common Name (Botanical Name) | Hardiness | Type | Bloom Time | Planting Time | Planting Depth |
|---|---|---|---|---|---|
| **Amaryllis** (*Hippeastrum* spp. and cvs.) | Zones 9 to 10 | Bulb | Force for indoor bloom | Fall, winter | In pot, 2/3 covered |
| **Autumn Daffodil** (*Sternbergia lutea*) | Zones 6 to 7 | Bulb | September to October | Summer to late October | 4 to 6 inches |
| **Bearded Iris** (*Iris* x *germanica*) | Zones 3 to 8 | Rhizome | May, early June; lasting foliage | Late summer, early fall | At soil surface, partly exposed |
| **Caladium** (*Caladium bicolor*) | Zones 9 to 11 | Tuber | Colorful foliage for part shade | Start indoors in spring | 3 to 4 inches |
| **Calla Lily** (*Zantedeschia* spp.) | Tender | Tuberous rhizome for containers | Summer | Late spring | 3 to 4 inches |
| **Canna** (*Canna* x *generalis*) | Zones 8 to 11 | Fleshy rhizome | Colorful foliage all summer | Start indoors in spring | 3 to 4 inches |
| **Colchicum, Meadow Saffron** (*Colchicum* cvs.) | Zones 4 to 9 | Corm | September to October | Summer or fall | 6 inches |
| **Crinum Lily, Spider Lily** (*Crinum moorei*) | Zones 8 to 11 | Bulb | Summer to fall | Spring | 6 inches |
| **Crocus, Autumn** (*Crocus* spp.) | Hardy | Corm | September to October | July, August | 4 to 6 inches |
| **Crocus, Dutch Crocus** (*Crocus vernus* cvs.) | Zones 3 to 7 | Corm | March to April (naturalizes) | Fall | 3 to 4 inches |
| **Crown Imperial** (*Fritillaria imperialis*) | Zones 3 to 8 | Bulb | April | Fall | 6 inches (set horizontally) |
| **Daffodil** (*Narcissus* spp. and cvs.) | Zones 3 to 9 | Bulb | March to May | Early fall (naturalizes) | 4 to 6 inches |
| **Dahlia** (*Dahlia* spp. and cvs.) | Zones 9 to 11 | Tuber | Blooms summer, early fall | Late spring (start early indoors Zones 3 to 5) | 4 to 6 inches |
| **Dogtooth Violet** (*Erythronium dens-canis*) | Zones 4 to 8 | Bulb | April (shade) | Early fall | 6 inches |
| **Flowering Onion** (*Allium* spp.) | Zones 3 to 8 | Bulb | May to June | Fall | To 18 inches, depending on species |
| **Gladiola** (*Gladiolus* x *hortulanus*) | Zones 7 to 11 | Corm | Mid- to late summer (plant at 2-week intervals) | Spring | 3 to 4 inches |

# Bulbs, Corms, Rhizomes, & Tubers

| Common Name (*Botanical Name*) | Hardiness | Type | Bloom Time | Planting Time | Planting Depth |
|---|---|---|---|---|---|
| **Glory-of-the-snow** (*Chionodoxa* spp.) | Zones 4 to 8 | Bulb | March to April | Fall (naturalizes) | 3 to 4 inches |
| **Grape Hyacinth** (*Muscari* spp.) | Zones 3 to 8 | Bulb | April to May | Fall (naturalizes) | 4 inches |
| **Greek Windflower** (*Anemone blanda*) | Zones 4 to 8 | Rhizome | March to April | Fall (plant in groups) | 4 inches |
| **Hyacinth** (*Hyacinthus orientalis*) | Zones 4 to 8 | Bulb | April | Fall | 6 inches |
| **Lily** (*Lilium* spp. and cvs.) | Zones 4 to 8 | Bulb | Asiatic: late May/July; Trumpet: June/July; Oriental: July/September | Spring or fall | 6 inches |
| **Lily-of-the-Nile** (*Agapanthus* and cvs.) | Zones 7 to 11 | Bulb | Late spring, summer | Spring; indoors in pots any time | 6 inches |
| **Resurrection Lily, Hardy Amaryllis** (*Lycoris squamigera*) | Zones 5 to 8 | Bulb | August, September | Late summer/ fall | 5 inches |
| **Reticulated Iris** (*Iris reticulata* and cvs.) | Zones 4 to 8 | Bulb | Early spring | Fall | 4 inches |
| **Snowdrop** (*Galanthus* spp.) | Zones 3 to 8 | Bulb | February to March | Fall (naturalizes) | 4 to 6 inches |
| **Star Flower** (*Ipheion uniflorum*) | Zones 5 to 9 | Bulb | April to early May | Fall | 3 inches |
| **Summer Snowflake** (*Leucojum aestivum*) | Zones 4 to 9 | Bulb | Late April to May | Fall | 6 inches |
| **Tuberose** (*Polianthes tuberosa*) | Zones 8 to 11 | Tuber | Late summer, early fall (plant at 2-week intervals) | Early June | 1 inch |
| **Tuberous Begonia** (*Begonia* x *tuberhybrida*) | Zones 9 and 10 | Tuber | All summer in baskets or pots | Spring; indoors anytime | 1 to 2 inches |
| **Tulip** (*Tulipa* spp. and cvs.) | Zones 3 to 7/8 | Bulb | April to June | Fall | 6 to 12 inches |
| **Winter Aconite** (*Eranthis* spp.) | Zones 3 to 7 | Rhizome | February to March | Fall | 3 inches |
| **Wood Hyacinth** (*Hyacinthoides hispanica*) | Zones 3 to 8 | Bulb | May, June (naturalizes) | Fall | 4 to 6 inches |

# JANUARY
## Bulbs, Corms, Rhizomes, & Tubers

 PLANNING

A pleasant way to satisfy the hunger for spring flowers is to take out favorite bulb catalogs, tear out garden pages that show bulbs you would like to try or add, and then to organize them into an album. Group together the spring-bloomers, summer-bloomers, fall-bloomers, and the bulbs that can be forced to bloom in winter indoors. Place a sticky note by each plant reminding you where to plant it. In spring and early summer when the catalogs for summer-flowering, then fall- and spring-flowering bulbs arrive, you can use your album to help make decisions on which bulbs to order for the next season.

John Elsley's list of plants that are first-rate companions for spring-flowering bulbs suggest where to look in your own garden for places to add spring-flowering bulbs. Your annuals garden log (see January, Annuals) will suggest tall hardy annual flowers that, started early indoors, can be good follow-on plants for the bulb flowers.

 PLANTING

If the soil is workable, diggable, plant **tulip** and **daffodil** bulbs that you didn't get into the ground last fall. The bulbs may produce plants that are stunted and small, but they have a chance of growing. One thing's for sure—if you don't get the bulbs in the ground now, they're toast. They won't last till next season.

 CARE

Early this month, check the dates and the timing chart on bulbs potted up for forcing last fall (see September). Move those that have finished chilling into a warmer room, and begin to water and fertilize them as you do houseplants. In two weeks or so, the shoots will grow tall and initiate flower buds. Place them in good light but out of direct sun. Feed a half dose of liquid fertilizer at every watering.

 PRUNING

When all the blooms are dead on **amaryllis** and other forced bulbs, cut the flower heads off, and move the plants to a bright sunny window to grow. Do not save the **paperwhites;** discard them.

 WATERING

Keep the soil just damp in pots of bulbs being forced, as well as in those that have finished blooming and that you are planning to plant outdoors in fall.

Don't allow the soil of pots of tender or tropical bulbs wintering in a protected place to dry out completely; they are semi-dormant.

 FERTILIZING

At every second watering, add to the water for bulbs growing on after blooming a half-dose of liquid fertilizer for flowering houseplants, African violet fertilizer, for example.

Save up wood ashes to dust over the soil for spring-flowering bulbs in early March. Do not sprinkle wood ashes on the soil around **Japanese irises** or **lilies,** except the **Madonna lily** (*Lilium candidum*).

PESTS

Aphids and fungus gnats can be a nuisance. Try rinsing aphids off with a kitchen sink spray or misting the plant with a horticultural soap.

Fungus gnats are tiny black gnats that hatch in potting mix and are a nuisance. Discourage them by allowing the soil to dry between waterings and by removing standing water from the plant saucers.

Discard forced bulbs you suspect of serious insect infestation, along with their soil.

*A pleasant way to satisfy the hunger for spring flowers is to take out favorite bulb catalogs, tear out garden pages that show bulbs you would like to try or add, and then to organize them into an album.*

## Did You Know?

### Horticulturist John Elsley's Pick of Companion Plants for Early Spring Bulbs

If you can't find the bulb mentioned, try to match the color and the time of bloom.

- **Daffodils** with perennials for all-season color.

- **Daffodils,** with **garden mums,** in front of **daylilies,** backed by **peonies,** backed by **willowleaf sunflowers** (*Helianthus salicifolius*), then **ornamental grasses.**

- **Giant snowdrop** with **shrubs** and **ground covers; giant snowdrop** (*Galanthus*) 'Atkinsii', and *Bergenia* 'Sunningdale' or 'Appleblossom', under **blood-twig dogwood** (*Cornus sanguinea*) 'Winter Beauty' or *C. stolonifera* 'Cardinal', or with red-stem *Salix* 'Erythroflexuosa'.

**Good Together:**

- **Bluebell** (*Hyacinthoides non-scripta*) with white **wake-robin** (*Trillium grandiflorum*) and *Rodgersia podophylla*.

- **Flowering onion** (*Allium* 'Purple Sensation' with **'Miss Kim' lilac;** or *Allium* 'Mount Everest') with **violets** or **violet-red cranesbill** (*Geranium sanguineum*), or **iris** 'Batik' or **blue false indigo** (*Baptisia australis*), or **peony** 'Red Red Rose'.

- **Glory-of-the-snow** (*Chionodoxa luciliae*) with *Magnolia* x *loebneri* 'Merrill'.

- **Grape hyacinth** (*Muscari armeniacum*) 'Blue Spike' with **hostas** and *Weigela* 'Wine and Roses'.

- **Narcissus** 'Delibes' with **tree peony** (*Paeonia suffruticosa*); *Narcissus* 'Scarlet OHara' with 'Crimson Pygmy' **barberry.**

- **Giant snowdrop** and **narcissus** 'Jet Fire' with **hellebore** hybrids.

- **Species tulip** (*Tulipa saxatilis*), with **bleeding heart** (*Dicentra spectabilis*) 'Gold Heart'; **tulip** 'Maureen' with **dogwood** (*Cornus alba* 'Aurea'); **tulip** 'Candy Club' with **Solomon's-seal** (*Polygonatum falcatum*); **tulip** 'Golden Parade' with **'Red Jade' crabapple; tulip** 'Monte Carlo' with **Colorado blue spruce** (*Picea pungens* 'Glauca'); **tulips** with **American arborvitae** (*Thuja occidentalis* 'Degroots Emerald Spire'); *Tulipa tarda* with **azalea** 'Staccato'.

**Shrubs That Complement Early Spring Bulbs**

**Azalea** 'Tri-lights'; **cornelian cherry** (*Cornus mas*) 'Golden Glory'; **crabapple** 'Louisa'; **dwarf witch alder** (*Fothergilla gardenii*) 'Beaver Creek'; **eastern ninebark** (*Physocarpus opulifoliu*) 'Diabolo'; **eastern redbud** (*Cercis canadensis*) 'Appalachian Red'; **giant arborvitae** (*Thuja plicata* 'Deerproof'; *Magnolia* x *soulangiana* 'San Jose', **magnolia** 'Butterflies'; and **Turkish filbert** (*Corylus avellana* 'Contorta').

# FEBRUARY
## Bulbs, Corms, Rhizomes, & Tubers

 PLANNING

As winter tosses its last really mean days your way, cheer yourself up by adding to your catalog album of summer-flowering bulbs. Some of these you will need to start indoors early, so be ready to order when the catalogs of summer-flowering bulbs arrive in March and April.

Have you tried any of the dazzling new **gladiolus?** They're easy! The big-leaved **cannas** and **ornamental bananas** are sensational accent plants in mixed borders and in containers on the patio. **Tigridia** blooms last just a day, but a tubful is a riot of color. *Amarcrinum howardii*, a recent cross between the **amaryllis** and **crinum,** bears gorgeous pink flowers. **Lily-of-the-Nile** puts up exquisite blue, white, or pink trumpets and thrives for years indoors. A mature plant is magnificent in bloom. Combine **oxalis, caladium, coleus, variegated canna,** and **Oriental lilies** in complementary colors in a group of containers.

This year take the **dahlia** plunge! They come in an exciting variety of shapes and colors. The 6-footers rival **sunflowers** in size, real showstoppers at the back of a mixed border. Massed in the front of the bed, the smaller, bushier cactus-flowered varieties like pink 'Park Princess' are sensational.

 PLANTING

There's still time to force **paper-whites** (see November), and many garden centers carry them this time of year.

 CARE

If the soil is workable, plant any **tulip** and **daffodil** bulbs you forgot last fall. They may or may not make it.

Clear leaves and remains of annuals and perennials from garden areas planted in bulbs as soon as you can work outdoors. Raking beds once the bulbs are up can damage the bulbs.

Bring the last of the spring-flowering bulbs potted up last fall for forcing into a bright, warm room. Water them when you do the houseplants. When they bloom, move them to bright light but not direct sun, and keep the soil barely damp.

**Daffodils, hyacinths,** and **muscari** forced indoors may prosper planted outdoors later if they are allowed to grow on indoors in a sunny spot. Water and fertilize as you do houseplants. When the weather is warm enough, plant them outdoors in an out-of-the-way place. If the foliage dies down before you can plant outdoors, allow the soil in the pots to dry, and plant the bulbs when the weather warms or next fall.

Check stored **cannas** and **dahlias** for disease, and remove and discard tubers showing mold or rot.

Move stored tubers of **tuberous begonias** that don't show a pink bud to a warm, dark place. When sprouts appear, but no later than March, set them in soil-less mix. (See Care, March.)

 PRUNING

Deadhead **amaryllis** blooms, and grow the plants in a bright sunny window.

The **tulips** and **paperwhites** go to the compost pile. These bulbs cannot be forced again.

 WATERING

Maintain some moisture in pots of bulbs that are being, or have been, forced and that you plan to replant later. Discard **tulips** and **paperwhites** that are finished, but continue to provide a sunny sill and to water and fertilize **daffodils** and **hyacinths** that look healthy.

Don't allow the soil in pots of tender or tropical bulbs wintering in a protected place to dry out completely; they are semi-dormant.

*This year take the dahlia plunge! They come in an exciting variety of shapes and colors.*

## Did You Know?

### About Lilies

In late summer afternoons the perfume of the **Oriental lily** 'Casa Blanca' permeates the garden—an invitation to try these most majestic flowers.

The three major lily categories—**Asiatics**, **Trumpets**, **Orientals**—bloom in that order starting with the Asiatics in June/July and ending with the big Orientals in July/August. They have overlapping flowering periods since there are late Asiatics and early Trumpets and Orientals. Each bulb produces one big flowering stem.

Mail-order suppliers ship lily bulbs at planting time in spring or in early fall. The early-blooming Asiatics are best planted in fall. The late-blooming Orientals and Trumpets also are best planted in the fall but may be planted in spring. Plant them as soon as possible. Container-grown lilies and lilies in bloom adapt to transplanting, but to plant a bare lily bulb that has sprouted a shoot over 2 inches long is bad news.

Give lilies a spot in full sun if your temperatures stay under 90 degrees Fahrenheit; in hotter areas, plant lilies in bright tall shade or provide protection from direct noon and afternoon sun.

Lilies do best in slightly acid, fertile soil rich in trace elements. The **Asiatic lilies** require a pH between 5.8 and 6.8. The **Orientals** prefer pH 5.2 to 6.2 and do well with **azaleas.** The **Trumpets** are less particular. All lilies like cold feet, so mulch heavily or underplant them with flowers, such as **coreopsis**, that do well in somewhat acid soil.

When the blossoms fade, pinch them off. When harvesting lilies, take no more than a third of the flower stalk, or it will be shorter next year. When flowering ends, cut the flower stalks to just above the leaves and allow the rest to yellow. Then cut the stalks to the ground—or leave them to mark the locations. In fall and again before growth begins in spring, fertilize the bed with Bulb-tone or Holly-tone at the rate of 4 pounds per 100 square feet. Mulch. Move or divide lilies every four years in the fall.

## FERTILIZING

**Outdoors.** As soon as the tips of the early bulbs show, assuming the ground isn't frozen, start watering them weekly with a diluted organic fertilizer; continue until they bloom.

**Indoors.** At every second watering, add a half-dose of liquid fertilizer for flowering houseplants to the soil for **amaryllis, daffodils,** and **hyacinths** still growing after blooming. Use bloom booster type fertilizers, like African violet food, which are high in phosphorous for promoting flower-bud initiation for next season.

Save up wood ashes to use as fertilizer for spring-flowering bulbs. They make lime and potash quickly available to the plants.

## PESTS

Get rid of aphids by spraying them with a kitchen sink sprayer or misting the plant with a horticultural soap. Discourage the little black fungus gnats that hover over potting mix by allowing the soil to dry between watering and removing standing water from the plant saucers.

When forced bulbs finish blooming, discard any you suspect of insect infestation.

# MARCH
## Bulbs, Corms, Rhizomes, & Tubers

 PLANNING

Now that the small early spring-flowering bulbs are showing their colors and the daffodils are inching up, consider where you'd like to see more or different colors and plants next spring. Write your ideas on sticky notes, and place them in your bulb album (see Planning, January) as reminders when preparing your order for spring-flowering bulbs this summer.

 PLANTING

Start tender summer-flowering bulbs and tropicals indoors late this month. Organize pots and potting mixes.

• Line trays or pots with a starter mix that is dampened 1/2 peat and 1/2 perlite, or use a well-drained commercial potting mix. Keep the pots in indirect light at about 70 degrees Fahrenheit.

• Arrange **tuberous begonia** tubers, hollow side facing up, 3 to 4 inches apart in a tray, round end down. Press the tubers 1 to 2 inches deep into the starter mix.

• Bury **caladium** tubers knobby side up 2 inches deep and several to a pot.

• Start **canna** rhizomes, eyes facing up, in small pots with the upper half of the rhizome above the soil.

• Clean and divide **dahlia** bulbs, making sure there is at least one eye with each division.

When the bulbs or rhizomes show several leaves, transplant to a suitable container.

## CARE

As soon as possible, clear leaves and the remains of annuals and perennials from garden areas planted in bulbs. Raking over beds once the bulbs are up can damage the emerging tips and even tear the little bulbs up by the roots; when that happens, just make a hole and poke them back in 2 or 3 inches deep, even if they've sprouted.

When the **tuberous begonia** tips appear, move them to bright light, but not direct sun, at temperatures between 60 to 75 F. When growth begins, move the containers to cooler temperatures, about 55 to 65 F. When they reach 4 inches, transplant them to 8- to 10-inch baskets or azalea pans. A single tuber leafed out will fill a 10-inch container. Maintain even moisture, but don't fertilize until they

have been potted—then fertilize every three weeks with a light application of something like African violet fertilizer.

Transplant forced **daffodils** and other forced bulbs that look healthy to an out-of-the-way place in the garden; do not remove the foliage as long as it is green and growing. If the foliage dies before you can transplant them outdoors, allow the soil in the pots to dry, and plant the bulbs outdoors when you can.

## PRUNING

Discard forced bulbs you suspect of insect infestation, along with their soil.

Deadhead early **daffodils, tulips,** and other large bulb flowers that have finished blooming; allow the foliage to remain. The small bulb flowers are self-cleaning.

## WATERING

**Indoors.** Keep the soil-less mix over bulbs started indoors moist by sprinkling the surface.

*As soon as possible, clear leaves and the remains of annuals and perennials from garden areas planted in bulbs. Raking over beds once the bulbs are up can damage the emerging tips and even tear the little bulbs up by the roots.*

Maintain the soil moisture in pots of tender or tropical bulbs wintering in a protected place.

# FERTILIZING

**Outdoors.** Sprinkle wood ashes over beds of spring-flowering bulbs, avoiding all **lilies** except for the **Madonna lily** (*Lilium candidum*).

Water spring-flowering bulbs nosing up with a diluted organic fertilizer.

Fertilize summer-flowering bulbs with Bulb-tone at the rate of 4 pounds per 100 square feet. For **lilies** use Holly-tone.

**Indoors.** At every second watering, add ½ dose of liquid bulb booster or African violet fertilizer to **amaryllis** and other forced bulbs you are growing on.

# PESTS

Protect **tulips** and **crocus** from deer with a repellent and change it every four to six weeks. A chicken wire cage is a sure way to keep critters out.

## Did You Know?

### You Can Start Dahlias Early Indoors

In Zones 3, 4, and 5, rooting dahlias indoors in late March or April—four to six weeks before the last frost is expected—gives them a head start out in the garden. Here's how:

***1*** Dahlia tubers wintered indoors at between 40 and 50 degrees Fahrenheit should be plump, firm, and still attached to their central stems. If no growth buds are visible, set them on 2 inches of damp soil in a warm place to stimulate growth. If growth buds appear on several tubers, you can separate those tubers from the central stem, taking a bit of the stem with each tuber, and plant them individually. If not, we plant the whole clump. You can start them early indoors either in the containers they are grow in permanently, or in bulb pans (half-pots) for later transplanting to the garden.

***2*** Line the containers with paper towels to cover the drainage holes, and top with 2 to 4 inches of damp soil-less potting mix, or a mix of 2 parts peat moss, 1 part perlite, and 1 part vermiculite. Set the clumps or tubers on top, with the growth buds facing up, and cover with a little potting mix.

***3*** As the shoots grow up, keep adding enough soil so that there is between 2 and 4 inches of soil over the base of the shoots. Move the containers to a sunny spot indoors.

***4*** When the shoots have opened two to four pairs of leaves, pinch out the central shoots to encourage side shoots. When the plants have six to eight side shoots, pinch out the top pair of buds and stake tall varieties.

***5*** Wait to move them outdoors until the air warms or the soil reaches 50 Fahrenheit. Place them in a protected spot for a week or so before planting them in the open garden. Provide richly fertilized soil and set the plants so there is about 4 inches of soil over the crowns. Provide stakes for the taller varieties.

***6*** In early fall, right after the first hard frost, cut the stems back to about 6 inches; either store the containers in a frost free place, or lift the crowns, dry them out of direct sun for a day or two, shake the soil off, and store the tubers still attached to their central stems in paper bags, cedar chips, vermiculite, sand, or peat moss. Label each variety. Store dahlias at temperatures between 40 and 50 degrees Fahrenheit.

# APRIL
## Bulbs, Corms, Rhizomes, & Tubers

## PLANNING

**Daffodils** and **forsythia** bushes come into full bloom this month—late or early according to your climate—and light up the day! If you haven't paired daffodils with forsythia, you can remedy that by planting a forsythia now. The forsythia varieties 'Meadowlark' and 'Northern Sun' will usually bloom even in Zone 4. The early **tulips** open as the daffs mature, along with the hardy **flowering plums, magnolias, pears,** and vivid lavender-to-pink **PJM rhododendrons** from Weston Nurseries in Massachusetts—and when the colors are coordinated, they are spectacular together.

## PLANTING

When temperatures reach 60 degrees Fahrenheit during the day, you can get ready to repot summer-flowering bulbs that wintered indoors—**ornamental banana, canna, ginger lilies, lily-of-the-Nile** (*Agapanthus africanus*). Set them in a sheltered spot, and begin weekly watering and fertilization. They can go into the garden when the soil temperature is between 50 **(dahlias)** and 60 degrees Fahrenheit (the others).

**Transplanting.** You can move spring-flowering bulbs around in the garden after the plants go out of bloom. Do it while the foliage is still green or starting to brown; once the foliage dies the bulbs are hard to locate. Prepare a new planting hole by loosening the soil and adding bulb fertilizer and compost. Then dig the clump, taking care not to damage the bulbs or roots, and plop it intact into the new planting hole. Allow the foliage to ripen naturally, just as you would have if you had not moved the bulbs.

You can lift and transplant the small fall-flowering bulbs, **autumn crocus,** for example, whose grass-like foliage comes up now.

**Dividing.** After the foliage has died down, but while you can still see it, is the best time to divide clumps of spring-flowering bulbs. If you plan to move them later, mark their positions now.

## CARE

When temperatures stay above 60 degrees Fahrenheit, move **amaryllis** pots to the garden and plant them up to their rims in a sunny spot.

When the early **tulips** show their tips, encourage them by watering them a few times with houseplant fertilizer. Any that send up foliage but fail to bloom, move to an out-of-the-way spot to mature.

## PRUNING

Deadhead the big spring-flowering bulbs, leaving the stems intact. Allow the foliage to ripen six to seven weeks before you remove it.

## WATERING

Maintain moisture in the container plants, the **tuberous begonias,** and the other summer-flowering bulbs started indoors and moved outdoors.

Keep the soil just damp in pots of bulbs that have finished blooming and that you hope to plant outdoors later.

## FERTILIZING

Every second time you water, include a half-strength dose of water-soluble fertilizer to the hardy bulbs growing in containers outdoors and to pots of **amaryllis.** Use African violet or bloom-booster fertilizer for flowering plants.

> *You can move spring-flowering bulbs around in the garden after the plants go out of bloom. Do it while the foliage is still green; once the foliage dies, the bulbs are hard to locate.*

## Did You Know?

### A Daffodil by Any Other Name

The immense variety of *Narcissus*, their easy ways, and their imperviousness even to deer make them spring's favorite bulb. Daffodil is used as a common name for the entire genus *Narcissus* but is most often associated with the large trumpet type. **Jonquils** are varieties of *Narcissus jonquilla,* late-bloomers that bear clusters of fragrant flowers on each stem.

Plant open woodlands with big, yellow daffodils in irregular drifts of twenty, fifty, or one hundred bulbs, and they will carpet it with gold. A dusting of wood ashes in early September is enough to keep naturalized daffs blooming.

Plant early daffs, like 8-inch 'Jack Snipe', to edge flower beds and in rock gardens, containers, in the shelter of boulders, and along fences.

For bouquets, grow show-stoppers like 12-inch orange-cupped 'Jetfire', and 18-inch pink-cupped 'Chinese Coral'. Bouquets of daffodils are long-lasting, but before combining just-cut daffodils with **tulips** or other flowers, be sure to place the daffodil stems in water overnight to detoxify.

For fragrance, in addition to **jonquils,** plant *Tazetta* **daffodils**. A favorite is 'Geranium', which has crisp white petals surrounding frilled orange cups. The perfumed **paper-whites,** so easy to force, belong to this group; they're not winter hardy here. Pot up paperwhites, a variety of **tazetta narcissus,** in late fall, and they will bloom and perfume your house in just a few weeks (see November).

**Planting daffodils.** Plant daffodils in the fall after the first hard frost. They thrive in full sun or partial shade in well-drained, slightly acidic soil. Set large bulbs 8 inches deep, 3 to 6 inches apart; small bulbs 3 to 5 inches deep, 1 to 3 inches apart. Add a handful of slow-release bulb fertilizer as topdressing after planting. Deadhead show daffs; naturalized daffs don't need it.

**Perennializing daffodils.** Most daffodils including jonquils perennialize. Allow the foliage to remain undisturbed until it has withered away. Binding the foliage while the leaves ripen cuts off light and oxygen the bulbs need to nourish the next year's flowers, so we advise against it.

You'll have bigger and more blooms next year if you fertilize spring-flowering bulbs as soon as they finish blooming with Bulb-tone at the rate of 4 to 6 pounds for each 100 square feet; repeat the dose in early September.

 PESTS

**Daffodils,** (*Narcissus*), **jonquils** are safe from deer, but other flowering bulbs may not be. For controls, see Pests, Diseases, and Controls in the Appendix.

If your **lily-of-the-valley** were ruined by rust late last summer, spray the bed now with a copper-based fungicide or Immunox.

## Bulbs, Corms, Rhizomes, & Tubers

 PLANNING

Unhappy with bare spots where the spring-flowering bulbs have gone by? When the air warms, hide them with pots of the big tropical-leaved **canna** and **ornamental banana** plants. They can be lifted in fall and wintered indoors. That will leave the space free for the spring-flowering bulbs to pop up next year. Also, if you set them in the garden in pots, moving the tropicals indoors to a frost-free place for the winter is easy.

 PLANTING

When the air warms and the **lilacs** bloom, Zone 6 and 7 gardeners can plant **dahlia** tubers outdoors. Set them 18 to 24 inches apart, according to the mature size of the plant, in well-worked soil enriched with a slow-release, low-nitrogen, four-month formulation fertilizer. Prepare sturdy stakes tall enough to support the upper third of the big **dahlias** that will grow up to be between 18 inches and 4 feet. Insert the stakes deep into the soil 2 inches away from the plants that need staking. Firm the plants in their holes, and water them. When the stems are 12 inches tall, tie the main stems to stakes. Tie on other branches as the plant matures.

You can start planting **gladiolus** when you plant sweet corn—ideal soil temper-ature is 50 F (air temperature 75 F). Plant sets of six to twelve for cutting, and repeat every ten days until the end of June. Standard glads flower in up to ninety days, depending on variety. Set the corms 5 inches deep, 5 inches apart in well-drained, fertile soil, pH 6.5.

 CARE

You can remove **tulip** foliage when it has yellowed halfway down; if you hope to perennialize **tulips,** fertilize them now. **Darwin hybrids** and **species tulips** should be encouraged. Tulips that sent up foliage but failed to bloom this year we recommend you discard or move to an out-of-the-way spot to mature.

Move pots of **tuberous begonias** and other bulbs started indoors out to a sheltered spot to harden off. In a week or ten days, you can move them to their permanent summer location.

In Zones 3 to 5, when temperatures reach 60 degrees and all danger of frost is past, move pots of **lily-of-the-Nile** and other tender bulbs and tropicals that wintered indoors in containers outside for a summer of R&R. Groom the plants. Repot those in small containers in fresh potting mix. Top-dress those too large to repot by replacing the top 2 inches of soil with compost.

Stake the tall **lilies** growing in the garden, and mulch them to keep their feet cool; or underplant them with flowers that do well in somewhat acidic soil, **coreopsis** or **lily-of-the-valley,** for example.

 PRUNING

Clear away the yellowing leaves of the **tuberous begonias,** and deadhead the flowers.

WATERING

Water potted **dahlias** often enough to maintain soil moisture, but avoid soaking them.

Keep the soil around the **tuberous begonias** evenly moist but not soaking.

Maintain the soil moisture of the **amaryllis** and other bulbs growing in containers. As the season grows warmer, plants in small pots and hanging baskets may need watering every day.

FERTILIZING

At every second watering, include a half dose of fertilizer in the water for all your potted and basket plants.

*Unhappy with bare spots where the spring-flowering bulbs have gone by? When the air warms, hide them with pots of the big tropical-leaved canna and ornamental banana plants.*

As the **tulips** finish blooming, spread bulb booster around those that you hope to perennialize.

You'll have bigger and more blooms next year if you fertilize spring-flowering bulbs as soon as they finish blooming with Bulb-tone at the rate of 4 to 6 pounds for each 100 square feet, and repeat in early September.

 PESTS

To cut down on Japanese beetle populations, plan to spread Milky Spore over the area and the surrounding garden in early September. For other controls, turn to Pests, Diseases, and Controls in the Appendix.

Rake or hoe weeds away. A swing-head hoe makes it easy. It's a push-pull oscillating hoe that cuts through weeds and cultivates the soil without disturbing the mulch.

To deter deer, spray with a new and different deterrent, or put up a barrier to keep the deer out. See Pests, Diseases, and Controls in the Appendix.

## Did You Know?

### You Can Start Your Caladiums Indoors

Start caladium tubers indoors about eight weeks before nights will be above 60 and day temperatures reach 70 degrees Fahrenheit.

*1* Fill a flat with 2 to 3 inches of moist peat moss or sterile soil-less potting mix.

*2* Set the tubers about 8 inches apart with the knobble side up and the little straggle of roots down.

*3* Keep the growing medium damp. The tubers are slow to start but do well under a grow light or in a sunny glassed-in porch.

*4* When they sprout, transplant them to containers filled with improved soil fertilized with Plant-tone. A container 8 to 10 inches in diameter can take four to five caladiums. Cover the tubers with 2 inches of fertile soil mixed with humus or peat moss.

*5* When daytime temperatures reach 70 degrees Fahrenheit and nights stay above 60, move the caladiums outdoors in their pots or transplant them to the garden. They do best in a semi-sunny or a lightly shaded location.

*6* When temperatures drop below 70 degrees in the fall, harvest the tubers, allow them to dry, and store them at temperatures between 70 and 75 degrees Fahrenheit.

Be warned: To a deer, a caladium is prime-time lettuce.

Starting Caladiums

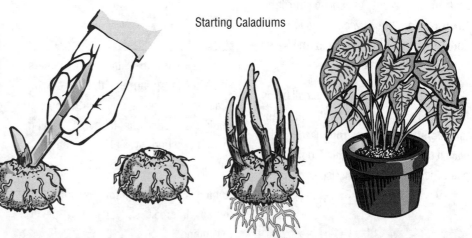

# JUNE
## Bulbs, Corms, Rhizomes, & Tubers

 PLANNING

Mail-order catalogs for spring-flowering bulbs for fall planting arrive about now. They offer discount prices on early orders for fall- and spring-flowering bulbs. They offer a wide selection and ship at planting time. You'll also find the most popular, and newest, varieties of bulbs at full service garden centers, but the selection may be more limited than that offered in catalogs.

Add those that interest you to your bulb album (see Planning, January); then make a planting plan that will keep bulbs blooming in your garden and indoors this fall, winter, and spring.

**Fall-flowering bulbs.** They are planted in summer or fall and bloom in September and October. Most are not much bigger than a **crocus.** Plan to plant them in drifts near paths to the house and in the front of shrub borders. **Resurrection lily** (*Lycoris squamigera*) and other full-sized late bloomers we suggest planting in containers.

**Spring-flowering bulbs.** The small bulbs flower in February and March, with **winter aconite** and **snowdrops** leading the way. It's a joy to watch their progress, so plant them in drifts by house entrances.

Intermediate-sized bulb flowers provide the next wave of color—**squill, oxalis, sapphire scillas,** luminous **species tulips,** dainty white **leucojum**—on stems 6 to 24 inches tall. Use them to fill spaces in flowering borders between perennials and where you intend to plant annuals later.

Many of the large bulbs bloom toward the middle and end of spring, but there are early, mid-season, and late varieties of most, including the **daffodils** and **tulips.** Order a few dozen to scatter in groups in your flower borders. Plan to plant **tulips** for cutting in the kitchen garden. Naturalized **daffodils,** which are deer-proof, light up shrub borders and woodlands. For their fragrance, plant groups of **hyacinths** near entrances. They are especially attractive planted in clusters with **lamb's ears** in front and **evergreen azaleas** behind.

 PLANTING

The leaves of the little fall bloomers come up in spring and then die down again in summer; before that happens, mark their positions to avoid digging them up when over-planting the area with flowers for summer bloom.

Continue to plant **gladiolus** corms at ten-day intervals so you'll have plenty for cutting.

 CARE

Move **tuberous begonias, dahlias, caladiums,** and other tender bulbs to their permanent place in the garden; they need some protection from noon and late afternoon sun.

Adjust the **dahlia** stakes as the plants grow.

PRUNING

Deadhead **tuberous begonias, irises,** and the other bulbs flowering now. Remove **caladium** flowers as they appear; they aren't showy and detract from the foliage.

Cut the yellowed foliage of the spring-flowering bulbs off at the base. If there are some you wanted to move but didn't get to, mark the spot with a plant marker or a golf tee so you'll know where to dig when you have time to move them.

 WATERING

Check the soil moisture of small containers of summer-flowering bulbs and the **tuberous begonias** every two days. Don't neglect pots of **amaryllis** summering in the garden.

*Cut the yellowed foliage of the spring-flowering bulbs off at the base. If there are some you wanted to move but didn't get to, mark the spot with a plant marker or a golf tee so you'll know where to dig.*

Where the hardy spring-flowering bulbs have bloomed, water only if you must; they are dormant now and most prefer to be rather dry.

**An underground automatic sprinkling system spells death to most bulbs unless it is adjusted to water deeply and only when moisture is needed— not every day, not every other day, not even every third day. This cannot be overstressed!**

# FERTILIZING

You'll have bigger and more blooms next year if you fertilize spring-flowering bulbs as soon as they finish blooming with Bulb-tone at the rate of 4 to 6 pounds for each 100 square feet, and repeat in early September.

Continue to fertilize **amaryllis** summering out in the open garden.

# PESTS

Handpick Japanese beetles into a jar of soapy water. Try applications of Neem to discourage them.

---

## Did You Know?

### About Fall-Flowering Bulbs

A handful of fall-flowering bulbs bloom when other flowers are about done, except **pansies, mums,** and **flowering cabbage** and **kale**. Try some of our favorites:

- **Autumn Daffodil** (*Sternbergia lutea*)

Planting time: late summer for fall bloom.

- **Colchicum** (*Colchicum* spp.)

Planting time: late summer/early fall for mid- to late fall bloom.

- **Fall Crocus** (*Crocus*, many fall-blooming spp. and cvs.)

Planting time: summer for September to November bloom.

- **Hardy Cyclamen** (*Cyclamen hederifolium*)

Planting time: July for late summer or early winter bloom.

- **Naked-lady Lily** (*Amaryllis belladonna* syn. *Brunsvigia rosea*)

Planting time: early summer for early fall bloom.

- **Oxblood Lily** (*Rhodophiala bifida*)

Planting time: early September for fall bloom.

- **Resurrection Lily, Hardy Amaryllis** (*Lycoris squamigera*)

Planting time: August for fall bloom.

---

If spring has been wet, keep an eye out for fungal diseases. Pick and discard infected foliage. A fungicide may help control the problem. Try applications of Messenger, new at this writing, which is said to stimulate the plant's own defenses. For controls, turn to Pests, Diseases, and Controls in the Appendix.

To deter deer, spray with a new and different deterrent because they become used to what's been around for a while, or put up a barrier to keep them out.

# JULY
## Bulbs, Corms, Rhizomes, & Tubers

## PLANNING

Take advantage of the quality mail-order bulb suppliers' discounts for early orders. They start shipping as early as mid-August and can run out of popular varieties.

When purchasing bulbs, buy the largest ones you can find. Smaller sizes are good for naturalizing. Medium and small **hyacinth** bulbs are a good deal as the shorter flower stalks are less vulnerable to late storms. Order **hyacinths** noted for perfume, such as 'Pink Festival'. Plan to try some of the beautiful little bulbs that bloom in fall.

To have a showing from the little bulbs, order enough of each variety to plant drifts of twenty, fifty, or one hundred. For the mid-sized bulbs to be effective you will need ten, twenty, or more of each. The big bulbs, the tall **Darwin tulips,** for example, make a big splash planted in groups of as few as five or ten. Order **hyacinths** in groups of three or five of one color. Choose several tulip varieties for cutting with bouquets in mind.

When ordering spring-flowering bulbs for forcing, select varieties recommended for forcing. You'll need five **daffodil** or **tulip** bulbs for each 6-inch pot and nine for a 12-inch pot. **Hyacinths** are planted three to a 5-inch pot. **Amaryllis** are planted one to a 6-inch pot or three to a 12-inch pot.

## PLANTING

Plant the little bulbs that bloom in the fall in a sunny spot in the shelter of a stone wall or a big rock. Most will perennialize.

Dig planting holes and beds for the small bulbs 3 to 5 inches deep. But first cover the area with 3 to 4 inches of humus, enough so that one quarter of the soil will be organic matter. Then add to the soil from the hole the following organic amendments and fertilizers:

> For every 100 square feet:
> Bulb-tone: 5 to 10 pounds
> Rock phosphate: 5 to 10 pounds
> Green sand: 5 to 10 pounds
> Clay soils: gypsum 5 to 10 pounds
> Osmocote four-month: 2 pounds

To foil voles and squirrels, line the bottom of the hole or the bed with 2 inches of VoleBloc™ or PermaTill. Set the little bulbs 1 to 3 inches apart. Fill in all around them with VoleBloc or PermaTill, so just the tip of the bulbs is showing. Cover with 1 inch of VoleBloc or PermaTill. Fill in with a mix that is 30 percent VoleBloc or PermaTill and improved soil.

## CARE

Tie tall **dahlias** and **lilies** to the upper third of their stakes. Hill the soil around **gladiolus** as they gain height, and stake the tallest.

Mulch around summer-flowering bulbs to keep their roots cool and to maintain moisture now that the year's driest season is upon us.

## PRUNING

Harvest or deadhead **dahlias, gladiolus,** and other flowering bulbs. Glads are long-lasting if cut when the lowest bud begins to show its color.

When harvesting **lilies,** do not take more than a third of the stem or the stem will be smaller next year. After deadheading bulbs that have finished blooming, let the foliage ripen naturally. The stalks of the **lilies** and the foliage of the **Japanese irises** turns gold and bronze in fall and can be quite beautiful.

Help flowers you harvest last longer by making an angled cut with clean shears, and immediately plunge the stems into a big bucket of tepid water containing floral preservative.

*To have a showing from the little bulbs, order enough of each
variety to plant drifts of twenty, fifty, or one hundred. For the mid-sized bulbs
to be effective you will need ten, twenty, or more of each.*

## Did You Know?

### About Summer-Flowering Bulbs

Summer-flowering bulbs are superb in big pots, planters, and barrels, and great fillers for empty spots in flower beds. Plan to lift those identified here as "tender" in fall, and store them indoors for winter.

- **Amarcrinum** (x *Amarcrinum howardii*), tender
- **Caladium** (*Caladium* spp. and cvs.), tender
- **Canna** (*Canna* x *generalis* cvs.), tender
- **Crocosmia** (*Crocosmia* spp. and cvs.), Zone 6
- **Flowering Onion** (*Allium* spp.), hardy
- **Gladiolus** (*Gladiolus byzantinus, G. hortulanus*), Zones 6a and 7b
- **Lilies** (*Lilium* spp. and cvs.), hardy
- **Mexican Shellflower** (*Tigridia*), tender

- **Ornamental Banana** (*Musa velutina*), tender
- **Peacock Orchid** (*Acidanthera bicolor*), tender
- **Peruvian Daffodil** (*Hymenocallis narcissiflora* syn. *Ismene calathina*), tender
- **Poppy Anemone** (*Anemone coronaria*), hardy
- **Rainlily** (*Zephyranthes* spp.), tender
- **Summer Hyacinth** (*Galtonia*), tender
- **Tuberose** (*Polianthes tuberosa*), tender
- **Wood Sorrel, Lady's Sorrel** (*Oxalis* cvs.), Zone 7

 WATERING

Check the soil moisture in hanging baskets and pots every two days or so, and water enough to keep the soil nicely damp.

Summer-flowering bulbs need sustained moisture to stay in top shape and resist the assorted pests and diseases that strike about now. In July and August, water deeply and regularly unless you have a soaking rain.

 FERTILIZING

Add a half-dose of water-soluble fertilizer to the water for bulbs growing in baskets and pots at every second watering.

 PESTS

Keep weeds gone.

Pinch off and discard (do not compost) leaves or blossoms that show infestations or signs of disease. Spray infested plants with Neem.

If **dahlias** show signs of powdery mildew, thin the interior growth to improve airflow. Spray with a solution of 1 tablespoon baking soda and 1 tablespoon of ultrafine horticultural oil mixed well in a gallon of water. See Pests, Diseases, and Controls in the Appendix for more information.

To deter deer, spray with a new and different deterrent spray or put up a barrier to keep the deer out.

PLANNING

Some mail-order houses ship spring-flowering bulbs for fall planting as early as mid-August. Some can be forced into bloom for winter indoors; these you can start in September. It's best to wait until after a hard frost to start planting the spring-blooming bulbs out in the garden. Store bulbs-in-waiting in a cool cellar, a crisper, or a cool garage.

**Caution: Don't store bulbs with apples. Apples, along with bananas and some other fruits and vegetables, give off ethylene gas, which ruins the blooms in flowering bulbs.**

Garden centers will soon be offering **shrubs** and **trees** at end-of-season sale prices, an invitation to consider starting a border of shrubs and bulbs. Spring-flowering bulbs do well under tall shrubs and deciduous trees and even in the shade of limbed-up evergreens that allows sun to reach the flowers. Don't top them with more than 2 or 3 inches of mulch; more will prevent the soil from draining, and that will harm the bulbs.

Turn back to January, and check out horticulturist John Elsley's excellent suggestions for combinations of flowers and shrubs that do well with spring-flowering bulbs.

 PLANTING

Late this month you can begin to transplant established spring-flowering bulbs that you marked in spring for moving. Use a pitchfork to lift them. Just outside the marked position, gently slide the tines straight down into the soil. If you feel resistance that could be a bulb, try the other side of the clump. When you have lifted a clump, ease it off the fork onto the ground. Pick out the largest bulbs, and replant them in their new spot in soil fertilized with Bulb-tone. Plant the little bulblets in an out-of-the-way place to grow up.

 CARE

**Crocosmia** doesn't need deadheading. The flowers are followed by attractive seed capsules that look good with the sword-shaped foliage.

 PRUNING

**Dahlias** need deadheading and are good cut flowers, so don't skimp on bouquets. The crisp, almost translucent petals catch the light and in the paler shades are truly luminous. The dainty long-stemmed cactus types are beautiful

massed as bedding plants and make lovely bouquets. Our favorite late-summer bouquet combines **dahlias, basil** (for the aroma), airy **cosmos,** plumes of **ornamental grasses,** and stems of **PeeGee hydrangeas.**

The best times to harvest **dahlias**—all flowers, really—is early morning or late evening. To give them a long vase life, re-cut the stems, and set them in water for a couple of hours or overnight, and then re-cut the stems for arranging. Harvest **gladiolus** when the lowest bud shows its color.

When harvesting **lilies,** leave behind more than two-thirds of the overall height of the stalk, or the plant will be smaller next year. If you do not harvest your lilies, deadhead faded flowers just to where the leaves begin. The foliage of summer-flowering bulbs, like that of spring-flowering bulbs, must be allowed to ripen. It's best to leave them to ripen into fall and then cut the stalks to the ground—or leave them to mark the locations if you plan to divide them later in the season.

If tall **bearded iris** foliage is browning at the tips, cut the tips back to healthy tissue.

> *Weed faithfully. We use a swing-head hoe for weeding. It's a push-pull oscillating hoe that cuts through weeds and cultivates the soil without disturbing the mulch.*

 WATERING

During droughts, **dahlias, lilies, crocosmia,** and the other summer-flowering bulbs need watering every week to ten days, as do the annuals and perennials. Watering overhead is okay.

 FERTILIZING

If you have incorporated organic or slow-release fertilizers in your soil, your bulbs shouldn't need fertilizing now.

 PESTS

Weed faithfully. We use a swing-head hoe for weeding. It's a push-pull oscillating hoe that cuts through weeds and cultivates the soil without disturbing the mulch.

Mildew can be a problem. Pick off and destroy infected foliage; do not compost it. Spray infected plants with a sulfur-based fungicide recommended by your garden center, or spray with a combination of 1 tablespoon baking soda and 1 tablespoon of ultrafine horticultural oil mixed well in a gallon of water.

## Did You Know?

### Iris Species Bloom Spring Through Summer

What a varied family!

The 3- and 4-inch high miniature **beardless iris** you see blooming in late winter and early spring is *Iris reticulata*. It is planted in the fall. They are charming in rock gardens and naturalized, set them out by the dozen, 2 to 3 inches apart, 2 to 3 inches deep in very well-drained soil. They do well in full or partial sun.

A second wave of beardless irises blooms toward mid-spring. These are the 20-inch tall **Dutch irises,** varieties of *I. hollandica*, and they also develop from bulbs planted the preceding fall. They need full sun and are planted about 5 inches deep with 3 to 4 inches between bulbs.

In late spring and early summer, the spectacular **bearded, Siberian,** and **Japanese** (Zones 4 to 8) **irises** come into bloom. These can be planted or divided in spring before growth begins or in early fall. The tall **bearded irises (German iris** hybrids) are divided in August and September.

The **bog irises** also bloom in late spring and early summer. The stately 5-foot **yellow flag** (*Iris pseudacorus*, Zones 5 to 8) bears bright yellow canna-like flowers. Rooted divisions are set out in early spring or fall in full or half sun in mucky, humusy soil that is moderately acidic. Lovely varieties of the many-hued **Louisiana iris** (*I. hexagona*, Zones 6 to 9) bloom at about the same time and in the same type of soil. These irises can be divided any time after they bloom.

Rust reduces **lily-of-the-valley** to brown rags; if this is happening, spray now and again early next spring with a fungicidal formulation of copper, Immunox, or mancozeb.

Spider mites can be a problem now that the weather is hot and dry. Inspect plants that are not doing well, and if they are under attack, spray in the early morning with a miticide.

To deter deer, spray with a new and different deterrent.

## PLANNING

Working with the Planting Guide for Forcing Bulbs, plan a schedule for potting up and forcing bulbs for indoors this winter. You can start planting **hyacinths** indoors for forcing when outdoor nighttime temperatures fall into the 50s. Wait until closer to the holidays to pot up **amaryllis** bulbs and **paperwhites.** There is a list of best bulbs for home forcing on http://www.bulb.com/spring/ homeforcing.asp. This list was compiled by the technical department of the International Flower Bulb Center in Hillegom, the Netherlands.

Prepare a timing guide for the bulbs you are forcing, so you'll know when to chill and when to bring them into warmth.

## PLANTING

Forcing bulbs for indoor bloom is a three-part project—pot up; chill twice; move to warmth to force blooming.

**Tulip** and **daffodil** bulbs take a standard pot, but the others are usually planted in bulb pans, which are half-pots, or else in shallow bowls, boxes, or water-proofed baskets. Before planting, soak the pots and water the soil thoroughly. To avoid the diseases that can assail forced bulbs, pot them in a mixture of one-half sterile

commercial potting medium and one-half good gritty garden soil. As an added precaution, you can soak or dust the bulbs with a broad-spectrum fungicide.

Plant **hyacinths** about three to a 5-inch pot; plant tulips and standard daffodils five to a 6-inch pot, or nine to a 12-inch pot. Set tulips with the flat side facing out. Plant as many **muscari** and other small bulbs as there is space for. Set the bulbs just touching. Plant big bulbs so just the tip shows; cover small bulbs with potting mix.

Label the pots with the plant's name, the date, and when the Planting Guide for Forcing Bulbs says to initiate forcing.

**Chilling.** For the first chilling period, place the pots in the dark where temperatures are 40 to 60 degrees Fahrenheit—an attached, unheated garage perhaps, or an unheated room. After the first chilling period, move the pots to colder temperatures—35 to 40 degrees Fahrenheit—such as a root cellar or the hatch-covered outside steps to a basement. Keep the soil damp; water when it feels dry to the touch.

**Forcing.** As the second chilling period ends, move the bulbs showing roots and shoots to temperatures between 50 and 60 degrees Fahrenheit and to good, indirect light. They take about two weeks to bloom. When they bloom, keep the soil moist but not soaking; they last longest in

temperatures between 55 and 65 degrees Fahrenheit and in indirect light.

This month you can plant **Asiatic lilies** in the garden for next summer's bloom.

## CARE

Keep bulbs waiting to be planted in a refrigerator crisper, away from fruit and vegetables, or in a cool garage or cellar.

When **tuberous begonias** begin to yellow, bring them indoors, let the soil dry to barely damp over five or six weeks, and then remove dead foliage and store the tubers in a cool, dry place.

Bring in pots of **amaryllis** that summered in the garden. You can let the soil dry, or keep them growing in a window. Either way, they need 55 degree temperatures for eight to ten weeks. (See how to rebloom an **Amaryllis** in the March pages of Chapter 4, Houseplants.)

Before real frosts arrive in Zones 3 to 6, harvest **gladiolus** corms, remove the stalks, and cure on screens for three or four weeks at room temperature. Break off and discard the old corms that are on the bottom, and store the new ones in mesh or paper bags at 40 to 60 degrees F.

After the first killing frost, lift and store the **dahlia** tubers. (See information about Dahlias, in March.)

*Keep bulbs waiting to be planted in a refrigerator crisper, away from fruit and vegetables, or in a cool garage or cellar.*

## Did You Know?

### Planting Guide for Forcing Bulbs

| Planting Time<br>Bulb | Container | Chilling Period<br>40/60 F | Chilling Period<br>35/40 F | Forcing Time |
|---|---|---|---|---|
| September/October<br>**Hyacinth (French, Roman)** | Bowl/half pot | 4–6 weeks | 6–8 weeks | 2 weeks at 65° F |
| October<br>**Crocus**, **Daffodil**,<br>**Narcissus** | Half or three-quarters pot | 6–8 weeks | 4–8 weeks | 2 weeks at 65° F |
| **Grape Hyacinth**,<br>**Muscari** | Half pot | 6–8 weeks | 8 weeks | 2 weeks at 65° F |
| **Hyacinth**, **Dutch** | Glass bowl, half or standard pot | 6–8 weeks | 6 weeks | 2 weeks at 65° F |
| **Tulips (large)** | Half, three-quarters, or standard pot | 6–8 weeks | 6–8 weeks | 2 weeks at 65° F |
| October/November/December<br>**Paperwhites** | Bowl and pebbles | 2–3 weeks | 3–4 weeks<br>(if shoots are<br>up, skip this) | 2 weeks at 65° F |
| **Tazetta Narcissus** | Bowl and pebbles | 2–3 weeks | 3–4 weeks | 2 weeks at 65° F |

Store cold-tender and tropical bulbs at temperatures specified by the grower. There's a best storage temperature for each species. For example, **caladiums** and **colocasia** need temperatures above 70 degrees; **tuberous begonias** and **crinum,** 35 to 41 degrees; **canna,** 41 to 50 degrees; **dahlias,** 35 to 50 degrees.

## PRUNING

Cut down **lily** stalks that are fully yellow; move or divide four-year-old **lilies** to keep them productive. Harvest **dahlias** before frosts get them.

## WATERING

Check the soil moisture weekly in pots of bulbs being chilled. Water when the soil is dry to the touch. Keep the soil damp in pots of tender perennials and tropicals wintering indoors; they are only semi-dormant.

## FERTILIZING

Spread Bulb-tone or fine wood ashes over established beds of spring-flowering bulbs at the rate of 4 to 6 pounds to 100 square feet.

## PESTS

Spread Milky Spore where Japanese beetles have been evident.

# OCTOBER
## Bulbs, Corms, Rhizomes, & Tubers

 PLANNING

As temperatures drop into the 50s, organize the planting of the spring-flowering bulbs. The best time is about six weeks before the ground freezes hard. If you plant them while the soil's still warm, bulbs risk developing fungus or disease. Bulbs planted too late risk not having sufficient root development to survive the winter.

The **daffodils** go in first, after the first hard frost. The **tulips** and other large bulbs go next, after two hard frosts. The small bulbs—**muscari, crocus**—go in after the tulips.

To get ready to plant, group the bulbs according to where you plan to place them in the garden. Their first year, spring-flowering bulbs will bloom even in shade. But to come back and to bloom, they need full sun, all-day light under deciduous trees, or bright shade under limbed-up evergreens.

Plan to plant the little bulbs in groups of twenty, fifty, or one hundred of each variety; mid-sized bulbs in groups of ten or twenty; big bulbs in sets of ten or fifteen; and **hyacinths** in sets of three or five of each color.

For a lasting show, plant a three-tier bulb garden. Plant big bulbs on the lowest level, cover them with a few inches of soil, then plant medium bulbs, add a few inches more soil, and plant small bulbs on top.

 PLANTING

**Bulbs for forcing indoors.** Continue potting up bulbs the Planting Guide for Forcing Bulbs recommends starting this month (see the September sidebar and Planting).

**Bulbs for the garden.** When you are planting groups of bulbs, prepare planting beds rather than individual holes. (See Planting in the introduction to this chapter.) As a generalization, set large bulbs 4 to 6 inches apart and 8 to 10 inches deep; set bulbs under 2 inches in size about 2 inches apart in planting beds 5 to 6 inches deep.

• When planting large **daffodils,** dig the holes 3 to 6 inches apart, 8 inches deep; set small daffs 1 to 3 inches apart, 3 to 5 inches deep.

• Plant very tall **tulips** 4 to 6 inches apart, 8 inches to 10 inches deep; set the **species tulips** 3 to 4 inches apart, 4 to 5 inches deep.

• Plant **hyacinths** about 3 to 4 inches apart, about 8 inches deep.

• Plant **wood hyacinths** about 2 to 4 inches apart, 5 to 6 inches deep.

**To create a naturalized drift.** Dig an irregularly-shaped planting bed, throw the bulbs out by the handful, and plant them where they fall.

To deter voles, moles, and squirrels, we urge you to plant all bulbs except daffodils, which are toxic to wildlife, with VoleBloc™ or PermaTill.

Early this month, plant **Oriental** and **Trumpet lilies** in the garden for next summer's bloom.

CARE

You can move **autumn crocus** and other fall-flowering bulbs after they finish blooming. Just lift the clump and transport it to its new location.

PRUNING

Cut the foliage of the **tall bearded** and **Dutch irises** down to 2 inches.

 WATERING

Monitor the moisture in pots of bulbs being forced for indoor bloom; if the soil is dry to the touch, water it. Keep track of the progress of the chilling periods.

*When you are planting groups of bulbs, prepare planting beds rather than individual holes.*

## Did You Know?

### The Sequence of Bloom for Spring-Flowering Bulbs

To help you find ideal places in your garden for spring-flowering bulbs, we have arranged them here in the order in which they come into bloom. This sequence of bloom has not been handed down from on high. Like all commandments about gardening, it needs to be taken with a grain of wisdom. The fact is that flowers, bulbs included, that are growing in shade will bloom later than those growing in full sun, even if they like shade. Ground that has a northern exposure or is heavily mulched will stay cold longer, and those plants are also likely to come into bloom later.

#### Late Winter/Early Spring

- **Early Crocus,** *Crocus* spp. and cvs.
- **Daffodils, Narcissus** Miniatures and early varieties
- **Snowdrops** (*Galanthus*)
- **Winter Aconite** (*Eranthis*)
- **Squill** (*Scilla tubergeniana*)
- **Dwarf Beardless Iris** (*Iris reticulata*)
- **Glory-of-the-snow** (*Chionodoxa luciliae*)

- **Grape Hyacinth** (*Muscari* spp. and cvs.)
- **Miniature Cyclamen** (*Cyclamen coum*)
- **Species Tulips** (*Tulipa saxatilis, T. tarda, T. turkestanica*)
- **Striped Squill** (*Puschkinia scilloides*)
- **Windflower** (*Anemone blanda*)

#### Mid- and Late Spring

- **Daffodils** (*Narcissus*) Mid-season, late varieties
- **Hyacinth** (*Hyacinthus*)
- **Late Crocus** (*Crocus*)
- **Lily-of-the-valley** (*Convallaria majalis*)
- **Fritallaria** (*Fritillaria persica*)
- **Silver Bells** (*Ornithogalum nutans*)
- **Spanish Bluebell** (*Hyacinthoides hispanica*)

- **Bluebell** (*Hyacinthoides non-scripta*)
- **Summer Snowflake** (*Leucojum aestivum* 'Gravetye Giant')
- **Starflower** (*Ipheion uniflorum* 'Wisley Blue')
- **Tulips** (*Tulipa*), Mid-season, late varieties
- **Wood Sorrel** (*Oxalis adenophylla*)

Maintain a little moisture in pots of tender perennials and tropicals wintering indoors.

rate of 5 to 10 pounds per 100 square feet. For **lilies,** spread Holly-tone at the rate of 4 pounds per 100 square feet.

you really want them to hang around and munch and come back for the **crocus** and **tulips** next spring.

## FERTILIZING

Clear dying foliage and dig up weeds from established beds of fall- and summer-flowering bulbs, and then fertilize them with Bulb-tone 4-10-6 at the

## PESTS

Clear the yard of anything that attracts deer—apples or pears, for example. Don't make pumpkins or ornamental bales of straw available to deer, unless

After planting tulips, be very sure to remove any fallen bits of the crackly brown jackets that protect the bulbs; squirrels spot them and assume you're inviting them to dig!

# NOVEMBER
## Bulbs, Corms, Rhizomes, & Tubers

 PLANNING

Kits of **amaryllis** bulbs for indoor blooming are sold this time of year, along with **paperwhites.** Both species take a few weeks to come into bloom.

 PLANTING

In Zones 5 and northward, it's late to be planting bulbs but not too late! As long as the earth is soft enough to dig in, plant any bulbs that haven't yet made it into the ground. In Zones 6 and 7, you can be planting tulips and other spring-flowering bulbs all month and even into December. However, next year try to get them in earlier so they have more time to develop a root system; the bigger the root system, the better next year's flowering will be.

Bulbs that don't get planted before the ground freezes may stay in fair condition if you can winter them in vermiculite in a place where the temperatures are between 35 and 45 degrees Fahrenheit. If the bulbs get through the winter looking plump and healthy, try planting them as soon as you can dig a hole in the ground, and they may flower some this year or live on to become healthy plants the following year.

 CARE

Clear away dead leaves and the remains of annuals and perennials planted over bulb areas so you won't have to rake over tender new bulb foliage in early spring. A light winter mulch of pine boughs makes a great leaf catcher.

**Crocosmia** may winter over in Zone 7 and even in warm Zone 6 gardens, if covered with a light winter mulch—pine boughs or salt hay for instance.

 PRUNING

Cut down any remaining stems of **lilies, irises,** and other summer-flowering bulbs.

 WATERING

Maintain the water level of bulbs being forced into indoor bloom in pebbles or water.

Continue to monitor the moisture in pots of bulbs being forced. Do not allow them to dry out. Plants drink their food through rootlets, and if they dry out the rootlets will die. Until the bulbs grow new roots, the bulbs go hungry as well

as thirsty. Growth will be severely checked and may not resume in time for forcing.

Maintain a little moisture in pots of tender perennials and tropicals wintering indoors; they are only semi-dormant.

 FERTILIZING

If you haven't already, fertilize established beds of bulbs now. Spread Bulb-tone 4-10-6 at the rate of 5 to 10 pounds per 100 square feet. For lilies, spread Holly-tone at the rate of 4 pounds per 100 square feet.

Save wood ashes to use to fertilize naturalized plantings of spring-flowering bulbs in early March.

 PESTS

If you mulch areas planted in spring-flowering bulbs, it may discourage squirrels.

*Bulbs that don't get planted before the ground freezes may stay in fair condition if you can winter them in vermiculite in a place where the temperatures are between 35 and 45 degrees Fahrenheit.*

## Did You Know?

### How to Force Paperwhites, Hyacinths, and Amaryllis

**Forcing paperwhites in soil.** These sensationally fragrant varieties of *Tazetta narcissus* need seven to nine weeks to come into bloom. Choose bulbs not yet sprouted and plant them within four weeks. Keep paper-whites waiting to be planted in a dry warm room, about 60 degrees.

Plant the bulbs in bulb pans—six bulbs to a 6-inch pan or twelve bulbs to a 10-inch pan. Set the bulbs up to their shoulders in gritty potting mix and, to hold them in place, add enough gravel to cover the necks. Soak the soil in the pots, let the water drain, and set them to root in temperatures between 45 to 60 degrees Fahrenheit. Water sparingly once a week until growth begins. See Planting in September for further instructions.

**Forcing paperwhites in pebbles.** We find that sprouted **paperwhites** come into bloom quickly when forced in pebbles and water. Here are general instructions:

Choose a bowl that has no drainage hole and that is about 4 or 5 inches deep. Fill it within 2 inches of the rim with marble chips, pea gravel, builder's sand, or PermaTill. Arrange the bulbs so they touch each other and are perfectly straight. Gently press the bottoms about an inch into the pebbles. Add water to just below the bottoms of the bulbs, and then add enough growing medium to cover the necks of the bulbs.

Store the containers in low light at cool temperatures, 45 to 60 degrees Fahrenheit, until they are well rooted and shoots are growing. Then move them to warmth and bright light; the warmer the room, the faster they grow—and go by.

**Forcing hyacinths.** Buy pre-chilled bulbs and "hyacinth glasses," glasses nipped in at the top so they suspend the bottom of the bulb just above the water. Fill the glass to just below the bottom of the bulb and proceed as for forcing paperwhites in pebbles.

**Forcing amaryllis.** Use well-drained gritty soil and regular pots, not bulb pans. Plant these immense bulbs one to a 6-inch pot or three to a 12-inch pot, with the top third or half showing above the soil. Water the pots and the soil thoroughly, and set them in a warm room. Maintain soil moisture and fertilize when you fertilize the houseplants. They should come into bloom in about five to six weeks at normal house temperatures. The flower stalk rises before the foliage and lasts up to two weeks.

# DECEMBER
## Bulbs, Corms, Rhizomes, & Tubers

 PLANNING

Catch up on entries for your garden log.

 PLANTING

If you have unplanted spring-flowering bulbs, plant them while the ground remains soft enough to dig in!

**Amaryllis** potted up at the beginning of this month may still have time to come into bloom for the end of the year.

 CARE

**Amaryllis,** the ones that summered outdoors and were brought indoors and were either dried down or allowed to grow on, will show signs of new growth within the next several weeks. When you see signs of new growth, repot the bulbs in fresh fertile potting mix in the same pots, (amaryllis does best somewhat potbound) and set them in bright indirect light in a warm room. Water and fertilize them when you do the houseplants. Wait to break off and repot offsets (baby bulbs) until the plants are in full growth in spring.

Monitor moisture in the soil of the bulbs being forced; water if the tops feel dry.

Mid-month, check the dates and the timing chart for bulbs being forced. Bring those that are showing roots and shoots into a warmer room and indirect light; water and fertilize lightly when you water houseplants. When they are growing well, move them to good light and out of direct sun. Keep the soil barely damp while they are blooming.

 PRUNING

When **amaryllis** finish blooming, cut the blossoms off and continue to grow the plants in a bright sunny window.

 WATERING

As they come into bloom, water the soil of forced bulbs so it's slightly damp.

Keep the soil damp in pots of tender perennials and tropicals wintering indoors.

 FERTILIZING

Include fertilizer when you water the **amaryllis.**

Save wood ashes to fertilize naturalized plantings of spring-flowering bulbs in early March.

 PESTS

Mold sometimes appears on pots of bulbs being forced when the growing medium is very wet. Move the bulbs to a place with good air circulation and allow the soil to dry down to barely damp.

Get rid of aphids by spraying them with a kitchen sink sprayer or misting the plant with a horticultural soap. Discourage the little black fungus gnats that hover over potting mix by allowing the soil to dry between waterings and removing standing water from the plant saucers.

# CHAPTER THREE

# Herbs & Vegetables

*Ripe, sun-warmed, aromatic, wholesome—herbs, vegetables, berries, and orchard fruit from your own garden richly reward the effort involved in creating and maintaining it. Add cutting flowers to the picture, and it will delight the eye as it does the palate.*

Our families are "foodies," so we grow herbs by our kitchen doors and plant big vegetable gardens. A kitchen garden is the best way to get children interested in gardening—they relate to food. When Mark and Scott Viette were still in high school, their vegetable baskets won first and second prizes in the county fair, and recently Mark's vegetable garden was featured in *Southern Living* magazine. We do it all—start seeds indoors in late winter and store long-season keepers when we put our kitchen gardens to bed in fall.

## PLANNING

The first step in making a kitchen garden appealing is to **set it off handsomely.** A picket fence adds charm. If deer and other four-footers love your food, you can install a six-foot high chicken wire fence inside the pickets—it will be almost invisible from a few feet away.

Make the entrance special with an antique gate or a gated pergola supporting one of the fragrant climbing roses recommended in Chapter 7; we love 'New Dawn'. Plan to train a **grape vine** over the fence and an espaliered **pear** if there's space. Gussy it up with ornate birdhouses, an antique sundial, and a water basin with a bubbler.

**Make it exciting.** Wake up your appetite. Grow **lemon cucumbers,** heirloom vegetables and fruits, exotic perfumed **Galia melons** from Israel, and pungent Oriental **tat-soi** greens. Pick baby **head lettuce** and tiny **squash,** or plant a giant variety of **pumpkin** and aim for 600 pounds! Serve real *haricots verts*, true *petits pois* without concern for the price. Grow your own **asparagus, rhubarb, strawberries.**

**Make it colorful.** Plant **bronze fennel, globe** and **purple basil** as well as the sweet varieties, and **variegated mint.** Plant red, not green, **romaine, bibb,** and **oakleaf lettuce;** red **scallions,** not white; yellow, purple, and orange **sweet peppers** along with red and green; scarlet, yellow, and purple runner **beans;** and violet **broccoli** (which cooks up green).

**Make it interesting.** Plant **summer squashes** with different shapes and colors—round 'Gourmet Globe', yellow 'Gold Rush', 'Butterstick', and **pattypan** 'Sunburst'. Add curly **Russian kale** for texture, **arugula, radicchio,** and **mache** for fall salads. Be tempted by little white and mauve **eggplants,** wildly colorful **hot peppers,** red **new potatoes, yellow watermelons, golden beets.**

**Make it beautiful and fragrant.** Plant **rhubarb,** and allow the magnificent flower heads to grow up. Edge the garden with aromatic perennial herbs—**chives, variegated thymes,** colorful **sages, golden oregano,** and fragrant **English lavender.** The flowers as well as the foliage of the culinary herbs are edible. Center the beds on a **dwarf apple** or a **plum tree,** and the air will be sweet when you arrive to plant the mid-spring crops.

Choose flowers whose colors and texture will enhance the beauty of the vegetables. Edge plain green vegetables such as **spinach** with brilliant

# Herbs & Vegetables

'Copper Sunset' mounding **nasturtiums,** whose flowers and foliage are edible. Grow red-stemmed **rhubarb chard** with deep red **'Empress of India' nasturtiums.** Back **bush beans** with pink or lavender **powder puff asters,** and edge the row with **blue ageratum** or **dwarf purple gomphrena** and **purple basil.** Plant late **tulips** in the fall, and over-seed the row in early spring with **leaf lettuce** and **johnny-jump-up violas.** For fragrant summer bouquets, plant aromatic **basils** with **cosmos, snapdragons,** and **dahlias.**

Intertwine **snap beans** with **morning glories,** and edge the row with **blue salvia, white cosmos Sensation Strain 'Purity',** and **blue ageratum.** Back the solid structures of the earth-hugging **lettuces, beets,** and **cabbages** with airy **bronze fennel,** tall **snapdragons, caraway,** or **cosmos.** These gardens can be prettier than flower gardens.

**Caution: Don't combine edibles with poisonous plants—for example, larkspur, foxgloves, and sweetpeas are toxic.**

## START WITH A PLANTING PLAN

A planting plan is the first step in planning a kitchen garden. To put together herbs, vegetables, and flowers that will enhance each other, you need to partner varieties that mature at about the same time. The information you need is in garden literature and in mail-order herb, vegetable, and flower catalogs. Match the early, mid-season, and late species and varieties of annual flowers (see the Introduction to Annuals) to the cool-season, warm-season, and hot-season vegetables.

**Cool-season vegetables** are offered in early and late varieties. Where the growing season is short, seedlings of the early varieties are started indoors, set out in spring fairly early, and mature before high summer heat. Seeds of the late, or long-standing, varieties are sown in the garden in late spring or early summer, and mature crops are planted in cooling fall weather.

**Warm-season vegetables** are available in early and late varieties. Tiny **cherry tomatoes** and small **Early Girl tomatoes** mature before the **Big Boy** and **long-keeper** types. Most New York gardeners set out seedlings.

**Hot-season vegetables** need a longer season to mature. Examples are **shell beans, peppers,** and **eggplant.** Some varieties are available in smaller, earlier varieties—**watermelons** and **cantaloupes,** for example—that have time to mature even in the frost-belt. These also are set out as seedlings.

**Intensive cropping.** When you know what you want to plant, the next step is to see how much of it will actually fit your space. With careful timing, you can get more than one crop from the same row. It's called "intensive cropping." Here's how to do it:

*1* Clear out early crops as soon as they have been harvested, and replant the rows with mid- and late-season varieties.

*2* Combine sowings of cold-resistant, quickie vegetables such as **radishes** and **lettuce,** with taller, slow-to-mature species such as **Brussels sprouts.**

*3* Plant together tall and short crops that mature at about the same time, such as **corn** or **sunflowers,** with long-standing, late-season ground-hugging **pumpkins** or **winter squash.** The rambling vines of the **pumpkins** and **winter squash** shade out weeds.

## PLANTING HERBS AND VEGETABLES

Because we are eager for early harvests, we start many vegetables and herbs indoors. How is explained in the section on Starting Seeds Indoors in the Planting section of January, in the Annuals chapter. The seedlings of **cool-season vegetables**

# Herbs & Vegetables

usually can be moved out to the garden within four to six weeks—**cabbage** and **broccoli,** for example. They're transplanted as quite young seedlings directly from the flats they were sown in.

**Warm- and hot-season vegetables and herbs** benefit from being transplanted from the flats they were started in and planted in individual 2- to 4-inch peat pots before being moved out to the garden. In cold regions, the bigger varieties of **tomato** may do best transplanted a couple of times to ever-larger containers. After transplanting vegetable and herb seedlings to larger pots, wait to fertilize until the appearance of two or three new leaves tells you the root system is growing again. At that stage, provide very good natural light all day in a cold frame, on a windowsill, or in a glassed-in porch. Or grow the seedlings under fluorescent light about sixteen hours a day and set about 3 inches above the seedlings. As the seedlings grow, raise the light to 4 to 6 inches overhead. Once the seedlings show strong growth, reduce the lights to twelve hours a day.

## GROWING HERBS AND VEGETABLES

Here's an overview of the year in a kitchen garden:

*1* In October or November, or in early spring as soon as the cold and moisture have left the earth, turn the rows by hand or with a rototiller.

*2* Then check and adjust the soil pH, and work in fertilizer and soil amendments.

*3* Plant hardy and half-hardy vegetables and herbs early to mid-spring (late March and April).

*4* Plant warm- and hot-season vegetables and herbs in May and June.

*5* As crops mature, harvest the rows; when a row is finished, clear it, fertilize, turn the soil, and replant the rows with fall season crops.

*6* In September, October, or November, clear the rows.

**Light.** Most herbs and vegetables do best in full sun. To provide as much sun as possible, arrange the planting rows in your kitchen garden to run east to west. At the north end set tall plants, like staked **tomatoes, sunflowers,** and **corn** (planted in groups to assure pollination). At the south end, set low-growing things so they won't be shaded by the taller plants. Some cool-season vegetables that bolt with heat—**lettuce, peas,** and **spinach,** for example—may produce longer if planted where the shade of taller plants cuts the heat of the late spring sun.

**Spacing.** Raised beds or rows, about 36 inches wide and 24 to 36 inches apart, gives you room to work from both side comfortably and enough width to plant low-growing crops like **lettuce** and **beets** in the same row with flowers. When the vegetable seedlings are up, thin them out around the strongest flower seedlings. As the early vegetables are harvested, the flowers will fill out.

Big, rapid growers like **eggplants, tomatoes,** and **summer squash** need 24 to 36 inches around each plant. To create a living mulch for these vegetables, plant spreading flowers like **sweet alyssum, nasturtiums,** and **multiflora petunias** about 12 inches away. Where mildew is a problem, avoid dense plantings, which cut down on air circulation.

## SOIL AND FERTILIZING

If you are starting **a new kitchen garden,** we recommend creating raised beds as described in the Introduction to the book under Starting a Raised Bed.

To support the lavish productivity of an **established kitchen garden,** every year before planting season begins it's a good idea to check and adjust the soil pH as described in the Introduction under Soil Preparation and Improvement.

# Herbs & Vegetables

In addition, before planting, work into the top 6 to 8 inches of the soil a generous helping of nutrients. (The exception is **nasturtiums.**) Use an organic fertilizer such as Plant-tone, or an eight-month formulation of a controlled-release chemical fertilizer for vegetables and annuals. (See Understanding Fertilizers in the Introduction to the book.) That will carry the plants through the whole growing season. In early spring before growth begins, scratch fertilizer into the soil around the kitchen garden perennials—**asparagus,** the **strawberry** patch, **rhubarb, bramble fruits,** and the others.

The long-season hot-weather crops, including **tomatoes,** benefit from a modest additional fertilization during the growing season. Use a water-soluble organic fertilizer such as fish emulsion or liquid seaweed. Prompts for fertilizing are given in the month-by-month pages that follow. In addition, before replanting a row that has already produced a crop, renew the fertilizer.

Planting a cover crop (see Annuals, Planting in the October pages) at the end of the growing season renews the organic content and fertility of the soil.

## WATERING

Seeds need consistent moisture to germinate and grow. **Before sowing seeds,** unless the garden is moist from recent rain, water the soil slowly and thoroughly. Use a sprinkler or a hose to lay down 1 to 2 inches of water. Set a coffee can or other container under the watering equipment to measure the time it takes to lay down that much water, and record it in your garden log. **After the seeds are planted,** water the area for half an hour or so.

Maintaining soil moisture keeps root systems growing, and big root systems deliver lots of produce and withstand summer drought and heat. Your kitchen garden needs a good soaking rain every week to ten days, or enough hose water to lay down 1 or 1½ inches.

In addition, water at any time seedlings show signs of wilting.

## PEST CONTROL

Integrated Pest Management (IPM), which is discussed in Pests, Diseases, and Controls in the Appendix to the book, is the new scientific and commercial approach to handling pests, and it includes some old-fashioned controls that many gardeners swear by. Some gardeners report greater success planting tall crops when the moon is rising and root crops when the moon is diminishing, but that's not proven whereas IPM methods are.

Organic gardeners also report some success with these plant combinations for combating pests:

Asparagus beetles. Try **basil, parsley, tomato** plants nearby.

Aphids. Try **garlic** and **nasturtiums** nearby.

Beetles. Try **nasturtiums** near your **radishes,** near **beans, cucumbers, eggplant, squash,** and **tomatoes.**

Colorado potato beetle. Try **marigolds** nearby.

Mexican bean beetles. Try **potatoes** near **beans.**

Mites. Try **radishes** near **beans, cucumbers, eggplant, squash,** and **tomatoes.**

Nematodes. Try **marigolds** nearby.

For information on common pests and diseases and their controls, turn to the section on Pests, Diseases, and Controls at the back of the book.

# Herbs & Vegetables

## Did You Know?

### How to Grow the Popular Culinary Herbs

**Arugula.** Annual. Sow seeds indoors in late winter or outdoors in early spring; repeat in mid-summer.

**Basil.** Annual here. Sow seeds indoors in mid-spring, or set seedlings out when you plant **tomatoes.** For flavor, plant **sweet basil;** for pesto and for freezing, 'Sweet Genovese'; for cooking and to make basil oil, **East Indian** or **Holy Basil;** for Oriental cuisine, and basil oil, plant **Thai basil;** for color and flowers, 'Purple Ruffles'; for containers, grow topiary-like tiny **bush basils.**

**Chives.** Perennial. Start seeds indoors in peat pots late in March, or set seedlings out in April.

**Dill.** Annual. Sow seeds in early spring in peat pots, or plant seedlings outdoors in May where the plants are to grow. Use the foliage fresh, or dry and store it. Allow flower heads to go to seed, then dry seeds for cooking.

**Cilantro/Coriander.** Annual. Sow seeds indoors in April, outdoors in May. The seed is the spice coriander.

**Fennel.** Annual. Sow seeds indoors in March, and set out seedlings in mid-spring where they are to grow. For flavorful leaves, plant **sweet fennel** (*Foeniculum vulgare dulce*); the cultivar 'Rubrum' is the **ornamental bronze fennel.** The vegetable is **Florence fennel** (*F. v.* var. *azoricum*).

**Lavender.** Perennial. Sow seeds indoors in January or February; transplant often. Transplant 12-inch seedlings in May, and coddle. 'Munstead' is the hardiest. Harvest the stems before the buds break.

**Mint.** Invasive perennial. Confine to a container. Plant root divisions in early spring, summer, or fall. **Spearmint** (*Mentha spicata*) is the best all-round culinary mint.

**Oregano.** Perennial. See **Sweet marjoram.** For flavor, plant **common oregano** (*Origanum vulgare*); for edging the garden, plant **golden oregano.** Sow seeds indoors in April, transplant seedlings in May,

**Parsley.** Biennial. Start seeds indoors in February. Set seedlings outdoors in April. About Labor Day, plant seedlings near maturing parsley plants. Choose **curly parsley** for garnishing, chopping, and floral bouquets. Plant flat **Italian parsley** for salads and cooking.

**Rosemary.** Tender perennial. Set out seedlings or rooted cuttings in mid-spring. North of Zone 7, winter rosemary indoors. For cooking, choose *Rosmarinus officinalis*; as a garden ornamental, *R. o.* 'Lockwood de Forest'.

**Sage.** Sow seeds indoors in March. Plant seedlings outdoors in April. For flavoring, plant *Salvia officinalis.* For color, plant **tricolor sage.**

**Sweet Marjoram.** Tender perennial. Sow seeds indoors in mid-spring or outdoors after the soil has warmed. A cousin to **oregano,** grow this one for use fresh.

**Tarragon.** Perennial. The best is **French tarragon** (*Artemisia dracunculus*), which is propagated from cuttings. For flavor, taste before you buy a plant. Set out rooted cuttings in April.

**Thyme.** Perennial. Start seeds February or March. Transplant outdoors in April after the soil warms. For flavor, plant **common thyme** (*Thymus vulgaris*); for display, 'Wedgewood English'; for containers, stepping stones, and in stone walls, **creeping thyme** (*T. serpyllum*). For edging, plant variegated 'Argenteus' and 'Aureus'.

## Vegetables

| Common Name | Sow Indoors* | Sow Outdoors | Approximate Time to Maturity | Our Picks |
|---|---|---|---|---|
| Asparagus Roots | — | Fall | 2 years to first harvest | 'Jersey Giant', Jersey Knight', 'Jersey King' |
| Beans, Snap | April (in pots) | After last frost/May | 54-58 days | 'Nickel', 'Vernandon', 'Goldkist' (yellow wax), 'Tenderette', 'Provider' |
| Beans, Pole | April (in pots) | May | 65-100 days | 'Emerite', 'Blue Lake' |
| Beets, Early | March | April-June | 50-75 days | 'Red Ace Hybrid' and specialty beets 'Chioggia', Golden Beet' |
| Beets, Late | — | June-July | 75-100 days | 'Long Season' (superb!) |
| Broccoli | March-May | March-April | 50-100 days | Early: 'Early Dividend', 'Early Emerald', 'Early Packman'; Summer: 'Saga', 'Small Miracle'; Late: 'Arcadia', 'Marathon', 'Pirate', 'Saga' |
| Brussels Sprouts | April-June | May | 90-150 days | Dwarf: 'Jade Cross E', 'Oliver' |
| Cabbage, Chinese | Late April | May-June | 50-65 days | Spring crop: 'Blues', 'Kasumi', 'Orient Express', 'Joi Choi' (Pak Choi) |
| Cabbage, Early | March-April | May | 65-100 days | 'First White Hybrid', 'Flat Dutch', 'Early Marvel', 'Chieftain Savoy', 'Tendersweet' |
| Cabbage, Late | — | May-June | 51-95 days | 'Storage No. 4', 'Scanbo' |
| Carrots, Early | March | April-May | 60-80 days | 'Chantenay', 'Danver Half Long', 'Baby Sweet', 'Nantes' |
| Cauliflower, Early | February | April | 50-100 days | 'Chartreuse', 'Burgundy Queen', 'Snow Crown', 'Orange Bouquet', 'Violet Queen', 'Alverda' (green) |
| Celeriac | March | April-May | 70-85 days | — |
| Collards | — | June | 60-85 days | — |
| Corn Salad (Mache) | — | April-May | 45-60 days | — |

# Herbs & Vegetables

## Vegetables

| Common Name | Sow Indoors* | Sow Outdoors | Approximate Time to Maturity | Our Picks |
|---|---|---|---|---|
| Corn, Sweet | — | After last frost and every 2-3 weeks for continuous crop | 65-100 days | 'Kandy', 'Peaches and Cream', 'Silver Queen'. Pop Corn: 'Tom Thumb', 'Shaman's Blue', 'Ruby Red' |
| Cucumbers | Late March-April (in pots) | May | 50-70 days | 'Sweet Success', 'Straight Eight', 'Burpee Burpless', 'Burpless #26', 'Sweet Slice' |
| Eggplant | Late March-April (in pots) | May-June | 65-90 days | 'Asian Bride' (white), 'Neon' (luminous purple), 'Rosa Bianca' (rosy), 'Little Fingers' |
| Endive | February | April | 65-100 days | — |
| Garlic Cloves | — | October-November | Late summer | 'Italian', 'Elephant', 'Softneck' |
| Kale, Spring Use | Late March-April | April-May | 55-65 days | — |
| Kale, Fall Use | — | June-July | 45-60 days | — |
| Kohlrabi | Late March-April | April-July | 45-60 days | — |
| Lettuce | Late March | April, May, August | 45-80 days | 'Black Simpson', 'Oak Leaf', 'Butter Crunch', 'Bib', 'Romaine', 'Redsails' |
| Leek | February | April-May | 120-150 days | — |
| Melons, Honeydew | April (in pots) | Pots in May-June | 70-100 days | 'Early Dew', 'Honeypearl' |
| Melons, Musk | April (in pots) | Pots in May | 90-120 days | 'Sweet 'n Early', 'Early Gold', 'Alaska', 'Ambrosia' |
| Melons, Water | April (in pots) | Pots in May | 65-90 days | 'Sugar Baby', 'Tiger Baby', 'Triple Crown Hybrid' (seedless) |
| New Zealand Spinach | April | May | 70 days | — |

# Herbs & Vegetables

## Vegetables

| Common Name | Sow Indoors* | Sow Outdoors | Approximate Time to Maturity | Our Picks |
|---|---|---|---|---|
| Okra | — | May | 55-60 days | — |
| Onion Seed | February-March | Late April-May, July | 70-115 days | — |
| Onion Sets | — | Late April-early May | 60-75 days | 'Candy' |
| Parsnip | — | April | 95-150 days | 'Lancer' |
| Peas (smooth), Early | — | Late March-May | 50-75 days | — |
| Peas (wrinkled) | — | April-May | 50-75 days | — |
| Peppers, Hot | April | Seedlings in May | 50-85 days | 'Anaheim', 'Mucho Nacho', 'Jalapeno', 'Hungarian Hot Wax', 'Habanero' |
| Peppers, Sweet | April | Seedlings in May | 50-85 days | 'California Wonder', 'Big Bertha', 'Better Bell', 'Sweet Banana' |
| Potatoes (sets) | — | April-June | 60-90 days | 'Yukon Gold', 'Red Sun', 'All Blue', 'Giant Peanut Fingerling', 'Gold Rush' |
| Pumpkin | April | May-June | 90-120 days | 'Baby Boo', 'Wee-Be-Little', 'Jack-O-Lantern', 'Jarradale' (baking) |
| Radish, Early | — | April, Sept | 25-50 days | 'Cherry Bell' (seed again in fall) |
| Radish, Winter | — | July-August | 25-50 days | — |
| Rhubarb | — | April-May | Spring | 'Valentine', 'Crimson Red', 'Strawberry' |
| Rutabaga | April | June-July | 70-90 days | 'American Purple Top', 'Gilfeather', 'Thomson Laurentian' |
| Salsify | — | April-May | 125-130 days | — |
| Spinach | Early April | April-May, Sept | 35-55 days | 'Bloomsdale', 'Tyee' |
| Squash, Summer | April | After last frost | 50-65 days | 'Zucchini', 'Scallop', 'Summer Crookneck', 'Starship', 'Spacemaster' |

# Herbs & Vegetables

## Vegetables

| Common Name | Sow Indoors* | Sow Outdoors | Approximate Time to Maturity | Our Picks |
|---|---|---|---|---|
| Squash, Winter | April | May-June | 60-110 days | 'Heart of Gold Acorn', 'Early Butternut', 'Waltham Butternut', 'Warted Green Hubbard' |
| Swiss Chard | April | April-June | 50-60 days | 'Bright Lights' |
| Tomatoes | April | Mid-May (plants) | 100-120 days | 'Sun Gold' (cherry), 'Early Girl', 'Goliath', 'Park Whopper', 'Beefmaster', 'Super Steak', 'German Johnson' (antique), 'Mr. Stripey', 'Oxheart' (heirloom), 'Roma', 'Italian Plum' |
| Turnips, Early | April | June | 40-75 days | 'All Top Hybrid', 'White Lady Hybrid' |
| Turnips, Late | — | July-Sept | 40-75 days | — |
| Turnips, Salad | — | April and Sept | 35-45 days | — |

* Use flats for sowing indoors unless otherwise specified.

## Culinary Herbs

| Common Name (Botanical Name) | Hardiness | Sow Indoors | Sow Outdoors | Harvest | Our Picks |
|---|---|---|---|---|---|
| Arugula (Eruca vesicaria) | Annual | April, July | Seedlings in April | Spring-summer | French arugula |
| Basil (Ocimum basilicum) | Zones 9 and 10 | April | Seedlings in May | Summer September | 'Sweet Genovese', 'Holy Basil', 'Thai Basil' |
| Chives (Allium schoenoprasum) | Zones 3 to 8 | March | Seedlings in April | All season | — |
| Cilantro (Coriander sativum) | Annual | April | Seedlings in May | All season | 'Santo Cilantro' |
| Dill (Anethum graveolens) | Annual | April | Seedlings in May | Spring/ early summer | 'Bouquet' |

# Herbs & Vegetables

## Culinary Herbs

| Common Name (Botanical Name) | Hardiness | Sow Indoors | Sow Outdoors | Harvest | Our Picks |
|---|---|---|---|---|---|
| Lavender (*Lavandula angustifolia*) | Zones 4/5 to 10 | February/ March | Seedlings in May | June/ may repeat | English lavender 'Munstead', 'Hidcote' |
| Mint (*Mentha spicata*) | Zones 3 to 9 | — | Root divisions spring/summer/ fall | All season | Spearmint (*M. spicata*) |
| Oregano/Sweet Marjoram (*Origanum vulgare*; *O. majorana*) | Tender perennial, Zones 5 to 10 | April | May; seedlings in May | All season | Common oregano (*Origanum vulgare*); sweet marjoram (*O. majorana*) |
| Parsley (*Petroselinum crispum*) | Biennial, Zones 3 to 9 | February | Seedlings in March/April; September | All season | Curly parsley; Italian parsley; *P. crispum* 'Neapolitanum' |
| Rosemary (*Rosmarinus officinalis*) | Zones 7 to 9 | Root cuttings, late summer | Seedlings | All season | Common rosemary |
| Sage (*Salvia officinalis*) | Zones 5 to 9 | April | Seedlings in May | All season | Common sage |
| Tarragon (*Artemisia dracunculus*) | Zones 4 to 9 | Root cuttings, summer | N/A | June | French tarragon |
| Thyme (*Thymus* spp. & cvs.) | Zones 3 to 9 | February/ March | April/May | All season | Common thyme (*T. vulgaris*), lemon thyme (*T.* x *citriodorus*), caraway thyme (*T. herba-barona*) |

## PLANNING

Gather your favorite mail-order catalogs for herbs, vegetables, and annuals, and sketch a planting plan. Plan to maximize your garden's productivity by closely spacing the plants and by interplanting and succession cropping.

**Interplanting** (or intercropping) is the planting of two or more crops in the same row at the same time, like fast-growing **radishes** with **lettuce,** which are both hardy early spring crops. Or **sweet corn** with **pumpkins,** which will remain to mature after the corn has been picked. Or **tomatoes** with **basil,** both warm weather crops set out at the same time.

**Succession cropping** refers to keeping a row planted with a sequence of vegetables; when the first crop is harvested, you remove it and reseed the row immediately. For example, **radishes,** followed by **lettuce,** followed by **snap bush beans,** followed by **late carrots.**

 ## PLANTING

If you plan to start seeds early indoors, begin to gather the equipment and the seeds you will need. (See Starting Seeds Indoors in the January pages of the Annuals chapter.)

**Seed Sharing.** Plan to share the seeds for herbs. Most families don't need a lot of any one kind. Our rule of thumb is this—for most annual and perennial herbs, we recommend two plants per household, or four if you dry herbs to give away. We plant six **parsley** and a dozen **basil** because we use it to scent bouquets and make basil oil. We use **lavender** buds in cooking, in bouquets, as well as to dry to scent linens, so we grow lavender in sunny sheltered corners everywhere.

 ## CARE

If you are overwintering herbs not quite hardy in your area in a cold frame (see September), as the days grow longer and the sun grows warmer during spells of thawing weather, monitor temperatures and ventilate to keep the interior moderately cool.

 ## PRUNING

Harvest and groom herbs such as **parsley** you brought indoors last fall. Discard plants that are failing.

 ## WATERING

Maintain the soil moisture in herbs growing indoors.

 ## FERTILIZING

Add 5 drops of houseplant fertilizer to the water for herbs growing indoors.

Save wood ashes to use later as a pH modifier for the kitchen garden. They make calcium and potash quickly available to the plants.

 ## PESTS

Damping off is a threat to seedlings started early indoors. It's a fungal disease that attacks the seedlings at the base of their stems. It rots the stems so the plants fall over. A sterile growing medium and good drainage help avoid the condition. Applications of the fungicide Arasam help control the problem.

# FEBRUARY

 PLANNING

**Prepare your garden tools for the season ahead.** Treat wooden handles with applications of boiled linseed oil, which is available in paint and hardware stores. Oil your shears and trimmers, shovels and spading forks. Service the rototiller or take it to be serviced, and have the blade changed if necessary.

If you plan to set vegetable seedlings out in the garden very early, best gather **protective covers** now. Various types of cones including those called "hot caps" and "walls of water" are available.

Plan to try tenting rows as a protective covering for early-start seedlings, and to keep insects and small pests away.

**Ordering vegetable seeds and plants.** Check your buying plans against your inventory of seeds left over or saved last year. List what you have, will order by mail, or plan to buy at a garden center. If prices are equal, buy perennials such as **asparagus** crowns (two or three years old for quick results), **rhubarb, strawberries, raspberries, fruit trees,** and **onion sets** from a garden center where you can see what you are getting.

Do a web search for items not found in your mail-order catalogs. We've had good luck with it. It's also worthwhile to check catalog prices against prices at online garden sites.

When your plan is final, prepare catalog orders and mail them, and prepare shopping lists for purchases to be made at garden centers.

Check your supplies of small pots suitable for transplanting seedlings you will start indoors. You can reuse pots, flats, and jars safely if you rinse them in a solution that is 1 part bleach to 9 parts water.

See if you need more seed starter or potting mix for head-start indoor plantings. For vegetables and herbs you plan to grow in hanging baskets and other containers, provide potting mixes that include water-holding gels. Check out the liquid and water-soluble organic fertilizers available . . . manure teas are in, in, in!!

 PLANTING

Late this month or early next month, Zone 7 and warm Zone 6 can start the perennial herbs that are slow to germinate or that must be fairly large before

they can succeed in the open garden—**lavender** and **thyme** come to mind. Cold-hardy **chives** and **parsley** can be started next month. Zones 3 through 5 would do best waiting until late March. (See the January pages of the Annuals chapter, Starting Seeds Indoors.)

## CARE

**Outdoors.** Late this month or early next month depending on your zone, prune the **grape vines;** don't wait until the sap runs as they will bleed, and that weakens the plants.

If you planted a cover crop in your garden in the fall (see the Annuals chapter, October, Planting), turn it under as soon as cold and moisture have left the earth.

## PRUNING

Groom, prune, and repot herbs brought indoors last fall.

**Outdoors.** Late this month you can begin to remove winter-damaged limbs from the fruit trees and prune out water sprouts, weak limbs, and any that cross.

*Check your buying plans against your inventory of seeds left over or saved last year. List what you have, will order by mail, or plan to buy at a garden center.*

## Did You Know?

### You Can Grow Herbs and Vegetables in Containers

Herbs and vertical vegetables make great container plants. Tidy herbs, like **parsley, globe basil,** and **thyme** suit a window box and make pretty edgers for tall or short potted flowers. **Tomato** seedlings perform beautifully growing in pots, planters, and even paper grocery bags.

**Shell beans** and **eggplant** climb from a container as readily as from the soil. Small **summer squash, gourds,** or **cucumbers** can be trained to a teepee (three or four long poles tied together at the top like a Native American tent). **Melons** and even **pumpkins,** too, but their fruits will need the support of a sling made of a mesh bag or a section of pantyhose tied to the teepee when the fruits get big. Varieties with medium- to small-sized fruits carried high on the plant are more attractive for container growing than are the low-growing, heavy-fruited types.

Some of the perennial kitchen garden plants do well in big tubs and planters—**artichokes, rhubarbs, strawberries, dwarf peaches,** and columnar **apple trees.**

For window box, basket, and container plantings, we recommend a humusy commercial potting mix enriched with slow-release fertilizer. Mix a polymer such as Soil Moist into the soil, and you'll find maintaining moisture much easier. Where summers are cool, place containers in warm microclimates, in the reflected heat from a south wall, for example.

---

**Raspberries.** If you didn't do it last fall, remove all the older canes that bore fruit last year, leaving six to eight new canes per hill.

**Blueberries.** Before growth begins, remove dead and broken branches and small bushy growth. For five-year-old plants, remove all but five or six sturdy branches.

 WATERING

Maintain the moisture levels of the herbs you brought indoors last fall.

 FERTILIZING

**Indoors.** At every watering, fertilize herbs growing indoors with a water-soluble houseplant fertilizer at half strength.

Save wood ashes to use as fertilizer for the kitchen garden. They make lime and potash quickly available to the plants.

 PESTS

Crowded seedlings growing indoors in soggy soil are vulnerable to the fungus called "damping off," which rots stems near the soil surface. Discard affected plants, reduce watering, and increase light and fresh air. If the problem persists, mist the seedlings with a fungicide such as Arasam or with 1 tablespoon of bleach to 1 quart of water (4 tablespoons to a gallon of water).

# MARCH
## Herbs & Vegetables

## 🗓 PLANNING

Look through your catalogs for inspiration and try a few bramble and orchard fruits and other delicious perennial food plants. **Asparagus,** red-stemmed **rhubarb,** and **Jerusalem artichokes** (sunchokes, the tuberous roots of tall, small-flowered **sunflowers**) are decorative and yummy. **Artichokes** aren't perennial here, even in Zone 7. **Alpine strawberries** are fun, but, if you love berries and cream, plant ordinary **strawberries** in a bed of their own.

A hardy **dwarf apple, pear,** or **peach** is lovely in bloom, the perfect central ornament for a kitchen garden; dwarf apples and pears also make handsome, productive espaliers. You can even grow a hardy dwarf fruit tree in a tub as long as it is at least 18 inches square or in diameter, and insulated inside with a double row of large bubble wrap or styrofoam.

**Grape vines** can be trained to a fence, a pergola, and as an espalier. To do it right, you'll need a book on the subject, or an informed neighbor.

The **bramble fruits** need a space of their own, off to one side.

**Highbush blueberries** are slow to produce, but their fall color is superb. They require an acidic soil, pH 4.5 to 5.5.

## 🌱 PLANTING

**Indoors.** In Zones 3 to 5, late this month and next, depending on your climate and the year, start seeds indoors for early **beets** and **turnips;** in late March you can start **eggplant** and **kale,** and others indicated on our plant lists. (See Starting Seeds Indoors under Planting in the January pages of the Annuals chapter.)

Any time after the second set of leaves opens, seedlings started indoors can be transplanted to individual 3- to 4-inch pots filled with a good potting mix.

A friend who lives in Vermont planted seed for **peas** outdoors at the end of March and beat all the neighbors to *petits pois.* But we have found that, while the seeds survive in cold soil, we get quicker growth and crops if we start them in early to mid-April depending on the year. The earth is ready to be worked when a ball of earth packed between your hands crumbles easily; if it sticks together, the soil is still too wet.

## 🌿 CARE

Protect seedlings planted early in the open garden from late frosts with hot caps or a lightweight fabric like Reemay. You can save seedlings from an occasional night frost by covering them with newspaper, coffee cans, drycleaner's dry cleaning plastic or plastic film, old sheets, blankets, bedspreads, or burlap.

When freezing night temperatures are over, remove the uppermost layer of straw used as winter mulch for **strawberry** plants. Leave the matted-down straw to make a clean bed for the berries to rest on.

After the annual fertilization, renew the mulch around the perennial food plants—**asparagus, rhubarb, bramble fruits,** and **fruit trees.**

## ✂ PRUNING

Cut back by half **thyme, chives, sage, tarragon, oregano,** and other perennial herbs.

Finish pruning **summer** and **everbearer raspberries** and **blueberries** before growth begins.

In late March begin pruning your **grapes;** we recommend the four-cane Kniffen system that trains canes to a top and bottom wire.

Thin **elderberries,** leaving only eight to ten of the thickest, healthiest canes.

*You can save seedlings from an occasional night frost by covering them with newspaper, coffee cans, drycleaner's dry cleaning plastic or plastic film, old sheets, blankets, bedspreads, or burlap.*

 # WATERING

Maintain the moisture for seeds and transplants—those indoors and those in a cold frame.

Maintain the soil moisture of herbs brought indoors last fall.

 # FERTILIZING

You can start fertilizing transplanted seedlings started indoors when the appearance of two or three new pairs of leaves indicates the root system is growing again.

Every two weeks, fertilize all the seedlings that will remain indoors another six weeks or more with a houseplant fertilizer at half strength.

 # PESTS

Protect plantings from rabbits and other pests with row covers or bird netting. A chicken wire fence is one sure way to keep rabbits out. If there are woodchucks, leave the chicken wire loose between posts; woodchucks can climb taut chicken wire.

## Did You Know?

### Preparing the Kitchen Garden for Planting

As soon as the snow is gone and winter moisture has left the soil, you can begin readying beds for planting. The earth is ready to be worked when a ball of earth packed between your hands crumbles easily; if it sticks together, the soil is still too wet.

A new bed needs the careful preparation described under Soil Preparation and Improvement in the Introduction to the book. Established beds for the annual vegetables and herbs must be reworked every year.

- If you didn't do it last fall, clear away the remains of last year's crops.

- Check the pH and apply whatever is needed to adjust the pH to between 6.0 and 7.0, the range suited to most food plants. The main exceptions are **basil** (5.5 to 6.5), **blueberries** (4.5 to 5.5), **dill** (5.5 to 6.7), **eggplant** and **melon** (5.5 to 6.5), **potatoes** (4.5 to 6.0), and **sorrel** (5.5 to 6.0). Vegetable gardens produce multiple crops, and over time the soil tends to become acid, so testing and adjusting the pH annually is important. Try a dusting of wood ashes over the rows to add lime, which sweetens the soil, and potash (potassium), which strengths stems and keeps growth healthy. Many garden soils have a potash deficiency. Retest, and if the pH still is off, follow the instructions for adjusting pH in Soil Preparation and Improvement in the Introduction to the book.

- Turn and loosen the soil, by hand or with a rototiller, and at the same time work into the soil whatever amendments you are adding.

- Fertilize the top 3 to 6 inches of the planting rows with a generous helping of nutrients (except for **nasturtiums**). If you are using an organic fertilizer such as Plant-tone, apply it four to six weeks before planting begins. If you are using a chemical fertilizer—granular or coated eight-month slow release—apply it just before planting.

You must also fertilize the soil around the perennials—**strawberries, orchard** and **bramble fruits.** For **asparagus,** use an organic fertilizer high in nitrogen.

# APRIL

## Herbs & Vegetables

## PLANNING

To make the most of your garden space, plan now for the crops that will replace the cool-season vegetables when their harvests are over.

When temperatures reach 65 degrees Fahrenheit, you can set out seedlings and sow seeds outdoors for **nasturtiums, summer savory, beans, cantaloupes, chard, corn, cucumbers, muskmelon, potatoes, pumpkin, squash, sweet corn, rutabaga, turnips.**

**Asparagus.** You can prepare a new bed as soon as the soil is workable and start planting three weeks before the last frost. In Zones 3 and 4, that's easier if you prepare the bed in the fall.

Order two- or three-year-old asparagus crowns for planting this month; fifty crowns should produce enough for the average family—and go on producing for about twenty years.

*1* In rows 3 to 4 feet apart, loosen the soil 18 inches deep. For open pollinated varieties like 'Martha Washington', make the planting bed 8 to 10 inches deep; for all-male **Jersey hybrids** such as 'Jersey Knight', make the beds 6 inches deep. Work 1 inch of compost into the top 2 inches of the planting beds, along with an organic fertilizer.

*2* Test the soil pH and, if needed, dig in amendments to bring the pH up or down to a range between 6.5 to 7.5.

*3* Spread the crowns over the soil 18 inches apart; cover them with 2 inches of soil.

*4* As the shoots grow, gradually fill the trenches, 2 to 3 inches of soil at a time.

*5* Mulch 2 inches deep.

*6* The second year, harvest only a few stalks. Stop when the stalks come in thin.

*7* Every year before growth begins and again after the harvest, retest and adjust the soil pH and fertilize the bed.

## PLANTING

Plant **bramble fruits** now, in very early spring; **fruit trees** while they are still dormant; **strawberries** after the ground has lost its winter cold; **rhubarb** as soon as plants become available; **asparagus** crowns (male plants) after danger of frost is past.

When danger of frost is over, you can also set out seedlings of **cabbage, cauliflower, chives, onion sets** (late April to early May), **fennel, sage, thyme.** You can sow seeds for **carrots, endive,** and

**sunflowers,** and you can plant **white potatoes.** Plant **broccoli** ('Green Comet') and **lettuce** seedlings or seeds now through early May. Plant **peas** as soon as the ground can be worked.

**Transplanting seedlings.** Before transplanting vegetable and herb seedlings to the open garden, set them in a sheltered spot outdoors to harden off for a few days.

**When you are ready to plant:**

*1* Wet the seedlings thoroughly with tepid water containing fertilizer.

*2* Dig a generous hole in the bed.

*3* Pour a little of the water into each planting hole. For:

• Seedlings growing together in a flat, separate intertwined seedlings by slicing them apart with a sharp knife.

• Seedlings in planting pockets, hold the flat a few inches above the soil, turn it on its side, and push one rootball at a time out of its pocket.

• Seedlings in peat pots, soak each peat pot thoroughly in a solution of 1 gallon of water to which you have added $1/2$ teaspoon of liquid hand dishwashing detergent and liquid fertilizer. Then gently tear open the bottom third of the peat pot so the roots can tie into the earth. Set the pot and the plant upright in the planting hole.

**4** Loosen roots that may be binding the rootball. Set each seedling upright and straight in its planting hole so the top of the rootball is just above the soil surface.

**5** Fill the hole with soil, and press it down firmly around the stem.

**6** Water well.

## CARE

Mulch the perennials 3 inches deep starting 3 inches from the trunk.

## PRUNING

Keep an eye on the rows where you have sown vegetables, and when the seedlings start to come up thick and fast, thin the rows as instructed by the seed packet.

Close, dense planting will shade out weeds; keep that in mind as you thin the rows.

## WATERING

If rain fails, be sure to water seeds and seedlings deeply.

## Did You Know?

### Crop Rotation Equals Better Health

You can avoid encouraging pests and diseases by rotating your crops annually. The rotation rule applies not only to individual species but also to members of that species' plant family.

**These six plant families benefit from crop rotation:**

**Cabbage group.** Broccoli, Brussels sprouts, cabbage, cauliflower, Chinese cabbage, collards, kale, kohlrabi, radishes, turnips.

**Carrot and parsley group.** Carrots, celery, coriander, dill, fennel, parsley, parsnips.

**Cucumber group.** Cucumbers, gourds, melons, squash, pumpkins, watermelons.

**Legumes.** Beans, peas.

**Onion group.** Chives, onions, garlic.

**Tomato group.** Eggplant, peppers, potatoes, tomatoes.

Water vegetables and fruits growing in containers every two to three days.

## FERTILIZING

Weekly, include a half-dose of a water-soluble organic fertilizer in the water for vegetables and fruits growing in containers.

## PESTS

Keep weed seedlings raked up when very young, then as the good plants grow up, they'll shade out the weeds.

**Be tolerant of a small infestation of the insects that are food for the beneficials.** The buzz of a nearby bee can scare you, but they are essential to pollinate crops. Wasps are mostly parasitic and destroy countless whiteflies and aphids. Yellow jackets feed their young many flies and caterpillars. Most lady beetles destroy aphids, mealy bugs, and spider mites. There are beneficial beetles, flies that attack corn borer and cutworms, and midges that devour aphids. Other insects considered beneficial are dragonflies, lacewings, spiders, and some mites.

To encourage these beneficials, avoid toxic sprays or dusts unless a crop is being truly harmed.

# MAY
## Herbs & Vegetables

## PLANNING

**Kitchen garden in a container.** Growing herbs, vegetables, even **dwarf fruit trees** in containers solves problems of space, light, temperature. They'll thrive as long as the soil is fertile and the moisture sustained.

Low-growing culinary herbs such as **miniature basils, parsley,** and **arugula,** and small and miniature vegetables like 'Tom Thumb', a tiny heading **lettuce,** do well in window boxes and big pots.

**Rosemary** thrives in a container. Train baby rosemary plants as topiary balls or trees this summer, bring them indoors before temperatures fall to freezing, and you'll have sensational gifts to give in December.

**Legumes and squashes** can be led to climb up into better light—**peas, beans** including the beautiful **scarlet runner** and purple-stemmed **hyacinth bean, eggplant, summer squash, melons,** even baby **pumpkins** will grow up a teepee, a pyramid, or a trellis stuck into a big container.

**Tomato** varieties do well in containers. Small varieties of **cherry tomatoes** thrive in 8-inch pots and hanging baskets. The big **heirloom** and late **keeper tomatoes** make it in 2- to 5-gallon containers filled with fertile planting mix.

## PLANTING

When temperatures head over 65 degrees Fahrenheit, you can set out seedlings of **tomatoes, eggplant, peanuts, hot** and **sweet peppers,** and **melons.** You can also sow seeds (Zone 7) or set out seedlings of **lima** and **shell beans.** If you want to plant these warm-weather crops sooner, use hotcaps or walls of water to protect them from cold.

**Sowing seeds.** The classic way to sow vegetable seeds is in shallow furrows (drills) created by dragging the edge of a rake or hoe handle along the planting line. Then you dribble the seeds into the drills at spaced intervals.

Small, fine seeds such as **lettuce** are broadcast over damp, well-worked soil. Cover them with seed starting mix and cover that with burlap to maintain the moisture during germination.

Seeds or seedlings of vining plants like **cucumbers** and **winter squash** may be sown around a supporting teepee in groups of four to six or three to five. Or, sow them at regular intervals front and back of trellising or chicken wire. If there's to be no support, sow the seeds in hills, that is, in groups, with lots of room all around for the vines to ramble.

If you sow seeds, when the seedlings are up, thin them so they are at least 3 to 5 inches apart.

## CARE

Pinch **herb** branches back to keep them shapely. Pinch out the growing tips of **basil** and flowers growing with the vegetables—**snapdragons, cosmos,** and other flowers with central stalks—to encourage branching.

## PRUNING

Harvest **asparagus, lettuce, radish, mesclun,** and other early crops. Check the **asparagus** every day and harvest spears as they reach 6 to 8 inches in height, or they will shoot up, get skinny, and "go to fern." They keep for a week at least in the crisper and freeze successfully.

Keep **peas** picked to keep the plants producing. Weed while thinning vegetable seedlings.

## WATERING

Seeds and seedlings need water right after planting and enough the first several weeks to maintain soil moisture.

*The classic way to sow vegetable seeds is in shallow furrows (drills) created by dragging the edge of a rake or hoe handle along the planting line. Then you dribble the seeds into the drills at spaced intervals.*

 ## FERTILIZING

When **asparagus** spears come in thin, stop harvesting and apply a high nitrogen organic fertilizer such as dried blood or cottonseed meal.

When cool-season crops are over, **peas** and **spinach,** for example, pull them out and compost them. Before replanting the rows, work an application of an organic or slow-release fertilizer into the soil.

 ## PESTS

If aphids appear at the tips of **tomato** stems, hose them off or pinch the tips out and put them in the garbage. Ladybugs should control them later in the season.

Asparagus beetle may be deterred by planting **tomatoes** and **basil** nearby. Spray or dust infestations with an insecticide containing rotenone.

Cabbage worms, the forebears of those small white moths, attack crops about now. Spray the foliage with Dipel, malathion, Pyrethrin, Rotenone, or a Sevin insecticide.

## Did You Know?

### About Choosing and Planting Tomatoes

Tomatoes are warm-season vegetables that flourish when nights reach 65 degrees Fahrenheit. The blossoms fall when days are above 90 and nights above 76 degrees Fahrenheit.

**Determinate tomatoes** are okay without staking, reach about 3 feet, and ripen a big crop in a short time. They bear all at once, not continuously. If you have a very short growing season—plant several determinate varieties.

**Indeterminate tomatoes** need staking or caging and produce continuously until stopped by cold. If you have a fairly long growing season and little space, choose indeterminate varieties.

**The letters VFNA** appear on the labels of plants resistant to the common insects and diseases that assail tomatoes.

**Planting.** You can start tomato seeds indoors six to seven weeks before the last frost is anticipated.

Set seedlings out only after all danger of frost is past, early to late May depending on your zone. They do best when temperatures are 65 degrees Fahrenheit. When buying tomato seedlings, bypass small containers with tall plants already fruiting and choose stocky, leafy, dark green plants just budding.

Two weeks before planting time, dig an organic or timed-release 5-10-10 fertilizer into the soil along with hydrated lime to prevent blossom-end rot. Add a handful of gypsum for each plant to provide calcium without changing the soil pH. Set stocky transplants so the first leaves are just above soil level; lay leggy plants in the ground horizontally with most of the stem buried and the head upright.

We set tomato seedlings so they have 4 feet all around.

When the plants start to set fruit, apply a water-soluble organic fertilizer.

Cutworms are the culprits when tender seedlings turn up topless. One solution is to create a collar to prevent the critters from climbing up to eat. When the crops are over, rototill the row, or hand-turn and fluff the soil. That brings the eggs to the surface where they die.

# JUNE
 ## Herbs & Vegetables

## PLANNING

**Wishing for more space in your kitchen garden?** Free up planting space by training your vining vegetables to grow with their heads in the air. Just provide a support and lead the first stems of **eggplant, pole beans,** and **small squash** varieties to it—the plants will do the rest. Even **melons** and **pumpkins** will ripen high on a vine, provided you support the fruit with a mesh bag as it grows large.

The **stylized wooden teepees** sold by garden centers are the strongest supports, and they last several years. But you can make a strong no-cost teepee by stripping the branches from eight to ten 8- to 10-foot saplings, gathering them teepee style, and securing them top and bottom with two rows of twine. String twine vertically in between the poles for vegetables to climb on, two to every two poles. Plant the beans just outside the teepee at 3-inch intervals

If you have a chicken wire fence or something similar around the garden, don't waste it! Use it to train **pole beans** and other vining vegetables to grow upward.

Don't waste wall space; an east- or west-facing-facing wall is a fine place to espalier **pears** and **apples.**

## PLANTING

When the weather heats up, the cool-season crops will play out. **Peas** are over now. **Lettuces** and **spinach** begin to "bolt," that is, they grow tall, produce seedheads, and taste bitter. So pull them all up and compost them.

Use the space freed up to start a few summer and fall crops—one or two sowings of **bush beans** two weeks apart, for example—and long-standing crops like **late beets, carrots,** and **turnips.**

Actually, you can replant the rows with seeds or seedlings (for a hurry-up crop) of any herbs and vegetables that have time to mature in the weeks remaining in your growing season: **basil, nasturtiums, summer savory, cucumbers, bush beans, chard, corn, cucumbers, muskmelons, okra, sweet peppers, potatoes, pumpkins, sweet corn, summer and winter squash, tomatoes.** Replace **spinach** that is bolting with seedlings of **New Zealand spinach,** which tastes very like spinach and grows on through summer.

## CARE

If your **strawberries** and **raspberries** are disappearing, protect your crops from hungry birds (they have excellent vision!) by covering the plants with nylon mesh, screening, cheesecloth, or a floating row cover.

## PRUNING

To encourage your herbs to bush out and be more productive, early on pinch out the tips of the main stems.

Continue to thin vegetable seedlings.

As **tomatoes** grow they branch upward, and they also develop sucker branches. Suckers aren't hard to spot once you know what you are looking for. A sucker is a new branch developing in the crotch between a "real" branch and the main stem. They can be productive, but letting them grow results in a big sprawling plant and reduces the amount of fruit the plant can ripen in our climate. So we recommend pinching suckers out regularly, working from the bottom of the plant to the top.

## WATERING

Later this month keep an eye on developments in your **corn** patch; when the silk is beginning to show, corn plants need a good deep watering.

**Peppers** need to be well watered as we head into summer heat. Maintaining moisture evenly in the **tomatoes** helps prevent blossom-end rot.

# FERTILIZING

When the **tomato** plants first start to set fruit, drench the foliage with a water-soluble organic fertilizer, such as fish emulsion. Water until it drips to the ground, wetting the soil beneath. The foliage absorbs nutrients quickly.

Repeat monthly until the fruits near mature size.

# PESTS

**Weed control is essential!** Any weeds allowed to mature and develop roots will be taking water and nutrients from the vegetables they are invading.

Watch out for corn borer and corn earworm. Corn earworm is also the tomato fruitworm, which winters in the soil as pupae. An environmentally-friendly solution is in late fall to dig up and turn over the soil in infested areas, which kills them. Genetically-engineered corn is resistant, but at this time there is a lot of controversy over genetically-engineered plants.

## Did You Know?

### About Thinning Vegetables

When you sow seeds by broadcasting them, the seedlings come up too closely spaced to mature individual plants. You must thin the sowings until each seedling has space enough all around to grow well. Seed packets indicate suitable spacing.

Thinnings of the root vegetables such as **beets** and **turnips,** and leafy vegetables such as **lettuce** and **spinach,** are good raw in salads, and they add nutrients to stews, sauces, and soups. So think of thinning as early harvests of the rows.

We use the thinnings of many vegetables in the kitchen. Here are some examples of our approach to thinning:

**Carrots,** like most root crops, don't transplant well. We broadcast the seeds over well-worked soil, and cover them $1/2$ inch deep. Germination takes several weeks. Then we thin the plants repeatedly until they stand about 3 inches apart. We use the thinnings in salads, stews, and soups.

**Kale** thinnings are excellent steamed. We scatter the seeds in a 4-inch band, then thin the seedlings several times until they are 8 to 12 inches apart.

We thin **beet** seedlings until the plants are 2 inches apart. Baby thinnings are good in salads, but we leave some of the thinning until the extra plants are large enough to cook up as **beet greens,** which we like even better than fresh **spinach.**

Planting **corn** early helps, as does planting varieties that have resistance to the pest. You can also protect the rows with floating row covers. At their feeding stage, they are discouraged by products that contain Sevin insecticide.

Asparagus beetles strip the foliage from the stems, and that prevents the plants from storing food for next season's production. Row covers may keep them away. Or, spray with a beetle control designed specifically for food plants, such as rotenone and Neem products.

Protect **tomatoes** from tomato hornworm by spraying with Sevin when the fruit is getting to be $1/2$ inch in diameter.

# JULY

## Herbs & Vegetables

### PLANNING

**Prepare to harvest** each species as it reaches peak flavor. Some vegetables maturing now must be kept picked to maintain productivity—notably **green beans**—something to consider when planning your vacation.

Individual seed packets offer guidance on harvest time. Here's an overview of when to harvest:

**Herbs.** The flavor of the perennial herbs is consistent all season. But **arugula,** an annual, is best in spring and sweetest harvested very young. Take no more than a third of any herb plant at one time. In hot weather, take only tip sprigs from your herbs. In extremely hot weather, the plants shut down.

**Leafy vegetables. Chard** and **kale** have the best flavor in late summer and early fall, and you can pick side leaves from these and the **leaf lettuces.**

**Beans. Bush** and **pole** (vining) **snap beans** must be picked as soon as the seeds fill the pods out. Left to grow big, the vegetables toughen and the plants will slow or stop producing. **Shell beans,** which are vining plants, can be harvested young and eaten like snap beans, or harvested after the pods swell out, or even left to dry on the vine.

**Melons.** Most melons are ripe when the fruit changes from greenish to buff yellow and the stem separates easily from the vine. When one melon on a vine is ready, the others on that vine will ripen soon after.

**Root crops.** There are early and late varieties. Spring **beets** are best harvested when about 3 inches around; winter keeper (late) varieties can stay in the ground until twice that size or more. Spring **carrots** are best harvested at 2 inches around. **Late carrots** can stay in their rows until hard frost threatens; the longer they stay, the sweeter the flavor. **Parsnips** taste best harvested after one or two hard frosts, and even better after a winter in the ground.

**Squash. Summer squash** and **zucchini** taste best harvested at 5 to 6 inches and must be kept picked continuously to keep the plants producing. The **winter squashes,** such as **butternut, Hubbard,** eating **pumpkins,** and others, develop full flavor after the stems begin to shrivel and dry, so leave them on the vine until just before the first hard frost. Even after a hard frost or two, all but the pumpkins will likely be okay.

### PLANTING

Zone 7 gardeners may still have time to ripen late crops started from seed sown early this month: **Brussels sprouts, cabbage;** late varieties of **beets, carrots,** and other root vegetables; **cauliflower, broccoli, chard,** and **kale.** In Zones 5 and 6, compare the days before the anticipated frost date with the days to maturity of these vegetables. Remember to work fertilizer into the soil before replanting a harvested row.

Gardeners in Zones 6 and 7 can try for a late **tomato** crop by starting seeds of quick-bearing **cherry tomato** varieties indoors or in a cold frame and transplanting them to a container that can be moved to a sheltered spot or a glassed-in porch.

### CARE

If you are losing crops of **bramble fruits,** cover them to protect them from birds and deer. The deer eat the tips of new **raspberry** branches, fruit and all. Bears love **blueberries.**

### PRUNING

Remove herb flowers as they develop—they're edible so you can use some as garnishes.

Harvest maturing vegetables to keep them producing, except for the **winter squashes** and the **root vegetables.**

Clear away fallen fruit from **orchard trees** to avoid attracting deer.

Thin squash blossoms and stir-fry them.

In cool areas, when most of the tops of the **onions** break over naturally, the crop is ready to harvest. In warm areas, you can begin harvesting when about a third of the tops break over.

Pinch out tips of melon vines bearing three or more blossoms and fruit.

# WATERING

A vegetable garden needs at least 1 inch of water per week in summer. The water from a hose hit by July sun is as hot as hot tap water. So, run the hose until the water is tepid before you turn it on the garden.

Check the moisture in large containers every three or four days; check small pots and hanging baskets every day or two.

Water your compost pile when you water the garden, and turn it weekly.

# FERTILIZING

When the **tomato** plants start to set fruit, drench the foliage and the soil with a water-soluble organic fertilizer,

## Did You Know?

### You Can Make Your Own Basil Oil

This is how my daughter Holly makes basil oil:

6 packed cups of just-picked sweet basil leaves
1 quart mild olive oil

To make: Strip off the leaves and discard the stems. Measure out 4 packed cups of leaves. Heat the oil until you can just bear to dip your finger in it. Bruise the leaves between your palms, and drop them into the oil. Remove the oil from the heat; cover the pot. Let the oil return to room temperature. Then add 2 more packed cups of bruised basil leaves, and reheat it as before. Turn the heat off, cover the pot, and let the leaves steep twenty-four hours. Reheat the oil as before, let it cool to room temperature, then strain out the leaves. Bottle, cap, and store the oil in the refrigerator.

and repeat every four weeks until the fruits near mature size.

# PESTS

Don't pull big weeds from bone dry soil—the upheaval can cost soil moisture. Water first, then tug gently but firmly to get all of the roots. Shake the soil into the garden, and compost the remains.

With summer's high heat and muggy air, fruits and vegetables become more susceptible to invasions of pests and diseases just as plants are crowding their rows. Thin the plants to let in more air. Next year, adopt a more open planting plan.

Spraying Japanese beetles now with a Neem product may help. Plan to treat the garden and the lawn around it with Milky Spore in late summer. It begins to be effective next year.

Since many fungal diseases thrive in a wet garden, water only in the early morning so the rising sun will dry the foliage. Spray **tomatoes** and **cucumbers** with a copper fungicide safe for food plants.

## PLANNING

Wilted leaves, cracked or discolored skin, and yellowed stems are often caused by natural stresses of the growing season. Plan to keep your eye on these developments. If symptoms worsen and you can't identify or solve them, ask your full service garden center for help or call a USDA Extension agent and apply the remedies recommended.

If you identify a symptom as a disease, remove and discard the affected foliage and stems, then apply the remedies to the plant itself. Wash your hands and tools well after handling diseased plants.

Be sure not to replant a crop that showed infection in the same spot next year, and don't plant any of its relatives there. (See April, Crop Rotation Equals Better Health.) Here's another area of gardening where a kept-up **garden log** is essential.

 ## PLANTING

As space becomes available, plant seeds or seedlings of cool-weather, short-season crops—**lettuce** and **radishes,** for example—that will mature before the first hard frost.

 ## CARE

In a drought, before pulling up roots of vegetables that are finished, water the garden and then tug the plants gently but firmly. Shake the soil clinging to the roots back into the garden and compost the plants.

 ## PRUNING

Pinch out **basil** flowers to keep the plants producing foliage.

Keep maturing **tomatoes, beans,** and **summer squashes** picked to keep the plants producing.

**Bramble everbearers.** Remove old canes when they finish bearing, and leave the new canes to produce a fall crop.

**Summer bearers.** Remove old canes as soon as they finish bearing.

**Herbs.** As the weather freshens mid-month, begin to harvest the herbs you wish to freeze or dry. You can strip **basil** and other annual herbs, but take no more than a third of the perennials.

 ## WATERING

Check the moisture in containers every four days; check small pots and hanging baskets every day or two.

A vegetable garden needs 1 inch of water per week in summer, by sky or by you.

 ## FERTILIZING

While the **tomato** plants are setting fruit, every four weeks drench the foliage and the soil with a water-soluble organic fertilizer; discontinue when the fruits near mature size.

 ## PESTS

Weed!

If mildew turns up on plant foliage, spray with a solution of 1 tablespoon of baking soda and 1 tablespoon of ultrafine horticultural oil mixed well in a gallon of water.

If the stems of your **cucumbers** and **summer and winter squash** are rotting and the leaves yellowing, the culprit is the squash vine borer. The moth lays her eggs at the base of the plant in early

## Did You Know?

### How to Harvest and Keep Culinary Herbs

Herbs are most flavorful harvested in the early morning before the sun dissipates the essential oils that give them flavor. Herb foliage stays fresh for a week or so in the crisper sealed in a vegetable bag lined with damp paper towels.

We renew our winter supply of herbs at the end of the growing season by drying or freezing. We use just-picked herbs. We rinse herbs only if they're muddy. Mulched herbs stay clean.

**Freezing herbs.** Pick the leafy tops of **parsley** and parsley-like leaves (**cilantro,** for instance), and chop them fine in a food processor. Turn them loosely into a plastic bag, seal, and freeze.

**Storing in oil. Basil, oregano, tarragon,** and the larger leafy herbs tend to darken when frozen. Pick the tiny tender leaves at the tips of the stems, pack them into a wide-mouthed jar, cover completely with good olive oil, seal, and store in the refrigerator. Both leaves and oil are good for cooking, and the oil makes an excellent salad dressing.

**Air drying leaves.** It's easy to do. Here's how:

*1* Pick fresh, healthy branch tips 12 to 14 inches long. Strip the coarse lower leaves and discard. Gather the stems in loose bunches, and hang them upside down in an airy, dry, preferably dark place.

*2* When the stems are crackling dry, strip the leaves off the stems by rubbing the stems between your palms.

*3* Pour the leaves into glass jars and cap tightly. After a few days, check to see whether moisture has appeared inside the glass. If yes, oven dry the herbs for two hours at 150 degrees Fahrenheit.

*4* Store the herbs in small jars, and write the date and the name on the label.

**Oven drying.** Spread the leaves out over paper towels, and heat them on Low until crackling dry. How long depends on the thickness of the herb and on your oven.

**Microwave drying.** Dryish herbs, like **thyme,** dry well in a microwave oven at half-power. Experiment with timing when you can afford to ruin a batch or two. Drying moist herbs such as **basil** in a microwave keeps the color and the flavor, but it's time-consuming. Prop several leaves on crumpled paper towel, and microwave 1 or 1$\frac{1}{2}$ minutes on High. A whole branch in our oven dries in three to four minutes.

**Drying seeds.** See How to Harvest, Dry, and Store Seeds, August, in the chapter on Annuals.

summer, and the worms eat the stalk and spread a virus that causes the stems to rot. Beneficial nematodes and *Bacillus thuringiensis* are controls.

To prevent this next year, dispose of the diseased plants now. Turn the soil and fluff it—that will kill the larvae. Next year, plant resistant varieties. Plant through a square of foil, and cover the row with floating row covers to keep the moths away. When the plants get too big or the weather too warm to keep the row cover on, mist the leaves regularly with garlic spray.

# SEPTEMBER
## Herbs & Vegetables

 PLANNING

In September in New York, we begin the battle to keep the kitchen garden going until Indian summer—a warm spell that occurs in late September or early October. The first light frosts can descend at night the first week in September, so get ready to prolong your harvests by covering vulnerable plants with old sheets, Reemay, newspaper, or anything to keep the frost off nights until warmer weather comes to give the plants another three or four weeks.

**Tomatoes.** When night frosts are predicted, pick the ripe tomatoes and half-ripe tomatoes that can be ripened indoors—those turning pink and those whitening. Set pink-reddish fruits on a sunny sill to ripen; wrap whitening fruits individually in newspaper, and set them in a cool place where they'll ripen in the next six weeks. Cover the plants at night to save them through Indian summer.

Freeze the fully ripe tomatoes; for cooking they're better than canned tomatoes. Select ripe, unblemished fruits, pop them dry into a freezer bag, and store them in the freezer. Before adding frozen tomatoes to a soup, a stew, or a sauce, run tepid water over the frozen skins to make peeling easy.

**Legumes and corn.** When real frosts are coming, pick the remaining **snap beans** and **corn,** prepare the vegetables for cooking, drop them into boiling water, wait two minutes; then remove, drain and freeze that portion you won't eat now. Cook the rest. You can shell beans and cook them fresh. Or, let shell bean pods dry, shell the beans, dry them on screens, and store in paper bags.

**Summer Squash.** Pick and rinse young squash, slice them into half-inch rounds, drop into boiling water, wait two minutes, remove the portion for freezing, drain, and freeze. Cook the rest.

**Strawberries, raspberries, blueberries.** Pick clean ripe fruit, remove the stems, toss the berries with granulated sugar, spoon them into freezer bags, and freeze.

 PLANTING

Clear out the remains of crops that have been harvested, and turn the rows. If you anticipate another six to eight weeks without freezing weather, replant them with seedlings of cool-season crops that mature in a short time—**lettuce, arugula, mache.** If you don't have enough growing weather ahead to mature crops in the open garden, try them in a cold frame or hot bed.

Plant **parsley** seeds or seedlings next to maturing parsley plants; they're biennial, and this year's parsley will go to seed as soon as the weather warms next spring.

You can divide perennial food plants this month.

## CARE

You can keep **tomatoes** and other cold-tender late crops through a cold spell by sheltering them from the first night frosts with row covers or old sheets.

To control Japanese beetles next year, spread Milky Spore on the soil and lawn around **raspberries** and **basil.**

In Zone 3, try wintering **sage, Italian oregano, savory,** and other cold tender perennial herbs in a cold frame.

Cold Frame

*You can keep tomatoes and other cold-tender late crops through a cold spell by sheltering them from the first night frosts with row covers or old sheets.*

## Did You Know?

### Making a Cold Frame or Hot Bed Is Easy

Cold frames and hot beds give plants a head start on the seasons. A handy person can make either.

**A cold frame** is just a bottomless box sunk into the earth and roofed over with glass or plastic. In its warmth, seeds and seedlings germinate and grow weeks before they can be started in the garden. Garden centers offer cold frames ready to assemble, and light-weight portable styles enable you to move them around to protect late and winter crops. Some are equipped with solar-powered frame openers triggered by high temperatures.

The ideal position for a cold frame is facing south on a slope that sets the cover at a 45 degree angle to the sun. That allows water and snow to slide off. The day's heat keeps the inside warm at night. When the air inside reaches 90 degrees Fahrenheit, prop the top up to vent the box or the heat will damage the plants.

**Making a cold frame:**

*1* Use concrete blocks, bricks, or rot-resistant boards to make a frame 5 to 6 feet long by 3 feet wide by 3 feet high.

*2* Make a cover for the cold frame from a pair of old storm windows. Or, staple heavy-duty plastic film to a wooden frame that fits onto the cold frame. Hinge the cover to the frame to make airing it easy.

*3* Place an outdoor thermometer inside the cold frame where you can see the temperature without opening the cover.

*4* In the cold frame, place flats, boxes, or pots filled with improved soil to plant in. Each season provide new improved soil.

**A hot bed** is much like a cold frame, but it has some insulation and is equipped with an underground heating cable regulated by a thermostat. The heat allows you to plant earlier than in a cold frame. When the heat is off, the hot bed serves as a cold frame. In horse and buggy days, hot beds were deeper, and bottom heat was provided by the decomposition of moist layers of straw, fresh horse manure, and leaves.

 PRUNING

Keep maturing vegetables picked to keep the plants producing.

When temperatures fall below 65 degrees Fahrenheit, pinch out the **tomato blossoms** to keep nutrients flowing to the remaining ripening fruits.

 WATERING

Plants in containers will need watering every ten days unless you have rain.

 FERTILIZING

As long as container plants are producing, continue to fertilize at half-strength at every watering.

PESTS

If mildew starts or continues to be a problem, clear the bed, rake out the remains of the plants, and dispose of it in the trash; do not compost.

# OCTOBER
## Herbs & Vegetables

 PLANNING

Continue the battle to prolong your harvest!

**Chard and kale.** Pick side leaves, rinse, bag them, and store them in the produce drawer. They will keep for a week or two.

**Root crops.** The flavor of mature **rutabagas** and **turnips** is improved by a light frost; **parsnips** are sweeter after a couple of frosts and can winter in the ground. **Beets** and **carrots** must be harvested before the ground freezes.

**For short-term storage,** harvest and clean the vegetables with their greens on; seal them in vegetable bags, and store them in the crisper. They will stay firm several weeks.

**For long-term storage,** remove the greens and layer the roots in damp sand in temperatures between 35 and 45 degrees Fahrenheit. You also can store **beets, carrots, parsnips, rutabagas,** and **turnips** in a pit in the ground; line the bottom with clean sand then layer in vegetables and sand, ending with a layer of sand. Cover the pit with bales of straw.

**Winter squash and pumpkins.** Keep maturing **winter squash** off the ground on hay or chicken wire to prevent the bottoms from rotting. Before frosts, harvest with a 3-inch stem. Wipe the skins with a damp cloth, and store indoors in a cool dry place; most varieties keep for two or three months, the big blue **Hubbard squashes** up to six months.

 PLANTING

Warm Zones 6 and 7 can plant **garlic** cloves now for harvest next spring.

Early this month you can plant, move, and divide most of the kitchen garden perennials and the **bramble** and **orchard fruits.**

Buy a few young **basil, parsley, bay leaf, chives,** and **rosemary** plants and grow them on a sunny sill indoors.

 CARE

In empty rows, plant a cover crop to improve the fertility, texture, and water-holding capacity of the soil. (See Planting, October, in the Annuals chapter.) Compost all the healthy vegetative material. (See Trees, October, Composting.) Now is the perfect time to refurbish or to start the compost pile. Air your cold frame or hot bed on hot days.

 PRUNING

Clear the rows of vegetables that have been harvested, and turn the soil.

Remove all the **raspberry** canes that bore fruit last summer, leaving six to eight strong new canes per hill. Cut these canes back by a few inches, and remove all weak canes and suckers.

 WATERING

Don't forget to water any newly divided or planted plants. Water seedlings in the cold frame or hot bed.

 FERTILIZING

Scratch a little organic fertilizer in around the kitchen garden perennials. Turn the compost pile weekly.

 PESTS

Discard remaining insect- or disease-infected garden debris in the garbage. Where infestations have been severe, turn the soil over; air destroys many of the organisms there.

**Basil** growing indoors may be attacked by whitefly. Shower the plants, and especially the undersides of the leaves, every two days for ten days. If the problem persists, spray four times every seven days with pyrethrum or Neem. If the problem still persists, discard the plants before they infect other houseplants.

# NOVEMBER
## Herbs & Vegetables

## Did You Know?

### How to Grow Strawberries

In cool regions, strawberry plants are set out in early spring as soon as the soil can be worked; in warm regions, they can be set out spring or fall. They need a bed of their own. Soon after planting, they send out runners that root new plantlets that can be used to start a new row or to renew the original bed. The beds should be renewed every six years. **One-crop varieties** bear early- or mid-season; **everbearer varieties** bear in late summer. A new type of everbearer described as **"day neutral"** produces its largest crop mid-season through fall. Plant two dozen of each for an all-season harvest.

A few weeks before planting, top a row 6 inches wide with 2 inches of compost or dried manure, and dig it in. Set the plantlets in rows in a zig-zag pattern. **Set the crowns at the level at which they were growing.** The first season remove all the blossoms that form in spring; allow the everbearers to bloom and to set fruit from July on. Keep day neutrals clear of blossoms until mid-season and let them produce from mid-season through fall. About six weeks after planting, strawberry plants send out runners. Remove all runners until the bed has been producing for three years. The fourth year allow them to root, and transplant them the following spring to start a new bed. The new bed will be in full production the following spring, and you can dig up the original bed. When the temperature heads towards 20 degrees Fahrenheit, cover the bed with a 6-inch straw mulch. After the ground has frozen hard, pile on a foot more of straw.

 PLANNING

If your soil is sandy or lacking in humusy material, take the time now to incorporate aged horse manure or chopped composted leaves. There are stables and farms in our region, so locating a source should not be difficult. Or dig in seaweed. Fall storms at sea usually leave drifts on the shore.

 PLANTING

About the only thing you can plant at this point are **Egyptian onions.**

 CARE

After the ground first freezes, cover **strawberries** with a 6-inch straw mulch; after the ground freezes hard, pile on a foot more straw.

 PRUNING

Clear the rows of everything but **parsnips,** which are improved by wintering in the garden. Turn the soil by hand or with a rototiller.

Cut fall-bearing **raspberries** back to the ground; remove dead and infested canes from summer and everbearer raspberries.

 WATERING

Maintain the soil moisture in herbs growing indoors.

 FERTILIZING

Save wood ashes to use as fertilizer for the kitchen garden. They make lime and potash quickly available to the plants.

 PESTS

**Basil** indoors may be attacked by whitefly. Shower the undersides of the leaves every two days for ten days. If the problem persists, spray four times every seven days with pyrethrum or Neem.

## PLANNING

Check last year's **garden log** for ideas for the coming season. Look over the accessories for kitchen gardens offered in garden catalogs. Early this month order the things you wish to give the gardeners on your holiday list. Do family and friends a favor by telling them about the seeds, tools, and accessories you'd enjoy receiving. A soil thermometer would be good to have.

**Organize a seed-saver file.** Each season, I usually use up at least one packet each of **beans, peas, lettuces,** and the **root vegetables.** But I always have left-over seeds for **basil** and other herbs, **tomatoes,** and **melons,** and others we plant several varieties of. Packets of seeds of space-consuming plants like **cabbages, Brussels sprouts,** and **kale** also take a few seasons to get used up.

I organize these left-overs in a spiral binder equipped with clear plastic sleeves. I mark the year on each packet, and place all the varieties of each species in the same sleeve. When I have one, I include a catalog image of the seed and any comments I have.

**Seeds are considered viable for at least five years.** The older the seed, the fewer will germinate. You can check out how well older seeds will do by scattering a half-dozen on a damp paper towel and covering them with another damp paper towel. With indoor warmth, they should sprout soon and tell you what percentage of the seed you can expect to see germinate if you plant them.

André and Mark have fewer leftover seeds than I do. They store their left-overs in the refrigerator.

 ## PLANTING

Planting is over for the year.

 ## CARE

As temperatures near 20 degrees Fahrenheit, cover the **strawberry** bed with a 6-inch straw mulch. When the ground has frozen hard, add a foot more.

 ## PRUNING

Groom **parsley** and other herbs growing indoors. Maintain the moisture of herbs growing in the cold frame or hot bed for as long as they are growing.

 ## WATERING

Maintain the soil moisture in herbs growing indoors.

 ## FERTILIZING

Nothing to fertilize this month.

Save wood ashes to use as fertilizer for the kitchen garden. They make lime and potash quickly available to the plants.

 ## PESTS

Continue whitefly alert for the **basil** plants growing indoors. Showering the plants, and especially the undersides of the leaves, may lick the problem. If the problem persists, spray four times every seven days with pyrethrum or Neem. If the problem continues to persist, discard the plants before they infect other houseplants.

# CHAPTER FOUR

# Houseplants

*Indoor gardens are populated with tropical plants and perennials that, like you, prefer their winters warm and cozy. We're beginning to learn they can do as much for our health as they do for our souls.*

Houseplants light up our lives during those long, long months between October and April when the weather shuts us away from our gardens. We get a lift when the **African violet** opens new blooms and **pothos** opens baby leaves. Pausing in a room scented by **Cape jasmine** improves the day's outlook. The value of plants in therapy is documented. Now science is showing how plants benefit our indoor environment by producing oxygen, adding moisture to the air, and, most importantly, filtering out the toxins given off by all manner of household synthetics.

## HOUSEPLANTS FOR HEALTH

In the 1980s a NASA scientist, Dr. B. C. Wolverton, conducted a scientific study of the effects of various houseplants on the air indoors and discovered houseplants do more than just cheer you up. His book, *How to Grow Fresh Air*, published by Penguin Books in 2003, confirms what indoor gardeners have long known—the beneficial effect of indoor gardens on minds and bodies in homes, offices, shopping malls, and hospitals.

Studies co-sponsored by Wolverton Environmental Services, Inc. and the Plants for Clean Air Council have graded popular houseplants according to their capacity to extract toxins from interiors of homes and commercial buildings.

On the whole, leafy plants like **spider plant** and the **peace lily** (*Spathiphyllum*) do the most air purifying, along with **areca** (*Chrysalidocarpus lutescens*) and other **palms.** But the flowering plants we grow indoors, including **tulips,** the lovely **moth orchid**—the most popular orchid as a houseplant—and **florists' mums,** also contribute to improving the air. So when you plan an indoor garden, know that it's an investment in health as well as a joy.

## LIGHT AND LOCATION

To be successful with houseplants, match the plant to the light available. Whatever your light potential, there are houseplants that can do well there.

The exposure—windows facing north, east, south, or west—is very important.

*1* **East-, northeast-, and north-facing** windows are cool and that's good. But in the dead of winter, the icy air right next to a windowpane can damage tender plants. Move them back at night if you are concerned.

**Flowering plants. Begonias, kalanchoe,** and some others get enough light from an east- or a west-facing window. **African violets** will bloom in a north-facing window that gets bounced light from snow cover or a white building—that can increase the footcandles (light energy) by as much as 30 percent.

**Foliage plants.** Generally, foliage plants do well in the bright light of east- and west-facing windows. Those whose plant tags describe their light needs as minimal can make do in a north-facing window.

*2* **West-, southwest-, and south-facing** windows are bright and very hot in summer; providing plants with protection from direct sun at noon is a good idea. Distance from the window, screens, and curtains

# Houseplants

greatly reduces the amount of light that gets through to the plant. Flowering houseplants do well here.

**Light gardens.** Tiered trays under fluorescent grow lights—light gardens—will bring **African violets** into bloom in a few weeks. Spot grow lights burned after dusk during the dark months add beauty to an indoor garden and help plants whose place indoors may not provide quite enough daylight. Additional light from incandescent bulbs helps plants during the darkest months of winter. Small plants such as **African violets** can make do under a desk lamp, providing it is on eight hours a day.

**Plant vacations.** New York houseplants benefit greatly from the additional light and air they get when you move them outdoors for the summer. **Ficus** and other indoor trees and shrubs can live with less than ideal light indoors for many months if they have a vacation outdoors.

In spring, as soon as the temperature at night stays consistently above 60 degrees Fahrenheit, you can start moving the plants to filtered light outdoors. A porch is ideal. Gradually expose **roses, geraniums, lemon trees,** and others that benefit from direct sun to brighter light before moving them into full sun.

## SOIL

The all-purpose houseplant potting soil suggested below is suitable for most plants. We start with a portion of a commercial potting mix suited to the plant, then add other ingredients. Here are suggestions:

**All-purpose houseplant potting soil.** For containers for foliage and most other plants growing indoors, use a combination of $1/8$ your own good garden soil or commercial bagged top soil, $1/8$ compost, $1/4$ Permatil or perlite, and $1/2$ commercial soil-less mix. Add in a modest application of Osmocote slow-release fertilizer. To reduce watering, for pots over 12 inches in diameter, add a water-holding polymer, Soil-Moist for example, at the recommended rate.

**African violets and other moisture-loving plants.** Use commercial African violet soil mix.

**Cactuses and other succulents.** These plants prefer a very well-drained soil with a slightly alkaline pH. For **desert cactuses,** combine $1/4$ garden loam, $1/4$ peat moss, and $1/2$ coarse sand, Permatil, or perlite. For **jungle cactuses** (Thanksgiving, Christmas, Easter), use the all-purpose potting soil above.

**Orchids.** Commercial potting mixes suited to various **orchids** are best for gardeners new to orchid culture. For orchids commonly grown as houseplants, a pH of between 5.2 and 6.5 is suitable. Use plastic pots and a potting mix of equal parts chopped and shredded redwood bark, coarse perlite, and sphagnum moss. **Humidity is very important:** Grow **orchids** on trays of moist gravel. Orchids are long-blooming and expensive. Several succeed as houseplants; if you are interested in them, invest in a book on the subject.

## POTTING, REPOTTING, AND TRANSPLANTING

**Small and medium houseplants.** Repotting is a constant necessity for small and medium plants. When you acquire a new houseplant and when you see roots creeping out the drainage holes of a plant you already have, check the rootball. If there still is soil around the rootball and in the bottom quarter or third of the pot, the plant doesn't need repotting. A rootball enveloped in roots needs to have its roots untangled and to be repotted in a container one size larger. We repot small- and medium-sized plants when we move them outdoors for the summer. If the roots become rootbound over the summer, we repot before bringing them back indoors in September (see September for more information).

# Houseplants

**Large plants.** Repotting very big trees and shrubs is difficult and necessary only every three or four years. Other years, in late winter before new growth begins, remove the top 2 inches of soil and replace it with 2 or 3 inches of compost or fertile potting soil.

**A radical facelift.** If a plant is languishing, give it a radical facelift. Slide the rootball out, unwind or cut through roots binding the sides, and cut off those matting the bottom. Add a layer of fertile soil mix to the bottom of the original container or to a container one size larger. Center the rootball inside and remove 2 inches of the soil on the top. Pack fresh soil mix all around the sides of the tub. Add 2 inches of fresh soil to the top. Water the soil thoroughly, including a half dose of fertilizer in the water.

## CONTAINERS

**Clay pots.** Unglazed clay lets excess humidity escape and is the best choice for plants needing very good drainage—**geraniums, cactuses,** and **succulents,** for example. Clay pots also give weight and stability to plants. Plants in clay pots need more frequent watering.

**Plastic pots.** Good-looking plastic pots and plastic look-alikes of ornamental clay and cement urns are available. They make excellent homes for plants that need sustained moisture. Plastic is lightweight and makes moving big shrubs and trees easier.

## WATERING

If the soil surface is dry to the touch, press into the soil; if the soil is still dry, water. Other signs a plant needs water are: the pot feels lighter than usual, and the leaves droop. **More houseplants die from overwatering than from any other cause.**

**Some signs of overwatering:**

*1* The plant is growing poorly.

*2* The **tips** of the leaves brown; the leaves curl, yellow, and wilt.

*3* The leaves are limp and soft.

*4* New and old leaves fall off the plant.

*5* The flowers are moldy.

**Some signs of underwatering:**

*1* The plant is growing poorly.

*2* The leaves are limp and wilted.

*3* The **edges** of the leaves turn brown and dry; the leaves curl, yellow, and wilt.

*4* Flowers fall off, or their color fades too early.

*5* The oldest leaves fall off, then newer leaves.

**Rules for watering:**

• Use water at room temperature.

• If your water is heavily chlorinated, use filtered or purified water, or let the water sit for twenty-four hours before using.

• Water the soil, not the foliage. Add water until it begins to seep into the saucer. An hour later check the saucer, and remove any standing water. (A bulb baster for pot roasts helps remove excess water from plant saucers.)

**Rehydrating a plant.** Drying to the point of total wilting will ruin some houseplants. However, others are forgiving. To help a plant recover, set it in the sink and shower the foliage with lukewarm water. Place the pot in a container partially filled with lukewarm water and leave it there for about forty-five minutes. Allow the pot to drain. Then return it to its usual place.

Propagating
by Air Layering

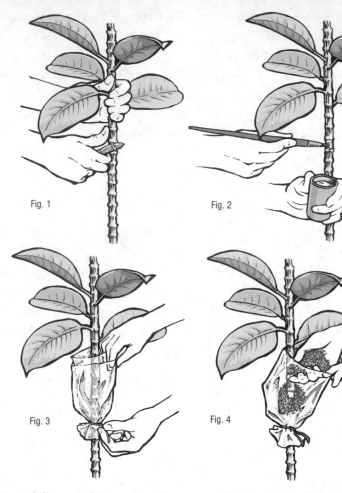

Fig. 1

Fig. 2

Fig. 3

Fig. 4

## FERTILIZING

For houseplants, use an organic fertilizer at half strength. Organic seaweed extract is an excellent choice. Follow the instructions on the fertilizer package conscientiously; too much fertilizer, like too much salt, doesn't improve the broth.

The rule of thumb is in fall and early winter at every fourth watering to fertilize plants showing little or no new growth. Increase that to every second watering for plants that are actively growing, and for all plants after January 15.

## PESTS

Plants growing indoors in optimum conditions will avoid most plant pests and diseases. But occasionally a new plant will import unwelcome guests and share them with your indoor garden. There are a few worthwhile safeguards:

*1* Keep the room cool and the air humid.

*2* Groom your plants often—deadhead, remove decaying and dead foliage—and inspect the undersides of leaves and crotches of branches for signs of pests such as mealybugs.

*3* During the heating season, spray or shower your plants often with room temperature water to clean them and to discourage critters, like spider mites that thrive in dry, still air.

Houseplants are often afflicted by aphids, mealybugs, red spider mites, scale, and whiteflies. For more information on how to control them, see Pests, Diseases, and Controls in the Appendix.

# Houseplants

## Did You Know?

### How to Propagate Houseplants

**Root division.** Multiply houseplants that have a crown, like **asparagus fern,** by dividing the rootball. Slice it cleanly in half, or thirds, and repot each piece in fresh soil.

**Stem cuttings.** Take cuttings of vining houseplants like **pothos;** make them 6 to 8 inches long, just behind a leaf node, and place them in trays filled with moist perlite, vermiculite, or peat-like mixes. When a mass of roots has formed at the ends of the stems, the cuttings are ready to transplant to potting soil. If resting in water, add 1 teaspoon of bleach per quart of water to prevent the growth of micro-organisms.

**Leaf cuttings. African violets** and **rex** and **other begonias** can be propagated by leaf cuttings. Press the stems of **African violet** leaves into 3 inches of moist vermiculite. Cover them with drinking glasses to maintain moisture and keep in low light until baby leaves develop. Wait two weeks, then transplant to African violet potting soil.

Pin a **rex begonia** leaf (with 2 inches of stem attached) right side up onto moist vermiculite or sphagnum moss. Make 2 shallow cuts on each vein on the underside of the leaf, and pin it to the soil with toothpicks. When baby leaves develop at the cuts, cut the plantlets out with a scrap of leaf still attached and grow the roots in water. When they are growing well, transplant.

**Air layering.** Air layering is used to multiply and to renew plants like **schefflera** and *Dracaena* which get leggy. Notch a stem (Fig. 1), smear the cut with rooting hormone (Fig. 2), and enclose the area in a handful of moistened sphagnum moss. Wrap the moss in plastic and tie it firmly, top and bottom (Fig. 3). Weekly, open the bundle and restore lost moisture (Fig. 4). When a mass of roots shows, cut the stem off an inch below the bundle (Fig. 5) and pot it to create a new plant (Fig. 6). Cut the trunk off at a suitable height above a bud or a pair of buds; new growth should develop just below the cut.

**Offsets.** Many plants that produce offsets (plantlets) are best propagated after the plant's resting period. Unpot the plant, separate the offset, and repot both parent and offset right away. **Spider plant** and many other leafy houseplants are composed of several individual offsets. You can pull the outer offsets apart and repot them to create new plants. **African violets** produce offsets that are rosettes of leaves growing on the main stem. Slice all around the offset and pot it.

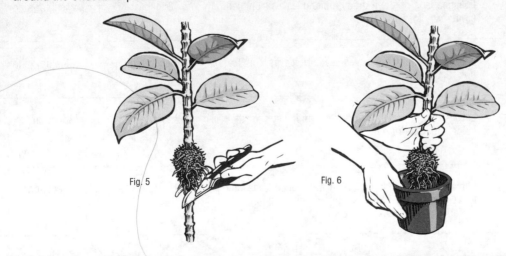

Fig. 5

Fig. 6

# Houseplants

| Common Name (*Botanical Name*) | Ornamental Features | Height | Light |
|---|---|---|---|
| **African Violet** (*Saintpaulia* spp. and cvs.) | Low; blooms year-round in shades of purple, rose, pink, white, or bicolors; some have variegated leaves; fairly easy. | 4 to 5 inches | Bright indirect/medium |
| **Asparagus Fern** (*Asparagus sprengeri*) | Arching stems fuzzed with flat green needles; needs a roomy pot and moisture. | 2 feet | Medium |
| **Begonia** (*Begonia* spp. and cvs.) | Showy, textural leaves, patterned; red, green, silver florets; angel-wing and rex begonia are among the most beautiful; fairly easy. | Various heights | Bright indirect/medium |
| **Boston Fern** (*Nephrolepis exaltata* 'Bostoniensis') | Spreading, arching, green fronds; finicky; 'Dallas' is best for the indoor garden. | 3 feet | Medium |
| **Calamondin, Orange or Lime** (*Citrus mitis*) | Shiny foliage; small, fragrant flowers; sour but edible citrus fruits; worm castings do wonders for citrus plants. | Shrub size and taller | Bright, full sun |
| **Cape Primrose** (*Streptocarpus* spp.) | Lovely biennial, blooms lavishly the second year; flowers usually lavender but there are rosy forms; arching strap-shaped leaves. | 6 to 8 inches | Full sun |
| **Cast-iron Plant** (*Aspidistra elatior*) | Tough, glossy, narrow, dark-green leaves; needs to be cool; easy. | 2 feet | Medium to low |
| **Chinese Evergreen** (*Aglaonema modestum*) | Foliage plant; medium-green, oblong leaves from central stem; easy for beginners. | 18 inches | Medium to low |
| **Corn Plant** (*Dracaena fragrans*) | Foliage plant with big leaves like corn leaves; trim leaf tips that yellow. | Ceiling-high in time | Medium to low |
| **Croton, Joseph's Coat** (*Codiaeum variegatum* 'Pictum') | Large, colorful leaves that depend on full sun for their color; mustn't dry out. | 2 to 4 feet | Bright sun |
| **Cyclamen** (*Cyclamen* spp. and cvs.) | Miniature and standard sizes; heart-shaped leaves and flowers in shades of pink, rose, or white, fall through spring; minis are easy to grow. | 6 to 12 inches | Direct sun |

# Houseplants

| Common Name (*Botanical Name*) | Ornamental Features | Height | Light |
|---|---|---|---|
| **Desert Cactus** (*Cactus* spp.) | Spiny rounds and oblongs in various sizes; almost drought proof. | All sizes | Sun/bright |
| **English Ivy** (*Hedera helix* cvs.) | Vining foliage plant with three-lobed leaves on trailing stems; keep cool. | To 3 feet | Bright to medium |
| **Ficus, Weeping Fig** (*Ficus* spp. and cvs.) | Finest indoor trees; leaves look like shiny birch leaves; fairly easy. | Ceiling height | Medium |
| **Fishtail Palm** (*Caryota mitis*) | Magnificent foliage plant whose leaves resemble fishtails; worth the effort. | Ceiling height in time | Medium |
| **Flowering Maple** (*Abutilon* cvs.) | Beautiful bell-shaped, drooping hibiscus-like flowers in white, coral, pink, deep pink; blooms repeatedly; needs sustained moisture. | 20 inches to tree size | Full sun indoors, part sun outdoors |
| **Gardenia** (*Gardenia jasminoides*) | Exquisitely perfumed white flowers in spring and summer; glossy dark-green leaves; needs sustained moisture. | Shrub size | Bright indirect/ medium |
| **Grape Ivy** (*Cissus rhombifolia*) | Drooping vine with beautiful leaves; fairly easy. | 1 to 2 feet | Medium or low |
| **Hibiscus, Chinese** (*Hibiscus rosa-sinensis*) | Gorgeous all-season blooms in red, yellow, orange, or pink; prone to whitefly. | Shrub to ceiling-high in time | Bright/direct sun okay |
| **Jade Plant** (*Crassula argentea*) | Beautiful fleshy, thick, oblong, dark-green leaves; airy pink flower heads; easy. | Tree-like shrub | Bright indirect |
| **Jasmine, Madagascar** (*Jasminum sambac*) | Vining flowering plant with small, white, fragrant flowers all year; maintain moisture. | Vine/shrub in time | Sun |
| **Jungle Cactus (Christmas, Thanksgiving, Easter)** (*Zygocactus* spp.; *Schlumbergera* spp.; *Rhipsalidopsis gaertneri*) | Drooping, flat-jointed, and spineless leaves; exotic tubular flowers in red, orange, white, and pink; easy. | Shrub size in time | Bright to medium |
| **Kaffir Lily** (*Clivia miniata*) | Arching strap-shape leaves with cluster of orange or, less commonly, yellow, lily-like flowers; needs space but worth it. | 24 inches | Bright |

# Houseplants

| Common Name (*Botanical Name*) | Ornamental Features | Height | Light |
|---|---|---|---|
| **Kalanchoe spp. and cvs.** (*Kalanchoe*) | Beautiful succulent foliage; produces airy flower heads from fall to spring; easy. | 6 to 24 inches | Bright light |
| **Lemon Tree, 'Meyer Improved' Lemon** (*Citrus limon* hybrid) | A real lemon-bearing tree with shiny evergreen foliage and year-round perfumed florets followed by full size lemons if the tree summers outdoors in the sun; needs to be cool indoors. | 6 feet | Full sun |
| **Lily-of-the-Nile** (*Agapanthus* spp. and cvs.) | Handsome, arching strap-shaped leaves topped in spring, summer, and fall by beautiful blue, white, or pink flower-heads; needs space but worth it. | 20 to 30 inches | Full sun |
| **Norfolk Island Pine** (*Araucaria heterophylla*) | Evergreen shaped like a narrow Christmas tree; must be kept cool. | Ceiling height in time | Bright to moderate |
| **Orchids, Moth** (*Phalaenopsis* spp. and cvs.) | Wide, dark-green, strap-like leaves; lasting flowers line the stems; easiest orchid to grow. | 20 plus inches | Bright indirect |
| **Parlor Palm** (*Chamaedorea elegans*) | Very attractive, airy bamboo-like foliage with 3-foot fronds; needs sustained moisture. | Shrub to 6 feet | Bright to medium |
| **Peace Lily** (*Spathiphyllum floribundum*) | Upright-arching, strap-shaped leaves; repeatedly bears white flowers that resemble calla lilies; easy. | 18 to 24 inches | Medium to low |
| **Peacock Plant** (*Calathea makoyana*) | Foliage plant; colorful leaves; easy but needs sustained moisture. | 12 to15 inches | Low |
| **Philodendron** (*Philodendron* spp. and cvs.) | Glossy-leaved foliage plant that stands much neglect. | Vine becomes shrub with support | Medium to low |
| **Pony Tail** (*Beaucarnea recurvata*) | Grassy leaves top a swollen base that stores water; easy. | 12 to 24 inches | Moderate to bright |
| **Pothos** (*Epipremnum aureum*) | Variegated vine with heart-shaped leaves; very easy. | 18 to 24 inches | Bright indirect |

# Houseplants

| Common Name (*Botanical Name*) | Ornamental Features | Height | Light |
|---|---|---|---|
| **Prayer Plant** (*Maranta* spp.) | Attractive leaves that fold together at night; very easy. | 12 to 18 inches | Shade, diffused |
| **Rubber Plant or Rubber Tree** (*Ficus elastica*) | Single stem with huge glossy leaves; nicest when new. | Ceiling-high in time | Bright indirect |
| **Schefflera** (*Brassaia actinophylla*) | Umbrella-shaped wth glossy leaflets; easy. | Tree size in time | Medium to low |
| **Shrimp Plant** (*Justicia brandegeana*) | Colorful, interesting shrimp-like bracts; fairly easy. | 12 to 18 inches | Medium |
| **Snake Plant** (*Sansevieria* spp.) | Upright lance-shaped leaves banded yellow and gray-green; stands much neglect. | 18 inches | Bright indirect |
| **Spider Plant** (*Chlorophytum comosum*) | Grass-foliage, and arching stems with plantlets; easy. | 8 to 12 inches | Bright indirect/ medium |
| **Split-leaf Philodendron** (*Monstera deliciosa*) | Large, deeply cut leaves; fairly easy but needs lots of space. | Shrub size | Low to medium |
| **Strawberry Begonia** (*Saxifraga stolonifera*) | Low-growing creeper that bears clusters of small white flowers on stems to 18 inches long; easy. | 6 to 8 inches | Full sun |
| **Wandering Jew** (*Zebrina pendula* 'Pendulosa') | Drooping stems with silver, purple, and green leaves; easy; keep it trimmed. | 12 inches or more | Medium light |
| **Wax Plant** (*Hoya carnosa*) | Drooping, vining stems; waxy oval leaves; perfumed white flowers form on old vines; easy. | 12 inches or more | Bright |
| **Yucca** (*Yucca elephantipes*) | Handsome stylized plant; clusters of sword-like leaves on woody stems; fairly easy. | 6 feet or more | Full sun |

## PLANNING

As you clear away the holiday trappings, **take the time to re-invent your indoor gardens.** Discard plants that aren't doing much to make space in good light for replacements. Then look over the plants that are growing well and consider which can be propagated to fill out your indoor gardens (see How to Propagate Houseplants in the introduction to this chapter).

 ## PLANTING

Give your out-of-bloom gift **azalea** a sunny spot on a sill since, along with **mums** and **poinsettias,** it is among those plants that test high as air purifiers. When it goes out of bloom, transplant it to a larger pot filled with all-purpose houseplant potting soil. Keep the soil moist, and when new growth appears, at every watering apply an acid type water-soluble fertilizer at one quarter the recommended strength. Increase that over a four-month period until you are fertilizing at the strength recommended on the container. Forced **azaleas** are not hardy, but if you summer it outdoors and expose it to several cool, but not freezing, nights before bringing it in, it may bloom again.

**Find time to repot plants outgrowing their current homes.** To avoid messing up the kitchen sink, invest in a plastic potting tray with high sides and back.

 ## CARE

Move plants that are doing poorly to brighter windows, or invest in grow lights to extend their lighting after dark.

Mist **gardenias, hibiscus, rosemary,** and other houseplants every day or two with water at room temperature. Air the room daily (except when it's freezing outdoors!) for ten minutes or so by opening a window or a door.

If **miniature roses** growing indoors aren't blooming, try giving them more footcandles by lighting them after dusk with grow lights. For more on care of **miniature roses** indoors, see the January pages of Chapter 7, Roses.

## PRUNING

Groom your plants: deadhead **roses, amaryllis, cyclamens,** and **African violets,** and remove yellowing leaves from **poinsettias,** foliage plants, **tropical hibiscus,** and other shrubs and trees wintering indoors. Snip off browned tips of foliage plants.

Deadhead and pinch back **flowering maples;** when they get leggy, they dry out quickly!

Thin and space out the tiny lemons developing on a **'Meyer Improved' lemon tree.**

 ## WATERING

Replenish the moisture in small pots every few days, medium pots every week, and big containers every ten days. Water until water runs into the saucer; remove any that remains after an hour.

Maintain the soil moisture in **flowering maples;** those thin leaves dry very quickly in a heated house!

Pruning Yellowed
Leaves

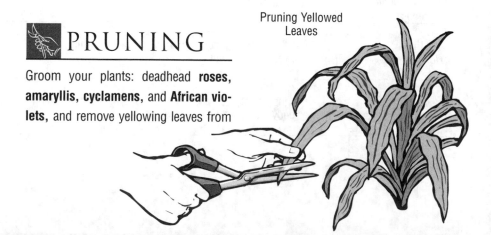

*Find time to repot plants outgrowing their current homes. To avoid messing up the kitchen sink, invest in a plastic potting tray with high sides and back.*

## Did You Know?

### The Ideal Temperature and Humidity for Houseplants

Most houseplants do well in daytime temperatures of 68 to 75 degrees Fahrenheit with a drop of 7 to 10 degrees at night and with humidity between 30 and 60 percent. Heating above 68 degrees takes the moisture out of the air. Miniature roses and other hardy plants do best when night temperatures are closer to 50. Most tropicals have problems when temperatures drop below 60. A humidifier helps.

Here are some additional ways to humidify the air:

- Mist the air around your plants daily.
- Open a window or door for about ten minutes daily except when outdoor temperatures are freezing.
- Group pots on big saucers, waterproof trays, or planters on wet pebbles; the water level must be below the bottom of the pots.
- Mulch pots with moist peat or sphagnum moss.
- Keep wet sponges among the pots.
- Double-pot the plants, and fill the space between the pots with moist sphagnum moss.

Shower **miniature roses** every two weeks and blow the plants dry with cool air from a hair dryer.

## FERTILIZING

Your houseplants and the **tropical hibiscus** and other tender shrubs brought indoors last September are, or soon will be, showing signs of growth; add a half-strength dose of water-soluble fertilizer at every second watering. Fertilize flowering houseplants and the **miniature roses** at every second watering. For **azaleas** and **gardenias,** use a fertilizer for acid-loving plants.

Light—and lack of it—influences fertilizing schedules for indoor plants because light governs growth. Our general take on fertilizing is, in fall and early winter when there is little or no new growth, fertilize all houseplants at every fourth watering; increase that to every second watering when plants are blooming and actively growing, and for all plants after January 15.

## PESTS

Check for spider mites, mealybug, and scale: controls are suggested in Pests, Diseases, and Controls in the Appendix. To avoid problems, mist your plants with water at room temperature, air the room often, keep temperatures down, and provide humidity.

Spider mites attack **miniature roses** growing indoors in hot, dry conditions. Rinse the plants every two weeks. Segregate infected plants. Air the room daily. Use a miticide.

# FEBRUARY
## Houseplants

 **PLANNING**

Visit nearby spring flower and garden shows and nurseries that stage indoor gardens. You'll find displays combining spring-flowering flowers, shrubs, and trees with the many types of cold-tender plants that can be grown indoors. Do it for the sheer joy of breathing plant-scented air and to get new ideas for your own indoor garden.

 **PLANTING**

Many garden centers still offer **paper-white narcissus** bulbs at this season, and you still have time to force them into bloom. For instructions, see the November pages in Chapter 2, Bulbs.

**Geraniums** brought indoors last fall are usually pretty leggy by now. Cut back ungainly branches to improve the structure of the plants. Branch ends that are 6 inches long root easily following the stem-cuttings procedure described under How to Propagate Houseplants in the introduction to this chapter.

A **geranium** that has a straight central trunk can be developed as a standard, or tree form, plant. How to Create a Geranium Tree Standard is described in the September pages of Chapter 1, Annuals.

**CARE**

**Aftercare of poinsettias.** Here are some hints:

*1* Best temperatures are 72 degrees Fahrenheit by day, no colder than 60 degrees by night. The plant will do best if given six hours a day of natural light bright enough to read by.

*2* Remove the foil and groom often.

*3* Keep the soil damp but not moist.

*4* When the plant shows signs of new growth, apply all-purpose houseplant fertilizer at half strength every other watering.

*5* **In mid-February** clear away fading bracts (the colored leaves at the top) and other dead leaves. Scratch up the soil surface and add 1 or 2 inches of sterile soil mix.

*6* If you have space, move the plant to a brighter location.

*7* **In mid-May,** when temperatures are above 60 degrees Fahrenheit at night, repot the plant, and move it outdoors to a partially shaded spot for ten days, and then to full sun for the summer. Or, plant it in the garden, pot and all.

*8* **In early September,** repot the plant and move it indoors to a sunny window in a cool room.

*9* To get the bracts to color up for Christmas, give the plant eight hours of daylight and sixteen hours of darkness from the time it comes indoors (no artificial light after dark).

*10* Fertilize at every other watering. We aren't saying getting **poinsettias** to color a second season is easy! But it's fun to try.

Mist indoor plants every day or two, especially **gardenias, rosemary, flowering maples,** with water at room temperature. Air the room daily for ten minutes or so by opening a window or a door—except when it's freezing out.

**Get rid of winter doldrums and lurking plant pests** by showering small and medium-sized plants in the sink. Shower the big plants in your shower. Use a gentle spray of lukewarm water so as not to shock the plant with a change of temperature and high pressure water. Allow the plants to drain thoroughly before moving them back.

**African violets** thrive with an occasional shower. Rinse the leaves clean in the sink with a gentle spray of lukewarm water. Keep the plants out of direct sun until the leaves are completely dry.

*Get rid of winter doldrums and lurking plant pests by showering small and medium-sized plants in the sink. Shower the big plants in your shower.*

##  PRUNING

Deadhead and pinch back **begonias, coleus, flowering maples,** and **ivy** to keep the plants shapely.

Deadhead **amaryllis, hyacinths,** and **daffodils** forced into bloom; cut off the flower heads, and grow the plants in bright sunny windows.

**Flowering maples** bloom when warmth and light levels are at summer highs. Indoors in winter, they may need you to supplement the window light with grow lights.

## WATERING

Water **African violets** from the bottom to avoid spotting the leaves.

February is the month **ficus** and all the other houseplants look their worst. Shower them all, small and large, with lukewarm water and cover the soil with moss, or Spanish moss, available at garden centers and florists, to maintain soil moisture.

Replenish the moisture in small pots every few days, medium pots every week, and big containers every ten days. Water until water runs into the saucer; remove any that remains after an hour.

##  FERTILIZING

By the beginning of this month, we will have almost fifty minutes more of daylight than we had at the beginning of January, so many of your plants will be growing. Add a half dose of liquid fertilizer to the water at every second watering for all your houseplants. For **amaryllis** and forced **spring-flowering bulbs** growing on, use a bloom booster fertilizer with a high phosphorous content. For flowering houseplants such as **miniature roses, cyclamen,** and **African violets,** use a liquid fertilizer for African violets. For **azaleas** and **gardenias** use a fertilizer for acid-loving plants.

Repotting the very big trees and shrubs is difficult and necessary only every three or four years. Other years in late winter before new growth begins, remove up to 2 inches of soil at the top and replace it with 2 or 3 inches of compost or fertile potting soil.

##  PESTS

Monitor plants that have been infested by pests in the past and renew treatments if symptoms reappear. Controls are suggested in the Pests, Diseases, and Controls section of the Appendix.

# MARCH
## Houseplants

 PLANNING

Prepare to repot your houseplants before moving them outdoors in May. Find the pots you will need for plants that will require bigger containers. Before reusing old pots, clean them up:

*1* Brush out the soil clinging to the sides and bottom.

*2* Scrub the pots in warm soapy water.

*3* Rinse away the soap and dip each pot in a solution of 1 part bleach to 9 parts water to disinfect it.

*4* Turn the pots upside down and let them air dry.

 PLANTING

Top-dress trees and shrubs too big to be repotted:

• Use a fork to gently loosen the top 2 inches of soil. When working with a **ficus** tree, be careful not to damage the roots that are close to the soil surface.

• Replace the missing soil with compost or with all-purpose houseplant potting soil that includes a dose of slow-release fertilizer.

 CARE

Mist your houseplants often and air their rooms daily for ten minutes or so by opening a window or a door.

Help a **gardenia** stay in good condition by growing it on wet pebbles, or double pot it: set the plant pot inside a cachepot about 2 inches larger, and fill the space between with moist moss. Grow it in full sun in a cool room, and air and mist the plant daily with water at room temperature. At every second watering, include a soluble fertilizer for acid-loving plants.

**Salt buildup** occurs in pots that have been long-time homes to plants. The symptom is a crusty, whitish substance around the edge of the pot. Scrape the stuff off and then water the plant until water runs out of the bottom. Wait a half hour and repeat. Allow the pot to drain, and repeat two or three more times.

The staining on unglazed clay is caused by a variety of substances. Try scrubbing the stain off with a plastic scrubber and white vinegar, or a lime remover, or a solution that is 1 part bleach to 9 parts water.

 PRUNING

Deadhead **African violets, pentas, kalanchoe, begonias,** and other flowering houseplants.

**Trim your hibiscus trees.** Cut back branches that cross or are growing into the center of the tree all the way to the main trunk. Then prune branches that are extending outward or upward enough to spoil the symmetry of the tree back to just beyond a healthy, outward-pointing bud. Do not remove more than a third of the tree.

Groom all your houseplants often, removing yellowing leaves, damaged stems, and unproductive branches. **Pruning and deadheading induce fresh growth.**

Cut back foliage plants that aren't producing a lot of new growth, and repot them in fresh soil.

 WATERING

Water small pots every few days, medium pots every week, and big containers every ten days. Use water at room temperature, and water until water runs into the saucer; remove any that remains in the saucer after an hour.

*Water small pots every few days, medium pots every week, and big containers every ten days (as needed). Use water at room temperature, and water until water runs into the saucer.*

 FERTILIZING

Fertilize foliage plants at every second watering with soluble complete organic fertilizer. For flowering plants and **miniature roses,** use African violet or bloom booster fertilizers. For **azaleas** and **gardenias,** at every second watering add a half dose of soluble fertilizer for acid-loving plants.

 PESTS

As the weeks grow warmer, there may be unwelcome activity around your houseplants. Watch out for aphids clustered at the tips of new shoots and buds of **miniature roses.** Those you can, rinse off in the sink. Pinch off infested shoots of larger plants. Then spray with insecticidal soap.

## Did You Know?

### Reblooming an Amaryllis

The amaryllis' spectacular trumpets brighten mid-winter rooms only once each season, but you can bring it back into bloom every year:

*1* When the last of the trumpets fades, cut off the flower stalk(s).

*2* Keep the plant in a sunny east-, south-, or west-facing window at temperatures between 62 and 72 degrees Fahrenheit.

*3* From January to August, at every other watering, apply a half-strength dose of bloom booster-type fertilizer high in phosphorous.

*4* When the outdoor temperature stays above 62 degrees Fahrenheit, put the plant outdoors in the sun.

*5* Keep the soil evenly damp and fertilize until the end of August.

*6* Between the end of August and September, when it turns cold, bring the amaryllis indoors. You can allow it to dry on a windowsill. It needs to be kept at about 55 degrees for eight to ten weeks.

*7* In two or three months a tongue of green will rise in the center of the bulb. Repot the plant in the All-Purpose Potting Soil for Indoor Plants described in the introduction to this chapter. **Always pot or repot an amaryllis in a container that is no more than 1 inch larger all around than the bulb and that has a drainage hole.** Set the bulb so it is one-third out of the soil, and fill the container with the potting mix to within 2 inches of the rim.

*8* Return the plant to a sunny east-, south-, or west-facing window in a room at average house temperatures, 62 to 73 degrees Fahrenheit.

*9* Moisten the soil every four or five days, and at every second watering add a half dose of a fertilizer for flowering houseplants to the water. The trumpets should unfurl in three to four weeks.

Your amaryllis may eventually send up offsets—baby bulbs—with slim new leaves. Break the babies off when you repot, pot them up, and grow them like the parent plant. They will take a few years to come into bloom.

# APRIL
## Houseplants

## PLANNING

The garden centers are readying their sales areas for plants for outdoor gardens, and many discount their larger houseplants rather than store them for the next six months. So, if you are in the market for a wonderful big **palm,** a braided **ficus,** a shrub-sized **jade plant,** this is a good time to shop around.

If you can find blue **lily-of-the-Nile** (*Agapanthus africanus*) or **kaffir lily** (*Clivia miniata*) as young plants, consider investing in them. These both can live for years indoors in winter and grow into big, elegant plants with beautiful flowers in spring and early summer.

The blue **lily-of-the-Nile** is an imposing flower from Southeast Africa. Late spring to early fall, a dense cluster of beautiful blue, white, or pink funnel-shaped flowers appears on a 3- to 5-foot stalk that stands well above a mound of strap-shaped leaves. It is highly regarded as a tub plant for terraces, steps, patios, and near outdoor pools.

The **kaffir lily** is from South Africa. It develops a fan of sword-shaped evergreen leaves topped in spring (indoors) or summer (outdoors) by big, showy, longlasting, amaryllis-like flower heads in brilliant orange-red or salmon. In

our region it blooms in spring or early summer indoors and may rebloom outdoors later.

## PLANTING

Repot small or medium-sized houseplants a few at a time this month to ready them for the move outdoors. It will be time to move them outdoors as soon as the weather stays above 60 degrees Fahrenheit at night.

## CARE

Continue to mist your indoor plants every day or two with water at room temperature. Air the room daily for ten minutes or so by opening a window or a door.

## PRUNING

Continue to deadhead the flowering plants. Keep pinching back the growing tips of **ivy, pothos,** and other vining plants to keep them bushy and beautiful.

Use clean, sharp scissors to trim away browning tips on *Dracaena,* **spider plants, Chinese evergreen,** and other leafy plants.

Some taller plants when mature, especially **Chinese evergreen,** *Dieffenbachia,* and *Dracaena,* end up with a naked trunk under awkward tufts of leaves. The same is true of **avocados.** To remedy this, cut the trunk back to about 8 inches from the pot. That will force new leaves to emerge, and the plant will be beautiful again. A **Norfolk Island pine** that has hit the ceiling has to be air layered to get a fresh start; topped, it won't regrow.

## WATERING

Replenish the moisture in small pots every few days, medium pots every week, and big containers every ten days. Water until water runs into the saucer; remove any that remains after an hour.

## FERTILIZING

Include a half-strength dose of soluble fertilizer at every second watering. For **azaleas** and **gardenias,** use a fertilizer for acid-loving plants.

*Repot small or medium-sized houseplants a few at a time this month to ready them for the move outdoors. It will be time to move them outdoors as soon as the weather stays above 60 degrees Fahrenheit at night.*

# PESTS

If you suspect spider mites are at work, shake the leaf over a piece of white paper. Specks that move are spider mites. A simple way to control spider mites on small plants is to turn the plants upside down in a basin of soapy lukewarm water. Follow by spraying with insecticidal soap.

Check for mealybug and scale; controls are suggested in the Pests, Diseases, and Control section of the Appendix. To avoid problems, mist your plants and air the room often, keep temperatures down, and provide humidity.

Removing Plant
from Container

## Did You Know?

### Repotting Houseplants

*1* A pot one size larger than the original container is best for most, but keep **amaryllis** and the **desert** and **jungle cactuses** (Christmas, Thanksgiving, Easter) slightly potbound.

*2* To keep the soil from dribbling through the drainage hole, cover the bottom of the pot with a square of fiberglass window screening, Reemay, or landscape fabric. A good brand of paper towel also works well.

*3* Add enough soil so that the crown of the plant will be 1 inch below the rim level for small plants and 2 inches for large plants. Then the water won't overflow when you water.

*4* If the rootball is encased in roots, make shallow slashes on all four sides, and slice off roots matting the bottom.

*5* Set the plant straight on the soil, and spoon soil in around the sides. Press it down with a wooden dowel, and continue adding soil and pressing it down until the sides are level with the crown and 1 to 2 inches below the pot rim.

*6* Groom the plant: remove fading flowers and leaves, prune back ungainly branches, and spray the foliage.

*7* Water well with water at room temperature containing a mild dose of starter solution.

*8* Set the plant in filtered light for a day or two to recover, and then return it to appropriate light.

Repotting Plant

PLANNING

Plan to give your houseplants a summer vacation in the fresh air and sunlight. To get ready for the move, locate places in your garden that will meet their light needs. And remember that they will need to harden off in a sheltered spot with moderate light before being moved to a permanent home.

 PLANTING

It's also a good idea to repot your plants before putting them outdoors. Most of them, that is. Don't repot your **amaryllis;** harden the plant off outdoors in indirect light for a week, and then set the pot up to its rim in the garden in full sun and well-drained soil.

Remove the flowering stems of **orchids** as soon as they finish blooming, and repot any that are crowding their containers. They can summer outdoors on a lightly shaded patio safe from high wind, or on a bright airy porch. Or you may attach them to tree branches protected from wind and safe from hot, direct sun.

**African violets** can summer outdoors in indirect light on an airy porch, but you will have to watch the moisture in those pots closely. African violet leaves suffer real damage if they dry out, and that can happen very quickly on a warm breezy day because they usually are growing in small pots. If you can, group several pots on a tray filled with pebbles and water, and check the water level in the tray and the moisture level in the pots daily.

Repot **miniature roses** in fresh soil, and put them outdoors in bright light.

 CARE

When nighttime temperatures stay steady at 60 degrees Fahrenheit and above, start moving your houseplants, including **poinsettias,** outdoors. Place them in good but indirect light in a sheltered spot for the first week. Like you, houseplants sunburn when exposed too long and too early to direct sun. Gradually move them into light suited to their needs.

Don't be alarmed if some drop leaves their first week or two outdoors. The change of light has that effect on some houseplants, notably **ficus.**

Several types of houseplants make wonderful fillers for window boxes and planters. Examples are the **Rex and other begonias,** most **ferns,** all **geraniums, aluminum plant, kalanchoe, ivy, grape ivy,** and other leafy and vining plants.

The sun's position in the sky changes during the year and becomes more intense in our hemisphere as spring advances. This may result in a significant change in the amount of direct sun and heat reaching plants in your windows. Adjust the placement of the houseplants remaining indoors accordingly.

 PRUNING

Deadhead flowering plants, and groom the leafy plants; that is, remove yellowing foliage and ungainly and damaged stems. Pinch back the tips of vining plants to keep them bushing out. Keep the soil clear of decaying vegetation.

*It's also a good idea to repot your plants before putting them outdoors. Most of them, that is.*

## Did You Know?

### Light Needs of Houseplants

**Full sun** means plants are good in or near sunlit windows or in strong reflected light. Examples are **croton, gardenias, jade plant, miniature roses, pineapple.**

**Bright indirect** means good in all of the above but not in full noonday sun. Examples are **aralia, fishtail** and **lady palms, episcia, wax plant.**

**Medium** means diffused light, out of direct sun, or with a sheer curtain between the plant and direct sun. Plants in this group do well inside the room, 4 to 8 feet from the windowpane, or on a north-facing windowsill. This light suits a majority of houseplants, including **African violets, asparagus fern, begonias,** *Dracaena,* **ficus** and **rubber plant, Norfolk Island pine, spider plant, Swedish ivy.**

**Medium to low** means indirect light. These plants are okay in dull corners and even more than 8 feet from a window. The group includes *Dieffenbachia,* **English ivy** (which seems okay in any light), **parlor palm, philodendron,** *Spathiphyllum,* and **snake plant.**

 WATERING

Maintain the soil moisture of the houseplants and **amaryllis** outdoors. As the season grows warmer, plants outdoors in small pots and hanging baskets will need watering every day.

**Don't forget to water plants remaining indoors!**

 FERTILIZING

Include a half dose of fertilizer in the water every second watering for all houseplants. For **azaleas** and **gardenias,** use a fertilizer for acid-loving plants.

 PESTS

In the fresh air, houseplants are less susceptible to the insects that trouble them indoors. Nonetheless, watch out for mealybug and aphids. Also watch out for signs that outdoor pests are after your plants. Cover the bottoms of pots buried in the garden with old nylon stockings to prevent centipedes, sow bugs, and such from invading through the drainage holes. Controls are recommended under Pests, Diseases, and Controls in the Appendix.

Squirrels are curious creatures that often dig in plant pots. If they are a persistent problem, spray the soil with a commercial repellent.

##  PLANNING

Plan to have flowers this winter by forcing spring-flowering bulbs to bloom indoors. Look over the bulb catalogs as they arrive and consider which of those recommended for forcing appeal to you. (See September and October in the chapter on Bulbs.)

Consider filling out your houseplant collection by starting your own **avocado** and **citrus trees.** Children enjoy the magic. The trees also make fine holiday presents.

**Avocado tree.** Avocado seeds/pits will root and produce a fine house tree, although we have yet to hear of one ripening fruit.

*1* Clean the pit under running warm water.

*2* Push three toothpicks into the seed at equal distances from each other around the circumference of the seed, mid-way between the pointed tip and the base, and use the toothpicks to suspend the seed at the top of a narrow glass or jar.

*3* Fill the container with water until a half-inch of the base of the avocado seed is immersed.

*4* Set the glass in a dark closet, and maintain the water level.

*5* When the seed has developed a good set of roots, a sprout will grow from the top. When the sprout opens leaves, move the glass to bright indirect light on a windowsill.

*6* When the sprout is 8 inches tall, cut it back to 4 inches.

*7* When the sprout again reaches 8 inches, plant it in moist all-purpose potting soil with the top third of the seed uncovered.

*8* Grow the seedling in bright indirect light, and pinch it back often to encourage it to bush out. Keep the soil evenly damp, and include a half dose of all-purpose fertilizer at every second watering.

*9* In May move the container to bright indirect light outdoors.

*10* In mid-September move the plant back to its indoor home. Maintain the soil moisture, and fertilize at half strength at every second watering.

*11* Avocado trees tend to get tall and lanky indoors, so the pinching is very important.

**Lemon tree.** Seeds of the various citrus fruits, **lemon, lime, orange,** and **grapefruit,** will germinate, and in a few years grow into a very respectable little tree that may bear fruit if summered outdoors.

*1* Choose six big whole seeds, and let them dry for a day or two.

*2* Plant the seeds in moist, all-purpose houseplant potting mix with about an inch of soil over the top.

*3* Cover the pot with a glass saucer or plastic film to help maintain the moisture. Keep the pot in a dark closet.

*4* Water often enough to maintain the soil moisture.

*5* When the seeds germinate, remove the cover, and move the pot to bright indirect light.

*6* Keep the soil evenly damp, and include a half dose of all-purpose fertilizer at every second watering.

*7* One-by-one, remove and discard the weakest seedlings until only the two sturdiest remain.

*8* When the two seedlings are crowding each other, discard one (unless you have time and space for two trees), and repot the other in a pot one size larger.

*Consider filling out your houseplant collection by starting your own avocado and citrus trees. Children enjoy the magic.*

**9** Grow the tree(s) in a south-facing window. Maintain moisture and continue to fertilize as before.

**10** In mid-May move the container to bright, indirect light outdoors.

**11** In mid-September move the plant back to its indoor home. If it fails to flower, keep it potbound for two or three years.

# PLANTING

Plant a young **tropical hibiscus** in the garden for summer color, and plan to pot it up and bring it indoors in September. It will eventually grow into a handsome flowering tree blooming almost non-stop.

# CARE

If you see sunburn—browned patches—on houseplants moved outdoors, move the plants to more shaded situations.

Move **miniature roses** grown as houseplants to a spot that gets six to eight hours of morning sun.

## Did You Know?

### A Flower and a Bract Are Not the Same

**Bracts** are leaves located immediately back of the petals in a flower. In most flowers, the bracts are small or scale-like leaves, but they can be very much larger and more colorful than the flowers themselves, as is the case with **poinsettias** and **dogwoods.**

# PRUNING

Deadhead **begonias,** and pinch back **coleus** and **vining plants.** Pinch back **flowering maple** to encourage bushiness. Deadhead **hibiscus, miniature roses,** and other flowering houseplants.

Thin some of the tiny lemons developing on a **'Meyer Improved' lemon tree.**

# WATERING

Check the soil moisture of containers of houseplants summering outdoors, and maintain soil moisture. Don't overlook pots of **amaryllis** summering in the garden. Feed them with a bloom booster fertilizer.

Maintain the soil moisture for houseplants summering indoors.

# FERTILIZING

Add a half-strength dose of water-soluble fertilizer at every second watering for houseplants and the **tropical hibiscus** and other tender shrubs summering outdoors. For **azaleas** and **gardenias,** use a fertilizer for acid-loving plants. Continue to use African violet fertilizer for flowering houseplants.

# PESTS

Check young shoots frequently, and spray away aphids clinging there. Watch out for scale on **spider plant, orchids, gardenias,** and houseplants with woody trunks. For controls, see the section on Pests, Diseases, and Controls in the Appendix.

## PLANNING

If you haven't yet, prepare and order spring-flowering bulbs to force into bloom indoors this winter. (See September and October in the chapter on Bulbs.)

Before your vacation, arrange to have the outdoor houseplants watered. Ease the chore by grouping the containers in a semi-shaded spot and making sure each has a saucer. Maybe investigate automatic watering systems.

Your houseplants are lush right now, so this is a good time to take cuttings to grow into holiday gifts. You will find instructions in the section on How to Propagate Houseplants in the introduction to this chapter.

Newly propagated or purchased houseplants will eventually need containers. In July and August, garden markets generally have sales on cachepots and ornate pots, planters, and other hard goods. Some quite beautiful imported pieces sell for modest prices, so check them out witha view to finding attractive homes for your own plants and those intended for giving.

 ## PLANTING

Multiply your holdings by rooting stem cuttings taken when you pinched back begonias, ivy, pothos, philodendrons, and other vining houseplants.

**Pineapple** is plentiful at this season. Rooting the top of a pineapple is an interesting project, and one that children enjoy. The pineapple we eat is *Ananas comosus*, a handsome **bromeliad** that can be grown as a houseplant. Here's how to root it:

*1* Cut a fresh, ripe pineapple top off including a half-inch of the fruit below the top.

*2* Tip it on its side and air dry it for forty-eight hours.

*3* Place it upright on barely moist sand or vermiculite with the fruit portion buried in the rooting medium.

*4* Set the plant in a bright northeast- or northwest-facing window.

*5* Keep the growing medium barely moist until the top starts to grow, and then provide a little more water.

*6* When it is growing well, transplant it to a standard cactus potting mix.

 ## CARE

Houseplants that remain indoors benefit from the cool created by air conditioning but may be harmed if the air blows directly on them. Move plants blowing in cool, artificial indoor breezes or screen them from the chill by placing furniture or some other obstruction between the plants and the air conditioner.

 ## PRUNING

A **ficus** tree needs pruning annually. It's best to do it when it is summering outdoors because the cuts ooze a sticky white sap—the ficus is related to the **rubber tree.** Prune out dried twigs and new sprouts developing at the base and along the main trunk, and remove branches crossing others. Then step back and consider what else can be done to thin out the crown.

Continue to deadhead flowering houseplants and to pinch back **coleus, ivy, pothos,** and the other vining houseplants.

 ## WATERING

If you are away on vacation for more than ten days and there's no one to water the small houseplants, which are most in danger of drying out while you are gone, try this: Fill a bathtub with about 4 inches of water and arrange clay pots upside down in the water, as many pots as you have small plants. Water the plants thoroughly shortly before you leave and set each one on a pot in the tub. The moist air around the pots may be enough to keep the plants in good condition while you are gone.

Maintain the soil moisture of the houseplants in pots outdoors, and **amaryllis** and tropical **hibiscus** growing in the garden. As the weather grows warmer, plants that are living outdoors in small pots and hanging baskets probably will need watering every day.

On very hot days, if the plants show signs of wilting, cool and moisten the air around the houseplants outdoors with a gentle spray from the hose.

Houseplants left indoors for summer need regular watering, and most benefit from a shower now and then as well.

# FERTILIZING

Add a half-strength dose of soluble fertilizer at every second watering for houseplants and the **tropical hibiscus** and other tender shrubs summering outdoors. For **azaleas** and **gardenias,** use a fertilizer for acid-loving plants. Continue to use African violet fertilizer for flowering houseplants.

## Did You Know?

### How to Handle a Desert Cactus

Some as are big as trees, others the size of a pincushion, and most are very prickly. They all can store enough water to carry on through the severe droughts of their native habitat. However, to flourish in an indoor garden, desert cactuses do need watering, and not just when it rains in west Texas.

Here are their requirements:

*1* Light is best in a south window—the most sun you can give the plant.

*2* House temperatures of 60 to 80 degrees Fahrenheit will suit most desert cactuses. But they can do quite well in an unheated room or sunroom where temperatures go as low as 38 to 45 degrees Fahrenheit. Some need a cold period to set flowers; growing instructions will say so.

*3* For soil, use commercial cactus potting soil, which is a very well-drained grainy mix, or make your own with the recipe in the Soil section in the introduction to this chapter.

*4* Water desert cactus when the soil feels dry. My dish garden of baby cactuses thrives watered with ice cubes—one for each plant. Shower the plants occasionally during the dry winter months indoors.

*5* Fertilize during spring and summer only, at every third or fourth watering, using a half-strength dose of an all-purpose plant food.

*6* Summer the plants outdoors: place them first in part light to acclimate and then move them to full sun.

*7* Bring them back indoors before temperatures fall below 60 degrees Fahrenheit. Many can take much more cold, but bringing them all in together is the easy, safe way to handle them in fall.

# PESTS

Aphids may be a problem. Check young shoots frequently, and spray away aphids clinging there.

Watch out for scale on **spider plant, orchids, gardenias,** and plants with woody trunks.

Pest controls are recommended in the section on Pests, Diseases, and Controls in the Appendix.

# AUGUST
## Houseplants

 PLANNING

**This is last call for ordering spring-flowering bulbs for winter forcing for your indoor garden.** Our current favorite is 'Pink Festival', a new breed of **hyacinth** that produces multiple stems over many weeks and whose perfume is totally worth the time and effort involved in potting and forcing the bulbs. A single stem can perfume an entire room!

You'll find step-by-step instructions for the timing and forcing of the flowering bulbs in the September pages of Chapter 2, Bulbs. A few dozen spring-flowering bulbs potted up this fall will provide flowers for many weeks this winter. Wrapped in white tissue paper and tied with colorful bows, bulb flowers about to burst into bloom make much-appreciated gifts.

Here's an overview of the forcing process:

*1* To avoid the diseases than can assail indoor bulbs, pot them in a mix of 1/2 sterile commercial potting medium and 1/2 good, gritty garden soil.

*2* Follow the instructions in the September and October pages of Chapter 2, Bulbs, particularly those instructions relative to temperatures for the various steps in forcing. Forcing bulbs for indoor bloom is a three-part project: pot up; chill twice; move to warmth to force blooming.

*3* Crowd the bulbs in their containers so they touch; that helps keep them upright, an important consideration. We've measured the height of forced **paperwhites** and found some get to over 36 inches tall. Once they reach that height we tie them loosely to a stake set in the center of the pot. Standard size **daffodils,** as opposed to miniatures, also get quite tall and may need staking.

*4* Keep the soil damp, but not wet, from beginning to end.

*5* Bring the flowers into bloom in bright light in a cool room. In temperatures below 72 degrees Fahrenheit, the flowers last longer.

 PLANTING

Begin now to prepare the in-ground plants that you will move indoors in fall: **basil, thyme, rosemary, browallia, coleus, geraniums, heliotrope, impatiens, lantana, pentas, kalanchoe,** and **wax begonias** are some that can winter over in an indoor garden. **New Guinea impatiens** may do well indoors if you can keep it in temperatures above 65 degrees Fahrenheit. Well-grown, these all make fine holiday gifts.

*1* Cut the tops and branches back to 4 to 6 inches.

*2* Dig up the plants, and pot each one in a container about an inch larger all around than the rootball.

*3* Water and fertilize the plants.

*4* Place them in a sheltered spot in indirect light to recover from the shock of transplanting. That will also prepare them for the lower light levels they will have when they are brought indoors.

## CARE

If your **hibiscus** drops flower buds, it's probably because the buds are too numerous for the amount of leaves processing nourishment. It happens—not to worry! This is nature's way of protecting it from over-production.

## PRUNING

If you plan to bring a **bougainvillea** standard or a hanging basket indoors for the winter, reduce fertilization now, keep the plant on the dry side, and prune back the wild growth until about September 1. In early fall, bring it indoors to a bright, cool room—about 55 degrees Fahrenheit. As the days get shorter and temperatures fall, the shoots that develop will flower all winter and into the following summer. In its native tropics, bougainvillea blossoms appear when day lengths are twelve hours or less.

 # WATERING

Maintain the soil moisture of the houseplants in pots outdoors and of **amaryllis** and **tropical hibiscus** in the garden. As the season grows warmer, those plants growing in small pots and hanging baskets will need watering every day.

On very hot days, cool and moisten the air around the houseplants outdoors by showering the area with a gentle spray from the hose.

Houseplants left indoors for summer benefit from a shower now and then as well.

## Did You Know?

### The Best Basket Plants for Indoors

Basket plants are the solution when there's no room on the floor for flower pots. To hang your baskets, invest in ceiling hooks with pulleys that allow you to lower the plants for grooming and watering.

Here's our pick of the most trouble-free and enduring basket plants for indoors:

- **Asparagus Fern** (*Asparagus densiflorus* 'Sprengeri') develops cascading stems with soft feathery needles.

- **English Ivy** (*Hedera helix* cvs.) has trailing stems. Small-leaved varieties and white-variegated varieties are the most decorative.

- **Grape Ivy** (*Cissus rhombifolia*) is an indestructible low-light cascading plant with beautiful bright green leaves.

- **Philodendron** cultivars have pointed glossy evergreen leaves and are drought-resistant and enduring.

- **Pothos** (*Epipremnum aureum*) has bright green, heart-shaped leaves beautifully splashed white or yellow.

- **Spider Plant** (*Chlorophytum comosum*) has arching stems that sprout tufts or nests of grassy leaves. An excellent air scrubber!

 # FERTILIZING

Add a half-strength dose of soluble fertilizer at every second watering for houseplants, the **tropical hibiscus,** and other tender shrubs summering outdoors. For **azaleas** and **gardenias,** use a fertilizer for acid-loving plants. Continue to use African violet fertilizer for flowering houseplants.

# PESTS

Whiteflies flock to houseplants summering outdoors in warm, airless corners on a porch or veranda. Spray the plants often with a hose on the gentle cycle to help control populations. Move plants you suspect of being infected to a breezy spot in the garden. Use insecticides labeled for whiteflies. See the Pests, Diseases, and Controls section of the appendix.

# SEPTEMBER

## PLANNING

When temperatures head for 60 degrees Fahrenheit, begin to bring the houseplants back indoors. Take cuttings of **coleus, begonias,** and **geraniums** if you do not have enough indoor space for the plants themselves. Potted up in a month or so, they'll make fine holiday gifts.

• Before moving plants indoors, plan to rinse them squeaky clean with a hose, and spray each with an insecticidal soap at least once. Twice is better. Dry warmth helps bugs breed! Spray plants that have been troubled with a product containing Sevin insecticide, or by using Pyrethrin or malathion, and a fungicide such as Daconil or Immunox.

• Repot plants growing in small containers in fresh soil—young plants, new plants, and plants that are rootbound.

• Be sure to bring plants finicky about changes in light indoors now, even if they can take colder temperatures. **Ficus** responds to light changes by dropping leaves—sometimes almost all its leaves—so bring it indoors while a lot of daylight still is reaching its indoor habitat.

• Bring **hibiscus** and **mandevilla** in to bright light. Don't prune them. Mist often, and keep the soil nicely damp but not moist. Cut **flowering maple** back by half and repot.

• Hardy plants that need full sun—**miniature roses, gardenias, geraniums,** and **jasmine,** for example—can stay outdoors in cities in Zone 7 until later this month. In the suburbs, frost comes sooner.

• Winter your **geranium** in a sunny window, or let it dry down and store it dormant where temperatures are 55 degrees Fahrenheit or so. Water the soil of semi-dormant geraniums once a month, just enough to keep the soil from drying out.

• When you move **amaryllis** indoors, they do not need repotting. See March for aftercare.

• Bring **poinsettias** indoors only for the foliage; they're difficult to rebloom.

• Allow **florist's azaleas** two to three weeks of cool nights outdoors (not colder than 40 degrees Fahrenheit) before bringing them inside to full sun. They may or may not rebloom.

• In early September bring **jungle cactuses (Christmas, Thanksgiving, Easter)** indoors to a cool room—65 to 70 degrees Fahrenheit by day, 60 degrees by night. For eight weeks let them rest—no artificial light at all, barely enough water to keep the soil from drying out, and no fertilizer.

## PLANTING

Potted up, some herbs and tender perennials make happy houseplants. **Basil, browallia, coleus, geraniums, scented geraniums, impatiens, kalanchoe, pentas, wax begonias** are some that do well indoors.

Begin potting spring-flowering bulbs for your indoor garden this winter (see September and October, in the Bulbs chapter).

## CARE

Mist **gardenias, hibiscus, rosemary,** and other plants moved indoors every day or two with water at room temperature. Air the room daily for ten minutes or so by opening a window or a door, unless it's freezing outdoors.

Don't worry about bud and leaf drop in plants you just brought indoors. They'll adjust to the change soon.

## Did You Know?

### About African Violets

African violets are winter favorites because they bloom for months on end. They can be propagated by leaf cuttings and by offsets, described in Propagating Houseplants in the introduction to this chapter.

*1* Light is ideal in winter in any bright window, but south-facing windows are too hot in summer. They flower best spring and fall when the day length is twelve to fourteen hours. African violets also flower well when growing 9 inches below fluorescent grow lights burning twelve hours a day.

*2* Temperatures are just right between 60 and 80 degrees Fahrenheit. A cool-vapor humidifier helps, and as with all houseplants, we recommend you air the room daily for five to ten minutes when the temperature outside isn't freezing.

*3* Humidity is necessary. These plants do well grouped on trays filled with pebbles and half filled with water.

*4* Use commercial African violet soil. For best flowering, keep the plants slightly potbound.

*5* Use plastic containers for these moisture-loving plants.

*6* Apply water at room temperature often enough to keep the soil evenly moist. Water from the bottom to avoid spotting the leaves; partially fill the plant saucer, and an hour later empty what remains. When they get dusty, rinse them gently under lukewarm water and allow the leaves to dry before returning them to direct sun.

*7* To encourage blooming, add a half-strength dose of African violet bloom booster fertilizer every second time you water.

 # PRUNING

Stems of tender perennials you cut back for the move indoors can be rooted in water. Group them in bouquets in a large glass bowl to save space and maintenance. Add a teaspoon of bleach to every quart of water.

Thin the fruit on your lemon tree! A **'Meyer Improved' lemon** typically creates a lemon for each flower, and it produces flowers all year, followed by too much fruit to ripen.

 # WATERING

Water the houseplants when the soil feels dry.

 # FERTILIZING

Add a half-strength dose of water-soluble fertilizer at every fourth watering for houseplants and the **tropical hibiscus** and other tender shrubs moved indoors. For **azaleas** and **gardenias,** use a fertilizer for acid-loving plants. Continue to use African violet fertilizer for flowering houseplants.

 # PESTS

To ward off problems, mist your plants and air the room daily or as often as practical, and keep temperatures as low as is comfortable.

At the first sign of spider mites, mealybug, scale, or other problems, apply the controls recommended in the Pests, Diseases, and Controls section of the Appendix.

# OCTOBER

## Houseplants

## PLANNING

Assess the health and beauty of your indoor garden, and then visit garden centers looking for fresh ideas for exciting new plants and indoor displays.

## PLANTING

With the gift-giving season ahead in mind, take stock of your houseplant assets. Plants potted up and cuttings taken in August and September make fine presents for family, friends, and co-workers. Houseplants make great gifts for office friends. You still have time to propagate many types of houseplants; see How to Propagate Houseplants in the introduction to this chapter.

Here are some suggestions:

• In new terracotta pots, plant cuttings, offsets, and plants you have propagated and move them to bright light or a light garden if you have one; a cool room is best for getting them into top shape for giving.

• For bulbs being forced, decide which will be far enough along in the forcing process to make worthwhile gifts in December. If some need a little hurry-up, move them to warmth a little sooner than scheduled. Scout for attractive inexpensive baskets to con-

ceal containers less appealing than you would wish for a gift.

• Fresh or rooted cuttings of desirable plants, grouped several to a small attractive vase, make a welcome gift.

## CARE

**Continue to mist the plants you brought indoors** with water at room temperature to help them to acclimate to the changed environment. Air the room daily for ten minutes or so by opening a window or a door. Avoid overheating.

You can encourage continued blooming in **miniature roses** by growing them under fluorescent lights and fertilizing at every other watering with a half-strength dose of African violet or bloom booster fertilizers.

## PRUNING

Deadhead your flowering plants. Pinch out flowers forming on **coleus.** Snip off browned leaf tips.

**Impatiens** may live through the winter given a cool, sunny window and providing they stay free of whitefly and aphids. When the plants get leggy, cut back the longer stems. Try rooting 6- to 8-inch cuttings in a jarful of water; every month

or so add a drop or two of liquid fertilizer. In late winter, pot up the cuttings that have the strongest roots.

**Growing bonsai.** Bonsai can be an enjoyable houseplant. Most need bright light and will do best in a room where the temperature is under 68 degrees Fahrenheit. Temperatures above 68 degrees dry the air, and that's hard on everything (you, too) except tropical plants.

There are two types of bonsai on the market. The most popular is a **juniper.** Junipers are hardy evergreens that need to be outdoors in a sheltered place in bright light 90 percent of the time. They can survive for a time on a sunny glassed-in porch or in a cold sunny room if you are faithful about watering and misting. Kept indoors 90 percent of the time, juniper bonsais won't live very long. Some merchants call them "temporary" bonsai.

The other type of plant commonly used for bonsai belongs to a group native to semi-tropical temperatures very like those produced by our year-round indoor heating. In this group we include **aralia, fatsia,** and **ficus** trimmed to look like bonsai and grown in shallow bonsai containers in gritty soil. That type of bonsai can live for a long time indoors if its watering and misting needs are met.

*Continue to mist the plants you brought indoors with water at room temperature to help them to acclimate to the changed environment.*

## Did You Know?

### Gardenias Will Bloom Indoors

The gardenia is a beautiful evergreen shrub whose flowers have a gloriously rich perfume. It can live for years as a houseplant and bloom well if you can summer it outdoors. Start with a young plant in fall, and it will acclimate.

Here's how to grow it:

*1* Give a gardenia full sun and a cool room—68 degrees Fahrenheit is ideal.

*2* Provide constant, even moisture by growing the plant on a saucer filled with pebbles and half-filled with water. Or double pot it and fill the space between the pots with moist moss. Mist lightly every day with water at room temperature. A shower and a good soaking every ten days or so in room-temperature water will help the foliage to stay crisp.

*3* Fertilize at every second watering with a half dose of acid-type fertilizer. Discontinue fertilizing when new buds appear.

*4* Watch for tiny webs indicating spider mites are setting up housekeeping. If they appear, shower the plant more often and spray with insecticidal soap.

*5* When flowering dies down, clean out imperfect leaves and branches, prune the tips of the branches back a few inches, and add an inch or two of fresh soil to the container. New growth in gardenias usually begins in March.

*6* Repot the plant in April, and move it outdoors in April or May.

*7* In September bring it back indoors.

Take your cue from the priceless bonsai collection at the U.S. National Arboretum. Those plants live most of the year in bright light in a sheltered place either in the bonsai house or in a sheltered area behind it. Some of them are hundreds of years old.

## WATERING

Check pots of **miniature roses** often, and keep the soil moderately damp. Rinse them every two weeks to discourage spider mites.

## FERTILIZING

Add a half-strength dose of water-soluble fertilizer at every fourth watering for houseplants, **bougainvillea, mandevilla, tropical hibiscus,** and other tender shrubs brought indoors. For **azaleas** and **gardenias,** use a fertilizer for acid-loving plants. Continue to use African violet fertilizer for flowering houseplants.

## PESTS

Check for spider mites, mealybug, and scale; controls are suggested in the Pests section of the introduction to this chapter. To avoid problems, mist your plants, air the room often, keep the temperature down, and provide humidity.

# NOVEMBER
## Houseplants

 PLANNING

Garden centers offer inexpensive baby sizes of many plants that make good indoor shrubs and trees—including **ficus, flowering maples,** and **hibiscus.** Our plant list tells you which will grow to shrub and to tree size: plan to buy these as babies for your own indoor garden, or to grow up to give to friends.

 PLANTING

**Creating a terrarium for shade-loving plants** is an interesting indoor garden project. Here's how to do it:

*1* Glass cases for terrarium gardens are available at garden centers, by mail order, and online; or use a fish tank or round bowl about 12 to 14 inches across. Whatever the container, to keep the moisture in, you will need a pane of clear plexiglass or glass to cover the top.

*2* Buy the following plants in the smallest pot size you can find, probably a 3-inch pot: **maidenhair fern; aluminum plant; selaginella;** one miniature flowering plant, such as *Begonia bowerae* or *B. hydrocotilifolia;* and one **creeping fig**—either *Ficus pumila* or *F. sagittata.*

*3* Line the bottom of the container with marble chips 1 inch deep, and top them with a thin layer of charcoal chips to keep the soil fresh.

*4* Scoop into the bowl 2 to 3 cups of moist, sterile commercial terrarium soil (African violet potting soil will do). Shape the soil into a miniature terrain with hills and valleys.

*5* Set the tallest plants in their places first, and add enough soil to cover their roots. Then tuck the roots of the little **begonia** and the **creeping fig** into the soil. Mulch with sphagnum moss.

*6* Dribble in just enough water to settle the roots. Add tiny statues, rocks, and other ornaments that suggest landscape scenes.

*7* Cover the top. When the inside fogs over, as it will, take the cover off for an hour or so. Repeat if needed. When the excess moisture is gone, the misting will stop. Mist monthly with water at room temperature. It should not need real watering for months.

*8* Keep the terrarium in dim light for ten days, and then gradually move it into brighter light in a west- or east-facing window.

*9* Fertilize once a year with a quarter dose of an all-purpose fertilizer.

 CARE

Mist **gardenias, hibiscus, rosemary,** and other houseplants every day or two with water at room temperature. Air their space daily for ten minutes or so by opening a window or a door.

If **miniature roses** aren't flowering, light them with spot grow lights after dusk and occasionally vacation them under fluorescents in a light garden for a few weeks.

If your thermostat is set higher than 68 degrees Fahrenheit, install a humidifier, or humidify the air by setting out vases, pans, or jars of water on radiators, or placing jars of water or wet sponges among your plants. Mist the plants and air their homes more often.

PRUNING

Deadhead **miniature roses, begonias, coleus,** and other flowering houseplants. Groom the foliage plants.

WATERING

The heat is on! Check the moisture in the houseplant pots weekly, small pots more often.

*When leaves look less than perky, a plant is telling you something. Pick up the pot: if it is lighter than you remember, press your finger into the soil and you'll find it needs watering.*

## Did You Know?

### Jungle Cactuses Are Easy to Make Rebloom

Those exotic cactuses that bear orchid-like flowers at Thanksgiving and Christmas are species of *Schlumbergera* and *Zygocactus* respectively. The varieties that bloom in spring, the **Easter cactus,** belong to the species *Rhipsalidopsis gaertneri.* All three jungle cactuses are *epiphytes*—plants that start life in a little humusy soil in the crotch of a tree.

All three grow well and bloom given similar care:

*1* Keep jungle cactuses where temperatures are 65 to 70 degrees Fahrenheit by day, no colder than 60 degrees by night. Set the plants in sunny east- or southeast-facing windows, or under fluorescent lights. When the plants go out of bloom, to encourage reblooming, do not allow artificial light to strike the plant.

*2* Water the plants lightly when the soil feels dry to the touch, about every four or five days. Use lukewarm water.

*3* Every other year, repot one size up in March or April. Use a mix that is a third coarse sand, a third perlite, and a third all-purpose, houseplant potting soil.

*4* When the weather warms in May, put the plants outdoors in indirect light for the summer.

*5* Water as needed to keep the soil damp, and at every second watering include a half-strength dose of African violet fertilizer.

*6* Towards the end of September bring the plants indoors to a cool room—65 degrees Fahrenheit by day, 60 degrees by night. For eight weeks let them rest—no artificial light, barely enough water to keep the soil from drying out, and no fertilizer.

*7* At the end of eight weeks, move the pots to sunny east- or southeast-facing windows and water as before.

*8* Just as new growth starts, you can root cuttings taken this month from a mature jungle cactus. Break off branch ends that include three or four of the claw-like segments. Let them dry three or four days. Press the ends into dampened cactus potting mix in an 8-inch pot. They'll be rooted in six weeks and can be individually potted.

When leaves look less than perky, a plant is telling you something. Pick up the pot: if it is lighter than you remember, press your finger into the soil and you'll find it needs watering.

 FERTILIZING

Add a half-strength dose of water-soluble fertilizer at every fourth watering for houseplants, the **tropical hibiscus,** and other tender shrubs brought indoors. For **azaleas** and **gardenias,** use a fertilizer for acid-loving plants. Continue to use African violet fertilizer for flowering houseplants.

 PESTS

Check for spider mites, mealybug, and scale; controls are suggested in the Pests section of the introduction to this chapter and in the Appendix. To avoid problems, mist your plants with water at room temperature, air the room often, keep temperatures down, and provide humidity.

# DECEMBER
## Houseplants

 **PLANNING**

A **Norfolk Island pine** can be your Christmas tree—but so can a **ficus,** or a **podocarpus** if it is decorated. Miniature Christmas lights sparkle the tree. You can also make a spectacular Christmas tree by arranging pots of **poinsettias** into a pyramid.

 **PLANTING**

The choice and early care of a **poinsettia** have everything to do with how well the plant will last.

*1* Choose a poinsettia with tightly clustered flowers, whose foliage is crisp and green all the way down to the soil.

*2* Protect the plant from cold winds while you are getting it home.

*3* Unwrap it, and remove the foil wrapping or cut away the bottom of the foil so water can drain. Keep it at about 72 degrees Fahrenheit during the day and 60 degrees at night.

*4* Provide six hours a day of natural light in a bright window. You can move it into the room for the evening, but get it back in its window in the morning.

*5* Keep the soil moist, but don't let water stand in the saucer.

 **CARE**

Mist **gardenias, rosemary,** and other houseplants every day or two with water at room temperature. Air the room daily for ten minutes or so by opening a window or a door, except in freezing weather.

If your **hibiscus** stops blooming, it's going into dormancy, probably from lack of sun and perhaps from lack of warmth as well. Water it only enough to keep the soil from drying out. Don't fertilize. The plant will drop lots of leaves, but it should live.

**African violets** flower best in spring and fall when the day length is twelve to fourteen hours. They'll also bloom this time of year when placed 9 inches below grow lights burned twelve hours a day. The leaves may not be as green, but they'll flower in eight to ten weeks.

 **PRUNING**

Deadhead flowering plants.

 **WATERING**

Maintain the soil moisture in all houseplants; **flowering maples** have thin leaves and dry out quickly! Shower **miniature roses** every two weeks.

 **FERTILIZING**

Add a half-strength dose of soluble fertilizer at every fourth watering for houseplants and the **tropical hibiscus** and other tender shrubs brought indoors. For **azaleas** and **gardenias,** use a fertilizer for acid-loving plants. Continue to use African violet fertilizer for flowering houseplants.

 **PESTS**

Check for spider mites, mealybug, and scale; controls are suggested in the Pests section of the introduction to this chapter and in the Appendix.

**Growing tropical hibiscus indoors means you may be challenged by whitefly and soft scale.** They raise families on a grand scale on the undersides of the leaves. Insecticidal soap controls them if you catch them early. The sticky yellow cards that nurseries use handle only minor infestations, but they do show you how fast the pests are multiplying. You may be able to control the infestation this way: shower each leaf on either side, let the plant dry, and then spray insecticidal soap over the tops and undersides of the leaves and in the nodes where branches and leaves meet.

# CHAPTER FIVE

# Lawns

*A good lawn is an enormous asset—to your family, to your budget, to your neighborhood.*
*And all it asks is to be fed properly and given good haircuts.*

To carpet your yard with a beautiful green lawn you must fertilize more than once, cut the grass at the right height, water correctly, and provide at least some protection from weeds and diseases. Aerating and de-thatching now and then are good.

The type of fertilizer you choose dictates the type of pest and weed controls you can use.

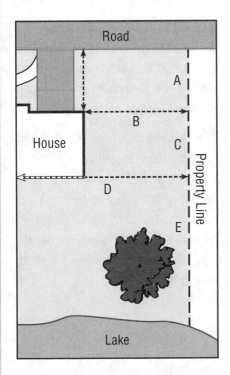

$$A \times B = X \qquad D \times E = Z$$
$$B \times C = Y \qquad X + Y + Z =$$

Total Square Feet

## FERTILIZING

**Organic fertilizers.** Organics release their nutrients slowly; two applications a year are enough. A Cornell University study found that using organic fertilizers may suppress some diseases, including brown patch, snow mold, dollar spot, and red thread. With organic fertilizers, any herbicides, pesticides, and fungicides you use are usually applied separately.

**Chemical fertilizers.** Balanced granular chemical fertilizers green the lawn overnight and are soon depleted, so you need to apply them four or five times a year. "Fertilizer-plus" products that include pre-emergent or post-emergent herbicides can be used to control crabgrass and broadleaf weeds. Insect and disease controls are usually applied separately.

**Herbicides, pesticides, and fungicides are applied only when needed.** Granular products applied with a drop-spreader are safest for the garden.

**To know how much fertilizer you need**: Measure the areas planted in lawn, multiply the width by the length to get the number of square feet in each, then add them all up for the total number of square feet you need to cover. Fertilizer bags tell you how many square feet the contents will cover. (See January.)

## SOIL PREPARATION AND IMPROVEMENT

**Soil pH.** If the pH of the soil is between pH 6.0 and 7.0, the lawn should do well. The ideal pH for turfgrass is 6.5. Heavily cropped lawn soils eventually become acidic and have a lower pH reading. However, do not lime by rote to raise the pH. Check the pH of your soil annually, but adjust it only when adjustment is needed. Sandy soil whose pH has been corrected is good for two years, clay soil for three. A pH check can be made any month.

**Aeration (coring).** Compacted soil has no space for water or air, nor does it have growing room for roots. The solution is to aerate the soil by cutting out core plugs of sod so that water, air, and fertilizer can get down to where they are needed. If the lawn is well used and beginning to bald or show a thatch buildup, then aerate. If all is

# Lawns

well, every two or three years aerate to keep it that way. You can do it by hand, and you also can rent power equipment to aerate and de-thatch. (See April and May.)

**Thatch and de-thatching.** Grass clippings landing on the lawn are decomposed by the microorganisms there, and that adds nutrients to the soil. That layer of clippings is called thatch, and it's a good thing as long as the clippings are less than 1/4 inch deep. However, if the lawn gets too much fast-acting, high-nitrogen fertilizer and water, it may grow quickly and the clippings may fall so thick and so fast the microorganisms can't keep up; that's when a layer of thatch a couple of inches deep accumulates, which is harmful. A lawn that feels spongy when you walk on it probably has thatch building to unhealthy levels. You can fix it by aerating and de-thatching. You can also prevent thatch buildup. (See April and May.)

## WATERING

Grass thrives on a good soaking every week to ten days. Soak it more often and it will grow, use up the nutrients in the soil, and need mowing almost twice as fast. If you make the mistake of watering the lawn frequently and shallowly—every one to three days—the roots will grow near the surface of the soil, which warms and dries out when the weather does and is a bad place for roots to be. The watering program in the July pages is easy on your time, effort, pocketbook, and lawn. Only your patience will suffer.

## CARE

The rule of thumb is that if 50 percent of a lawn needs fixing, then you need a new lawn. If 30 percent or less is in trouble, it can be patched or restored. From 30 to 50 percent, you must renovate. For lawn patching or restoration to succeed, you must mix humus and fertilizers into the soil before you seed or sod the area.

**Repair.** You can repair a small area with sod, new or stripped from somewhere else in the lawn, or by seeding the area. Lawn-patching products include mulch and nutrients and are easy to apply.

**Restoration.** This involves sowing seed into an existing lawn after vigorously cultivating the ground with rented power equipment. (See August for more details.)

**Starting a new lawn.** To seed or to sod, that is the question. It is not nobler to seed, just less costly. Sodding is faster, but the soil needs the same deep preparation and patient watering until it is established. Also, sod won't keep weeds out forever, and sod varieties are limited.

**Seeding saves money**. The bigger the lawn, the greater the savings. To seed 1,000 square feet costs about $10, not including the humus, fertilizer, and other soil amendments the soil will need to get a good start. If you seed, you can choose from among the varieties of grasses in our turfgrass table.

**Sod if you enjoy making magic.** It's the way to have an instant lawn. The cost for 1,000 square foot area is about $200, if you do the work yourself. Your choice of grasses will be limited.

**Timing for a new lawn.** Cool-season grasses peak in spring, go semi-dormant in mid-summer, and peak again in fall. They're best started around Labor Day. Early spring is second best. Most seeds germinate when daytime temperatures are 68 to 95 degrees Fahrenheit.

# Lawns

## MOWING

The rule of thumb is to mow every five to seven days during the peak season, and as needed at other times. Keep the mower blades sharpened, cut the grass high, and don't let the mowing get away from you. Mow at the right height for the grass and the season. (See June.) The table of grasses for New York includes the mowing heights of each grass recommended.

**About mowers.** There are many sizes and types of mowers, but only two ways of cutting—reel or rotary. The reel mower does a slightly better job but is slower. The rotary mower does a fine job and is faster. The most important thing to know about a mower is that it must be sharpened throughout the mowing season. Dull blades tear and damage the grass, and that shows up in the appearance of the lawn and the health of the grass plants. (See December for more about mowers.)

**Leaves and your lawn.** If there's just a scattering of leaves on your lawn, they'll dry and crumble into bits that the microorganisms in the soil will reduce to nutrients. The residue will blow away with winter winds and weather. But, matted accumulations of leaves rob the grass of the sunlight it needs as growth continues through fall. Crunch the leaves under the lawn mower, rake, and bag them—or grind them, and distribute the bits over the garden with a blower-vacuum. (See October.)

## CONTROLLING WEEDS, PESTS, AND DISEASES

Weeds, pests, and diseases attack lawns made vulnerable by lack of fertilizer and poor garden practices. There are ways to control them.

**Cultural practices.** Feed, mow, and water your lawn wisely.

**Biological methods.** Apply agents such as beneficial nematodes, bacteria, and other organisms. A biological control becoming more available is endophytes—fungi bred to live within grasses and stop insect pests.

**Chemical controls.** Pre-emergent and post-emergent herbicides, and pesticides and fungicides—some natural, some man-made—are used to control weeds, pests, and diseases. Many now on the market are considered environmentally sound. Once again we caution you to apply these only if really needed. For an overview of how and when to do what, turn to the March pages.

## WEEDS

All post-emergent liquid weed killers work best when the dose called for on the label is combined with 1 teaspoon of liquid dish detergent to each gallon of water.

**Broadleaf weed seeds.** These weeds, including dandelions, can be controlled by applications of a **pre-emergent** broadleaf weed killer when the forsythia petals drop. Repeat in fall.

**Broadleaf weed plants.** If a variety of weeds leaf out in May and June, apply a **post-emergent** broad-spectrum herbicide.

**Chickweed, bindweed, violets, sorrel, and clover plants.** Kill these weeds by applications of a post-emergent control such as 2,4-D+TurflonD, Dicamba 2,4-D+BanvelD, or Gordon's Trimec Broadleaf Herbicide. Repeat in the fall.

**Crabgrass seeds.** When the forsythia petals drop, stop the weed seeds by applying pre-emergent weed killers such as Betasan, Tupersan, Balan, Dacthal, Team, or Sidriron.

**Dandelion, plantain, and other broadleaf weed plants.** Control them by individual applications in April and May of 2,4-D and 2,4-D combinations.

# Lawns

**Wild onion (garlic).** Apply a post-emergent control such as 2,4-D+ Dicamba (Banvel D) or 2,4-D+TurflonD in early spring when the onions first emerge, and repeat two weeks later.

## PESTS

November through April, pests and diseases appear to be on vacation. They're with you the rest of the year.

**Grubs.** To control the larvae that become rose chafer or Asiatic beetle, in May and June and again in August and September, apply biological controls such as beneficial nematodes. Or apply chemical controls such as Merit or Marathon.

**Ants.** Use Permethrin.

**Chinch bugs.** Apply Sevin, Permethrin, or Baygon in April and May, and again in August and September.

**Cutworms.** Use beneficial nematodes, Sevin, or Safer soap in spring.

**Japanese beetles.** Apply rotenone, Neem, or Sevin. For Japanese beetle grubs, use Milky Spore.

**Moles.** Runs of heaved sod ending in mounds of dirt are signs that moles are shopping for grubs. Apply a grub control such as Merit or Marathon to kill off the grubs, and chances are the moles will find another supermarket.

**Sod webworms.** In late June and again in late August and early September, apply *Bt*, Sevin, Permethrin, or Baygon.

## DISEASES

To control a variety of diseases at one time, apply a broad-spectrum fungicide or, better yet, a broad-spectrum systemic fungicide such as Daconil, Mancozeb, Chipco, Clearys 3336, and Bayleton. Make the applications when the disease appears and twice a month in May, June, July, and August.

**Fusarium blight (now called necrotic ring spot), copper spot, and dollar spot.** They show up as a circle of dead grass with some green tufts in the middle. The disease will likely run its course. The controls are fungicidal copper, sulfur, Bayleton, or Cleary 3336.

**Helminthosporum leaf spot and melting out.** These diseases cause brown and black spots on the blades, and the grass dies in irregular patches. Treat with a fungicide labeled for use on turf and melting out diseases, such as Fore or Heritage, every two weeks from the first appearance of the problem until it is gone.

**Powdery mildew.** It looks as though the leaves have been powdered. Powdery mildew turns up in shady spots, so try to get more light to the area. Or control with applications of fungicidal copper or sulfur, or a systemic fungicide such as Bayleton or Banner Maxx, applied twice a month from June through September.

**Red thread and pink patch.** Patches of grass turn light tan to pink, and pink threads bind the blades. As soon as it appears, treat the lawn with a contact fungicide twice, seven to ten days apart.

**Rust-infected leaves.** These leaves are spotted yellow, orange, or brown. Rust is common in new lawns with a high percentage of ryegrass. It generally fades as other grass varieties take over from the rye. Control with applications twice a month of sulfur, mancozeb, or manzate, or a systemic fungicide such as Bayleton and Banner Maxx, from the time it appears—usually May through September.

**Snow mold.** This causes small to large gray or white matted patches of grass. Rake the lawn in early spring, and avoid overuse of nitrogen fertilizers.

# Lawns

| Types of Grass (*Botanical Name*) | Description | Problems | Start As | Sow Per 1,000 sq. ft. | Mowing Height |
|---|---|---|---|---|---|
| **Creeping Red Fescue** (*Festuca* species) | Glossy green, fine texture, shade-, drought- and foot traffic-tolerant. Choose modern mixes with Kentucky bluegrass and perennial rye for genetic diversity and disease tolerance. Needs less fertilizer. | Disease-prone unless well drained. Tends to lie flat and cause uneven mowing. | Seed in spring or fall | 3 to 4 pounds | 2 to 2½ inches |
| **Hard Fescue** (*Festuca longiflora*) | Tough, low-growing bunch-type grass; used for erosion control. Tolerates shade, cold, drought, salt, poor soil. Disease-tolerant mixes. Needs little feeding or mowing. | Stiff | Seed in spring or fall | 3 to 4 pounds | 3+ inches |
| **Tall Fescue** (*Festuca arundinacea*) | Popular, wide bladed, durable. Choose modern mixes including bluegrass and perennial rye. These are finer and withstand foot traffic, drought, disease. Grows in sun or shade, sandy soil, and can be used for erosion control. | Older versions tend to clump and are subject to many problems | Seed in spring, early summer, or fall | 4 to 8 pounds | 3 to 4 inches |

# Lawns

| Types of Grass (*Botanical Name*) | Description | Problems | Start As | Sow Per 1,000 sq. ft. | Mowing Height |
|---|---|---|---|---|---|
| **Kentucky Bluegrass** (*Poa pratensis*) | Most popular. Rich blue-green, medium to fine texture. Repairs well under normal use. Mixed with perennial ryegrass and fine fescues, it has a higher tolerance for cold. Full sun best. Use only improved cultivars. | Labor intensive, heavy feeder, needs lots of water. Vulnerable to powdery mildew, fungal diseases, chinch bugs, cutworms, grubs, sod webworms. | Seed or sod, spring or fall | 1 to 2 pounds | 2 to 2³/₄ inches |
| **Perennial Ryegrass** (*Lolium perenne*) | Nice texture and color. Germinates quickly; the pop-up "starter" grass in mixtures and used to patch bare spots in summer. Good permanent grass mixed with other grasses. Likes cool climates. Often added to bluegrass and fine fescue mixes. Some varieties tolerate some shade. | Suffers in extreme heat. Vulnerable to brown patch, red thread, rust, snow mold, dollar spot. | Seed or sod in spring, early summer, or fall | 14 to 15 pounds | 2 to 2¹/₂ inches |
| **Zoysia** (*Zoysia japonica*) | Warm-season coarse grass that spreads rapidly and vigorously, resists weeds. Great summer grass for high traffic. Tolerates drought, sandy soil, and some salt spray. | Brown half the year in our area. Chronic heavy thatch buildup. Prone to assorted pests. | Plugs or sod in spring | Plugs or sod | 2 inches |

# JANUARY
## Lawns

 PLANNING

If your lawn mower was serviced when mowing ended last year, great! If not, see December for suggestions.

 PLANTING

It's too early even for grass seed.

 CARE

Walking on frozen grass damages it. Shovel walk and driveways before applying snowmelt salts. Otherwise you risk damaging the lawn.

 MOWING

None needed.

 WATERING

None needed.

 FERTILIZING

If you are using an organic fertilizer, a late winter fertilization benefits a lawn not growing well. A light coat of granular fertilizer can be applied over a light snow.

### Fertilizing and Fertilizers

Save $$ by leaving grass clippings on the lawn. Reduced to their elemental forms by microorganisms in the soil, clippings can lower the amount of fertilizer needed by as much as 30 percent. Clippings from a 1,000 square foot lawn contribute $1/2$ to 2 pounds of nitrogen depending on how much the lawn was fertilized.

**When to fertilize.** Avoid fertilizing when temperatures are over 90 degrees.

**Organic fertilizers.** Organic fertilizers are applied twice a year. They can be applied in any season without danger of burning. Organics do not include herbicides, pesticides, or fungicides; these are applied separately and only when needed.

The first fertilization is best made before grass starts into growth in early spring. For Zones 6 and 7 that could be as early as late March, but for most of New York it will be in well into April.

The second fertilization is best applied in early September. A third fertilization can help lawns doing poorly and can be made in late fall or even late winter.

**Chemical fertilizers.** Granular chemical fertilizers are applied four times a year. Formulations are available that include pre-emergent or post-emergent controls for crabgrass and broadleaf weeds. For a new lawn, choose a fertilizer with an NPK of 1-1-1, or 1-2-2. For an established lawn, choose a fertilizer whose NPK ratio is 3-1-2 or 4-1-2.

The first fertilization is best made as grass starts into growth in early spring. For warm Zones 6 and 7 that can be as early as March, but for most of us it is during the month of April.

The second fertilization is May to June; the third is made in July or August; the fourth in August or September. The fifth fertilization is optional and can be made October or November.

Save wood ashes to use as fertilizer for the lawn. They make lime and potash quickly available and can be applied over a few inches of snow.

## PESTS

If snow mold appears, just rake the patches clear and avoid overuse of nitrogen fertilizers in the future.

# FEBRUARY
## Lawns

# PLANNING

If your lawn mower needs servicing, take it to the dealer now, during the dealer's quiet season. Keeping the blades sharp is essential to giving the lawn a good cut, one that will help to keep it healthy and looking good.

# PLANTING

You can over-seed thin areas in late winter or early spring. It's okay to sow seed on a few inches of snow. For suggestions on how to repair damage—where a tree limb has fallen or a delivery truck has gouged the turf—and how to seed a lawn, see August. If your lawn has developed low spots, top-dress it with improved soil as soon as the snow is gone, and seed it. (See September.)

# CARE

Check the pH of your lawn soil this month or wait until next month if you still have deep snow, and adjust it if needed.

# MOWING

Not likely!

## Did You Know?

### Soil pH and Lime

To keep your soil in top condition for growing grass, check the pH annually and adjust it only if needed.

The ideal pH for turfgrass is pH 6.5, but between 6.0 and 7.0 is okay. Some gardeners lime their lawns every year, but you shouldn't lime by rote. Where limestone is prevalent, soils are naturally alkaline, and even the hose water may contain lime. There the pH may need to be lowered periodically, not raised. The pH can be adjusted any time the lawn isn't in full growth, but checking it as soon as the snow goes gives you time to correct the pH before the grass-growing season begins.

A sandy soil whose pH has been corrected is good for two years; a clay soil is good for three years. Kits for analyzing pH are sold at garden centers and by mail-order suppliers, as are products used for adjusting the soil pH.

- To raise the pH by 1 pH point, apply dolomitic limestone:
  Sandy soil—50 pounds per 1000 square feet
  Clay soil—100 pounds per 1000 square feet

- To lower the pH by 1 pH point, apply elemental sulfur (water-soluble garden sulfur):
  Sandy soil—50 pounds per 1000 square feet
  Clay soil—100 pounds per 1000 square feet

Other acidifiers are aluminum sulfate and iron sulfate; they act faster but do not last as long in the soil as elemental sulfur.

# WATERING

Maintain the moisture in the soil of areas that have just been seeded or sodded. (See September.)

# FERTILIZING

In warm Zone 7, the first application of an organic fertilizer can be made between now and April. If you are using a chemical fertilizer, wait until shortly before the grass begins to grow.

# PESTS

If wild onion (garlic) was a problem last spring, plan to apply a post-emergent control such as 2,4-D+Dicamba (Banvel D) or 2,4-D+TurflonD when the pesky onions first appear.

## Did You Know?

### About Herbicides, Pesticides, and Fungicides

**Herbicides.** The best defense against weeds is a thriving lawn cut high. If a few weeds do appear, pull them by hand before they set seed. If crabgrass has been spreading, control with a **pre-emergent** crabgrass killer. If broadleaved weeds such as violets and dandelions are spreading, use a **broad-spectrum, pre-emergent** herbicide that kills weeds as well as crabgrass. Crabgrass germinates in April, about the time forsythia petals fall and dandelions fluff out their seedheads. If broadleaf weeds develop, apply a **post-emergent, broad-spectrum** herbicide. If the lawn is infested with a particular weed, apply a product specific to that weed, as and when the label directs.

**Pesticides.** Lawns are home to insects, most of them beneficial so don't overdo the use of biological and chemical controls. To get rid of harmful insects, you can use a combination of a granular chemical fertilizer plus a pesticide. If you are using an organic fertilizer, apply a broad-spectrum pesticide (insecticide) from June to August. To control a specific insect infestation—Japanese beetles, for example—**apply a control specific to the insect when and how the label directs.**

**Fungioides.** Fungi can cause lawn diseases. Most feed on dead vegetation, recycling it as soil nutrients. However, a few fungi feed on live plants. Symptoms and controls are described in this chapter's introduction. The best defense is a healthy lawn—fertilize adequately, mow at the right height, water wisely, adjust the pH as needed by aerating (coring, plugging) every two or three years and by avoiding thatch buildup. Treat problems immediately.

## PLANNING

Get the lawn mower sharpened and the trimmer ready to go. Decide on a lawn feeding and weeding program.

## PLANTING

When the snow has gone, check the lawn over for areas that need repair and overseed them. You can begin repairs when the soil stops being squishy.

## CARE

When the snow has gone, clear fallen branches from the lawn. Reposition pavers keeping ground covers from invading the grass areas.

## MOWING

Usually too early for mowing. See April.

## WATERING

Not needed.

## FERTILIZING

Organic fertilizers can be applied as early as the end of this month. If you are using chemicals, wait until closer to the time the grass begins to grow.

## PESTS

Get together last year's leftover herbicides and pesticides. Figure out what you'll need this year and ask your garden center for advice—there may be new products worth trying. If you've had crabgrass, when the forsythia petals fall next month you will need to apply a pre-emergent crabgrass killer. If dandelions and other broadleaf weeds bloom with the forsythias, plan to use a control that deals with broadleaf weeds as well as crabgrass. If wild onion (garlic) pops up, you can wait and apply a post-emergent control such as 2,4-D+Dicamba (Banvel D) or 2,4-D+TurflonD, and repeat two weeks later.

 PLANNING

When the grass begins to grow, keep an eye on emerging weed and pest populations. If mole runs appear, apply a grub control such as Merit or Marathon to send them elsewhere for their food.

 PLANTING

Repair areas in the lawn that have been damaged by falling branches, snow-blowing equipment, and so on. (See August.)

 CARE

When the soil has warmed and dried, check the soil pH and lime it if needed. Aerate if you haven't in the last two years. Check and correct thatch buildup. (See May.) Use a grass rake to fluff the soil. Clear away debris.

 MOWING

By the end of this month, your lawn may need mowing. Begin to mow when the grass tops the height our turfgrass table recommends for your variety. Set your mower at the height recommended in the table for your type of grass. If you don't know what type you are growing, set the mower at 2½ inches.

## Did You Know?

### About Aeration (Coring)

To solve compaction, avoid thatch buildup, and condition the soil, aerate every two or three years. Aerating equipment punches 2- to 3-inch-deep holes in the soil and lets fertilizer, air, and water penetrate. Aerators that are "corers" have hollow tines and are more effective than aerators with solid tines.

To aerate 1,000 square feet or less, you can use a manual aerator. It looks like a spading fork, but the tines are hollow tubes. For a larger area, you need a drum-mounted aerator, or hire a firm that is equipped to do the job.

- The best time to aerate is in the early spring or fall when the grass isn't actively growing.
- The day before, lightly water the grass so the tines will enter the soil.
- Before using the aerator, a light application of fertilizer is beneficial.
- Be thorough, and make two passes at right angles to each other with the aerator.
- Spread grass seed over the aerated area at the rate recommended on the bag and water slowly and gently.

 WATERING

If you have a sodded or seeded area, maintain soil moisture.

 FERTILIZING

**Organic fertilizer.** The first of the two annual applications is best made a few weeks before the grass begins to grow.

**Chemical fertilizer.** Make the first application just before the lawn begins to grow.

 PESTS

If crabgrass or nutgrass is a problem, when the forsythia petals drop, apply a pre-emergent control; if they do leaf out, apply a post-emergent control. This month and next, keep an eye out for chickweed, bindweed, violets, sorrel, clover plants, dandelions, plantain, and other broadleaf weed plants. If there are only a few, pull them by hand. If there are many, kill them before they go to seed. If you spot chinch bugs, apply controls this month and next, and again in August and September. Controls for each of these problems are suggested in the introduction to this chapter.

# PLANNING

If you want to reduce the amount of water you use on the lawn, consider replacing outlying areas with a drought-tolerant ground cover.

# PLANTING

You can still seed or over-sow areas of the lawn this month. (See August.)

# CARE

May is the time to aerate and de-thatch.

# MOWING

Begin to mow when the grass tops the height our turfgrass table recommends for your variety. Set the mower at the height the table recommends for your type of grass. If you don't know what type you have, set the mower at 2$\frac{1}{2}$ inches. Mow often enough so you never have to cut off more than a third of the grass to maintain the height recommended. Keep the mower blades sharpened.

# WATERING

Water newly sodded or seeded areas.

## Did You Know?

### About Thatch and De-thatching

Grass clippings left on the lawn are returned to an elemental state by microorganisms in the soil and recycled as nutrients. A $\frac{1}{4}$-inch layer of clippings is good; more is not. Clippings build too high when overdoses of pesticides kill the soil microorganisms and when soluble high-nitrogen (N2) fertilizers and excessive watering push grass growth. Your lawn may need de-thatching if it feels spongy to walk on.

- Look before you leap. Cut out a pie-shaped plug of turf that includes dirt with the roots. If the spongy layer between the grass and the soil measures more than $\frac{1}{2}$ inch, de-thatch.

- The best time to de-thatch a cool-season grass is in early fall.

- A convex rake with short knife-like blades in place of tines can be used to de-thatch a small lawn. For a big de-thatching job, a gas-powered vertical mower and power rake attachment is needed. If the thatch is thick, make two passes at right angles to each other.

# FERTILIZING

**Organic fertilizer.** If the first application hasn't been made yet, do it now.

**Chemical fertilizer.** If your first application was six weeks ago, repeat now. If weeds are a problem, use a fertilizer that includes a post-emergent herbicide.

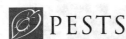
# PESTS

If you suspect grubs are a problem, here's how to check it out. Cut out and remove a square foot of turf 8 inches deep. If you find three or four grub larvae in the top 6 inches, apply a grub control. Check again in mid-August or early September.

If dandelions, plantain, chickweed, bindweed, violets, sorrel, clover plants, or other broadleaf weeds appear, apply post-emergent controls before they go to seed.

Apply controls this month for the larvae that become chinch bugs, rose chafer, and Asiatic, Japanese, and other beetles.

Rust may appear in new lawns with a high percentage of ryegrass. If rust shows up, spray immediately.

White Grub

# JUNE
## Lawns

## PLANNING

Time to assess your mowing equipment and perhaps take advantage of sales to upgrade.

## PLANTING

Sod installed from now on will likely need watering daily until it begins to root and grow again.

## CARE

Keep your mower blades sharpened!

## MOWING

Check the mowing height of equipment, and make sure it is at the height recommended for your type of turfgrass in the table in the introduction to the chapter.

## WATERING

Keep the soil for newly planted seed or sod moist by watering every day or two until it is growing well.

## FERTILIZING

**Organic fertilizer.** If the first application hasn't been made yet, do it now. Organics can be applied any time, but grass grows rapidly in spring and needs to have the nutrients replenished.

**Chemical fertilizer.** The second application is best made about six weeks after the first.

If weeds are a problem, you can use a fertilizer that includes a post-emergent herbicide. If insects are a problem, use a fertilizer-plus product that includes a broad-spectrum pesticide.

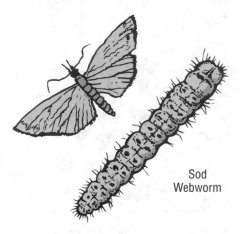

Sod Webworm

## PESTS

If you see broadleaf weeds in the lawn, apply a **post-emergent** broad-spectrum herbicide. If you've had problems with rose chafer, Asiatic beetle, Japanese beetle, or other white grubs, apply controls now. Watch out for sod webworms; initiate controls immediately. Powdery mildew can appear about now. It occurs most often in shaded areas of the lawn. Initiate controls now, and continue throughout the summer.

Fertilizer Spreaders

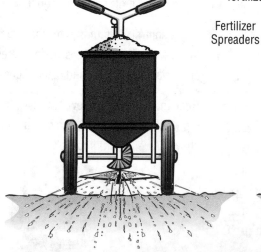 

*Sod installed from now on will likely need watering daily until it begins to root and grow again.*

## Did You Know?

### Mowing: The Six Commandments

Good mowing practices help to keep the lawn beautiful and healthy.

*1* Mow when the lawn is dry.

*2* Keep the mower blades sharpened throughout the cutting season.

*3* Cut the grass high. For the ideal height for your grass, turn back to the turfgrass table. Turfgrass mowed higher than 2 inches develops extensive roots, reducing the need for water and nutrients. A Virginia research study showed:

- Cut grass 1 inch high: 43.1 weeds per 100 square feet (a plot 10 by 10 feet).

- Cut grass 2 inches high: 2.5 weeds per 100 square feet.

- Cut grass 3 inches high: 0.2 weeds per 100 square foot.

*4* Mow often enough that you never have to cut off more than a third of the grass to maintain the height recommended in the turfgrass table. If your mower is set at 2$\frac{1}{2}$ inches, mow when the grass is 3$\frac{1}{2}$ inches high.

*5* Use a mulching mower to make it easy for soil organisms to recycle clippings.

*6* Vary your cutting pattern; that's easier on the grass.

### To Avoid Thatch Buildup

- Remove less than 1 inch of the grass blade when you mow. Use a mulching mower to double cut the clippings, which makes it easier for the microorganisms in the soil to break them down.

- Avoid excessive dosing with pesticides that kill the soil microorganisms.

- Avoid soluble high-nitrogen (N2) fertilizers and excessive watering.

- Aerate every two or three years. Aeration helps avoid a big thatch buildup although it isn't enough alone to solve one.

- Beneficial insects speed the breakdown of thatch, so be conservative in your use of pesticides.

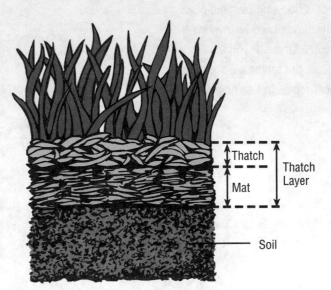

# JULY
## Lawns

 ## PLANNING

As summer reveals the pests and diseases that love your lawn best, plan fall and spring strategies for reducing their numbers.

 ## PLANTING

You can repair with sod now, but wait until September for any serious seeding project.

 ## CARE

The little moths hovering over the grass are laying the eggs of sod webworms—soon to become larvae. If you applied a control in June, the moths are a prompt that you must repeat in late August and in September.

 ## MOWING

**When you will be away for more than a week, arrange to have the lawn mowed.** The growth rate of the grasses is slowing, but if on your return you have to cut more than a week's worth of growth, the lawn will suffer.

Keep the mower blades sharpened.

 ## WATERING

The lawn needs a good soaking every week, especially in very hot weather. . . by rain or by you.

 ## FERTILIZING

**Chemical fertilizer.** The third application can be made this month or next.

 ## PESTS

**Summertime, and the living is easy... for lawn diseases.** Look out for fusarium blight (now called necrotic ring spot), copper spot, and dollar spot; helminthosporum leaf spot and melting out diseases; powdery mildew; red thread and pink patch; and rust-infected leaves. As soon as you have identified a disease, apply the controls recommended in the introduction to the chapter, and repeat twice this month and next.

Measuring
an Inch of Water

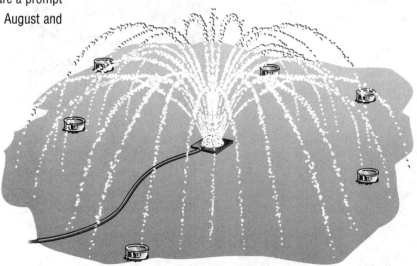

*When you will be away for more than a week, arrange to have the lawn mowed. The growth rate of the grasses is slowing, but if on your return you have to cut more than a week's worth of growth, the lawn will suffer.*

## Did You Know?

### How to Water Your Lawn

Lawns need water every week. When you water, imitate a slow soaking rain. Then it will go deep, and the roots will grow down, away from the heat and drought at the surface.

- When you water, lay down 1½ inches **slowly and gently.**
- Purchase a sprinkler that delivers the water slowly, avoiding wasteful runoff. Or, put down 3/4 of an inch of water, wait an hour, and then repeat.

- Between 5 a.m. and 10 a.m. is the most efficient time to water. But water any time your lawn retains footprints or grass blades curl inward. Where soil is thin—over rock outcroppings, for example—the grass dries out first and turns a bluish color, signaling that the lawn needs water.

- Watering systems deliver water at highly individual rates. To time how long it takes for your system to deliver 1½ inches of water, do this:

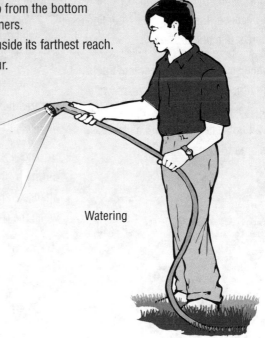

*1* With a waterproof marker, draw horizontal lines 1½ inches up from the bottom of the interior of five empty 1-pound coffee tins or other containers.

*2* Arrange them in a straight line out from the sprinkler to just inside its farthest reach.

*3* Turn the sprinkler on, mark the time, and run it for half an hour.

*4* Check the water levels in the cans.

*5* Repeat at 15-minute intervals until the water reaches the 1½ inch marker lines.

*6* Compare the amounts of water in the cans. If some have less than others, overlap the areas the sprinkler reaches. Average the amounts and the time.

*7* Record the timing in your garden log. You think you'll remember but likely you won't.

Watering

# AUGUST

 ## PLANNING

If you have a coastal home and lawn, you can offset the damage potential of exceptionally high tides by flooding the lawn until the soil is so saturated it can't absorb much of the salt water.

 ## PLANTING

After mid-August is a good time to begin repairing and over-seeding problem spots because the weather is cooling and there's rain ahead.

You can also lay sod over problem spots this month, but you will have to water daily to keep the new sod from drying out. Wait until late this month if you have a large area to sod.

 ## CARE

Dry periods reveal grub damage; prepare to apply grub controls.

 ## MOWING

Mowing high is especially important during the hot, dry months.

 ## WATERING

Remember to keep newly seeded or sodded areas well watered.

A lawn that is consistently and deeply watered has deep roots and will be just fine in spite of the heat and drought.

If patches over rocks turn brownish during a dry spell, try not to be upset; chances are the grass will turn green when the weather changes.

 ## FERTILIZING

**Chemical fertilizer.** If you haven't applied your third fertilization yet, do it now.

 ## PESTS

Repeat controls for chinch bugs, rose chafer, and Asiatic or Japanese beetles. Apply pre-emergent controls for annual bluegrass. Treat again for sod webworms.

Chinch Bug

Japanese Beetle

*A lawn that is consistently and deeply watered has deep roots and will be just fine in spite of the heat and drought.*

## Did You Know?

### Repair and Restoration

**Patching.** If 30 percent or less of the lawn is poor, patch.

*1* Level the sod and soil in the damaged area.

*2* Cut away jagged pieces of sod.

*3* Top with 3 to 4 inches of humus or topsoil. For each 10- by 10-foot area, add: Espoma Organic Lawn Food 5-3-5— 5 to 10 pounds; Rock phosphate—5 to 10 pounds; Green sand—5 to 10 pounds; for clay soils—gypsum 5 to 10 pounds. Mix this into the soil.

*4* For seeding or using a patching product, tamp it level with the lawn. For sod, tamp it down $1/2$ to $3/4$ inch below grade.

*5* Sow seed, spread the patching product, or install sod using, if possible, turfgrass matching the existing grass.

*6* Fertilize the entire lawn lightly.

*7* If you have seeded, cover it with straw so that only 30 to 50 percent of the soil is visible.

*8* Water slowly and often to keep the soil moist until the seeds have (nearly) all germinated. When the grass is an inch high, reduce watering to every four or five days. After the first mowing, water deeply every seven days unless it rains.

*9* Mow when the grass is $1/3$-inch taller than its optimum height. For seeded lawn, avoid the riding mower until the soil is firm underfoot. For sodded lawn, use the riding mower after two or three weeks.

**Renovation.** If 30 to 50 percent needs fixing, renovate. Mow the lawn as low as possible, then:

**Option one.** If the soil isn't compacted, rent a slit seeder, which drops seed onto the soil after slicing it. Use half the seeds to plant in one direction, and then go over the area again in the other direction dropping the remaining seeds.

**Option two.**

• Cultivate compacted soil with a power rake to slice through thatch and into the soil so the seeds can touch with the earth.

• Use a hollow tine core aerator to bring soil to the surface.

• Go over it again with the power rake to smooth out the cores and prepare for seeding.

• Distribute seed evenly with a mechanical spreader, preferably drop-style. Make two passes at right angles to each other.

After the lawn has been seeded, follow steps 6 through 9 for Patching.

**Reestablish**

If more than 50 percent is no good, kill the existing grass and start a new lawn from scratch, as described in the September sidebar.

# SEPTEMBER
## Lawns

 PLANNING

If you wanted to aerate the lawn this spring but didn't get around to it, plan to do it in mid-fall, after the grass stops actively growing.

 PLANTING

Labor Day is the beginning of the best season for repair, renovation, and starting a new lawn.

 CARE

The best time to de-thatch is in early fall.

 MOWING

Expect the lawn to slow its growth, but keep the mower blades sharpened anyway. The mowing isn't over yet!

 WATERING

Water if you have more than seven or eight days without rain, especially newly seeded or sodded areas.

 FERTILIZING

**Organic fertilizer.** The second fertilization can be made this month.

**Chemical fertilizer.** If you have not yet made the fourth application, do it now.

 PESTS

For chickweed, bindweed, ground ivy, violets, sorrel, clover, and other broadleaf weeds, apply a **post-emergent** weed killer now. Controls for sod webworm, rose chafer, and Asiatic or Japanese beetles must be applied in September. Repeat the spring treatments for chinch bugs this month and next. Start or continue treatments for powdery mildew and rust, fusarium blight, helminthosporum disease, red thread, and dollar spot.

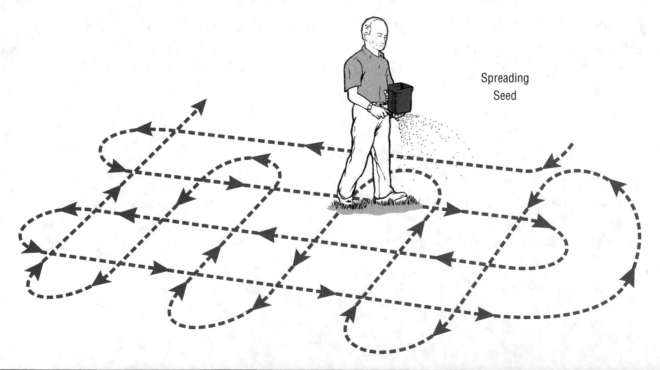

Spreading Seed

*Water if you have more than seven or eight days without rain, especially newly seeded or sodded areas.*

## Did You Know?

### About Starting a New Lawn: Seed or Sod

September is the best month to sow seed for the type of grasses used in New York. Early spring is second.

**Seed**

*1* Spray the area with RoundUp to kill existing weed seeds. Wait seven to ten days, and then repeat.

*2* Wait seven to ten more days, check the soil pH, adjust it if needed, and add the amendments and fertilizers described in the section on Repair and Renovation in the August pages.

*3* Rototill all this into the soil.

*4* Sow the seed evenly using a mechanical spreader, preferably drop-style. Make two passes, at right angles to each other using half the seed allotted on each pass.

*5* Rake the seed into the top few inches of the soil.

*6* Rent a lawn roller, and roll the seeded area.

*7* Apply a straw mulch, and spread it thin enough so only 30 to 50 percent of the soil shows.

*8* Water and mow. (See Repair and Renovation on the August pages.)

*9* Fertilize following the annual schedule given in the months of this chapter.

**Sod**

*1* Prepare the soil as for seeding; see steps 1, 2, 3, above.

*2* Lay the sod in a staggered brick pattern so that the seam on one row of sod falls in the center of the previous row. Butt the edges firmly together and standing on a board laid over the previous row, tamp the seams firmly in place with the back of a rake.

*3* Water enough to wet 4 to 6 inches of the underlying soil. For the next month, water deeply every four to five days unless you have rain.

Sod Placement

*4* Mow when the grass is a third taller than its optimum height. Use a hand mower rather than a riding mower for the first season.

*5* Fertilize following the annual schedule given throughout the months of this chapter.

# OCTOBER
## Lawns

## PLANNING

A healthy lawn is its own best defense against the weeds, pests, and diseases that cause deterioration. **Use your experience with the lawn this year to plan a lawn-care schedule that will build on current successes.**

## PLANTING

The soil still has warmth, though the air is cooling. A happy time for our lawns which are cool-season grasses. You can still seed or sod, repair, over-seed, or renovate early this month.

## CARE

The best time to de-thatch a cool-season grass is in early fall. **The best time to aerate is when the grass isn't actively growing, early spring or mid-fall.** Now, while you are still expecting lots of fall rain, is a good time. Also, rake up or use a blower-vacuum to clear leaves accumulating on the lawn. Leaving a few leaves to decompose is okay.

## MOWING

Grass growth is slowing. Mow only when the grass is a third taller than the cutting height we recommend for your type of plant. Keep the mower blades sharpened.

## WATERING

October should be wet, but if it isn't, water. For new lawns, water if you have more than seven or eight days without rain.

## FERTILIZING

**Organic fertilizer.** If you didn't make the second fertilization last month, do it now.

**Chemical fertilizer.** If your lawn hasn't done as well as hoped, consider a fifth fertilization a few weeks after the fourth to carry the lawn through winter.

## PESTS

To be effective, a September application of **pre-emergent** broadleaf weed killer to control broadleaf weeds must be repeated in October. That goes for controls for chickweed, bindweed, violets, sorrel, and clover plants. Repeat the September treatment for chinch bugs this month. For controls, turn back to the Pests and Diseases sections in this chapter's introduction.

## Did You Know?

### Leaves and Your Lawn

Leaves are assets. Not one should leave your property. However, matted leaves rob the grass of the sunlight it needs as it continues to grow through fall. Grass grows when the soil is warm, and it will remain warm in our region at least through November, and in Zone 8, even later.
- As long as you can still see the grass blades through the fallen leaves, you can shred them with a mower and leave them on the lawn to decompose into nutrients. To crumble, they must be mowed when dry.
- If or when the leaf layer is such that you can see just a little of the grass, mow, rake up the mess, spread it over annual beds and kitchen gardens, and dig it into the top 6 inches; that's next spring's supply of humus!
- When the leaf layer is about 4 inches deep, suck the leaves up in a blower-vacuum and blow the residue over the surrounding lawn. Or bag the ground leaves, and store them to use next spring as mulch.
- If the leaves get deeper than 4 inches, gather them into leaf bags and put them on your compost pile. (See October in Chapter 9, Trees.)

# NOVEMBER
## Lawns

 ## PLANNING

**If your winters include heavy snow,** lay in a supply of sand, non-clumping kitty litter, or environmentally friendly de-icing products that will enable you to have skid-proof paths and walks without harming the surrounding lawn.

 ## PLANTING

It's too late to seed or sod this year.

## CARE

**Inventory your supply of herbicides, pesticides, and fungicides,** and put them away for the winter.

- Seal herbicides, pesticides, and fungicides in their original containers. It is unwise to transfer them to unmarked containers, and in some states it's illegal.
- Store all in a locked cupboard where they will be safe from the curiosity of children and pets.
- Store granular formulations of all kinds, including fertilizers, in a cool, dry location to keep them in good condition for next year.
- Store liquid formulations away from direct sun and where temperatures do not go down to freezing—otherwise they may deteriorate.

 ## Did You Know?

### About Turfgrasses

Turfgrasses are divided into two categories—cool-season grasses and warm-season grasses.

**Cool-season grass.** Cool-season grasses are those that make the most popular, and appealing, lawns in our region. They peak in spring, go semi-dormant in summer, have a second peak season in mid- and late fall, and go semi-dormant for the winter. The grasses we have recommended in our turfgrass table are cool-season grasses. They come in varieties for full sun, for part-shade, varieties that are okay in both some sun and some shade, varieties for damp spots, for dry spots, and for sand and for clay soils. A knowledgeable person at a nearby nursery or hardware store can help you choose the grass variety that is doing best in your neighborhood. Chances are they are stocking what is working best. The best time to plant a cool-season grass is in late summer around Labor Day. It thrives in early fall's still-warm soil and cool, moist weather. Early spring is the second best planting season. Seed will germinate as long as daytime temperatures are 68 to 95 degrees Fahrenheit.

**Warm-season grass.** A warm-season grass peaks in summer and gets its best start planted in late summer. The most familiar warm-season grass is **zoysia,** which turns to gold from the time the temperature hits 55 to 50 degrees Fahrenheit until late May. Once established, it is almost impossible to get rid of, and it will take over any other grass you plant. It has virtues—it is a coarse but rich green spongy mat all summer, resists drought, and is almost immune to weeds. It might be a good choice for a warm Zone 7 summer vacation property.

 ## MOWING

Mow the late-late leaves and let the wind blow the chaff away.

 ## WATERING

Keep areas recently seeded or sodded watered if early November runs dry.

 ## FERTILIZING

Fertilizing is over for the year.

 ## PESTS

Weeds, pests, and disease should be hibernating; you're on vacation!

# DECEMBER
## Lawns

 PLANNING

The giving time is near; draw up a lawn wish list.

 PLANTING

Planting season is over.

 CARE

Get all your lawn gear together and in good shape before you store it. If you have a gas-powered lawn mower, run it until the tank is dry. Drain and replace the oil. Clean the air filter. Oil the spark plugs. Clean and store the engine. Rinse the spreader. Oil the wheels and put it away. Clean spraying equipment too. Store insecticides, fungicides, and such in a frost-free location.

Shovel snow away before spreading de-icing products, and you will use less. Use snowmelt products safe for concrete and safe for grass and plants. Even better, use sand or non-clumping kitty litter.

 Did You Know?

### About Lawn Mowers

A lawn that is more than a half-acre calls for a gas-powered mower. The blades have to be of good enough quality to hold an edge because dull blades harm the grass. Electric mowers are lighter and quiet but suited only to smaller lawns; the farther you drag the cord, the lower the voltage, the slower the mower. Battery-powered electric mowers are heavier but not limited by the length of the cord. Riding mowers make sense if the lawn is over an acre. If you have several acres to maintain, make it a tractor mower that can till, scoop snow, and pull large loads.

**Reel mower.** A reel mower cuts with a scissor-like action and does the best job when the blades are sharp. Dull, it tears and mashes the leaves and causes the tips to brown. A reel mower is a good choice for a lawn that is level and cut regularly. The cost and maintenance may be higher than a rotary mower.

**Rotary mower.** A flat, circular blade rotating very quickly lops off the grass. The machine is easily maneuvered and does a fine job if the blades are sharpened regularly. If the blades aren't sharp, the lawn next day may look scorched or singed. Also, the whirling blades can be dangerous, so allow only adults wearing closed-toe shoes to operate it.

**Mulching mower.** A mower built for mulching has four blades rather than two, and re-cuts the grass as it moves, leaving behind very fine clippings that decompose and feed the lawn. It also grinds dry leaves finely in the fall. To work most efficiently, it must move slowly, and the turf must be dry.

 MOWING

Mowing is long ceased.

 WATERING

Watering season is over. Drain and store the hoses before freezing weather.

 FERTILIZING

**Organic fertilizer.** An optional third application can be made this month or next if you find your lawn can use extra help.

PESTS

They're waiting for spring. Happy holidays!

# CHAPTER SIX

# Perennials

*The garden's jewel box is filled with perennials. Given a good start, a perennial grows more beautiful every year.*

Choose perennials suited to your zone and place them where their light needs are met, and you'll love the results. Where winter comes early and stays late, look for late-blooming varieties of spring-flowering species. Where frosts can happen as early as September, choose early-blooming varieties of the summer flowers.

Most flowering perennials need a full sun location, six to eight hours of direct sun from 10 a.m. through mid-afternoon. Plants that can take shade need the bright shade under a tall tree or all-day dappled light under a tree with open branching. In Zones 3 and 4, perennials growing in full sun generally can stand a little more cold.

**The ideal perennial garden includes:**

• Flowers that bloom in spring, summer, and fall. Our perennials list can help you locate those that are just right for your garden.

• Foliage plants for color and diversity, including ornamental grasses (see Chapter 10) and ferns.

• Small evergreens to anchor the composition and to keep it green in winter.

## PLANNING

**When will it bloom?** Most perennials come into bloom their second season and grow fuller each year until they need dividing (see below). Only a few perennials will bloom the first year from seed. To be sure of a show of flowers the first season, buy big container-grown root divisions or second-year seedlings. Generally speaking, the larger the crown (and container and price) the fuller will be the floral display that year. If the perennial that you are interested in blooms in early or mid-spring—**columbine,** for example—you'll get more flowers the first spring if you set out a container-grown specimen the preceding late August or early September than if you plant it in early spring.

Some catalogs ship perennials in spring "bare root," with planting instructions—**astilbes,** for instance. In our experience, these often flower fully only in the second or even third season.

When you need lots of a particular perennial—**catmint** to edge a big bed, for example—seeds are the way to go. You can start seeds in flats indoors or in a cold frame, but most don't germinate as quickly as seeds for annuals. (See the January pages of the Annuals chapter.) Perennials can also be started from seed in the garden or a cold frame, either in spring two weeks after the last frost date or in early summer up to two months before the first frost date. When fall sowing is recommended on a seed packet, it usually means those seeds will benefit from a chilling period. The process, called "stratification," is described in November.

## PLANTING

**Soil for perennials.** The "good garden loam" perennials thrive in is more often created than inherited. The solution to assorted soil problems, including rocky soil and poor drainage, is to grow

# Perennials

perennials in raised beds enriched with organic additives. You will find information about adjusting soil pH, additives for soil, and creating new and raised beds under Soil Preparation and Improvement in the Introduction.

**Planting procedures.** Whether you are planting in the soft soil of a new raised bed or preparing a planting hole in an established perennial border, make the hole three times the diameter of the rootball, and twice as deep.

If you are preparing a planting hole in an established bed, test and amend the soil pH as when preparing a raised bed (see Soil Preparation and Improvement in the Introduction to the book) and then mix in 3 to 4 inches of humus, enough so that a quarter of the soil is organic matter. Mix in a slow-release organic fertilizer, half-fill the hole with the amended soil, and tamp it down firmly.

Free the plant from matted roots circling the rootball. If you can't untangle them, make four shallow vertical slashes in the sides and slice off the bottom half inch. Dip the rootball in a bucket containing starter solution. Half-fill the hole with improved soil. Set the plant a little high in the hole. Fill the hole with improved soil, and tamp firmly. Water slowly and deeply, and then apply a 2- to 3-inch layer of mulch starting 3 inches from the crown.

The spacing between perennials depends on the size of the plant when mature. Edging plants under a foot tall need 12 to 18 inches all around. Intermediate sizes—1 to 1½ feet tall—which is most perennials—need 18 to 24 inches between plants. Larger plants need be about 3 feet apart. **Hostas** and **daylilies** need 24 to 30 inches. **Peonies** need 3 to 4 feet. Cool climate gardeners find that close planting shades out weeds.

When summer is over, we like to leave in place healthy seed-bearing perennials with woody upright structures, like **black-eyed Susans**. They're interesting in the winter, and they provide seeds for the birds. Some self-sow and will refurnish your bed.

In the fall, clear away perennials' dead foliage; cut it off, don't pull it off because pulling may damage the crown beneath. Look before you leap; be careful not to damage burgeoning stems.

**Maintenance.** To sustain growth and satisfying bloom, your perennials need a continuous supply of nutrients. The fertilization schedule for established beds begins in late winter or early spring. After that, how often you fertilize depends on the type of fertilizer you are using. (See Understanding Fertilizers in the Introduction to the book.)

Here's an overview of the annual maintenance needs of a perennial bed:

*1* Before growth begins in late winter and early spring, clean up the beds, test and adjust the pH, fertilize and refurbish the soil. (See Soil pH in the Introduction to the book.)

*2* Maintain a year-round mulch to protect plant roots from heat, cold, and drought. A winter mulch of pine boughs applied after the second hard frost in fall catches leaves and blown debris and saves some tricky raking in spring.

*3* Deadhead and groom the plants during the growing season.

*4* Every few years divide the crowns to keep plants producing and healthy.

*5* Control the problems described in the section on pests and diseases.

*6* Make a final application of fertilizer as growth slows at the end of the growing season: Zones 3 and 4, usually about August 15; Zone 5, early September; Zones 6 and 7, early September to early October.

*7* Throughout the season, early spring to mid-fall, edge beds that are not protected by some form of barrier to prevent grasses and weeds from invading. Use an edger to create a trench 4 to 8 inches deep.

# Perennials

In addition to an annual check of the pH, every three to five years we recommend an application of rock phosphate, green sand, and where there is clay, of gypsum. These are the granular soil additives recommended for preparing a new planting bed. Just measure the products into a bucket, mix them, and with your fingers scratch them into the soil a quarter inch deep.

## FERTILIZERS

**If you are using organic fertilizers,** such as Holly-tone or Plant-tone, then you will need to fertilize the first time about four to six weeks before growth is due to begin in spring, and then again as the growing season is ending.

**If you are using time- or controlled-release chemical fertilizers,** you will need to fertilize just before the plants start to grow and to repeat according to the formula inscribed on the fertilizer container. If you use a nine-month formula, that should carry you through the whole growth season.

**If you are using granular chemical fertilizers,** then you will need to fertilize just before growth begins in spring, and repeat every six weeks until the end of the growing season.

## STAKING

Most tall perennials that are spaced properly, fertilized organically, and not stuck on a windy hill won't need staking. Wide spacing improves the plants' access to light and air, and that strengthens the stems. Weak growth is often the result of force-feeding with non-organic fertilizers. However, **delphiniums, lilies,** the tallest **dahlias,** and some other very big perennials usually do need staking.

When you set out a new plant that needs staking—or when an established plant that will be very tall starts to grow—insert a stake in the soil as close as possible to the crown and as tall as the plant will grow to be. Tie the

Staking
Perennials

main stem loosely to the stake with soft green wool, raffia, cotton string, wool yarn, or strips of pantyhose. As the plant grows, keep tying the main stem and branches onto the stake higher and higher.

## PRUNING, SHEARING, AND DEADHEADING

You can improve the performance and health of some perennials by selective pruning, shearing, and deadheading. Our suggestions appear in the month-by-month pages that follow.

For some perennials, pruning or shearing early in the growth cycle keeps plants compact and encourages later and more, though usually smaller, blooms. Removing fading and dead blooms—deadheading—stops the development of seeds and, in most cases, results in more flowers.

Shearing is the way to deadhead plants with very small flowers—**creeping phlox, miniature pinks, baby's-breath,** for example. The quick and easy way to deadhead larger blooms is by pinching them out. Just place your thumbnail and forefinger in back of the bracts—the small scale-like leaves behind the petals—and squeeze the flower head off. If the flower stems are too thick to pinch out, snip them off with small pruning shears sold for the purpose.

# Perennials

Pruning and shearing also helps the health of some plants attacked by leafminer and mildew. Cut the diseased foliage to the ground and discard it. The new foliage should grow in clean.

## WATERING AND MULCHING

**Watering.** Sustained moisture makes nutrients in the soil available and is essential to the unchecked growth and health of perennials.

When you plant a perennial, put down 1½ inches of water right after planting. New plants and established flower beds need 1½ inches of gentle rain or slow, deep, gently watering every ten days to two weeks.

Between July and August, you will likely have to water perennials regularly. In fall, just before the ground freezes, water the perennials thoroughly.

**Mulching.** We recommend keeping a 2- to 3-inch layer of mulch around perennials. Deeper mulch may bury the crown and kill some perennials. (See Mulch in the Introduction to the book.) Start the mulch a few inches from the crown, and spread it out over an area wider than the plant's diameter. That is enough to minimize the loss of soil moisture—saving water and the time applying it—and to moderate soil temperatures. For year-round use, we recommend organic mulches such as shredded bark and pine needles (which can be piled a little deeper) because they add humus and nutrients to the soil as they decompose.

Replenish the mulch after the late winter/early spring fertilization.

The need for a winter mulch depends on the severity of your climate, the hardiness of the plants, and the exposure of the beds. In Zone 6, the main purpose of winter mulch is to keep the perennials from heaving out of the ground as the ground freezes and thaws in winter and early spring. In Zone 7, a winter mulch can save perennials that are borderline hardy during especially severe winters. Apply a winter mulch only after the ground has frozen hard, and remove it when you first spot signs of active growth in the plants.

We recommend airy organics such as straw or pine boughs as a winter mulch. Apply the mulch so you can see the plant through it. For coastal dwellers, marsh hay and salt hay from the shore are excellent winter mulches as they are weed free, and they can be saved, covered in a pile, from year to year.

## DIVIDING AND MOVING PERENNIALS

You can help your perennials stay healthy and productive by dividing and replanting them every few years. Division forces the crowns to grow new roots, and replanting provides an opportunity to refurbish the soil. A new planting hole generally has freshly amended soil—and the plant benefits.

We divide when we need more of a plant, typically **heuchera, catmint,** and other edgers.

A plant needs dividing when it is producing fewer and smaller blooms or when the crown is pushing up and stems look crowded and leggy. **Many perennials benefit from division every five or six years.**

You can divide in early spring before growth begins. But the best time to divide most perennials is toward the end of the growing season—late summer, before and around Labor Day. The soil will be warm enough for several weeks ahead to keep existing roots growing while new roots are developing. In Zones 3 and 4, divide around August 15. In Zone 5, about September 1. In Zone 6, most perennials can be divided September 1 to September 15. In Zone 7, divide September 1 to mid-October.

**There's more than one way to divide a crown.** For the gardener who wants to multiply his/her supply, the most profitable way is to lift the whole crown with a spading fork, and with a shovel or an edger, divide the crown into two or more pieces. While waiting to replant, keep the divisions moist and out of the sun. This method is best for perennials that have very hard crowns.

For the method that is easiest on the gardener: with a shovel, chop through the center of the crown and dig up one half. Amend and fertilize the soil around the section that is to remain where it is; it will grow on in lively fashion. Replant the other section in improved soil. We recommend this method for **peonies** and other perennials slow to recover from being moved. This method allows for reproduction without interrupting the blooming cycle of the garden.

## PESTS AND DISEASES

**Weeds.** Keep weeds out of flower beds to eliminate competition for water and nutrients, to keep air moving in the garden, to avoid pests and diseases inherent to some perennials, and to keep the garden looking beautiful.

**Deer and rodents.** Deer prefer most all perennials, and especially **hostas.** So far they are snubbing **ornamental grasses, ferns,** and perennials with dainty foliage and tiny flowers, **baby's-breath,** for example. The deterrents we've tried keep deer away only until

they realize smelly sprays and flashing lights are not hazardous to their health. Changing the deterrent every six weeks is some help. Dogs, electric fences, and deer fences work . . . up to a point.

To keep **rabbits, woodchucks,** and other rodents away from your flower beds, try chemical fungicide formulations such as Thiram (Arasan) and hot pepper wax.

**If you see signs of vole or mole activity, bait the main runway with a rodenticide. See the October pages for more information.**

**Insects and diseases.** Pests, such as aphids, caterpillars, beetles, and mealybugs, and diseases, such as powdery mildew, root and stem rot, rust disease, and spider mites, can afflict perennials. Keep an eye out for these problems. Look in Pests, Diseases, and Controls in the Appendix for solutions.

## Did You Know?

### The Love Language of the Flowers

For the Victorians, floral valentines spoke volumes because each flower has meaning in the language of the flowers. The language was invented by Persian courtiers, and its influence is present whenever a lover sends roses to a sweetheart.

- **Anemone**—abandoned
- **Bachelor's-button**—single and blessed
- **Bluebell**—faithfulness
- **Blue salvia**—think of you
- **Carnation white**—love
- **Carnation red**—alas, for my poor heart
- **Forget-me-not**—love that is true
- **Hyacinth white**—beauty
- **Jonquil**—desiring a return of affection
- **Lily-of-the-valley**—happiness returns
- **Pansy**—my thoughts are with you
- **Peach blossom**—I am captive
- **Pink single**—love that is pure
- **Rose**—love
- **Rose yellow**—jealousy
- **Tulip**—love

# Perennials

| Common Name (*Botanical Name*) | Hardiness Zones | Bloom Time | Light | Height | Description |
|---|---|---|---|---|---|
| **Adam's Needle** (*Yucca filamentosa* 'Bright Edge') | 5 to 9 | Summer | Full sun | Foliage 2 feet; flowers 5 feet | Rosette of spine-tipped, sword-shaped leaves; spikes of creamy bell-shaped flowers. |
| **Artemisia** (*Artemisia* spp. and cvs.) | 3 to 8 | Foliage plant | Sun | 12 to 36 inches | Luminous all-season silver or gray foliage. |
| **Aster** (*Aster* x *frikartii*) | 5 to 8 | July and August | Sun, part sun | 18 to 30 inches | Small ray-flowers. Recommended are dark blue 'Monch' and lavender-blue 'Wonder of Staff'. In Zone 4, plant *A. novae-belgii* cultivars. |
| **Astilbe** (*Astilbe* x *arendsii* and cvs.) | 4 to 8 | Summer | Part sun | 14 to 36 inches | Fernlike foliage; feathery flower spires in off-white, pastels, deep reds, burgundies, fuchsias. A favorite: little *A. chinensis*. |
| **Baby's Breath** (*Gypsophila paniculata*) | 3 to 8 | June to August | Full sun | 3 to 4 feet | Tiny white or pink florets on airy stems. A favorite: trailing *G. repens*. |
| **Balloon Flower, Japanese Bellflower** (*Platycodon grandiflorus* var. *mariesii*) | 3 to 8 | Summer to early fall | Full sun | 12 to 24 inches | Starry flowers in blue, white, or lilac pink. |
| **Barrenwort** (*Epimedium* spp. and cvs.) | 5 to 8 | Spring | Bright shade | 12 to 15 inches | Attractive foliage. The flowers are graceful sprays in red, pink, lavender, yellow, or white shapes like miniature columbines. Forms a lovely mat. |
| **Beebalm** (*Monarda* spp. and cvs.) | 4 to 8 | Late June through August | Sun, part shade | 2 to 4 feet | Attracts butterflies and bees. Red, pink mop-head flowers. Plant mildew-resistant cultivars. A favorite: 'Raspberry Wine'. |
| **Bellflower** (*Campanula* spp. and cvs.) | 3 to 8 | Late May, early June | Sun, part shade | 4 to 36 inches | Many sizes of bell-shaped flowers in blues, white, pink. May rebloom if deadheaded. |
| **Black-eyed Susan** (*Rudbeckia fulgida* 'Goldsturm') | Most 3 to 9 | July through September | Sun | 2 to 3 feet | Classic yellow daisy flower. Attracts butterflies and goldfinches. Disease-resistant. |
| **Blazing Star, Spike Gayfeather** (*Liatris spicata*) | Most 4 to 9 | July and August | Sun | 2 to 3 feet | Fuzzy purple or white flower spikes, grassy foliage. Long-lived, reintroduced native. A favorite: 'Kobold'. |
| **Bleeding Heart** (*Dicentra eximia*) | 3 to 8 | April/May sporadically in summer | Part shade or shade | 12 to 18 inches | Very pretty, heart-shaped pink or white flowers dangle from thin stems above feathery foliage. |
| **Blue False Indigo, Wild Blue Indigo** (*Baptisia australis*) | 3 to 8 | Spring | Sun | 24 to 30 inches | Shrub-like. Spikes of indigo-blue flowers followed by dark blue pods' handsome foliage. |
| **Bluestar** (*Amsonia hubrechtii*) | 6 to 9 | Spring | Sun | 1 to 3 feet | Drooping or upright clusters of pale blue flowers. The foliage turns bright gold in fall. For Vermont try *A. tabernaemontana*. |
| **Brunnera, False Forget-Me-Not** (*Brunnera macrophylla*) | 4 to 7 | Spring | Sun, part shade | 12 to 16 inches | Airy stems of dainty, blue florets; handsome foliage. Good ground cover. Needs moist soil. |

# Perennials

| Common Name (*Botanical Name*) | Hardiness Zones | Bloom Time | Light | Height | Description |
|---|---|---|---|---|---|
| **Bugbane** (*Cimicifuga racemosa*) | 3 to 4 | July | Part shade | 4 to 6 feet | Spikes of bottlebrush blooms. *C. simplex* blooms in fall. |
| **Butterfly Weed** (*Asclepias tuberosa*) | 3 to 9 | Spring, summer | Sun, part sun | 24 to 30 inches | Flat heads of fragrant orange florets attractive to butterflies and bees. Good for a wild garden. |
| **Candytuft** (*Iberis sempervirens*) | 3 to 9 | Late May | Sun | 8 to 12 inches | Beautiful, dark green edger; white flowers. May rebloom if sheared after flowering. |
| **Catmint** (*Nepeta faassenii* 'Walker's Low') | 3 to 9 | June till frosts | Sun, part shade | 12 to 15 inches | Aromatic foliage covered with lavender blue florets from late June on. |
| **Chrysanthemum, Garden Mum** (*Chrysanthemum* x *morifolium*) | 3 to 7 | August to October | Sun | 1 to 3 feet | Lots of bright fall colors, shapes. In cool Vermont try the most reliable, 'Clara Curtis' and 'Mary Stoker'. |
| **Columbine** (*Aquilegia* spp. and cvs.) | 3 to 8 | May | Sun, part shade | 1 to 3 feet | Elegant, delicate plants. Flowers are cups with spurs in blues, white, yellow, reds. |
| **Coral Bells** (*Heuchera* spp. and cvs.) | Most 3 to 8 | May and June | Sun, part shade | 2 feet | Low; sprays of tiny bell flowers on long stems. 'Purple Robe' and 'Chocolate Ruffles' are favorites. 'Marmalade' is brilliant. |
| **Cranesbill, Hardy Geranium** (*Geranium* spp. and cvs.) | Most 4 to 8 | May to July | Sun, part shade, shade | 6 inches to 2 feet | White, pink, blue, magenta flowers. Try *G. sanguineum striatum*, *G. macrorrhizum* 'Ingwersen's', and *G. cantabrigiense* 'St. Olga'. |
| **Daylily** (*Hemerocallis* cvs.) | Most 4 to 9 | June through September | Sun, bright shade | 1 to 4 feet | Trumpet flowers in yellow, red, orange, salmon, pink, lilac, and cream above fountain-like foliage. |
| **Evening Primrose, Sundrops** (*Oenothera* spp. and cvs.) | 4 to 9 | Spring and summer | Sun | 18 to 24 inches | Showy, enduring cup-shaped flowers. *O. fruticosa*, and other evening primroses, are mostly golden, bloom evening, and close in morning. Sundrops are day-bloomers; *O. speciosa* 'Rosea' is a soft pink. |
| **Foamflower** (*Tiarella* spp. and cvs.) | 3 to 8 | April and May | Bright shade | 8 inches | Dainty attractive foliage and fluffy flower spikes in white or pink. |
| **Globe Thistle** (*Echinops ritro* 'Taplow Blue') | 3 to 7 | Summer to early fall | Sun, part sun | 2 to 4 feet | Thistle-like foliage, globe-shaped bluish flowers. Great for texture and a lasting late-season display. |
| **Goldenrod** (*Solidago* spp. and cvs.) | 4 to 9 | Mid-summer to fall | Sun, part shade | 2 to 4 feet | Feathery spikes of yellow. Attracts butterflies and beneficial insects. Good cut, fresh, or dried. |
| **Heliopsis** (*Heliopsis helianthoides* cvs.) | 3 to 9 | Summer, fall | Sun | 3 to 4 feet | Showy, bright yellow, ray flowers; coarse foliage. Reseeds. |
| **Hellebore, Lenten Rose** (*Helleborus orientalis*) | 6 to 8 | March to April | Part shade, shade | 15 to 20 inches | Nodding cream, maroon, green speckled, open-cupped flowers among glossy, deeply divided leaves. Winter interest plus early flowering. |

# Perennials

| Common Name (Botanical Name) | Hardiness Zones | Bloom Time | Light | Height | Description |
|---|---|---|---|---|---|
| **Hosta, Plantain Lily** (*Hosta* spp. and cvs.) | 3 to 8 | July to September | Part shade, shade | 6 to 36 inches | Variegated, ruffled, or rippled foliage in greens, blue-green, yellow, chartreuse. Deer and slug favorites. |
| **Japanese Anemone** (*Anemone hupehensis* var. *japonica*) | 5 to 8 | Summer and early fall | Sun, part shade | 2 to 3 feet | Multi-branching stems of airy flowers in pink, rose, white. *A. tomentosa* 'Robustissima' survives in Zone 4. |
| **Lady's Mantle** (*Alchemilla mollis*) | 3 to 7 | Spring and early summer | Sun, shade | 1 foot | Beautiful foliage; clusters of yellow flowers. After rain the leaves hold luminous beads of water. Charming. |
| **Lamb's Ear** (*Stachys byzantina*) | 4 to 8 | Foliage plant | Sun, part shade | 12 inches | Almost luminous silver-gray foliage with a furry texture. |
| **Lavender, Common Lavender** (*Lavandula angustifolia*) | 4/5 to 9 | Late spring and summer | Full sun | 10 to 24 inches | Sweetly aromatic foliage. Entire plant is perfumed. 'Hidcote' is one of the hardiest. Cut back hard in spring. |
| **Lily** (*Lilium* spp. and cvs.) | 4 to 8 | Early to late summer | Sun | 30 to 40 inches | Stately stems topped by large, bugle-shaped flowers. Colors are white, yellow, crimson, and combinations. |
| **Lilyturf** (*Liriope muscari* cvs.) | 5 to 10 | Spring to mid-summer | Sun to part shade | 12 to 18 inches | Grassy clumps topped by spikes of blue, purple, lavender, or white florets. Cultivars include 'Royal Purple', 'Gold Banded', and 'John Burch'. |
| **Lupine** (*Lupinus* Russell cvs.) | 4 to 9 | Spring to summer | Sun, part shade | 3 to 4 feet | Tall stately spires; pea-like flowers in many shades and bicolors. |
| **Marsh Rose Mallow** (*Hibiscus moscheutos*) | 4/5 to 9 | Mid-summer | Sun, bright shade | 3 to 6 feet | Shrubby; flowers 6 to 10 inches across in deep crimson, white, pink, and bicolors. |
| **Meadow Rue** (*Thalictrum aquilegifolium*) | 4 to 8 | Spring | Sun | 3 to 4 feet | Scalloped blue-green foliage topped by sprays in tender lavender-blue. Tall. Favorites: *T. flavum* and *T. rochebruniaum* 'Lavender Mist'. |
| **Monkshood** (*Aconitum* spp.) | 3 to 7 | Late summer and fall | Sun | 2 to 3 feet | Tall with deeply divided foliage topped by spires of white or blue flowers. All parts are poisonous. *A. napellus* blooms early July to August. |
| **Montauk Daisy** (*Nipponanthemum nipponicum*)) | 5 to 9 | Late summer | Sun | 2 to 5 feet | Glossy foliage and white daisies. Excellent shore plant naturalized on Long Island. |
| **Oriental Poppy** (*Papaver orientalis* and cvs.) | 2 to 7 | Spring, early summer | Sun | 2 to 3 feet | Big, silky flowers with a dark central blotch; colors are red, orange, pink, salmon, white, and bicolors. |
| **Peony** (*Paeonia* spp. and cvs.) | 4 to 8 | May to June | Sun, part shade | 2 to 3 feet | Fragrant silky flowers in reds, pinks, white, and yellow. Long-lived and carefree. |
| **Phlox, Garden Phlox, Summer Phlox** (*Phlox paniculata*) | 4 to 8 | July and August | Full sun | 24 to 40 inches | Strong pastels and white flowers. New mildew-resistant cultivars white 'David' and 'Miss Lingard'; pink 'Eva Cullum' and 'Rosalinde'. |
| **Pinks, Cottage Pinks** (*Dianthus plumarius*) | 4 to 8 | June and July | Sun | 12 to 18 inches | Narrow, grayish foliage. Fragrant white, red, pink, bicolored flowers. |

# Perennials

| Common Name (*Botanical Name*) | Hardiness Zones | Bloom Time | Light | Height | Description |
|---|---|---|---|---|---|
| **Primrose** (*Primula* x *polyantha*) | 3 to 8 | April to May | Part shade | 6 to 12 inches | Enduring, open-faced flowers in pastels and crayon colors with yellow centers. |
| **Purple Coneflower** (*Echinacea purpurea* and cvs.) | 3 to 9 | July to August | Sun | 2 to 4 feet | Purple-petaled daisy with dark orange center. 'Fragrant Angel' is a new luminous white. |
| **Russian Sage** (*Perovskia atriplicifolia*) | 5 to 9 | Summer, early fall | Full sun | To 36 inches tall | Fine, branching stems covered with powder-blue florets. Silver in winter. |
| **Salvia** (*Salvia nemerosa* 'May Night') | 5 to 8 | Late spring, early summer | Sun | 18 to 24 inches | Bushy perennial that bears masses of dark blue-purple flowering spikes. 'Snow Hill' is a new white. |
| **Shasta Daisy** (*Chrysanthemum* x *superbum*) | 4 to 8 | July to frosts | Sun, part shade | 1 to 3 feet; there are dwarf varieties | Big classy white daisy. Attracts butterflies and beneficial insects. Easy care and very long blooming. |
| **Siberian Iris** (*Iris sibirica* and cvs.) | 3 to 8 | Late spring and early summer | Sun to part sun | 24 to 40 inches | Slim, grassy leaves and clusters of two and three flowers. Fall foliage is russet-gold and an asset in winter. |
| **Solomon's Seal, Variegated Japanese** (*Polygonatum odoratum* 'Variegatum') | 3 to 9 | Spring | Shade | 2 to 3 feet | Arching woodland plant; variegated foliage and bell-shaped flowers that dangle in pairs, followed by blue-black fruits. |
| **Spotted Dead Nettle** (*Lamium maculatum* cvs.) | 3 to 8 | Spring flowers and colorful foliage all season | Bright shade or shade | 12 to 15 inches | Variegated foliage plant; makes an attractive ground cover with perennials. Reddish, purple, pink, or white flowers. |
| **Spurge** (*Euphorbia epithymoides, E. dulcis, E. griffithii*) | 5 to 9 | Spring | Sun | 15 to 18 inches | Clumping foliage plant; narrow leaves and yellow flower-like bracts all spring. Foliage turns reddish in fall. Okay at the seashore. |
| **Stoke's Aster** (*Stokesia laevis* cvs.) | 4 to 9 | Summer, late summer | Sun | 12 to 14 inches | Big, sprawling; large lavender blue flowers that combine the beauty of a thistle with the charm of a fluffy aster. |
| **Stonecrop** (*Sedum* 'Autumn Joy') | 3 to 8 | August to October | Sun, part shade | 2 feet | 'Autumn Joy' is tall; flower heads change from jade green to rosy russet in fall. Many other hybrids and species are useful. |
| **Tickseed** (*Coreopsis verticillata* cvs.) | 6 to 9 | All summer | Sun | 1 to 2 feet | Dainty mounds of airy foliage covered with masses of small airy flowers in yellow or pink. |
| **Veronica Speedwell** (*Veronica* spp. and cvs.) | 4 to 8 | June and July | Sun | 1 to 3 feet | Spires of blue, pink, or white florets. Attracts butterflies. Self-seeding can be a problem. |
| **Yarrow, Fern-leaved Yarrow** (*Achillea filipendula* cvs.) | 3 to 8 | July until frost | Full sun | 18 to 24 inches | Aromatic foliage and flat canary-yellow flowerheads. *A. millifolium* cultivars come in glowing colors. |

See November for the plants that have been selected Plant of the Year by the Perennial Plant Association.

## PLANNING

We've visited and written about hundreds, literally, of exceptional gardens. Most needed between eight and fifteen years to mature before they even began to satisfy the gardener's vision. The first few years, the gardeners spent getting the foundation plants into the ground—placing the blocks of major flowering and foliage plants. The next many years they spent moving the plants around, trying for situations and combinations that would fulfill the dream of a garden colorful and interesting, spring through fall.

If you have in mind moving some plants this spring, spend some time now with your garden books and catalogs and make a spring planting and moving plan. If you will be adding plants, try for species and cultivars that have more than one asset.

If you haven't yet grown **daylilies,** make a New Year's resolution to explore their potential. Daylilies bring a lot to the party. From spring through fall, the foliage adds the grace and movement of an ornamental grass, and the flowers keep blooming in the garden in the difficult mid-summer months. Most varieties bloom July through August, but a few flowers open as early as June. **Large-flowered** daylilies typically open one to three blossoms per stem every day; the **miniatures** open three to seven blossoms per stem every day. Daylilies thrive in clay, loam, or sandy soils and tolerate heat, wind, cold, and seashore conditions.

Here's how to grow daylilies:

- **Planting season.** The best planting time is spring. Soak the bare-root divisions two to six hours before planting; plant container-grown daylilies any time, but early spring is still best.

- **Light.** Daylilies bloom most fully in full sun but do well in bright shade.

- **Planting.** Prepare beds or planting holes in improved soil (see Soil Preparation and Improvement in the Introduction to the book). For fertilizer, use Plant-tone.

- **Bare-root.** Fan the roots out in the planting hole, and set the crown so it is about 1 inch below the soil surface.

- **Container-grown.** Set the crown so it is about an inch above the surface of the surrounding soil.

- **Spacing.** Set them 24 inches apart for miniatures, 36 inches apart for large daylilies.

- **Watering.** Water gently and thoroughly after planting. The first season, water weekly unless it rains. Water established daylilies in periods of drought.

- **Mulch.** Spread pine needles, pine bark, or hardwood bark 2 to 3 inches deep, starting 3 inches from the crown.

- **Fertilizing.** Fertilize in early spring and in fall as recommended in the introduction to this chapter.

- **Watch out for deer!** Cover the plants with chicken wire or mesh when they start to grow. Deer also gobble the blooms of cultivated daylilies but can't be bothered with wild daylilies.

## PLANTING

It's too early to plant anything but not too early to decide whether you want to try starting seeds indoors. Seed packets and the blurbs in many garden catalogs tell you whether and when the seeds can be started early indoors. (See starting seeds indoors in the January pages of the Annuals chapter.)

*If you have in mind moving some plants this spring, spend some time now with your garden books and catalogs and make a spring planting and moving plan. If you will be adding plants, try for species that have more than one asset.*

## CARE

If you are without snow cover, make the rounds of your perennial beds to see if there are crowns that have been heaved. If yes, gently heel them in, and cover them with a winter mulch of evergreen boughs to keep the ground cold until winter ends. If there has been heaving, also cover the crowns of **mums, veronica,** and other perennials with foliage showing.

Use only snowmelt products that don't harm plants, turf, and concrete.

## PRUNING

Prune back **ornamental grasses** that are looking weather-beaten. Use shears to cut back the low-growing grasses and new plantings of the big grasses to within a few inches of the crown. When a big grass begins to mature, simplify the annual haircut by roping the leaves together with sisal twine. Tie them all the way to the top so that they end up looking like a telephone pole. Then saw the top off a few inches above the crown. If you use a chain saw (as you must when a big grass reaches full size) take care not to catch the twine in the teeth!

## WATERING

**Indoors.** Water often enough to sustain moisture in big containers of tropical (cold-tender) perennials stored indoors for the winter.

## FERTILIZING

No fertilizing this month.

## PESTS

Damping off is a threat to seedlings started indoors. It's a fungal disease that attacks the seedlings at the base of their stems. It rots the stems so the plants fall over. A sterile growing medium and good drainage help avoid the condition. The fungicide Thiram (Arasan) is a good preventative against damping off.

# FEBRUARY
## Perennials

 **PLANNING**

While the cold keeps you housebound, **look through garden catalogs for summer-flowering bulbs, tender tropicals, aromatic herbs, dwarf evergreens, and flowering trees** that can enhance the seasonal color, structure, and texture of your perennial borders. Study your garden through the windows and decide what to order now. It's time.

 **PLANTING**

**Indoors.** You can start some perennials indoors from seed this month and next. Some we've had good luck with are **garden mums, delphiniums, catmint, sweet rocket, hollyhocks,** and **phlox.** For instructions, see Starting Seeds Indoors in the Planting section of the January page of the Annuals chapter.

**Outdoors.** If the weather permits planting, by the end of the month you could sow seeds outdoors of perennials that need to be stratified, or chilled, in order to germinate. The November pages explain stratification.

 **CARE**

**Indoors.** When seedlings started indoors become crowded, transplant each to an individual 3- to 4-inch pot filled with a sterile, commercial potting mix. Give seedlings to be grown indoors six weeks in the best light available. An installation of grow lights burned fourteen to sixteen hours a day is helpful.

Check snow-free flowers beds for plants heaved by thaw and freeze cycles, and press the crowns back into place. Add a light, winter mulch to plants that have been heaved and those that retain green foliage during winter—for example, **garden mums, candytuft, basket-of-gold.**

 **PRUNING**

Cut off battered **hellebore** foliage to make space for new growth and flowering.

Cut back the **ornamental grasses** before growth begins.

 **WATERING**

Water transplanted seedlings started indoors when the soil is dry to the touch.

Maintain the soil moisture in containers of **tropical perennials** stored indoors.

 **FERTILIZING**

**Indoors.** Every two weeks fertilize (with a soluble houseplant fertilizer at half strength) all the seedlings that will remain indoors another six weeks or more. Do not fertilize transplanted seedlings until the appearance of two or three new leaves tells you the root system is growing again.

 **PESTS**

**Indoors.** Seedlings started indoors that are crowded or lack good drainage and air may show symptoms of damping off, which rots stems near the soil surface. Discard affected plants, reduce watering, and increase light and fresh air. If the problem persists, mist the seedlings with a fungicide, such as Thiram (Arasan).

# MARCH
## Perennials

## PLANNING

Take advantage of sales early this month to buy fertilizers, other soil additives, and mulch. But be cautious. If the price is a steal, make sure the bag is unbroken. Moisture that gets into bags of coco hulls, for example, encourages mildew.

When the snow leaves the garden beds, take a set of markers to the garden and reserve space for the plants you have ordered. Outline planting bays reserved for annuals, and plant row markers indicating the flowers you plan to put there.

Take advantage of a warm spell to clean the birdhouses. If mosquitoes have been a problem, consider installing houses for purple martins and also for bats.

## PLANTING

If bare-root perennials arrive too soon for planting, store them in their packaging in a dark, cool but frost-free place.

## CARE

As soon as you can, rake up the perennial borders to get them ready for their first annual application of fertilizer. Adjust or repair barriers that are edging beds. Edge beds that are not protected by some form of barrier.

## PRUNING

**Indoors.** Transplant seedlings as they outgrow their planting pockets. Pinch out the growing tips of leggy seedlings.

**Outdoors.** When the snow has gone, prune the cold-season **ornamental grasses** (those that shoot up early).

## WATERING

**Indoors.** Continue watering seedlings started indoors. Keep the soil damp in containers of cold-tender and tropical perennials wintering indoors.

## FERTILIZING

Perennials need to be fertilized every year. When to fertilize depends on the type of fertilizer you are using. The section on Understanding Fertilizers in the Introduction to the book explains that. You can start preparing the beds for their annual fertilization as soon as winter cold and moisture have left the ground.

Clear away and discard the plant debris from the previous year. Then:

- Check and adjust the soil pH.

- If you are using organic fertilizers, apply them as soon as you can work the ground.

- If you are using chemical fertilizers, apply them just before growth begins.

- If you are using time-release fertilizers, wait until just before growth begins and apply a nine-month formulation.

**Container gardens of perennials.** Before growth begins, top-dress the soil by scratching in an inch or two of humus and potting soil that includes a nine-month formulation of a slow-release fertilizer.

Fertilize the soil around **ornamental grasses** before growth with a slow-release, organic fertilizer such as Hollytone or Espoma, an organic lawn food.

We find it beneficial to dust wood ashes from our fireplaces over the soil around the crowns (but not the crowns themselves) of **peonies, delphiniums, campanula, dianthus, lamb's ears,** 'Silver King' and other **artemisias, Madonna** and **Martagon (turk's cap) lilies;** don't get wood ashes (or lime) near the other **lilies** or **Japanese irises.**

## PESTS

When the forsythias come into bloom, apply a pre-emergent weed killer to the beds of perennials.

If you think you see signs of voles, have a look at October and what is said there about moles and voles.

## PLANNING

As your perennials come into bloom, record the dates in this book or in a garden log; it will help you plan your garden next year.

## PLANTING

**Indoors.** Transplant seedlings started indoors that are outgrowing their containers to larger pots.

**Outdoors.** As soon as the earth has dried some and warmed, you can move plants around in the beds and add new perennials when available. We usually start planting those that are the most cold hardy when the **forsythia** starts to bloom towards the end of the month or early next month. That includes moving **peonies,** though common wisdom says to do it in September.

Plant **astilbe** crowns and other bare-root perennials shipped by mail order as soon as possible after they arrive. Here's how:

*1* Remove the wrapping. Clear away the moist packing materials. Soak the roots as directed by the supplier.

*2* Dig a roomy planting hole large enough to accommodate the roots spread out to their fullest extent.

*3* Improve the soil from the hole with the amendments recommended in the Introduction to the book under Soil Preparation and Improvement.

*4* Build a firm cone of soil in the center of the hole. Make it high enough to place the crown of the plant a half inch or so higher than the level of the surrounding ground.

*5* Center the roots over the cone and spread them out into the hole.

*6* Half-fill the hole with improved soil, and tamp it down. Fill the rest of the way, and tamp that down.

*7* Create a saucer around the crown.

*8* Water the planting slowly, gently, and thoroughly.

*9* Apply mulch 2- to 3- inches deep starting 2 to 3 inches or so from the crown of the plant.

## CARE

In spring the best time to divide or move perennials is before growth begins. Fast-growing perennials—**asters,** *Eupatorium, Helianthus, Heliopsis,* **monarda,** for example—need dividing every four to six years. For how-to information, turn back to the section titled Dividing in the Introduction to this chapter.

In late April, lift and divide the roots of last year's **garden mums.** Discard the old centers, and plant the young shoots in well-prepared soil. You'll get a better show than if you leave them in the same place for years on end.

## PRUNING

**Indoors.** Pinch out the tips of leggy seedlings still growing indoors.

**Outdoors.** Experiment with pinching back branching perennials by half an inch or so to encourage shorter, bushier growth and more (though smaller) flowers. Perennials that benefit from this include **pink turtlehead,** *Veronica spicata,* and **'Autumn Joy' sedum.**

Remove old tired-looking stems from the **hellebores,** but allow the flowers to remain and go to seed as the seeds will drop to the ground and germinate. In May, look for seedlings at the base of the plants and transplant them to a humusy, semi-shaded site.

Your **asters** will be gorgeous if you divide and replant the crowns annually before growth begins: they're heavy feeders and benefit from newly fertilized planting holes rich in compost.

Prune **lavender** back hard to encourage new growth. Cut back **Russian sage** leaving just 6 to 12 inches of woody stem. Pinch out the tips of the new growth when it emerges to encourage bushier growth.

## WATERING

Maintain the soil moisture for seedlings indoors and outdoors and for perennials in containers.

## FERTILIZING

If you are using only chemical fertilizers that are quickly available, you will need to fertilize garden and container plants every six weeks from beginning to end of the growing season.

## PESTS

If your **peonies** were affected by botrytis last year—ugly, blackened patches on the stems and foliage—spray emerging peony tips with Mancozeb or Manzate, fungicides, or ask your garden center to recommend a control for botrytis.

Hoe and rake weeds, particularly around crowns of perennials towards the back of the border where the weeds are less apparent when the garden fills out.

## Did You Know?

### Worm Compost

Worm compost and manure tea made from worm compost are excellent fertilizers. Worm compost kits are available, but you can make one and produce your own. Here's the method recommended by one supplier, the Down to Earth Worm Farm of Greensboro, Vermont:

*1* Provide a waterproof wooden box about 20 x 30 inches. No top needed.

*2* Keep it in a warm basement or closet—60 to 80 degrees Fahrenheit.

*3* Line the box 3 inches deep with damp, shredded and rotting leaves, newspaper, or corrugated cardboard.

*4* Spread over the bed a pound of red wiggler worms, surface-feeding worms recommended for this project.

*5* Mist the bed often enough to keep the top layer damp.

*6* Feed the worms by spreading garbage over the bedding—any soft, moist foods including grains such as cornmeal, **but no** meat, fish, fat, cheese, fruit, vinegar, or vinegar chips. Keep the food moist by covering it with soggy strips of paper. Do not add new food until the previous batch is gone.

*7* Keep the box loosely covered with black plastic: worms prefer the dark.

*8* When the contents of the box have risen to near the top some months later, scoop the upper layer, including the worms, into a holding bed of moist shredded leaves. Harvest the dark grainy compost below—worm castings. Then restart the project.

*9* Worm castings enrich soil and include microbial forms that give it "life." Scratch it in around the plants or make a "tea" and spray over plant foliage.

**Worm castings tea**
- Mix 1/2 cup of worm compost into 1/2 gallon water
- Steep two days
- Strain through a coffee filter and pour into a misting bottle.

Deer graze on emerging **daylily** foliage. Spray with Deer-Off or some other evil-smelling liquid to keep them away while the plants grow up. Or, lay chicken wire loosely over the tops. You can remove it when the leaves grow up and get tough.

The ants that crawl over **peony** buds are harmless; let them be.

When the **hostas** break ground, watch out for slugs and snails.

# MAY
## Perennials

## PLANNING

As your perennials come up, evaluate the performance of the older plantings. Plan in fall or next spring to divide any that are producing fewer and smaller blooms and those with leggy stems and crowded crowns. For most perennials, the best time for dividing is toward the end of the growing season—late summer and early September—but you can also divide before growth begins in early spring.

## PLANTING

May and early June are excellent for planting container-grown perennials and root divisions. Replace perennials whose performance isn't satisfying with new container-grown plants mature enough to bloom this year.

You can also start perennials from seed. Though most need two or three years to bloom from seed, some will bloom sooner: large-flowered **tickseed** varieties *Coreopsis grandiflora* 'Goldfink' and 'Early Sunrise', **shasta daisies, speedwell, purple coneflower, oxeye daisy,** *Veronica spicata, Heliopsis helianthoides*, **violet sage,** *Salvia* x *superba*, and **yarrow.**

As the spring-flowering bulbs in your perennial borders go out of bloom, screen the area with big seedlings of colorful annuals, aromatic herbs, and potted tropical foliage plants like **canna** and **hardy banana.**

When the air warms, move seedlings of perennials started indoors to a sheltered corner outside to harden them off in preparation for planting in the open garden.

## CARE

When temperatures reach 60 degrees Fahrenheit, move containers of **cold-tender** and **tropical** perennials outdoors for the summer. Repot the small plants; topdress the soil of plants too large to repot. Move containers of **hardy perennials** wintering in protected spots to their summer locations.

**Prepare sturdy stakes** tall enough to support the upper third of your taller plants (**delphiniums** and **lilies,** for example) that will grow to between 18 inches and 4 feet tall. Insert the stakes deep into the soil, 2 inches away from the crowns. Firm the plants in their holes, and water them. When stems are 12 inches tall, tie the main stems to the stakes. Tie on other branches as the plants grow taller.

Restore edging around beds not protected by a barrier.

## PRUNING

Thin the seedlings of perennials sown out in the garden.

When **Cheddar pinks** and **creeping phlox** reach a height of 4 to 6 inches, shear back by an inch or so to encourage bushiness.

When **candytuft, rock cress,** and other low-sprawling perennials finish flowering, shear them back at once to keep the plants bushy and beautiful.

When the new shoots of **beebalm** and **phlox** are 8 to 10 inches high, remove all but four or five stems per plant to keep air circulating through the plants and help prevent powdery mildew.

Pinch back (by half) about half of the shoots in crowns of **phlox, beebalm,** and **shasta daisies;** this will delay the flowering of the pinched-back stems and spread the flowering over a longer period.

Divide and replant **primroses** when they finish blooming.

## WATERING

As the month warms up, begin biweekly checks of the moisture in large plant containers; check the moisture level in small pots and hanging baskets every day or two.

*Maintain the moisture in newly planted seeds and seedlings. Unchecked growth is essential to the development of root systems so they'll be strong enough to withstand summer heat.*

Maintain the moisture in newly planted seeds and seedlings. Unchecked growth is essential to the development of root systems so they'll be strong enough to withstand summer heat. If you do not have a good soaking rain every week to ten days, water planted beds gently and slowly to a depth of 1 or 2 inches.

 ## FERTILIZING

**If you are using chemical fertilizers,** you will need to fertilize the garden and container plants every six weeks from beginning to end of the growing season. If you are using an organio fertilizer and haven't yet applied it, do it now.

 ## PESTS

Slugs and snails haven't surfaced yet, but they may be preparing an unwelcome appearance. Diatomaceous earth, a natural control, works in dry soil but isn't effective on moist spring soil. In moist soil, apply iron phosphate (Sluggo), slug and snail bait, or set out traps to do them in. You can make your own slug trap by pouring a little beer in shallow aluminum plates or empty tuna fish cans.

Weeds really take off early this month; use a scuffle hoe or rake to get rid of them—every last one. Get those in the

middle and back of the border before they disappear behind a screen of foliage.

To remove aphids on the new growth of **mums, coreopsis, sedum,** and **verbena,** spray with a garden hose or remove the infested tips and discard them.

Early spraying with fungicidal formulations of copper will help to save susceptible perennials from blackspot, powdery mildew, rusts, and bacterial diseases such as bacterial leaf spots and wilt.

If your **peonies** were affected by botrytis last year—ugly, blackened patches on the stems and foliage—spray emerging peony tips with Mancozeb or Manzate, fungicides.

If traces of leafminers appear on **columbine** foliage, remove and discard the affected leaves. If the condition persists, cut the foliage to the ground when the plants finish blooming. It will regrow free of leafminers and be beautiful all summer. If leafminers are a continuing problem, replace your plants with *Aquilegia canadensis,* which is more resistant.

PLANNING

When the spring flowers have peaked, areas where more summer color is needed will begin to show up. Make a planting plan showing those areas along with potential solutions to try when the fall planting season comes around.

As you become aware of how spring growth has thickened clumps of **monarda, peonies, daylilies,** and other big perennials, you may be tempted to move the plants to give their neighbors breathing room. You could, without doing much harm, move **irises** soon after they bloom instead of waiting until late August or early September. However, this is not a good time to move most perennials. Those that have already

bloomed are preparing next year's show, and those that haven't bloomed are getting ready to do so. If the garden is really getting crowded, let a little air in either by digging up and moving a small outside portion of the some perennials or by simply cutting off the outside stems that are crowding the neighbors.

 PLANTING

There is still time to start seeds of perennials in the open garden. Where the growing season is short, even quick-to-bloom perennials may not have time to do much this year, but they'll be mature and bloom next year.

Sow seeds indoors or in a cold frame in the next few weeks for perennials you want quantities of next year—edgers and ground covers like **candytuft** and **catmint,** for example, and garden staples like **shasta daisies, coneflowers,** and **coreopsis.** The seeds and seedlings will be easy to care for if started in trays or flats. When the seedlings are growing sturdily, transplant them to an empty row in your kitchen garden or to a sheltered spot in the flower beds. When the weather cools in late August, move them to permanent homes in the garden.

 CARE

Every few weeks adjust the ties on the tall flowers you have staked.

Perennial Garden Plan

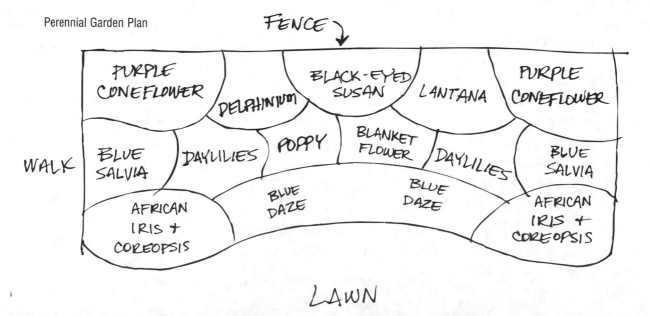

*When the spring flowers have peaked, areas where more summer color is needed will begin to show up. Make a planting plan showing those areas along with potential solutions to try when the fall planting season comes around.*

To keep roots cool and weeds down, renew the mulch on flower beds.

If you have plants in your cold frame or hot bed, keep the top open as the weather warms.

## PRUNING

Deadhead flowers as they fade.

Shear back 'Silver Mound' *Artemisia*, *Amsonia*, and *Baptisia* by half when they reach half their mature height. This should keep them from flopping later in the summer.

Deadhead **catmint, lavender,** and other repeat bloomers to encourage a second round of flowers.

Trim back stems and shoots of perennials crowding their neighbors to maintain the definition between individual groups of perennials.

To keep the plants compact and improve flowering, around June 1 (and repeat July 15) pinch and prune back **garden mums** by a third, along with **asters, baby's-breath, beebalm,** 'Snow Bank' *Boltonia*, *Eupatorium*, *Helianthus*, *Heliopsis*, and *Scabiosa*.

## WATERING

Every day, check and adjust the soil moisture in small pots and baskets; every week, in your cold frame or hot bed.

In hot, windy weather, check the soil moisture in big containers often, and water as needed to keep the soil nicely damp.

As the weather warms and dries, maintain moisture in all new plantings.

## FERTILIZING

Every two weeks, add a half-dose of fertilizer to the water for small containers. Use compost or potting soil to top off large containers of perennials whose soil level seems to be shrinking.

If you are using only granular chemical fertilizers, then you will need to fertilize garden plants every six weeks from beginning to end of the growing season.

## PESTS

Watch out for aphids and mites.

Handpick Japanese beetles—they're sluggish in the cool of early morning. Drop them into soapy water, and flush them down a drain. If they multiply, spray the plants with Neem, which will discourage feeding by adults. Try placing Japanese beetle traps far from the plantings you wish to protect, not among them. Insecticides containing Neem, rotenone, or Sevin insecticide are controls.

Protect **phlox, beebalm, veronica,** and other plants that have shown signs of powdery mildew in the past by spraying with a mixture of 1 tablespoon baking soda and 1 tablespoon of ultrafine horticultural oil, combined in a gallon of water.

PLANNING

Before your vacation, arrange to have containers of perennials watered. Ease the chore by grouping the containers in a semi-shaded spot and providing smaller containers with saucers.

Investigate automatic watering systems.

 PLANTING

Plant "fillers"—big pots of annuals, herbs, summer-flowering bulbs like **crocosmia** and **canna**—in places where the passing of spring-flowering bulbs leaves gaps in the flower beds.

 CARE

Tie tall **delphiniums, dahlias,** and **lilies** to the upper third of their stakes.

Replenish the mulch in the perennial beds to keep their roots cool and to maintain moisture now that the year's driest season is about here.

If you are starting seedlings in a cold frame, keep the lid open.

 PRUNING

Go through your garden with hand-held head shears and deadhead spent flowers. Deadhead daily if you enjoy it, but at least every two weeks, except for perennials whose seed pods you are planning to let develop—the **coneflowers,** for example.

Shear to the ground plants showing the irregular serpentine tracings of leafminers. **Columbine** is very susceptible. The new foliage should grow in clean.

July 15 or so, to keep the plants compact and improve flowering, repeat the early June reduction of **asters, baby's-breath, beebalm,** 'Snow Bank' *Boltonia, Eupatorium, Helianthus, Heliopsis, Scabiosa*.

Deadheading and Pruning

Groom the garden and trim back stems and shoots of perennials invading their neighbors.

 WATERING

Every day, check and adjust the soil moisture in small pots and baskets. On hot, windy summer days, check the soil moisture in big containers of perennials, and water as often as needed to keep the soil nicely damp.

If there's no rain for a week or ten days, slowly and gently apply $1\frac{1}{2}$ inches of water to the garden, measured in a one-pound coffee tin or rain gauge.

Take care to check, and when needed, to water seeds started indoors or in a cold frame. These baby plants need attention.

 FERTILIZING

If you are using only chemical fertilizers, such as 5-10-5, which are quickly available to the plants, then you will need to fertilize every six weeks from beginning to end of the growing season.

Frequent watering quickly leaches the nutrients from the soil in small containers, so you must fertilize to compensate.

*Before your vacation, arrange to have containers of perennials watered. Ease the chore by grouping the containers in a semi-shaded spot and providing smaller containers with saucers.*

Include a half dose of a water-soluble fertilizer every second time you water.

 # PESTS

Continue to control infestations of Japanese beetles, aphids, mites, and whiteflies.

Keep an eye on **asters, beebalm, phlox, dahlias,** and other flowers susceptible to powdery mildew. It often starts on the older, denser foliage at the base of the plant where there is less air. If you see a smoky film forming, thin the interior growth to improve airflow. Spray all the foliage of that plant, any other susceptible nearby plants with a solution of 1 tablespoon baking soda and 1 tablespoon of ultrafine horticultural oil mixed in a gallon of water. When the affected plants finish blooming, cut them back to the ground to promote clean, healthy new growth. Destroy the prunings. Spray the clump and the surrounding soil with a fungicide for mildew.

In plantings where rust is a problem, **lily-of-the-valley** for example, you can to some extent avoid the condition by keeping the plants watered during

## Did You Know?

### Pruning Encourages Reblooming

Deadheading—removing faded and dead blooms—encourages almost all flowering perennials to bloom on. To keep the plant shapely, cut off the stem of the spent bloom just above the next node on the stem. That's where the next flowering stem will arise.

In some plants cutting out-of-bloom stems to the ground and reducing deteriorating foliage by four to six inches or more will encourage regrowth and reblooming. Some perennials that respond to this treatment are **catmint,** *Campanula carpatica, Centranthus, Echinops, Chrysanthemum* 'May Queen', and cultivars of the **shasta daisies, daylilies** that are rebloomers, **delphiniums,** *Salvia nemerosa, Scabiosa, Stokesia, Tradescantia, Verbena, Veronica,* and **yarrow.**

Shearing tall fall-blooming perennials by half their height June 1 and again by July 15, or no later than eight weeks before their scheduled bloom time, results in more attractive plants and better blooms. Some that benefit from this treatment are **asters,** *Boltonia, Chrysopsis, Helianthus, Heliopsis,* **mums, Russian Sage,** *Salvia grandiflora,* and *Saponaria officinalis.*

Shearing spring bloomers soon after they finish blooming keeps them from getting leggy and promotes fuller bloom next season. Some that benefit from this treatment are **candytuft, creeping phlox,** and **sweet alyssum.**

droughts and in good condition. Applying an anti-transpirant every other week may help avoid the condition. Spraying with a horticultural oil, such as Mancozeb, manzate, sulfur or copper, helps control outbreaks. If the condition cannot be brought under control, remove all the foliage and dispose of it,

and then clean the bed and spray the soil with a rust deterrent.

For other controls, turn to Pests, Diseases, and Controls in the Appendix.

## PLANNING

This month some garden centers stage great sales. They sell off not only good-sized perennials, but many also begin to put hard goods on sale. So this is the moment to consider stocking up on flower holders, pots, and cachepots, as well as mulch, compost, wood chips for paths, tiles, stones for hardscaping, garden benches, birdhouses, and so on.

Evaluate the light reaching the flower beds. If some flowers are flopping forward, they may be short of light. Tree branches may have grown out and be casting shade on flower beds that were once in full sun. You can prune culprits now, the sooner the better. It takes full sun for most flowers to bloom up to their potential.

Bring your garden log up to date: record the effect of staking taller plants and the result of cutting back **asters**, *Boltonia*, and others to delay blooming.

## PLANTING

In spite of the heat and drought, container-grown perennials and root divisions can be planted successfully this month as long as you water them every week or so, and hose them down gently if they show signs of wilting on especially hot days.

In New York's cool Zones 3 and 4, we recommend dividing and replanting perennials that need it around August 15. Warmer areas can wait until later.

When the weather cools mid-month, start transplanting seedlings started in your cold frame to the open garden.

## CARE

If you have seedlings in a cold frame, be sure to keep it aired enough to avoid overheating.

Check and adjust the stakes supporting *Boltonia*, the big **dahlias, lilies, Japanese anemones,** and other very tall flowers. Tie on straggling branches, and add stakes as needed to help the plants carry the full weight when they bloom.

Restore edging around beds not protected by a barrier.

## PRUNING

**Dahlias** need deadheading and are excellent vase flowers.

Continue to harvest or deadhead **phlox, perennial salvia**, *Scabiosa*, **purple coneflower,** and other summer-flowering perennials.

Remove dead, damaged, diseased, and insect-infested stems wherever they occur.

Shear 'Silver Mound' *Artemisia* to keep it from collapsing in hot weather.

## WATERING

**Every day,** check and adjust the soil moisture in small pots and baskets. On hot, windy summer days, check the soil moisture in big containers of perennials and plants in the cold frame or hot bed, and water as needed to keep the soil nicely damp.

## FERTILIZING

Include a half-dose of a water-soluble fertilizer every second time you water small containers.

In Zones 3 and 4, if you are using organic fertilizers, make a final application to in-ground perennials as growth slows—usually about August 15.

If you are using granular chemical fertilizers, continue the regular six-week applications now until the end of the growing season.

*Evaluate the light reaching the flower beds. If some flowers are flopping forward, they may be short of light.*

## PESTS

High humidity and heat encourage powdery mildew; drought weakens plants and makes them more vulnerable to diseases such as rust. Apply sulfur, ultrafine horticultural oil, copper fungicide, Immunox, or Bayleton to afflicted plants not yet finished blooming. Cut down to the ground infected plants that have finished blooming, clear all fallen foliage and mulch, and spray the area with a control.

Make a note in your garden log for next season to move the affected plants farther apart to increase air circulation. Or, if the infestation is very bad, in early spring replace the affected plants with mildew-resistant varieties. Make a note in your garden log to apply controls early and often.

Check perennials for fungal leaf spot, and apply a fungicide if needed.

If you see continuing signs of mites, hose the plant down regularly and spray with insecticidal soaps or ultrafine horticultural oils.

## Did You Know?

### When Your Perennials Need Watering

Climates and microclimates and the weather patterns from year to year, affect the size, color, and health of perennials, their bloom time, their hardiness, and their seasonal performance.

Understanding how heat and humidity affect your perennials helps you to water correctly.

• The hotter and drier the air, and the windier the weather, the more water your plants need. Don't water by rote; water when the soil feels dry.

• The sandier the soil, the more often your garden will need watering. You can offset sandy soil by incorporating plenty of humus in the soil before planting new plants. The windier the exposure, the sooner container and plants and garden soil will dry out.

• The higher the heat, the drier the air will be, and the more likely you are to encounter spider mites infesting your plantings. Overhead watering humidifies the air and can help. Perennials growing in moist humusy soil and mulched 2 to 3 inches deep can stand considerably more heat, sun, and drought than plants without mulch,

• The wetter the season, the higher the humidity, and the more likely the soil is to become waterlogged, especially in beds that don't drain well. Humidity encourages mildew and other negative conditions.

The first line of defense against disease in areas of high heat and humidity is to plant perennials advertised as disease resistant. Equally important is to provide your plants with very well-drained soil, a must for most perennials. Uncrowded, well-spaced plants have better drainage and good air circulation. The solution to finding a wet spot right where you want to put your flower bed is to create a raised bed as described in the Introduction to the book.

# SEPTEMBER
## Perennials

##  PLANNING

This month, make places in your flower beds to add **colorful foliage plants** and **ornamental grasses** next spring — some up front, some behind, but not directly behind those up front, and some farther back.

The silver-gray fuzz of **lamb's ears** lightens the front of a border. Clumps of **dwarf bamboo** (*Pleioblastus fortunei*) add variety to the texture of middle rows. To change the texture at the back of the border, plant *Verbascum*, a tall candelabra of a plant with felted gray foliage. In shady areas, make room for colorful **hosta** varieties. The colorful new **heucheras** and hostas are luminous, and some bluish hostas have wonderfully textured ribbed or quilted leaves.

##  PLANTING

In Zone 5, around September 1 is a good time to plant, divide, and transplant perennials. In Zone 6, most perennials can be planted and divided September 1 to September 15. In Zone 7, plant and divide September 1 to mid-October. This gives the crowns time to develop roots before the soil cools and growth stops.

Use these same dates as a guide to transplanting the seedlings started earlier to a nursery row or to permanent places in the flower beds.

##  CARE

After the first killing frost, you can lift and store **dahlias.** (See You Can Start Dahlias Early Indoors in March in the chapter on Bulbs.)

When temperatures fall below 60 degrees Fahrenheit, move tender and tropical perennials growing in containers to a frost-free shed or garage.

In Zones 3 and 4, move big containers of hardy perennials to sheltered locations for the winter. Add insulation by packing bags filled with dry leaves around them.

##  PRUNING

Continue to deadhead spent blooms.

Cut **peonies** to the ground before the first frost and discard the debris.

##  WATERING

September rains should keep the garden well watered, but check and, when needed, water small pots and baskets

Dividing Perennials

still outdoors. There should be enough rain this month for the garden and containers of hardy perennials.

*September rains should keep the garden well watered, but check and, when needed, water small pots and baskets still outdoors.*

 FERTILIZING

Include a half dose of a water-soluble fertilizer every second time you water window boxes and small containers still outdoors.

In Zones 5, 6, and 7, if you are using organic blend fertilizers, such as Holly-tone or Plant-tone, make a final application now.

If you are using granular chemical fertilizers, fertilize garden and container plants for the last time just as the growing season ends, some time between early September and early October.

If you are using time-release fertilizers, earlier applications should carry the plants through the end of the growing season.

 PESTS

We believe in radical weeding this month. Edge the flower beds to keep grass from creeping in. Then scratch up the soil around clumps of perennials and get all the weeds out. This has the added virtue of opening up the soil so fall rains can give the plants a deep watering.

If **hostas** show signs of slug or snail damage, bait them with small saucers of stale beer or with Sluggo.

Remove and discard every scrap of infected foliage and mulch from under plants that have been attacked by insects or diseases.

## Did You Know?

### Astilbes Love the Shade

Astilbes are among the loveliest—and most useful—of all the perennials that bloom in the shade. In late spring and summer the plants raise graceful plumes in mostly pastel shades. The deeply cut, fernlike foliage is green or bronzed, attractive both before and after flowering.

Astilbes are excellent fillers for the middle of the border and perfect for edging a woodland path, stream, or pond. You can achieve a lasting show by planting early, mid-season, and late bloomers. For instance: plant the white early-blooming favorite 'Deutschland', red 'Fanal', and pink 'Europa' with mid-season 'Ostrich Plume' ('Straussenfedder'), and late bloomers such as the lilac 'Superba' and little 'Pumila'.

'Pumila', a variety of *Astilbe chinensis*, spreads by underground runners. The others spread by clump enlargement, and in time make large, dense mats. Catalogs ship bare-root astilbe crowns in early spring. Follow their planting instructions and be patient. For a quick show, set out a series of container-grown astilbes from early spring to late summer. Astilbe grows best in light shade in well-drained, rich, moist humusy soil. Summer drought and winter wetness are their worst enemies—except for voles, which love them. For vole controls, see Pests in the October pages of this chapter.

# PLANNING

This is an excellent month to start new beds for planting next spring—doing it now gives the soil and its amendments fall and winter to settle in. For instructions, see Soil Preparation and Improvement and Starting a Raised Bed in the Introduction to the book.

 # PLANTING

In Zone 7, you can plant, divide, and transplant perennials until mid-month. See Dividing and Moving Perennials in the introduction to this chapter.

 # CARE

In Zones 6 and 7, move hardy perennials in containers to a sheltered location. Add insulation by packing bags filled with dry leaves around them.

Clear dead leaves from the flower beds, and do not compost them. They may shelter pests and diseases that will flourish in spring.

Continue to root out weeds. Dandelion seeds germinate well in compost and must be rooted out, not just chopped off at the surface, because they re-grow from the roots.

 # PRUNING

Let perennials that are attractive in winter remain. Even old flower stalks can be interesting. The seed-bearing **coneflowers** feed the birds and add color with their architectural branches of rust or rich brown or, in the rain, sooty black. **Sedum** 'Autumn Joy', **Siberian iris** in its rusty winter brown, the **coreopsis** bramble, and the dry leaves of *Allium tuberosum* give the garden form while the earth rests.

 # WATERING

**Outdoors.** The most important preparation for winter is a deep and thorough watering of new, established, in-ground, and container perennials before the soil freezes. If the sky doesn't do it, then you must compensate.

**Indoors.** Water the soil in big containers of tropical perennials stored for winter. Add just enough to keep the soil from drying out.

 # FERTILIZING

In Zones 6 and 7, the growing season slows in early October. If you are using granular chemical fertilizers, make the last fertilization early this month.

 # PESTS

**Outdoors.** Apply or change whatever deer deterrents you are using. See Pests, Diseases, and Controls in the Appendix.

**About moles and voles.** You think "moles" when you see tunnels heaving the lawn, and you blame them when perennials disappear and bulbs move around. Wrong: Moles are meat eaters (grubs, worms); Voles are vegetarians, active October through March. Members of the *Microtus* species, these short-tailed pine or meadow mice are most active October to March. These small rodents are reddish-brown to gray, 2 to 4 inches long, and have short tails, blunt faces, and tiny eyes and ears. They live in extensive tunnel systems usually less than a foot deep with entrances an inch or two across.

Protecting the plant is easier than getting rid of voles. They dislike tunneling through coarse material, so you can discourage them by setting plants out in VoleBloc or PermaTill, bits of non-toxic, light, long-lasting aggregates rather like pea gravel with jagged edges.

**Established plantings.** Dig a 4-inch wide, 12-inch deep moat around the drip line of perennials under attack, fill it with VoleBloc, and mulch with VoleBloc.

*Let perennials that are attractive in winter remain. Even old flower stalks can be interesting.*

## Did You Know?

### What to Plant for Winter Interest

In winter, ornamental grasses dance with the wind, woolly betonies stand tall above fallen leaves, and evergreen edgers and ground covers rimmed with ice catch the sun and sparkle—if you have planted for winter interest.

Here are a few of many perennials that stand out when storms of falling leaves give way to ice-blue skies and crisp winter air.

- **Astilbe** species and varieties keep their rich brown flower stalks in winter.
- **Blue False Indigo, Wild Blue Indigo** (*Baptisia australis*) maintains its gunmetal gray or black seed pods and leaves.
- **Blue Oat Grass** (*Helictotrichon sempervirens*) is a small grass whose gray-blue leaves last year round.
- **Boltonia** (*Boltonia asteroids*) 'Snow Bank' has rich brown stalks and leaves that last through winter.
- **Carpet Bugle** (*Ajuga reptans*) 'Burgundy Glow' maintains its variegated foliage—white, pink, rose, and green.
- **Chinese Chives** (*Allium tuberosum*) keeps white seedheads usually until spring.
- **Coneflowers** (*Echinacea purpurea* varieties) and the **rudbeckias** ripen seeds the birds love.
- **Coreopsis** (*Coreopsis verticillata*) 'Moonbeam' retains its stems in winter.
- **Edging Candytuft** (*Iberis sempervirens*) remains dark green through fall and later.
- **Hellebore** (*Helleborus orientalis* and cultivars) keep their evergreen, deeply divided foliage most winters.
- **Russian Sage** (*Perovskia atriplicifolia*) is like a huge white bird's nest all winter.
- **Siberian Iris** (*Iris sibirica*) develops attractive seedpods and the grassy foliage turns rusty brown in fall.
- **Silver Grass** (*Miscanthus sinensis*) can soar to 6 or 8 feet, and the foliage in winters turn gold; lovely with snow at its feet.
- **Woolly Betony, Lamb's Ears** (*Stachys byzantina*) has big, semi-evergreen, gray leaves that remain in fall.
- **Sedums** 'Autumn Joy' and 'Vera Jameson' (*Sedum spectabile*) retain their seedheads all winter.

**New plantings.** Prepare a planting hole 2 inches deeper than the rootball, and layer in 2 inches of VoleBloc. Set the rootball in place and backfill with VoleBloc. Mulch with more VoleBloc.

If vole activity appears in late winter:

- Bait the main area around the plants with a rodenticide.
- Pull the mulch apart, spray the crowns lightly with a repellent, and put the mulch back in place.

**Indoors.** Check tropical perennials moved indoors for whiteflies and spider mites. If you find problems, apply the controls recommended in the Pests, Diseases, and Controls section in the Appendix.

PLANNING

During this gray month take the time to enlarge your horticultural knowledge. Here's the way horticulturists talk about flowers along with explanations of what the words represent:

**Anatomy of a flower.** Buds are enclosed in sepals; together they make up the calyx.

Petals develop next. All of the petals make up the corolla, and sometimes these come together and make a tube or cup, as with daffodils. Sepals and perianth make up the perianth. Bracts are the leaves immediately below the perianths; they are small or scale-like leaves in most flowers but are very much larger than the flowers themselves in poinsettias.

Organs are inside the petals: The male organ is made up of stamens, and each stamen includes a filament (stalk) tipped with an anther; anthers form pollen.

Female organs are the seed-bearing carpels; when they fuse together in a blossom, the organ is called an ovary. Pistils may have three parts: an ovary in which seeds are formed, a slender style, which ends in a stigma. The stigma usually is either rough or sticky to hold the pollen that falls on it. That's what fertilizes the seed.

 PLANTING

There is still time to sow seeds that require stratification.

**Stratification.** Some seeds are programmed to withhold germination in the fall when they can be killed by winter frosts. They will germinate only after being exposed for a specific time period in the garden—typically four to eight weeks—to winter cold and moisture. Seed packets designate these seeds as needing "stratification" to germinate and tell you for how long. You can sow the seeds now in the garden, and they will germinate in the spring.

For more control of the stratification process, you can start them in containers. Here's how that works:

*1* Sow the seeds in pots or trays, as described in starting seeds indoors under planting in the January pages of Annuals. Label and date the containers. Cover them with plastic film (plastic bags from the drycleaners, for example) to keep the moisture from evaporating.

*2* Keep the containers for the period designated on the seed packet in an unheated garage, shed, porch, or cold frame where they will be exposed to cold temperatures of less than 40 degrees Fahrenheit but safe from snow, rain, and wind.

*3* When the temperature climbs to between 45 and 60 degrees Fahrenheit, the seeds will begin to germinate—each species in its own time frame. Once the seedlings pop, remove the plastic, and begin the care program for seedlings described in starting seeds indoors (January, Annuals).

*4* Plan to have enough large containers for each seedling so you can grow them on until outdoor planting weather arrives in May or June.

 CARE

After the first hard frost, protect perennials that are borderline hardy in your zone, and those that have just been planted, by applying a winter mulch of pine boughs or straw.

PRUNING

To encourage **garden mums** to perennialize, let the old stems stand as insulation for the new growth emerging at the base of the plants.

*After the first hard frost, protect perennials that are borderline hardy in your zone, and those that have just been planted, by applying a winter mulch of pine boughs or straw.*

# WATERING

Water container plants wintering indoors often enough to keep the soil from drying out.

Make sure the soil in containers of perennials wintering outdoors remains damp until covered by snow or until the soil freezes.

# FERTILIZING

Fertilizer is not needed now because the growing season is over.

# PESTS

If you see signs of vole activity, bait the main runway with a rodenticide. See the October pages of this chapter.

## Did You Know?

### PPA "Best-of-the-Best" Perennials

The Perennial Plant Association (PPA) is a professional trade association dedicated to improving the industry. André Viette has served as president. Each year the PPA chooses a Plant of the Year rated according to multi-seasonal interest and low maintenance. Here are recent choices. To keep up with Plant of the Year choices to come, check out www.Perennial plant.org.

- **Astilbe** (*Astilbe chinensis*) 'Sprite' 1994
- **Coral Bells** (*Heuchera*) 'Palace Purple' 1991
- **Coneflower** (*Rudbeckia fulgida* var. *sullivantii*) 'Goldsturm' 1999
- **Coreopsis** (*Coreopsis*) 'Moonbeam' 1992
- **Creeping Phlox** (*Phlox stolonifera*) 1990
- **Feather Reed Grass** (*Calamagrostis acutiflora*) 'Karl Foerster' 2001
- **Japanese Painted Fern** (*Athyrium nipponicum*) 'Pictum' 2004
- **Penstemon** (*Penstemon*) 'Husker Red' 1996
- **Perennial Salvia** (*Salvia nemerosa*) 'May Night' 1997
- **Phlox** (*Phlox*) 'David' 2002
- **Purple Coneflower** (*Echinacea*) 'Magnus' 1998
- **Russian Sage** (*Perovskia atriplicifolia*) 1995
- **Scabiosa** (*Scabiosa columbaria*) 'Butterfly Blue' 2000
- **Shasta Daisy** (*Leucanthemum*) 'Becky' 2003
- **Veronica** (*Veronica*) 'Sunny Border Blue' 1993

## PLANNING

Tools that make gardening easier become dearly held companions. You get attached. Good tools are expensive, but they last well and make welcome gifts. Here's a handful—arranged in order of importance to us—that we use all the time when we work in the flower beds:

• A tool every seasoned gardener (and farmer) carries, but no one thinks of as a tool, is a **sharp little knife,** a pocket knife, or a folding pruning knife, for digging up dandelions, cutting twine, impulse pruning—a thousand little jobs. It should be a size that is very comfortable in your palm, opens and closes easily, and is so well made it will last a lifetime.

• A pair of **tiny shears** for deadheading and harvesting flowers. Fiskars, manufacturers known for their line of pruning tools, make the little shears, and you can find the same type in shops with fabrics and sewing materials.

• For planting, the two most basic tools are a **hand cultivator** and a **garden trowel.** The broad fat-bellied type of trowel is the most versatile: the narrow variety incised with inches is mainly for planting bulbs. Painted trowels tend to peel. Cast aluminum is homely but light and durable; choose models whose handles are sheathed in plastic so they won't blacken your palms.

• The broad flat tines of a **short-handled spading (turning) fork** are the gardener's best friend when it comes to lifting and dividing perennials and loosening soil.

• A **shovel** gets less use than a spading fork, but you'll need it to dig planting holes and move dirt and gravel.

• A **hand rake** (as opposed to a long-handled rake) for cleaning up flower beds.

• A **hoe** for weeding. A circle hoe makes weeding much easier. So does a swing-head scuffle hoe which works with a push-pull movement. They cut through weeds on the forward and backward stroke and cultivate the soil without disturbing the mulch.

 ## PLANTING

Seeds that need stratification can be planted as long as the soil can be worked. See Planting, in the November pages.

## CARE

Use only snowmelt products that don't harm plants, turf, and concrete.

 ## PRUNING

Clear away and discard perennials that frost has reduced to mush. Leave plants with interesting structures and seedheads the birds will browse—**coneflowers,** for example.

 ## WATERING

Maintain soil moisture in containers stored indoors, and also in containers of hardy perennials outdoors if there's neither snow nor rain. The soil needs just enough moisture to keep the roots from drying out.

 ## FERTILIZING

Fertilizer is not needed now because the growing season is over.

 ## PESTS

**Indoors.** Keep an eye out for spider mites, mealybug, and scale on perennials wintering indoors. To avoid problems, mist the plants and air the room daily towards noon when the outside air is warmer.

# CHAPTER SEVEN

# Roses

*Roses can be both a great joy and a great challenge.*
*It's a good idea to look before you leap.*

A richly perfumed **tea rose,** a **pillar rose** in bloom, a hedge spangled with **sweetheart roses**—why resist? Well, most need repeat fertilization and pruning. Many need spraying. Know what you want the rose to do for you and what you are willing to do for it, and choose accordingly. When the right rose is in the right place, it performs beyond all expectations.

## COLD HARDINESS IS ESSENTIAL

The hardiness of a **rose** variety depends on the hardiness of its understock (the roots). **Multiflora rose** roots (which do well in acidic soils) are very hardy, so a rose budded (grafted) on a multiflora understock is very hardy. Hardy rose varieties growing on their own roots are also very hardy. The most widely used understock, 'Dr. Huey', is not very hardy, so even hardy rose varieties budded on Dr. Huey understock are not very hardy. The **species roses,** the wild roses from around the world that are the parents of all garden hybrids, and many once-blooming **old garden roses,** are

## Did You Know?

### About ARS and AARS Ratings

Two major influences on the U.S. world of roses are the non-profit American Rose Society (ARS) and All-America Rose Selections (AARS). The ratings given roses are national ratings based on how roses do nationwide. Some do better or worse regionally than the national rating. Local rose societies and growers will know.

The ARS is an association of rosarians who rate rose introductions on a scale of 1 (worst) to 10 (best). The ratings average individual ratings given by beginners as well as experienced rose growers. They are printed yearly in the "Handbook for Selecting Roses" available from the ARS. The highest rating given even the enduringly popular roses, 'New Dawn', 'Double Delight', 'Iceberg', 'The Fairy', and 'Bonica', reach no higher than 8.7.

The rose gardens near ARS headquarters in Shreveport, Louisiana, are open to the public during the growing season. Their web site, www.ars.org, can help you locate local rose societies.

The AARS (www.rose.org) is a nonprofit association of rose growers and rose producers that introduces and promotes roses judged exceptional in their trial programs. They are headquartered in Chicago. The roses judged go through a two-year field trial. The AARS seal of approval has influenced rosarians since 1938.

generally cold-hardy. Of the repeat bloomers, **rugosas** are very hardy. **Miniatures** and the modern roses including **hybrid teas** whose tags say they are growing on their own roots and are hardy in your zone will most likely succeed. **Own-root roses** are the best bet for New York because if one of our exceptionally nasty winters kills the top, the rose that regrows from the rootstock will be the one you fell in love with and planted. Winter protection is wise no matter how hardy the rose. You'll find suggestions in Winter Care for Roses on page 192.

# Roses

## PLANTING

The humidity present spring and fall is kinder to new roses, but they'll succeed planted even in hot dry summer months if given adequate care. For a rose to bloom up to its potential, it must be placed where it has full sun, air all around it, well-drained top quality soil to grow in, and adequate fertilizer and water.

Roses are sold bare root, container-grown, and in plantable containers.

- **Bare-root roses** are available when it's time to plant them, early spring before growth begins. Follow exactly the suppliers' instructions for planting.

- **Container-grown roses** are available throughout the season, and in most of New York you can plant them late April through to October.

- **Roses in plantable containers** are easy to plant, but they are available only in spring and early summer.

**Light and spacing.** Roses need at least six hours of direct sun, and eight is better. Morning light is especially valuable because it dries the leaves, and that helps prevent disease. The most shade tolerant roses are hybrids of the **musk rose, albas, rugosa roses,** the lovely **floribunda** 'Iceberg' (which may die back but likely will regrow in spring).

In addition to full sun, roses need air. Be sure to give your roses enough space all around for good air circulation. The rule of thumb is, **compact roses** need to be 2 to 4 feet apart. **Climbing** and **heirloom roses** need 5 to 10 feet between them. **Miniature roses** do well with just 18 to 24 inches all around.

**Soil.** The ideal soil for roses has good drainage, has lots of water-holding humus, and is very, very fertile. The soil pH that favors roses is between pH 5.8 and 6.8. Instructions for changing pH are given in the Introduction to the book.

The hole for a bush rose needs to be at least 24 inches deep. If your soil is less than wonderful or if you have difficulty digging deeply enough, create a **raised bed** for roses. The project is described in the March pages. For instructions on preparing a **new planting hole or bed** for roses, turn to March.

## FERTILIZERS FOR ROSES

Rose soil needs refurbishing in early spring every year.

*1* Check and adjust the soil pH (see above).

*2* Fertilize:

- If you are using an organic fertilizer, apply it four to six weeks **before** growth begins.

- If you are using a granular chemical fertilizer, apply it **just before** growth begins.

- If you are using a time-release fertilizer, **just before** growth begins apply an eight-month formulation.

*3* Renew the mulch. This organic blanket will stabilize soil temperature and renew the humus content of the soil.

*4* Every three to five years improve the soil by applying rock phosphate, green sand, and if your soil has a lot of clay, gypsum. These are the granular soil additives used in preparing a new bed for roses. (See March). Measure it all into a pail, mix it, and scratch the mixture into the soil around the rose. Rain will do the rest.

In addition, in the Introduction to the book in the section titled "Understanding Fertilizers" there's a complete explanation of fertilizer. **When you use them** depends on the type of fertilizer you are using—organic, chemical, slow- or time-release.

**Organic-blend fertilizers.** Every six weeks spread Rose-tone, Plant-tone, or your favorite organic fertilizer blend over the inside perimeter of the watering basin at the rate of 10 pounds per 100 square feet.

*1* Make the first application four to six weeks before growth begins;

*2* Second application six weeks later, in early summer;

*3* Third application six weeks later, in mid-summer;

*4* Last application when growth slows, somewhere between mid-August in the colder zones and late September.

**Chemical fertilizers.** If you are using granular chemical fertilizers, apply these every six weeks beginning just before the roses come into bloom and ending with a final application of an organic, not chemical, fertilizer when growth slows.

**Time-release fertilizer.** Just before growth begins, apply an eight-month formulation.

In addition, roses that have been producing masses of blooms benefit from an occasional foliar feeding with a solution containing a liquid fertilizer. You'll find soluble organics such as fish emulsion, liquid seaweed, compost, and manure teas available at garden centers, as well as water-soluble chemical fertilizers.

## PRUNING, DEADHEADING, AND HARVESTING

Roses must be pruned to remain shapely and stay healthy and productive. The best time is late in their dormant period before the buds begin to swell and new leaves appear—April and May. But late is better than not at all. The exception: **one-time bloomers are pruned after they have finished blooming because next year's flowers develop on this year's new growth.**

Prune to remove any cane thinner than a pencil and all damaged, weak, and nonproductive canes. That allows the plant's energy to go into flower production and larger, healthier canes. **Hybrid teas** and **exhibition roses** are pruned hard when the goal is to encourage a few large blooms. The **cluster-flower roses** and **compact roses** are pruned lightly to encourage growth and maintain their shape. For detailed information on when and how to prune the various categories of roses, turn to February.

**Deadheading and harvesting.** If you remove spent blooms that encourages the bushes to produce. Harvesting roses for bouquets is a form of dead-heading—so indulge!! If you don't, blooms that were pollinated may begin to form seed pods (hips), which takes away energy needed for growth and flower production. **Miniatures,** small **polyanthas, species, carpet roses,** and 'Knock Out' series generally do not need deadheading.

Let the last roses stay on to produce hips. That causes the plant to undergo chemical changes that slow growth, inhibit blooming, and generally prepare for dormancy by focusing on "hardening" the canes. The formation of hips tells the plant that it's done its job and can now rest.

## WATERING AND MULCHING

What roses need—what all plants need—is deep watering because that encourages the roots to grow deep into the soil. A deep root system survives dry spells and winter freezes. By "deep watering" we mean a slow, gentle, and thorough watering with a sprinkler, a soaker hose, a bubbler, or by hand. Water deeply after planting, then every week for the next eight weeks unless you have a soaking rain.

In good soil in average summer weather, both new and established roses need 1 to $1^1/_2$ inches of water each week, by rain or by you. During a hot summer, each established bush needs a 5-gallon bucket of water each week. Roses growing in sandy soil need more frequent watering than roses in clay soil. One of the most important winter preparations is a deep and thorough watering before the ground freezes.

We favor installing a drip irrigation system or soaker hoses for roses. These two methods release water directly to the plant roots and not to the foliage, which helps avoid some diseases, and you don't waste water in runoff.

**Mulch.** After planting or transplanting a rose, spread mulch 2 to 3 inches deep starting 3 inches from the main stem and out to a point wider than the plant's diameter. Replenish the mulch in later winter after fertilizing, in early summer, and in late fall.

## WINTER CARE FOR ROSES

To help roses harden off and mature for winter, about six weeks before the first frost we recommend making a last fertilization of a slow-release, organic product such as Espoma Rose-tone or Plant-tone. It will work slowly over winter without promoting top growth that can be harmed by fall frosts.

Remember when cold weather threatens to stop deadheading and allow the flowers to go to seed and form rose hips. When the bush is bare of leaves, to prevent disease and fungus from overwintering, remove the petals and leaves and other debris on the ground. Spray with dormant oil to kill insects and diseases on the bush and on the ground. Water the plant thoroughly before the ground freezes hard.

**Winter mulch.** Once the ground has thoroughly frozen, in Zones 3, 4, 5, and 6, we recommend adding about a foot to the mulch to stabilize the soil temperature and prevent heaving. Use straw, salt hay, leaves, compost, or pine bark mulch. If the site is windy, encase the plant in a cage of wire and straw, or wrap it with burlap and straw and tie together.

You can also use styrofoam rose cones as a protection. First, trim and defoliate the bush and mound it up with 12 inches of soil and mulch. Tie up the canes, place the protective cone over it, and weight the cone down.

When the forsythias bloom, remove the mulch and other protection.

## PESTS

**Weeds.** Rake away weeds, including grass and dandelions, early and often.

**Deer and voles.** For controls, turn to Pests, Diseases, and Controls in the Appendix to the book.

**Insects and diseases.** The first line of defense is to plant pest- and disease-resistant roses, to give your roses lots of air all around, to fertilize, and to water well. **When you encounter an infestation, treat it, and immediately remove every scrap of infected vegetation from the plant and the ground.**

**Blackspot and powdery mildew.** Blackspot causes black spots about $1/16$ to $1/2$ inches in diameter on the leaves and sometimes the stems. The infected leaves later turn yellow around the spots and fall off. It is promoted by wet foliage, splashing water, and warm temperatures. The new 'Knock Out' shrub roses seem impervious, but most others are not.

Powdery mildew covers buds, stems, and leaves with a white-gray powdery substance. It cannot reproduce in water. It thrives during high humidity but forms on dry leaves.

You may succeed in warding off these two diseases if you:

• Spray with a combination of $1 1/2$ tablespoons of baking soda and either 2 tablespoons of horticultural oil or a few drops of dishwashing liquid in 1 gallon of water. The first application is made before foliage appears. It must be reapplied after rain.

• Remove leaves close to the ground (the first 6 to 8 inches), which are likely to be wetted. Mulch well to minimize water splashing onto the leaves.

• Remove all diseased leaves from the plant or ground immediately to prevent spreading the disease.

# Roses

Prune infected canes all the way back to healthy tissue in late winter.

• Prune to open the center of the bush to allow sunlight and air to reach all the plant.

• Remove the old mulch in early spring of plants that had a lot of problems the previous year. Allow the area to dry, and spread clean new mulch.

• Keep the plant well watered. A weak or stressed plant is more susceptible to disease.

• Apply chemical fungicides to prevent blackspot and mildew. Spray every seven to fourteen days—especially the undersides of the leaves. **Follow the label directions exactly.**

**Remember:** Using a single fungicide over and over may cause the fungus to build a resistance to it. Alternate between two fungicides, Triforine (Funginex) and Daconil for example, to keep resistant fungi from building up. Fungicides generally can prevent blackspot, but do not cure an existing case of blackspot.

**Japanese beetles, aphids, spider mites.** See Pests, Diseases, and Controls in the Appendix.

**Leafcutter bees.** These busy bees cut semi-circle shaped holes in the leaves of roses. They pose no real threat to rose health, but they drive exhibitors crazy.

**Viral diseases.** Symptoms are a mottling or mosaic discoloration of the leaf or ring spots. In most cases, removing the infected plant is the only control. Another suggestion is to buy roses from growers who are committed to producing resistant plants. These growers, including Jackson & Perkins, make cuttings from "indexed" blocks of mother plants. An "indexed" block is a group of plants that has been tested and has a high likelihood of not being infected with a virus.

For additional information, turn to Pests, Diseases, and Controls in the Appendix.

Pruning Roses

# Roses

## Climbers

| Name | Color | Comments |
| --- | --- | --- |
| 'Fisherman's Friend' | Red | Repeat bloomer; English type rose; fragrant |
| 'Fourth of July' | Red and white striped | Blooms all season; clusters of large open flowers; 8.8 ARS rating |
| 'Gertrude Jekyll' | Rich pink | Blooms all season; fragrant 4-inch flowers; slight scent |
| 'Heritage' | Gentle pink | English/David Austin type; repeat bloomer; intense fragrance |
| 'Improved Blaze' | Cherry Red | Semi-double blooms all season. Mild fruity scent |
| New Dawn'/ 'White Dawn' | Silvery pink/white | Fluffy blooms all season. Mild fruity scent |
| 'Othello' | Dark red | Repeat bloomer; recommended for fragrance |
| 'Pilgrim' | Yellow | All season; David Austin type; perfumed |
| 'William Baffin' | Pink/Red | Semi-double mid-season blooms and repeats. Very hardy |

## Cluster-Flowered Garden Roses

| Name | Color | Comments |
| --- | --- | --- |
| 'Iceberg' | Ice white | Blooms mid-season and repeats; ARS 8.8 rating; very fragrant; stands some shade; there's a climbing 'Iceberg' |
| 'Scentimental' | Red/cream blend | Blooms all season; ARS 7.7 rating; slight fragrance |
| 'Sunsprite' | Deep yellow | Blooms mid-season and repeats; ARS 8.5 rating; very fragrant |
| 'Travemunde' | Red | Repeats; floribunda |

## Ground Cover Roses

| Name | Color | Comments |
| --- | --- | --- |
| 'Starry Night' | White | Blooms all season; mild fragrance |
| 'Scarlet Meidiland' | Scarlet | Blooms all season; ARS 7.7 rating; slight fragrance |
| 'White Meidiland' | White | Blooms all season; slight fragrance |

## Hybrid Tea Roses

| Name | Color | Comments |
| --- | --- | --- |
| 'Bella'roma' | Golden-yellow blushed pink | All-season blooms with strong rose perfume |
| 'Earth Song' | Deep pink | Repeat bloomer; sweet scent |
| 'Electron' | Deep pink | Double; ARS 7.7 rating; intense fragrance |
| 'Elina' | Ivory | Blooms all season; AARS winner 2003; light musk scent |
| 'Fragrant Cloud' | Coral red | All-season blooms; tea rose scent |
| 'Olympiad' | Ruby red | Blooms all season; slight sweet scent |
| 'Queen Elizabeth' | Clear pink | Blooms mid-season and repeats; ARS 7.7 rating; fragrant |
| 'Tiffany' | Yellow-centered pink | All-season blooms; rich rose scent |

# Roses

## Hedge Roses/Shrub Roses/Old Garden Roses including Rugosa Rose (*Rosa rugosa*)

| Name | Color | Comments |
| --- | --- | --- |
| 'Alba' | White | Rugosa rose; blooms all summer—may repeat; fragrant; showy fruit |
| 'Baronne Prevost' | Blush pink | French Alba many-petalled rose; blooms once early summer; moderate perfume |
| 'Belle de Poitevin' | Magenta pink | Old garden rose, many-petalled; large showy fruit |
| 'Bonica' | Shell Pink | Shrub. Blooms all season. Tolerates cold winters |
| 'Celsiana' | Soft pink | Damask; blooms once; semi-double introduced before 1750; delicious scent |
| 'Frau Dagmar Hastrup' | Silvery pink | Compact Rugosa rose; blooms all season; showy fruit; intense clove scent |
| 'Knock Out' varieties | Shell pink; bright pink; ruby red | Hot new shrub rose; single blooms all season; light sweet scent; most free-flowering disease-resistant rose to date |
| 'Linda Campbell' | Clear red | Rugosa rose; repeat bloomer; large clusters of blooms; some scent |
| 'Madame Hardy' | White; green button eye | Damask rose; blooms in spring; one of the most beautiful roses; lemony scent |
| 'Morden Blush'/ 'Morden Ruby' | Peach/red | Shrub. Double, all-season bloom. Very cold hardy |
| 'Rose de Rescht' | Deep rose | Old Bourbon many-petalled rose; blooms all summer; superb perfumed |
| 'Rosa Mundi' | Light crimson | Gallica rose; blooms in spring; very fragrant |
| 'Rubra' | Red | Rugosa rose; blooms all summer—may repeat; fragrant; showy fruit |
| 'Salet' | Pink | Moss rose; repeat bloomer; double-flowered; very fragrant |
| 'The Fairy' | Bright pink | Hedge rose. Small fluffy blooms from mid-summer |
| 'Therese Bugnet' | Lilac pink | Shrub rose; some repeat; almost thornless; slight fragrance |

## Miniature Roses

| Name | Color | Comments |
| --- | --- | --- |
| 'Black Jade' | Near black red | Repeat blooms through fall |
| 'Cachet' | White | Large miniature; cluster-flowered rose, exhibition quality |
| 'Jean Keneally' | Apricot | Shrubby miniature; blooms mid-season and repeats; ARS Award of Excellence 1986; mild scent |
| 'Jeanne Lajoie' | Two-tone medium pink | Climbing miniature; grows to at least 6 feet |
| 'Magic Carrousel' | Red blend | Cascading climbing miniature; ARS Award of Excellence |
| 'Raindrops' | Lavender | Flowers have a cream reverse |
| 'Red Cascade' | Dark red | Climbing miniature; blooms all season |
| 'Rise 'N Shine' | Yellow | Upright miniature; repeat bloomer; ARS Award for Excellence; slightly scented |
| 'Starina' | Orange red | Shrubby miniature; inducted into the Miniature Hall of Fame; fragrant |

PLANNING

Take this respite from the garden to learn more about roses. Mai-order catalogs from the rose specialists named in the Appendix are great teachers. Make an album of catalog pages of roses you would like to try. Go out to the garden and find likely places to plant them.

**Roses that climb (CL) need 5 to 10 feet between plants.** Train them to climb or ramble, and the canes will cover split rail fences, stone walls, pillars, posts, pergolas, or arches. A large flowered **climber** trained to a trellis makes a beautiful backdrop for a rose garden. **Ramblers** and **miniature climbers** are excellent basket and container plants.

**Large-flowered bush roses need 3 to 4 feet between plants.** These roses are all about big, breathtakingly beautiful flowers, ideal for exhibition and for collectors. The group includes **modern hybrid tea (HT)** and **grandiflora (GR)** roses. The plants are large, upright, leggy, and need a bed of their own. In formal gardens **hybrid tea roses** are set off, parterre style, in geometric shaped beds edged with low hedges of clipped **boxwood** or **lavender cotton** (*Santolina chamaecyparissus*).

**Cluster-flowered bush roses need 2 to 3 feet between plants.** Medium sized, these easily managed roses bear clusters of flowers all season. They're excellent in big perennial borders and grouped in transitional spaces. Some can be pruned just with hedge shears. The **floribundas** (many-flowered) are planted in Europe along the roads and in parks. The **modern bush roses,** including the peachy-pink AARS 1987 winner 'Bonica' and other **Meidilands,** are hybrid everbloomers growing on their own roots. Smaller **polyanthas** like the rambling, fragrant seashell pink 'The Fairy', make pretty, low, carefree hedges. The **English** and **David Austin roses** are graceful plants that bear very pretty flowers in the style of old garden roses but with more modern disease resistance built in.

**Compact and patio roses need 2 to 4 feet or more.** Compact, 2 to 4 feet tall, somewhere between **miniatures** and **floribundas,** these bloom freely all season. They are planted in perennial borders, for hedges, as ground cover, as edgers, and as fillers for rose beds. The **flower carpet** group has a 5-foot spread.

**Miniature roses need 18 to 24 inches between plants.** The enchanting **minis** bloom all season, are winter hardy, disease-resistant, and are easy to grow indoors, too. The upright forms are 12 inches high and 6 to 18 inches across, and make pretty edgers. Those with trailing branches are lovely basket and container plants.

**Heirloom, rugosa, and species roses need 5 to 6 feet or more between plants. Heirloom roses** are **old garden roses,** a passport to "time travel." Many are exceptionally fragrant. Most bloom once for about four weeks in early or mid-spring, on canes 3 to 6 feet long. The modern trouble-free **rugosa roses** are tall stiff bushes with spiny upright canes, perfect for tall hedges, as windbreaks, keep-outs to intruders. Deer don't trouble them, and they are excellent at the seashore.

Some rose species are excellent subjects for a naturalized garden. The magenta-pink **Virginia rose** (*Rosa virginiana*) is extremely cold hardy and has brilliant autumn foliage.

PLANTING

If there is no snow, you could go out now and lay out a new rose bed, but you won't be able to dig until the soil dries.

*If there is no snow, you could go out now and lay out a new rose bed, but you won't be able to dig until the soil dries.*

## CARE

**Indoors.** If **miniatures** growing indoors aren't blooming, add grow lights for the evening.

**Outdoors.** Where there is no snow cover, check and adjust the winter mulch and other forms of protection for in-ground roses.

## PRUNING

Deadhead **miniature roses** indoors; remove crossing and crowded stems to keep the center open.

## WATERING

**Indoors.** Keep the soil moderately moist for **miniatures**. Moisten only the soil, not the leaves. Shower them every two weeks.

Maintain the soil moisture of roses in containers overwintering in a frost-free shed or garage.

## Did You Know?

### You Can Grow Miniature Roses Indoors

Miniature roses that do well indoors are available from florists and garden markets. Some favorites are 'Rise 'n Shine', 'Little Jackie', 'Red Beauty', and 'Starina'. To grow a mini indoors:

- Repot it in a clay pot lined with pebbles or PermaTill and filled with a potting mix that includes a water-holding polymer.

- Grow it on a south-facing windowsill, under grow lights, or in a window greenhouse.

- Keep the plant cool at night.

- Water when the surface feels dry to the touch.

- Fertilize at every watering with a half-dose of a water-soluble fertilizer.

- Deadhead back to the first five leaflet set.

- Prune out crowded and crossing stems to keep the center open.

- Remove infected foliage and stems at once.

- Shower every two weeks.

- In May move the plant outdoors to a semi-sunny spot for a summer vacation.

## FERTILIZING

Fertilize **miniature roses** growing indoors at every watering with a half-dose of a soluble plant food for flowering plants, African violet, or some other bloom booster.

## PESTS

If spider mite webs show up on **miniatures** growing indoors, rinse the plants every two weeks. Air the room daily. Segregate infected plants. See also Pests, Diseases, and Controls in the Appendix to the book.

# FEBRUARY
## Roses

 PLANNING

When ordering new roses, make sure they withstand your winters. Be wary of roses that have no hardiness rating; growers don't always know how new roses will perform. It's also a good idea to be skeptical of winter ratings based on experience in the United Kingdom—plants perform differently there.

Hardiness trials conducted over a period of years at Rogers Farm (University of Maine, Stillwater, Maine, under Dr. Lois Berg Stack, of the UM Cooperative Extension Service) have shown that the **species roses,** and once-blooming **old garden (heirloom) roses** on our plant list are among the hardiest. Of the repeat-bloomers in the trials, **rugosas** proved very hardy, as well. Whenever possible, especially in Zones 3 through 5, buy only **hybrid teas and other hybrid roses labeled as growing on their own roots and hardy in your area.** Their hardiness depends on the roots' natural resistance to cold. Killed to the ground, shoots from the rootstock will regenerate and bloom "true" to the parent variety.

If you want to try a **hybrid tea** or other rose, whose hardiness is iffy in your zone, grow it in a container that can be sheltered in a frost-free garage or shed for the winter.

 PLANTING

**Miniature roses** that aren't doing well may benefit from repotting in a larger container.

 CARE

Check your rosebushes for signs of heaving: it can happen in our milder zones during January and February thaws. Gently press the crowns back into the ground and cover with a light mulch.

Check and adjust winter mulches and other forms of protection.

 PRUNING

**Indoors.** Continue to deadhead and groom the **minis.**

**Outdoors.** During warm spells, go out and evaluate the when and how of the pruning job ahead for your roses. Wait until the last of the really cold weather to prune away dead or damaged branches.

If you want to slow the growth and promote flowering in some roses, plan to **root prune** them. The best time for it is ahead, in early spring before growth begins. Root pruning is easy once the ground has thawed. With a spade sever the roots in a circle all around the bush to where the roots are about the size of your little finger. If you encounter roots you need a saw to cut, you are too close. If the roots are web fine, you are too far out.

 WATERING

Maintain the soil moisture of **miniature roses** growing indoors and roses in containers overwintering in a frost-free shed or garage.

 FERTILIZING

As long as the ground is frozen it's too early to fertilize.

 PESTS

When the soil dries, remove the mulch layer under roses that were troubled by **blackspot** and **mildew** last year. Wait until you have tested the pH and fertilized to spread a fresh mulch.

As winter ends, get ready to smother insect eggs overwintering in the roses by spraying them with an ultrafine (dormant) horticultural oil spray; labels describe the temperature limits for effectiveness.

*When ordering new roses make sure they withstand your winters. Be wary of roses that have no hardiness rating; growers don't always know how new roses will perform.*

## Did You Know?

### The When and How of Pruning Roses

Wear thick leather gloves, and use sharp, clean pruning shears for small canes, and a small pruning saw for large canes.

- Pruning can begin before or as the buds swell:

  Zone 7: in March
  Zone 6: mid- to late March
  Zones 3, 4, 5: early to late April

**Basics**

- Place pruning cuts so the center of the bush remains open for maximum air circulation.
- Make cuts $1/4$ inch above an outward-facing bud or leafset. Cut at a 45-degree angle with the high side on the side the bud or leafset is on—the outward facing side.
- Squeeze a drop of white glue over the cut ends of larger canes to keep borers out.
- Scrub the woody surface of the bud union with a brass wire brush (sold by hardware stores) to clear dead tissue and stimulate growth.

**Pruning Established Roses**

- **All but one-time bloomers.** Before or as the buds swell, remove dead canes, growth skinnier than a pencil, and canes crossing the center that are growing in the wrong direction and crowding others. Cut winter-damaged canes back to healthy green wood. Leave enough stem above the bud union for new growth to develop. **The exception to this rule: one-time bloomers are pruned after the roses have faded.**
- **All roses.** Saw off old woody canes as close to the bud union as possible.
- **All grafted/budded roses.** Remove suckers growing from below the bud union of **hybrid teas, grandifloras,** and other grafted roses, or they will take over.
- **Hybrid teas, grandifloras.** Cut **hybrid teas** back to six well-placed canes and **grandifloras** back to eight canes. Reduce the canes a third, to 14 to 18 inches long.
- **Floribundas, polyanthas.** Cut three-year-old canes off at the bud union or to the crown. Cut two-year-old stems back by half. Cut back new canes by a third, or to just below where they bloomed last year.
- **Modern bush roses, 'Bonica', the Meidiland family.** Trim branch tips back to shape the plant.
- **Cluster-flowered bush roses, heirloom,** and **species roses.** Prune lightly to shape the plant.
- **Miniatures.** Remove all but the best four or five canes, and cut those back by a third.
- **Climbers.** For the first two years, prune to remove unproductive canes. After that, prune out the oldest canes leaving five or six healthy canes, and shorten their side shoots by two-thirds.
- **Carpet roses.** Prune the canes back to 6 inches.
- **Rugosa roses.** Cut unproductive older canes back to the ground.

# MARCH
## Roses

 ## PLANNING

Look your roses over and determine which survived winter. That may impact your order for new rose bushes. If you have lost a lot of roses, order early because the weather that killed your roses may cause a run on the most desirable plants.

 ## PLANTING

Except for sheltered especially warm microclimates, it is still too early to plant roses, but you can begin to bone up on planting procedures.

**Preparing a rose for planting:**

• **Bare root.** Keep the rose in its package in a dark, cool place until planting time. The roots need to be soaked in tepid water before planting—usually six to twelve hours.

• **Container grown.** Make shallow slits in the container sides, and peel the pieces away. If roots wrap the rootball, make four shallow vertical cuts in the sides of the rootball, and slice of the bottom 2 inches.

• **Roses in plantable containers.** Open the top, and maintain the soil moisture until you are ready to plant. Follow the package directions for planting.

 ## CARE

Adjust the leads and supports for **climbers.**

Adjust winter protection for roses before the last storms hit.

Check for heaving, and press the crowns back into the soil.

 ## PRUNING

**Indoors.** Deadhead **miniature roses.**

**Outdoors.** Roses are best pruned before the buds swell (see February); if the winter was mild, gardeners in Zones 6 and 7 had best keep an eye on their progress.

 ## WATERING

Maintain the soil moisture of **miniature roses** growing indoors and roses in containers overwintering in a frost-free shed or garage.

 ## FERTILIZING

When the winter cold and wet have left the ground, prepare clean **established rose beds** and prepare them for fertilization by checking and adjusting the pH. How to fertilize is explained in the April pages.

 ## PESTS

As soon as mud season is over and before you fertilize or mulch, remove and discard old mulch under plants that had blackspot or mildew last year.

Apply an ultrafine dormant oil spray **to smother overwintering insect eggs.** There are temperature limits for effectiveness, so read the label.

If vole runs appear around the roses, bait the main runway with a rodenticide.

*Maintain the soil moisture of miniature roses growing indoors and roses in containers overwintering in a frost-free shed or garage.*

## Did You Know?

### How to Plant Roses

**Preparing a New Rose Bed**

Any airy, sunny, well-drained site soil can be made into a fine bed for roses. Start three to four weeks before planting season so the soil amendments will settle in before you plant.

*1* Choose a site with full sun—at least six to eight hours.

*2* Lay out the bed.

*3* Check and adjust the pH.

*4* Thoroughly water the turf.

*5* Spray with RoundUp Weed and Grass Killer. The turf will be completely dead in about two weeks. Or, remove the turf (and compost it).

*6* Cover the bed with 3 to 5 inches of organic material—any combination of decomposed bark, compost, partially decomposed leaves, sphagnum peat moss, black peat humus, well-rotted animal manure.

*7* For every 100 square feet of garden bed, spread on these long-lasting organic fertilizers and amendments:
Rose-tone or Plant-tone: 5 to 10 pounds
Rock phosphate: 5 to 10 pounds
Green sand: 5 to 10 pounds
Clay soils: gypsum 5 to 10 pounds

*8* With a rear-tine rototiller, which you can rent from a garden center, mix all this as deeply as the rototiller will go.

*9* Rake the bed smooth, and discard rocks, lumps, and bumps.

**Preparing A New Planting Hole for a Rose Bush**

*1* Outline a hole at least 20 inches wide. Dig a hole twice as deep as the rootball.

*2* Test the pH of the soil. Bring to the site the products needed to adjust the pH, along with the fertilizers and amendments recommended for new 100 square foot bed, above. If the area you are planting measures only 10 square feet, combine one-tenth of the amount of each supplement given for a bed over 100 square feet.

*3* As you dig, every 4 or 5 inches mix a portion of the fertilizer and amendments into the soil from the hole. The soil by the side of the hole is now "improved" and ready for the next step.

*4* Pack in enough improved soil to place the graft (bud union—a thickened node at the base of the stem) if there is one, or the crown, at the right depth.

**Planting A Rose Bush**

*1* **Depth.** The right depth depends on your plant-hardiness zone. In Zone 6 and north, grafted/budded roses do best planted if the graft lies 2 to 3 inches below the soil surface. In Zone 7, the bud union can be at soil level.

*2* **Arranging the roots. Bare-root rose.** Firm a cone in the center of the mound, drape the roots over it, and spread them out in the hole. **Container rose.** Settle the rootball on packed improved soil. **Plantable container rose.** Set the container on firmly packed improved soil. Make sure the plant is sitting straight and its crown is level with the surrounding soil, fill the hole half-way with improved soil, and pack it down. Water. Finish filling with improved soil, pack it down, and water again.

*3* **Watering.** Shape the soil around the crown into a wide saucer (water basin), and create a rim around it that will keep rain or hose water from running off. Water the soil slowly, gently, and thoroughly with a sprinkler, a soaker hose, a bubbler, or by hand. You need to put down 1½ inches of water. Or, slowly and gently pour on 10 to 15 gallons of water from a bucket.

*4* **Mulching.** Mulch 2 to 3 inches deep starting 3 inches from the main stem.

## PLANNING

As the roses begin to wake up, record in your garden log which ones did what and when. That information will be helpful next year when you are getting ready to prepare the bed and prune your roses.

## PLANTING

If you have a sunny, sheltered porch or patio, you soon may be able to plant a few container roses. The **miniatures** thrive in moss-lined baskets, planters, and clay or cement containers. **Compact** and **patio, cluster-flowered** varieties and **tree roses** bloom non-stop in a container.

## CARE

If you did not prepare the soil in established rose beds last month, clear your rose beds of old mulch, and check and adjust the pH to get ready to fertilize. Remember: Every three to five years enrich the soil by applying phosphate, green sand, and gypsum if the soil has a a lot of clay.

If the last frost has gone by, you can return containers that sheltered in a garage or shed to a sheltered corner in the garden. Top-dress the soil, fertilize, and prune the branches.

## PRUNING

**Indoors.** Continue to deadhead **miniature roses.**

**Outdoors.** If you have not yet pruned your in-ground roses, do so now. The rule is to prune before the buds break. But late is better than not at all. See the February pages for recommended timing. **The exception to the early spring pruning rule** is one-time bloomers. Prune this type **after** blooming as they bear their flowers on the previous year's growth.

Prune **first year plants** only lightly to allow them to concentrate on establishing a strong root system.

When the **forsythia** blooms, cut 'Knock Out' series roses back to 10 inches to keep them shrub size; otherwise, they can grow 9 to 10 feet tall.

## WATERING

**Indoors.** Keep the soil for **miniatures** moderately moist. Wet the soil, not the leaves.

**Outdoors.** Maintain soil moisture for **tender roses** still sheltering in a garage or shed and those moved outdoors—in-ground roses, too, especially climbers under an overhang or pergola where rain and snow don't quite get to them. Roses are growing now and must have 1½ inches of water every week—that's two to three 5-gallon buckets.

## FERTILIZING

Before growth begins, fertilize the soil around in-ground and container roses. How far in advance depends on the type of fertilizer you are using. **Mark the date in your garden log, and note on your calendar when the next application is due.**

• **Organic fertilizers.** Early this month and three more times this year—about every six weeks—to every 100 square feet of bed, apply 5 to 10 pounds of Rose-tone or Plant-tone.

The next application is due in early summer, about six weeks from now, and every six weeks until growth slows, about August 15 in Zones 3 and 4, in September farther south.

*If you have a sunny, sheltered porch or patio, you soon may be able to plant a few container roses. The miniatures thrive in moss lined baskets, planters, and clay or cement containers.*

• **Slow-release fertilizers:** Four to six weeks before growth begins, apply an eight-month formulation.

• **Granular chemical fertilizer.** Make a first application just before growth begins. The next application is due in six weeks; repeat every six weeks after that until growth slows. The last application of the year should be an organic fertilizer.

Supplement this with foliage feedings of water-soluble organic or fast-acting, liquid fertilizers if the roses fail to bloom up to expectation or show a lack of vigor.

## PESTS

Weeds are popping. Rake them away.

Spray with an anti-desiccant spray or the Cornell remedy for blackspot and mildew (see June). If you have had serious infestations, start spraying with a rose fungicide.

## Did You Know?

### How to Prune Roses

Where you cut—whether pruning, deadheading, or harvesting—shapes the bush's future. Roses tend to send a strong lateral (sideways) cane (branch-stem) out from the node just below a cut. You can keep the center of the bush open by **making all cuts about ¼ inch above an outward facing bud or leaf cluster.** Use **sharp** bypass shears.

• Always cut at a diagonal, a 45-degree angle. Make the top of the cut on the side the bud or leafset is on.

• When deadheading or harvesting roses, make the cut just above the first five- or seven-segment leaf below the flower or above an outward-facing bud. If this would cause too much of the cane to be removed, make the cut at a three-segment leaf instead.

• The first year cut back to the first three- or five-segment leaf. In following years, cut far enough down to get to a five-segment or seven-segment leaf or bud that is facing outward. This will open up the plant.

Aphids cluster on rosebuds and cane tips. Spray them off every morning with a hose, or spray with Neem or insecticidal soap.

Deer are busy, hungry, and enjoy tender new shoots and rose foliage. For controls see Pests, Diseases, and Controls in the Appendix to the book.

# MAY
## Roses

 PLANNING

Other gardener's roses, like someone else's grass, always look better. That's because we see them from a distance.

To get a notion of how stunning roses can be, **visit some of the public rose gardens** in our area since roses are coming into their glory period. Bring a notebook, and write down the names of those you must have—then look for them at garden centers. They're brimming with roses this time of year, all in top condition.

 PLANTING

A fine month for planting new roses.

Fill gaps in the rose bed with leafy annuals to hide the legginess of the roses—**salvias, 'Wave' petunias, sun coleus. Lavender** is our favorite perennial used as a rose companion.

 CARE

Repot **miniature roses** growing indoors in fresh soil, and put them outdoors in bright light, but not in direct sunlight, to prepare them for full sun later.

 PRUNING

Prune **one-time bloomers** when they finish blooming. See the February pages for recommended timing.

To keep specimen roses looking good and producing flowers, **deadhead religiously**—that is, remove spent blooms—**hybrid teas** and **grandifloras** especially. **Miniature roses** and the small **polyanthas, carpet roses,** and **species roses** generally do not need deadheading.

To deadhead, make the cut a 45-degree diagonal just above the next five- or seven-segment leaf down the stem. The first year cut back to the first three- or five-segment leafset. In following years, cut far enough down to get to a five-segment or seven-segment leafset or bud that is facing outward. This keeps the plant's new growth headed outward.

 WATERING

As the weather warms, begin daily checks of the moisture in the soil of **container roses** growing in small pots and baskets. Water enough to keep the soil from drying out.

From late spring to early fall, **roses growing in big tubs** may need watering every four to five days, or weekly. The larger the container, the less often it will need watering.

Make sure **in-ground roses** receive 1½ inches of water every week—that's two or three 5-gallon buckets.

 FERTILIZING

Liquid-feed roses **growing in containers** every two weeks with a half-strength dose of a soluble rose fertilizer.

For **in-ground** roses, six weeks after your first application of organic-blend fertilizers or granular, chemical fertilizer, repeat the application. The usual timing is early summer, but it depends on when you make the first application.

**Supplement this with foliage feedings of water-soluble organic or chemical liquid fertilizers if the roses fail to bloom up to expectation or show a lack of vigor.**

 PESTS

Use a hoe to root out weeds creeping into the mulch under the roses.

If blackspot or powdery mildew appear, remove and discard (do not compost!!) every leaf and spoiled blossom on the plant and petals on the ground. Prune out diseased canes. Apply a rose fungicide according to the label directions.

Aphids cluster on rosebuds and cane tips. Use a strong spray of water to blow them away in the early morning. If they persist, spray with Neem or insecticidal soap.

Aphids

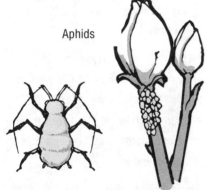

Roses that are wilting, yellowing, and seem stunted may be troubled by nematodes. The control is applications of ground crab shells which to date only wholesalers sell with names like Clandosan. However you can make your own. Save up and grind lobster and crab shells and scatter it around and dig it into the soil around affected roses.

## Did You Know?

### How to Grow Roses in Containers

Smaller roses do well in containers. **Miniatures, rose trees,** smaller **Meidilands, floribundas,** and some **hybrid teas** are all candidates.

- **Light.** The roses will need six but better eight hours of sun each day. Be prepared to turn the pot often to keep the bush growing evenly all around. A movable container makes it easy to take advantage of shifting light. Garden centers offer plant saucers and containers equipped with casters.

- **Container size.** For a **miniature rose,** a 6-inch pot that's 5 inches deep is sufficient. For **standard roses** provide a tub that is at least 18 inches in diameter and 14 inches deep. Save watering time by planting in a container with a built-in water reservoir or water ring that lets the plant soak up the water from the bottom.

- **Preparation.** Soak porous containers—clay and wood—before adding soil, or they will take moisture from the soil you put into them. For winter protection, wrap the interior with a double row of large bubble-wrap or Styrofoam™.

- **Soil.** Line the bottom with PermaTill®, then fill with this mix: $1/4$ good garden soil or bagged top soil, $1/4$ commercial soil-less mix, $1/4$ compost, and $1/4$ sand, or $1/8$ perlite and $1/8$ PermaTill. Add a modest application of Osmocote® slow-release fertilizer and a water-holding polymer such as Soil Moist to help maintain moisture. Soak the growing medium before you plant.

- **Watering.** After planting, water well and maintain soil moisture thereafter.

- **Fertilizing.** Liquid feed every two weeks with a half-strength dose of a good rose or container-plant fertilizer.

- **Winter care.** Before freezing cold temperatures, store the container in a detached, unheated garage, shed, or cool basement. A potted rose needs to be cold enough to go dormant but must not freeze. Water lightly once a month.

Deer nibble the tender new wood and leaves on roses and eat the flowers and the buds; the Pests, Diseases, and Controls section in the Appendix to the book has suggestions for controlling them.

PLANNING

The roses that didn't sell this spring may be on sale now—or soon. Be tempted but be wise. Check out the rootball, and go for plants whose leaves are shiny, green, plentiful, no yellowing, no stippling, and no spider mite webs.

 PLANTING

If you haven't tried **miniature roses** yet, see what's on sale at the garden centers this month. The minis bloom freely and will almost surely come back better than ever next year. The little blossoms are somewhat reserved about sharing their scent, but it's there. Orangy red 'Starina' is known for its fragrance.

Many **miniatures** are hybrids of 'Minima', a selection of the **China rose** (*Rosa chinensis*). One of the wonderful characteristics the China rose imparted to modern roses is summer-long bloom. If you've grown a miniature indoors, plant it in the ground for the summer to encourage a better root system.

 CARE

Top up the mulch around the roses before heat gets intense.

Attach the new growth of the **climbers** and **ramblers** to their supports.

 PRUNING

Check budded/grafted roses, and remove new canes coming from the rootstock below the bud union.

Deadhead **hybrid teas, grandifloras,** and other show-time roses.

Prune one-time bloomers as soon as possible after they finish blooming. See February for likely timing.

Cutting a Rose

**How to harvest roses.** Here are some hints to help you get the most from your roses.

- Harvest roses early, before the sun gets to them.

- Take to the garden a 5-gallon plastic bucket filled with lukewarm water containing floral preservative, clean sharp pruning shears, and thick gauntlets.

- Choose stems whose buds haven't fully opened.

- The first year make the cut just above the first three- or five-segment leafset. In following years cut far enough down to get to a five-segment or seven-segment leaf or bud that is facing outward.

- Immediately plunge the cut stem into the water bucket. Then remove the foliage that will be below the water line, and condition the roses in fresh water overnight in a cool place.

- Scour the bucket and vases with a dilute bleach solution ($\frac{1}{2}$ teaspoon of bleach per gallon of water) each time after they are used.

*Check budded/grafted roses, and remove new canes coming from the rootstock below the bud union.*

 ## WATERING

Growing in good soil, new and established roses need 1 to 1½ inches of water each week—from the sky or your watering system. Or, slowly pour two or three 5-gallon buckets of water around and in the water basin.

**Miniature roses** growing in small pots and baskets probably need water daily. Check the roses growing in **big containers** every couple of days, and water when the soil feels dry a few inches down. Water until the water runs out the bottom.

 ## FERTILIZING

Liquid feed roses growing in containers every two weeks with a half-strength dose of a rose fertilizer.

The second application of organic blend fertilizer or chemical water-soluble fertilizer was due six weeks after the early spring application. Do it now if you haven't done it yet.

 ## PESTS

Deer nibble roses, buds, and leaves; deterrent sprays may not keep them away. See the section on Pests in the Appendix to the book.

Continue to root out weeds, and look out for aphids, spider mites, thrips, blackspot, and powdery mildew. If you have already sprayed without effect, switch to another control.

Japanese beetles get busy now. This rather handsome metallic green and coppery maroon insect wrecks the flowers and chews the leaves and stems as well. In early morning, knock them into soapy water, and destroy them. If there are wild grape vines on your property, root them out; they are an attractive host plant for the Japanese beetle. Apply Milky Spore or a grub

control product to the lawn and gardens now, and there should be fewer Japanese beetles next year. But that won't stop them from flying in. **Beetle traps are effective, only if they are placed far away from the roses.** If Japanese beetles become a real problem, apply insecticides containing Neem, rotenone, or Sevin.

## PLANNING

This month and next, visit public gardens and gardens noted for roses—and smell the roses. Note the names of those that are really fragrant, and plan to try them. For the perfumed roses to be truly fragrant, we find they need to grow in full sun—eight hours.

## PLANTING

You can plant **container roses** at home and even at the shore. If Japanese beetles are ruining your roses, try one they don't pay much attention to, the **rugosa rose.** *Rosa rugosa* is a tall (5 feet or more) native of China, Russia, Japan, and Korea that does so well at the sea it is used to create wind breaks in very exposed positions. (But can be invasive so don't plant it where it can go wild and take over native plants.)

Yes, it's tall and thorny, but modern cultivars bear clove-scented single or double flowers that are quite lovely, and the rose hips are spectacular. Most bloom for quite a while in spring, and some repeat bloom.

The roses are very cold-hardy and resist not only the Japanese beetle but also many other pests. The only pruning needed is the removal in early spring of older canes to encourage new growth.

One of the most beautiful is white 'Rose Blanc Double de Coubert'; another beauty is deep pink almost thornless 'Therese Bugnet'. They are among several that tested very hardy.

When filling containers for a seashore garden, use commercial potting soil instead of the sandy soil of the area. The humidity in the air reduces the need to water, but check the soil moisture often.

## CARE

Heat is here. Check and replenish the mulch under the roses.

## PRUNING

Harvest—and deadhead—**hybrid teas** and **grandifloras.** The **everblooming roses** that bear clusters of small flowers generally do not need deadheading, but if they aren't producing as expected, groom and deadhead them, and apply a liquid fertilizer.

## WATERING

This month and next, **check the soil moisture daily in pots and baskets.** They may need a good soaking almost every day. Water until you see water dripping from the bottom of the container.

Make sure **in-ground roses** receive 1½ inches of water every week—that's two to three 5-gallon buckets.

Keep roses that suffered from powdery mildew well watered. Unlike blackspot, wet conditions actually inhibit the development of powdery mildew. While it thrives in high humidity, it forms on dry leaves. Warm dry days and cool dry nights are ideal for powdery mildew. A weak or stressed plant is more susceptible to disease.

If blackspot is a problem on the same plant, water the roots and avoid wetting the foliage.

## FERTILIZING

Liquid feed roses growing in containers every two weeks with a half-strength dose of a good rose or container-plant fertilizer.

The third application of organic-blend fertilizer or chemical, water-soluble fertilizer is due six weeks after the second application in mid-summer.

If roses fertilized with a time-release, chemical fertilizer are failing to bloom as expected or look peaked, supplement with foliar feedings of water-soluble, organic or fast-acting, liquid fertilizers.

*This month and next, check the soil moisture daily in pots and baskets. They may need a good soaking almost every day.*

## PESTS

Weed! Don't let them grow up inside the bushes!

Mites attack roses stressed by hot weather and drought. Make them miserable with vigorous hosing of the leaves, and especially the undersides of the leaves, every day or two for a week. If there are signs of webs on twigs and leaf stems, apply Neem or an insecticidal soap.

If caterpillars become numerous, spray with a biological control such as *Bacillus thuringiensis*. Other controls are Sevin or malathion insecticide, pyrethrin, or rotenone.

If Japanese beetles persist, spray their bodies with a pyrethrum product. It's a contact sport!

The rose midge larvae causes deformed buds and dead branch tips. Prune the branches, and destroy infested buds and tips. Spray with Neem every five days or as directed.

Deer may be eating your roses and their foliage; see Pests, Diseases, and Controls in the Appendix of the book.

## Did You Know?

### You Can Root Cuttings to Multiply Your Roses

Propagating roses by softwood cuttings is a fascinating project, and a thrill when you succeed. Some considered easy to propagate from softwood and semi-softwood cuttings are **old roses**, **English roses**, and **miniatures.** Take cuttings from the ends of new canes that are green to semi-green and whose flowers have lost almost all their petals.

*1* Set a 1-gallon clear freezer bag upright, and pack the bottom with 6 inches of sterile potting mix well-moistened with water containing 1 teaspoon of soluble rose food for every 4 quarts.

*2* Shake about 2 inches of rooting hormone powder Number 3, or Roottone, into a small glass.

*3* Take the cutting in early morning. From the blossom end, count down four leafsets to a five-leafset, and cut the stem off about an inch below.

*4* Working in the shade, cut the top off about a half-inch above the top leafset. Remove the leaves from the bottom 2 inches. Mist the foliage. Score the bottom inch of so of the stem vertically. Dip the wounded end in the rooting powder, and knock off the excess.

*5* Bury the cut end upright in the middle of the potting mix deep enough to cover the wounds. Press the soil up around the stem.

*6* Mist the cutting, blow the bag full of air, and zip it closed.

*7* Place the plastic bag in bright, indirect light.

*8* Sometime between two and six weeks, there should begin to be roots showing along the bottom of the bag.

*9* When top growth begins, acclimate the cutting to the air in the room. Each day for the next two weeks, unzip the bag a little more, and leave it open a little longer. Start with four hours the first day.

*10* Fill a pot as big as the bag to within 4 inches of the top with half potting soil and half peat. Set the bag on top, slit the bottom, and carefully remove it. Gently firm the soil up around the roots.

*11* In about a week, move the pot outside, and week by week expose it to increasingly stronger light. Maintain the soil moisture. In September, transplant the plant to the garden, and cover it with an open mulch of hay or evergreen boughs.

# AUGUST
## Roses

# PLANNING

Late afternoons in August the scent of perfumed roses is heady because the fragrant oils have been volatilized by a whole day of hot sun. Once upon a time, oils drawn from the scented florals were our only source of fragrance. The roses that scented the old potpourris are still available. **It's fun on a lazy summer evening to dream of planting a garden of roses for making potpourris.** You could interplant the roses with **English lavender** (*Lavandula officinalis*) 'Hidcote'. Lavender's lasting scent when dried makes it a "must" in recipes for dry perfumes.

Some scented candidates for your dream garden are the scented **Bourbon roses,** in general, and the very fragrant pink 'La Reine Victoria' in particular. Many of the cabbage roses, and the fairly hardy species, *Rosa centifolia*, are sweetly fragrant, including the cultivar 'Fantin Latour'. The damask roses are fragrant, including the beautiful white 'Madame Hardy' which did quite well in hardiness tests. If you have room for only one rose for potpourri, choose the rose grown commercially for its scent, *Rosa gallica* 'Officinalis', the **Apothecary rose.** This rose is unique in that the petals are more fragrant after drying, and it did pretty well in the Maine tests men-

tioned under Planning in the February pages. Before indulging, check their hardiness in your area!!

# PLANTING

**If roses go on sale and you haven't the inclination to plant your purchases** in August's high heat, buy now anyway, and grow them in their containers until September brings cooler and better weather for planting. A **miniature rose** is safe in its original container as long as you keep it watered. The larger roses will do better while waiting if they are repotted in a larger container.

# CARE

If the foliage of the **hybrid teas** wilts in temperatures over 90 degrees Fahrenheit, help them recover by misting the leaves with a mild solution of liquid seaweed. Apply it in early morning before the sun starts to climb.

# PRUNING

In Zones 3, 4, and 5, you can begin allowing rose hips to form to encourage your plants to go dormant, notably the **hybrid teas** and **grandifloras.**

Remove suckers growing up from under the bud union of your grafted **hybrid roses,** along with any diseased or damaged canes.

# WATERING

This month and next check the soil moisture daily in small pots and baskets. They may need a good soaking almost every day. Roses growing in big containers in hot windy places may need watering every third or fifth day. Water until it is dripping from the bottom of the container.

Make sure **in-ground roses** receive $1\frac{1}{2}$ inches of water every week—that's two to three 5-gallon buckets.

**Keep roses attacked by powdery mildew well watered.** Wet conditions actually inhibit the development of powdery mildew. If blackspot is a problem in the same plant, water the roots, and avoid wetting the foliage.

# FERTILIZING

Liquid feed **roses growing in containers** with a water-soluble fertilizer every two weeks.

*Late afternoons in August the scent of perfumed roses is heady because the fragrant oils have been volatilized by a whole day of hot sun. Once upon a time, oils drawn from the scented florals were our only source of fragrance.*

The third application of organic blend fertilizer or chemical water-soluble fertilizer was due six weeks after the second application, in mid-summer. If you haven't done it yet, do it now. If the roses look as though they need a quick pick-up, spray a liquid fertilizer on the foliage.

If roses fertilized with a time-release chemical fertilizer are failing to bloom as expected or look peaked, supplement with foliar feedings of water-soluble organic or fast-acting liquid fertilizers.

 PESTS

Roses weakened or stressed by hot dry weather are especially vulnerable to mites, aphids, and Japanese beetles.

**Control rust** by avoiding overhead watering, and disposing of infected foliage and twigs, applying an anti-transpirant every other week, or spraying with a horticultural oil.

**Control powdery mildew** by applying an anti-transpirant, and by maintaining good air circulation.

## Did You Know?

### Rose Potpourri Is Easy to Make

The ancient recipe that follows is from my book *Potpourris and Other Fragrant Delights*, which was published here and in Europe some years ago. Gum storax is from the resin of the tree *Styrax officinalis*, and it is the "benjamin" mentioned in the old stillroom potpourri recipes. Gum benzoin and oil of benzoin are substitutes, and are offered by several online suppliers.

3 cups dried petals of a fragrant rose
2 cups dried **lavender** buds
1 cup **lemon verbena** leaves
1 tablespoon ground allspice
1 tablespoon fresh-ground cinnamon
1 tablespoon fresh-ground cloves
$1/4$ ounce or more gum benzoin, gum storax, or oil of styrax

Combine all the dry ingredients, then add the gum benzoin, gum storax, or oil of styrax, mixing as you go until the scent seems satisfyingly strong. Seal the mixture in a container, and set it to cure in a dark, dry place, shaking the contents every day. Put the potpourri into a decorative container that has a close-fitting lid.

Uncap the container when you wish to scent a room, but keep it well covered at all other times.

**Control blackspot** by removing fallen leaves, pruning out diseased twigs, and avoiding wetting the foliage.

Viral diseases may strike now. There's no remedy. Symptoms are a mottling or mosaic discoloration of the leaf or ring spots. In most cases, removing the infected plant is the only control.

Continue weed patrol.

Deer may be eating your roses and their leaves; see Pests in the Appendix of the book.

# SEPTEMBER

## PLANNING

**It is time to begin planning winter protection for your roses.**

Roses growing on their own roots will need less attention than those grafted/budded onto hardy rootstock. The first line of defense for vulnerable roses is to plant the bud union at the proper depth as described in the March pages. Check bud unions now of budded plants, and, if need be, dig and replant the roses this month. The Care section of the November pages have detailed instructions on winter care.

## PLANTING

As the weather cools, repot the **miniature roses** that usually live indoors, rinse and spray them with insecticidal soap, and bring them indoors to a sunny sill.

September is a fine month for planting as well as transplanting roses, so take advantage of end-of-season sales to complete your rose collection.

## CARE

To help roses harden off and mature for winter, stop the use of high nitrogen fertilizers about six weeks before the first frost.

If you did not **check and adjust the pH of the soil in your rose beds** in March or April, you can do it now. Roses prefer a slightly acidic soil, pH 5.8 to 6.8. To raise the pH, use 5 to 10 pounds of limestone per 100 square feet of garden bed. If the pH is too high, lower it with an application of elemental fertilizer sulfur, (water-soluble garden sulfur) at the rate of 5 to 10 pounds per 100 square feet. Aluminum sulfate or iron sulfate are acidifiers that act faster but do not last as long in the soil.

## PRUNING

Let the last blossoms on **hybrid teas** and **grandifloras** develop into rose hips. It causes the plant to undergo chemical changes that slow growth, inhibit blooming, and generally prepare for dormancy by hardening the canes. The formation of hips tells the plant that it's done its job and can now prepare to rest.

## WATERING

**Indoors.** Keep the soil for **miniatures** moderately moist. Moisten the soil, not the leaves. Shower them every two weeks.

**Outdoors.** Continue to check soil moisture daily in roses growing outdoors in small containers. Water **big containers** every week or so unless you've had a soaking rain.

Make sure **in-ground** roses receive 1 to 1½ inches of water every week—that's two to three 5-gallon buckets. If you are using a watering system or a hose, measure the amount in a 1-pound coffee tin, or use a rain gauge, available from garden centers and catalog suppliers. The plants must be well watered before the ground begins to freeze.

## FERTILIZING

If you are using organic or water-soluble chemical fertilizers, make the last application between the first of this month and early October. If you are using a time-release fertilizer and applied an eight-month formulation in early spring, it will carry the roses all the way through.

*If you did not check and adjust the pH of the soil in your rose beds in March or April, you can do it now. Roses prefer a slightly acidic soil, pH 5.8 to 6.8.*

Even if you have been using a quick-release chemical fertilizer, make this last application of the year an organic fertilizer that will carry the roses through the rest of the growing weather and into winter in good shape.

 PESTS

Continue to check your roses for signs of aphids and spider mites.

Powdery mildew remains a threat. Remove and destroy the leaves on the plants affected, and replace the mulch beneath with fresh mulch.

**Rake away and destroy mulch under roses that have had blackspot, mildew, and other problems.** Let the soil air and dry, then apply fresh mulch.

Root out weeds and grasses that have crept into the mulch under big roses.

Deer may be eating someone else's apples instead of your roses, but don't count on it.

## Did You Know?

### Some Roses Make Good Hedges

A rose hedge is a pleasure and an effective barrier. The height you want to achieve indicates the variety to plant. As always—make sure your choice is winter hardy, not just almost, but completely!

**Low borders. Miniature roses** make pretty borders for rose gardens, and they bloom all season. 'China Doll' tops out at about 18 inches, and covers itself with clusters of 1½-inch light pink, semi-double blooms.

**Low hedges.** The rose most often advertised as the "living fence" hedge is 'The Fairy', a **polyantha** under 30 inches that blooms all season. It is borderline hardy in my garden, Zone 5. 'The Fairy' and other **polyanthas** grow into brambly hedges covered with clusters of roses under 2 inches.

**Medium hedges.** The vigorous **floribundas,** which are cluster-flowered bush roses that bloom all season, make fine hedges 4 to 5 feet tall. Our favorite is 'Betty Prior' whose vivid pink flowers and emerald green foliage stay beautiful all summer. The **Meidiland** group of roses develops into wide-spreading naturalized hedges that bloom all season with little care. 'Bonica', an upright 4- to 5-foot bush, bears 3-inch, fully double, shell pink flowers set off by rich deep green glossy leaves.

**Tall hedges.** The **rugosa roses** grow into tall, very thorny hedges that withstand strong winds and sea spray. Very hardy, they do not appeal to deer. The only pruning they need is the removal in early spring of older canes to encourage vigorous new growth. The flowers of the modern cultivars are quite beautiful, and many produce spectacular rose hips.

PLANNING

If you lose roses when winter temperatures fall to 10 degrees, plan to cover them for the winter. (See the Care section of the November pages.) The time to do it is just before or just after the ground begins to freeze.

Be wary of covering roses before the temperature falls to 28 degrees Fahrenheit as that may keep the rose from hardening properly and will slow the onset of dormancy, leaving the plants vulnerable to frost. Cover a rose too late, however, and it may be damaged by the cold.

 PLANTING

This month, apply potassium to the soil to help winterize your roses.

When tree leaves start to change color is an excellent moment to plant new roses, and to start digging and transplanting roses. In Zone 7, you can still plant roses in November depending on the year. In Zone 6, you can plant roses in October and into the very beginning of November. In Zones 3, 4, and 5, best plant before Indian summer.

 CARE

Begin to prepare **climbers, roses growing in containers**, and **tree roses** for winter; protection for other roses is described in the November pages.

**Climbing Roses.** Climbers exposed to high winds will do better with protection in winter. Spray the canes with a rose fungicide or dormant oil, and use an anti-desiccant, such as Wilt-Pruf®, to help them withstand winter dryness. Clear fallen leaves and mulch from the soil beneath the climber, and apply new mulch about a foot deep.

Untie the canes from the trellis or fence. Wrap them with an insulation material (such as you use to keep pipes from freezing), and then retie them in place. If the stems are very flexible, you may find it easier just to lay them along the ground, and cover them with a foot of soil or mulch.

**Container Roses.** Before air temperatures reach 28 degrees, be sure to move roses growing in containers to an unheated garage or shed. First, remove the leaves, cut the canes back to 36 inches, tie them together to make the container easy to move, and clear the mulch away from the soil surface. Add new mulch, move the containers to their winter quarters, then water the container thoroughly.

**Standard or Tree Roses.** Prepare **tree roses growing in containers** for winter as recommended for **container roses**, above. Before temperatures reach 28 degrees Fahrenheit, move them to an unheated garage or shed.

A **tree rose growing in the ground** needs to be given winter protection. Remove the leaves, clear away old mulch, and replace it with new mulch. Tie the canes together loosely. Enclose the plant in hay or salt hay wrapped in burlap, translucent white plastic, or roofing paper, and tie the bundle together with a cord to keep everything in place.

North of Zone 6, an **in-ground tree rose** growing in an exposed location may need even more help. Cut free one side of the roots, then tip the entire tree rose over into a trench. Cover it with a foot of soil topped by mulch.

## PRUNING

As the weather cools, allow the last of the roses to form rose hips. That encourages the plant to slow growth and blooming, and to harden the canes, all in preparation for dormancy.

*Be wary of covering roses before the temperature falls to 28 degrees Fahrenheit as that may keep the rose from hardening properly and will slow the onset of dormancy, leaving the plants vulnerable to frost.*

 # WATERING

**Indoors.** Check pots of **miniatures** every day or two, and keep the soil moderately damp. Shower them every two weeks to discourage spider mites.

**Outdoors.** One of the most important winter preparations for all roses is a final deep and thorough watering before the ground freezes.

 # FERTILIZING

Fertilizing is over for now.

 # PESTS

When the roses have lost their leaves, prevent disease and fungus from over-wintering by removing fallen leaves, old mulch, and weeds under the roses. Spray with dormant oil to kill bacteria on the bush and on the ground.

Renew the mulch; it protects the ground from freezing, which keeps moisture available for roots.

## Did You Know?

### Rose Hip Jam

When you plan to make rose hip jam, avoid spraying the roses whose hips you want to use with anything bad for your health. The **rugosa roses** produce the biggest and most colorful rose hips, and generally are pest- and disease-resistant, so their hips are good candidates for jam making. Wait until after the first frost to pick the hips, and choose the biggest.

This recipe was given to me by my friend, the late Sally Erath.

**Frances Chrystie's Rose Hip Jam**

4 cups rose hips
1 cup water
Sugar (as needed, see below)

Place the rose hips and the water in a large pot over medium heat. Cover, and simmer about 30 minutes, until the fruit is very tender. Force the pulp through a fine sieve.

Measure the pulp then return it to the pot. For each cup of fruit pulp, stir in 1 cup of sugar. Simmer for ten to fifteen minutes, or more, until the mixture is thick. Remove the pot from the heat, and skim off the foam. Pour the jam into jelly glasses cleaned and dried in your dishwasher. Fill the glasses to within 1/2 inch of the rim, and seal with melted paraffin.

Store in the fridge.

If vole runs appear around your roses, bait the main runway with a rodenticide.

If you've been troubled by rodents in winters past, wait until after a hard frost, then mound VoleBloc or PermaTill all around the main stem of each rosebush, and cover that with a winter mulch.

# NOVEMBER
## Roses

 PLANNING

Now that the leafy season is over and the garden bare, evaluate the setting you've given your roses, and consider which might do and look better moved to another spot.

 PLANTING

In Zone 7, you can plant and transplant roses as long as the weather stays comfortable.

 CARE

Winter protection for roses is meant to keep the canes from drying in bitter winds, and to avoid cold damage to the canes and bud union and damage to the crown when alternate thawing and freezing cycles cause the soil to heave it.

Protect **newly planted roses** and the **miniatures,** even those rated winter hardy in your area, when the temperature heads toward 28 degrees Fahrenheit:

*1* Cut the canes back to 36 inches, and tie them together with string. These canes will be trimmed back further in the spring to remove portions winterkilled.

*2* Spray the canes with an anti-desiccant.

*3* The "thaw/heave" cycles that can occur when warm spells hit can heave the crown from the ground. Mulch will prevent the ground from thawing. So:

• Cover the crown or the bed at least a foot deep with tree leaves. Do not use rose leaves as they may harbor disease. Oak leaves are best as they are more resistant to rot and seem to drain better.

• Or, cover the bed with straw.

• Or, spread a mound a foot deep of soil from another part of the garden over the base of the plant. Bark, fresh compost, or shredded leaves can be used instead of soil.

*4* Along with any one of the above, in Zones 6 and north, and in sites exposed to stiff wind, protect the canes:

• Wrap the whole plant in burlap or Reemay®.

• Or, encase the plant in a cage of wire and straw.

• Or, wrap the plant in straw covered with burlap and tied with rope.

• Use rose cones made of Styrofoam™ as protection. You need to trim and defoliate the rose first, then mound the crown with 12 inches of soil and mulch. Tie up the canes, place the protective cone over them, and set a weight on the cone to keep it from blowing away.

Really do it! Whatever happens, you will know you have done your best to protect the plant.

 PRUNING

Save pruning of long canes for late winter and early spring as branch tips generally have some winter dieback, and you'll have to prune them then anyway.

 WATERING

**Indoors.** Keep the soil for **miniatures** moderately moist. Shower them every two weeks, but the other times you water them, wet the soil, not the leaves.

**Outdoors.** A major danger to roses in winter is lack of water before the plant is completely dormant. Be sure before the ground freezes to give your roses a deep and thorough watering.

Maintain moderate soil moisture for hardy roses in containers, and for containers of hardy roses sheltering in a cold garage or shed.

*A major danger to roses in winter is lack of water before the plant is completely dormant. Be sure before the ground freezes to give your roses a deep and thorough watering.*

 # FERTILIZING

To encourage blooming, fertilize **miniature roses** growing indoors under grow lights with a light application of African violet or another of the liquid bloom booster fertilizers.

 # PESTS

**Indoors. Spider mites** are a threat to **miniature roses.** Pale, fine stippling on leaves is the give-away. Spray affected plants in a kitchen sink every day or two for a couple of weeks. If that doesn't work, spray with insecticidal soap. Air the room every day.

**Outdoors.** To prevent disease spores of infected roses from infecting new growth when it comes along in the spring, before protecting roses for winter, strip off the leaves, and pick up all fallen leaves. Remove the mulch below diseased plants, and replace it with fresh.

If vole runs appear around your roses, bait the main runway with a rodenticide.

## Did You Know?

### Most Successful Roses in Zone 3 Trials

Rachel Kane, of the Perennial Pleasures Nursery in East Hardwick, Vermont recommends these for Vermont's Zone 3 and cold climates. They were the most enduring roses in trials conducted at Rogers Farm, University of Maine, in the years 2001-2003.

*1* *Rosa rugosa* 'Hanse', reddish purple flowers, sweetly scented makes a good hedge.

*2* 'Blanc Double de Coubert', 4 feet, white double that blooms all summer.

*3* 'Therese Bugnet', an almost thornless, double rugosa rose, 5 to 6 feet tall that repeat blooms in soft pink flowers.

*4* 'Harrison's Yellow', a late spring floriferous bloomer; rather scraggly plant but a good yellow.

*5* The Explorer series, 6 to 8 feet, repeat bloomers: Red 'John Cabot'; deep pink 'William Baffin'; medium pink 'John Davis'.

*6* Pale pink 'Grootendorst'; deep pink 'Grootendorst Supreme'; shrubs about 5 feet tall that bear clusters of small flowers with pinked edges.

*7* 'Iceberg' white; pure white floribunda blooms twice a season. It dies back but regrows in spring to 30 inches.

# DECEMBER
## Roses

 PLANNING

Bring your garden log up to date.

 PLANTING

A raised bed for roses solves drainage problems and gives the roses a very good start. You can start a bed for a rose garden any time before the ground freezes hard. If you don't get around to it now, do prepare the bed at least four weeks before you plan to plant in spring.

See Starting a Raised Bed in the Introduction to the book for complete details.

CARE

If **miniature roses** growing indoors aren't flowering, increase the light by adding grow lights after dusk and putting them under fluorescents in a light garden until they begin to bud.

 PRUNING

Deadhead **miniature roses** indoors.

 WATERING

**Indoors.** Keep the soil moderately moist for **miniatures** growing indoors.

**Outdoors.** Don't let the containers of hardy roses sheltering in a cold garage or shed dry out. As long as the ground isn't frozen, water roses in containers that are under eaves or pergolas.

If December is short of snow or rain, before the ground freezes, water the roses overwintering in the open garden thoroughly.

 FERTILIZING

To encourage blooming, fertilize **miniature roses** that are growing indoors under grow lights with a frequent light application of African violet or another bloom booster fertilizer.

## Did You Know?

### Gifts Rose Gardeners Appreciate

Grooming and pruning roses is essential to their health and beauty. Here's a set of tool rose growers love to give—and to receive:

*1* For pruning and cleaning up—a set of bypass pruners, the scissor type, not the anvil type that crush the stems.

*2* For removal of large woody canes at the graft—a pruning saw small enough to access the graft area so the cut can be made flush with the main stem.

*3* For cutting canes $1/2$ inch diameter or greater—lopping shears with 18-inch handles.

*4* To scrub loose bark away from the bud union—a brass wire brush about 2 inches wide by 3 inches deep. Hardware stores sell them.

*5* To seal pruning cuts on canes greater than $1/4$ inch diameter to prevent cane borers from entering—clear nail polish or white glue.

*6* To save hands and arms from scratches—long heavy leather gauntlets.

PESTS

**Indoors.** Dry air invites spider mites to adopt **miniature roses;** air the room every day. When you water **container roses,** water the soil, not the foliage.

**Outdoors.** If vole runs appear around the roses, bait the main runway with a rodenticide.

# CHAPTER EIGHT

# Shrubs

*Shrubs are summer's visual link to the trees and the sky, an airy presence in winter, home to the garden's first spring flowers.*

Once established, a shrub needs little attention. Annual fertilizing, water during droughts, and pruning. Your shrubs will do the most for you if you learn when and how to prune them.

When choosing a shrub for a New York garden, **make sure it really is winter hardy** in your zone. A shrub that is borderline hardy might survive many winters and mature into a handsome specimen, then break your heart by succumbing in an especially bad year. Our winters are uncertain—some years deep snow insulates the roots and keeps the plants safe; other years there's little snow cover, and the soil is bare to a biting cold that can last many weeks. Another thing is that flowering shrubs planted north of their hardiness zone may grow well enough but not bloom satisfactorily. An example is common **forsythia,** hardy in Zone 5, which lived in our northern Vermont garden but seldom bloomed. (Happily, there are modern cultivars that flower reliably in the north.)

## DESIGN

Because of a shrub's size and mass, it makes a major impact on garden design. The shrub's structure—the branching and central stems—is the first thing you notice. Some shrubs we tend to think of as being arched **(bridal wreath),** others as rounded **(barberries),** others as upright **(Japanese kerria 'Pleniflora'),** others as drooping **(Japanese andromeda),** yet others as conical **(dwarf Alberta spruce).**

You will find your garden most interesting if you include shrubs that introduce considerable variety in structure and size, in flower, foliage, and berry texture, and color. A thoughtful mix of evergreen and deciduous types will keep your grounds appealing in all four seasons.

Since few properties can accommodate every shrub you fall in love with, when adding a shrub to your foundation plantings or designing a shrub border, look for species that have more than one asset. In addition to lovely flowers, some shrubs enchant with their fragrance—the **lilacs, mock orange,** and **Burkwood viburnum** are outstanding examples. Some broadleaf evergreen shrubs bear beautiful flowers—among them are the **rhododendrons** and **mountain laurel.** Some shrubs delight the gardener and the birds with berries late in the season—the **hollies** and **cotoneaster.**

## PLANTING

The best planting seasons are early spring when the ground becomes workable and especially fall. For deciduous shrubs, that's from the time the leaves start to turn in October through November. Evergreens are best planted or moved late August, September, and early October, depending on your zone. How a shrub is packaged has everything to do with when it can be planted. Shrubs are sold bare root, container grown, and balled and burlapped—B&B.

# Shrubs

**Bare-root shrubs.** In early spring before growth begins, mail-order suppliers ship some shrubs bare root. Ascertain the size of a mail-order purchase before deciding it's a bargain since you'll have to pay shipping. Follow the nursery's instructions for planting exactly.

**Container-grown shrubs.** You can plant container-grown shrubs from early spring through summer and fall into November when fall lingers. Buying locally allows you to select shrubs whose flower and foliage color, and structure are exactly what you expect.

**Balled-and-burlapped shrubs.** You can plant B&B shrubs from early spring into November. Evergreens are best moved August, September, and early October. In summer, avoid buying B&B shrubs dug in spring that have been sitting for months in the open air with their bare rootball drying and baking. B&B shrubs dug in spring and "heeled in," that is protected by mounds of mulch or soil, stay in good condition. We recommend paying extra to have large B&B shrubs planted and guaranteed by the supplier.

## LIGHT AND SPACING

Many shrubs got their start in light shade under tall trees in a forest or at its edge. So most can do with less than a full day of sunlight. **Azaleas, rhododendrons,** and **mountain laurel** do very well in the tall shade at the edge of a woodland area.

**Spacing is critical.** Shrubs planted at distances that allow plenty of space for the lateral development of branches grow into beautiful mature specimens. To calculate the best spacing for two or more young shrubs, add together the widths given on the plant tags, and divide by the number of plants. To occupy the bed while young shrubs fill out, plant shade-tolerant **hostas** or **ferns,** and annuals such as **impatiens, pentas,** and **caladiums.**

**Soil.** The information on Soil Preparation and Improvement and pH given in the Introduction to the book applies to shrubs. Suitable pH varies widely. For **azaleas,** it's between pH 4.5 and 6.0; for **dwarf burning bush** (*Euonymus alatus* 'Compactus'), pH 6.0 to 7.5 is suitable. Most **lilacs** thrive when the soil pH is near 8.0, a figure attainable in acidic soils by applying a biannual dusting of lime; instead of liming **lilacs,** in spring we sprinkle wood ashes around them—to raise the pH.

You can grow a small shrub successfully in soil whose pH is not perfect because its roots are modest. A big shrub needs lots of growing room and will have an edge if it is growing in soil with composition and pH compatible to its needs.

**Digging the hole.** Make the planting hole three times as wide and twice as deep as the rootball. Loosen the sides of the hole, and blend the soil taken from the hole with the organic amendments described in Soil Preparation and Improvement in the Introduction to the book. Half-fill the bottom of the hole with improved soil, and tamp it down to make a firm base for the roots.

Set the shrub so the crown will be an inch above ground level. Half-fill the hole once more with improved soil. Tamp it down firmly. Finish filling the hole with improved soil, and tamp it down firmly. Shape the soil around the crown into a wide saucer so water won't run off as quickly.

After planting, water the soil slowly, gently, and thoroughly with a sprinkler, a soaker hose, a bubbler, or by hand. You need to put down 1½ inches of water (see Watering). Or, slowly pour on 10 to 15 gallons of water from a bucket.

# Shrubs

Mulch newly planted shrubs 2 to 3 inches deep starting 3 inches from the main stem. Replenish the mulch as needed to keep it 2 to 3 inches deep.

**Growing shrubs in containers.** You can grow a shrub in a container outdoors indefinitely—a hardy shrub, that is—providing the container is large enough to insulate the roots from winter cold. (See April, Growing Shrubs in Containers.)

**Transplanting shrubs.** Spring and especially fall through November are the best seasons to move deciduous shrubs. Evergreen shrubs can be transplanted spring and fall through October. You will find information on moving large established shrubs under Planting, in the February pages. Move flowering shrubs well before, or after, they have bloomed.

## CARE AND PRUNING

The major maintenance involved in growing shrubs is pruning. Correct pruning and pinching or deadheading enhances a shrub's "habit" or natural form, and it encourages productivity. Pruning a shrub takes thought because when and how differs with each species and cultivar. We've given simple, basic guidelines to when and where to prune deciduous and evergreen shrubs in the March and May pages, and they will help. But we urge you to get a really well-illustrated guide to pruning shrubs and trees; the titles of our favorite books on the subject appear in the bibliography.

You can reduce the amount of pruning your shrubs will need by selecting **dwarf** and **slow-growing** varieties. This is most important when choosing **shrubs for hedges.** But even dwarfs grow, albeit slowly, so they may need some pruning to maintain their size. See the introduction and January pages to the Trees chapter for the proper ways to prune.

**Pruning.** We prune shrubs with a variety of goals in mind:

• **To rejuvenate.** Prune drastically in late winter while still dormant to rejuvenate leggy shrubs. Take away no more than a third or a quarter of the branches in one season. Make the cuts about a foot from the ground. Repeat the process the next two years until the pruning project is complete.

• **To encourage flowering.** Prune shrubs that flower on the current season's wood—**butterfly bush** and **vitex,** for example—well **before growth begins** to encourage the production of many new flowering shoots. Prune shrubs that bloom on last year's wood—**azaleas,** for example—when they **finish blooming,** because they soon start initiating flower buds for the next season.

• **To stimulate fullness.** Prune shrubs when they are **growing actively** to encourage more, bushier growth. Fresh, young shoots that are cut back by half immediately begin to grow lateral shoots.

• **To encourage branching.** To encourage more foliage in broadleaf evergreens that branch—**azaleas** and **abellas,** for example—prune succulent new shoots while they are **growing actively** back by half. **Rhododendrons** are different; cut just above a whorl of leaves.

• **To limit growth.** Prune leafy plants **after the season's growth** to reduce the leaf surfaces, which limits the sugar synthesized and sent to the roots, because that limits next year's growth.

• **To top a plant.** Top a shrub or a hedge **after the season's growth** has been completed to maintain the height.

# Shrubs

## FERTILIZING AND MULCHING

**Fertilizing.** A new shrub in improved soil rich in long-lasting organic fertilizers doesn't need fertilizing until the following year. The **first** annual application of fertilizer should be made **before growth begins** in spring. The **last** application should be as growth slows toward the **end of the growing season.** The number of applications in between depends entirely on the type of fertilizer you are using. (See Understanding Fertilizers in the Introduction to the book.)

**The rule of thumb is to make a final application of fertilizer as growth slows at the end of the growing season—in Zones 3 and 4, usually about August 15; in Zone 5, early September; and in Zones 6 and 7, early September to early October.**

**Mulching.** Mulch shrubs 3 inches deep (no more!) after planting, starting 3 inches from the central stem(s). Top it off as needed to maintain the 3-inch height in spring after fertilizing, and again before summer heat arrives, and once more before winter cold sets in.

**Watering.** Once established, most shrubs will require less extra watering than perennials; when the weather isn't supporting growth, they adapt by slowing down unless forced by shallow watering and inappropriate fertilizing to grow. Always water slowly and gently, and try to pour on 1½ inches. Set a one-pound coffee can or other container under the sprinkler or the hose, and record how long it took to put 1½ inches in the can—then you'll know for future waterings.

Newly planted and transplanted shrubs need sustained moisture. For the first eight weeks, apply two or three 5-gallon buckets of water around the roots once a week unless you have sustained soaking rains. In summer, every week or ten days, unless you have a soaking rain, slowly and gently lay down 1½ inches of water. In fall, even after cold sets in, shrub roots continue to develop, so water often enough to prevent the soil from drying out. In fact, one of the most important winter preparations is a deep and thorough watering before the ground freezes.

## PEST CONTROL

**Weeds.** In naked earth, weeds sprout from April to October. Mulch helps keep them out, and the few that do get started are easy to hand pull.

**Critters.** Bears harvest the berries of the handsome **highbush blueberry** (*Vaccinium corymbosum*), which we plant for its autumn color. Deer graze on **rhododendrons, arborvitae, hydrangeas, shrub althea,** and many other favorite shrubs. Rabbits can girdle stems especially above the snow line. For solutions to these and other pests, see Pests, Diseases, and Controls in the Appendix.

**Insects and diseases.** Choose shrubs that are disease-resistant, and be willing to accept a normal amount of insect damage. See Integrated Pest Management under Pests, Diseases, and Controls in the Appendix of the book.

Good garden practices help keep problems away—air, space, light, good soil, water as needed. Avoid planting shrubs in airless corners. Whitefly and spider mites love hot, airless spots and will spoil the leaves even if they don't do permanent damage. Neem-based products control them; spray the plants two or three times at intervals of ten days or so. See Pests, Diseases, and Controls in the Appendix for more information.

# Shrubs

## Deciduous Shrubs

| Common Name (*Botanical Name*) | Hardiness Zones | Light | Bloom Period | Blooms On | Ornamental Features |
|---|---|---|---|---|---|
| **Azalea, Deciduous** (*Rhododendron* spp. and cvs.) | 4 to 9 | Part sun/ shade | Spring | Old wood | 'Northern Light' hybrids hardiest; 'Golden Lights' hardy in Zone 3; favorites are 'Jane Abbott', 'Frank Abbott', 'Parade', 'Pink and Sweet', 'Golden Showers', 'Innocence'. |
| **Beautybush** (*Kolkwitzia amabilis*) | 4 to 9 | Part sun/ shade | May/June | Old wood | Upright shrub with masses of showy pink flowers. |
| **Butterfly Bush** (*Buddleia davidii* and cvs.) | 5 to 9 | Sun/ part sun | Late summer to frost | New wood | Lilac-like blooms in lilac, pink, white, or purple. Attracts butterflies and hummingbirds. |
| **Bush Cinquefoil, Shrubby Cinquefoil** (*Potentilla fruticosa* cvs.) | 2 to 7 | Sun/ part sun | June through early frost | New wood | Nice texture, all-season blooms like single roses. |
| **Daphne 'Carol Mackie'** (*Daphne* x *burkwoodii* 'Carol Mackie') | 4 to 8 | Sun/ part sun | Mid-spring | Old wood | Very fragrant flowers and semi-evergreen creamy variegated foliage. Another favorite is trailing rose daphne (*D. cneorum*). |
| **Deutzia** (*Deutzia gracilis* 'Nikko') | 5 to 8 | Sun/ part shade | May | Old wood | Small white flowers. Fine-textured blue-green leaves turn red in fall. |
| **Flowering Quince, Japanese Quince** (*Chaenomeles speciosa* and cvs.) | 5 to 8 | Sun/ part sun | Early spring | Old wood | A truly beautiful woody shrub with broad spreading branches and flowers like apple blossoms. |
| **Forsythia** (*Forsythia* x *intermedia*) | 4 to 8 | Sun/ part sun | Early spring | Old wood | Harbinger of spring. Upright 'Lynwood Gold' is superb. For Zone 4, 'Vermont Sun' 'New Hampshire Gold', 'Northern Gold'. |
| **Fothergilla** (*Fothergilla gardenii*) | 5 to 9 | Sun/ part sun | Spring | Old wood | Scented bottlebrush flowers and colorful fall foliage. *F. major* is hardy in Zone 4, as is 'Mount Airy', an intermediate size. |
| **Glossy Abelia** (*Abelia* x *grandiflora*) | 5 to 9 | Sun/ part sun | May through frost | New wood | Fragrant white or pink flowers and semi-evergreen foliage, tinged maroon in fall. |
| **Honeysuckle** (*Lonicera* sps. and cvs.) | 3 to 8 | Sun/ part sun | Varies by species | | Winter honeysuckle, *L. fregrantissima* (March and April), and *L. japonica* 'Hall's honeysuckle' (July and August) are perfumed shrubby forms. |
| **Hydrangea** (*Hydrangea* spp. and cvs.) | 4 to 9 | Sun/ part sun | Summer | New or old wood | 'Annabelle' has 12-inch white flowers that pale to green. For Zone 4, *H. paniculata*, which blooms late, and *H. p.* 'Praecox' with sterile and fertile flowers. Mopheads and lacecaps belong to *H. macrophylla*. |
| **Japanese Kerrla** (*Kerria japonica* 'Picta') | 4 to 9 | Sun/ part sun | Early to mid-spring | Old and some new wood | A 3-foot shrub with variegated leaves and small yellow flowers that last for weeks. |
| **Japanese Maple** (*Acer palmatum* cvs.) | 5 to 9 | Sun/ part sun | Foliage plant | N/A | Many sizes, shapes, and colors available—weeping, upright, and tall shrub or small tree; green, pink, red, or black-red foliage. |
| **Lilac, Common Lilac** (*Syringa* spp. and hybrids) | 4 to 7 | Sun/ part sun | Early and mid-spring | Old wood | Old-fashioned lilacs are the scent of spring. Showy modern forms are less fragrant. Late-bloomers are Meyer lilac (*S. meyeri* 'Palabin') and Preston hybrids such as 'Minuet'. |

# Shrubs

| Common Name (*Botanical Name*) | Hardiness Zones | Light | Bloom Period | Blooms On | Ornamental Features |
|---|---|---|---|---|---|
| **Oakleaf Hydrangea** (*Hydrangea quercifolia*) | 5 to 9 | Sun/ part sun | Late spring, summer | Old wood | Cones of creamy florets and deep-red fall foliage. Try 'Snowflake' and 'Snowqueen'. |
| **Rose-of-Sharon** (*Hibiscus syriacus* cvs.) | 5 to 8 | Sun/ part sun | Late summer | New wood | White, dark-pink, blue, or lilac flowers. 'White Chiffon' and 'Lavender Chiffon' are beautiful. |
| **Shadblow, Serviceberry** (*Amelanchier* spp.) | 3 to 8 | Part sun/ shade | Early spring | Old wood | *A. arborea,* trained as a tree or shrub, lights up our woods with small white flowers and then edible fruits. 'Autumn Brilliance' and *A. canadensis* are favorites. |
| **Smokebush** (*Cotinus coggygria* cvs.) | 5 to 8 | Part sun/ shade | Early summer | Old wood | Airy flower-like clusters in June become puffy plumes on pink or gray stalks so the bush seems enveloped in smoke. The big native smoketree (*C. obovatus*) is superb. |
| **Spirea** (*Spiraea* spp. and cvs.) | 3 to 9 | Part sun/ shade | Summer | Depends on the species | Spireas have arching branches with clusters of tiny flowers. Arching *S. nipponica,* blooms on old wood. Pink-flowered *S. bumalda* cultivars bloom on new wood. 'Little Princess' is suited to the front of a border. |
| **Summersweet, Sweetpepper Bush** (*Clethra alnifolia* spp. and cvs.) | 4 to 9 | Part sun/ shade | Summer | Old wood | Fragrant white or pink florets July into August. *C.* 'Ruby spice' has deep rose flowers and excellent fragrance. |
| **Viburnum** (*Viburnum* spp. and cvs.) | 4 to 8 | Sun/ part sun | Early and mid-spring | Old wood | *V. carlesii* (Zone 6) and others with globe-shaped flowers are noted for fragrance and colorful fall foliage. Doublefile viburnum is larger; recalls dogwood when in bloom. |
| **Weigela** (*Weigela florida*) | 4 to 8 | Part sun/ shade | Mid- to late spring | Old and some new wood | Arching branches bear tubular white, pink, or red flowers in late May and June. |
| **Winterberry Holly** (*Ilex verticillata*) | 3 to 9 | Part sun/ shade | Fall and winter berries | New wood | Tiny white flowers in June followed by red berries; females need a compatible male pollinator. For small gardens use 'Red Sprite' and the male 'Jim Dandy'. |

## Evergreen Shrubs

| Common Name (*Botanical Name*) | Hardiness Zones | Light | Bloom Period | Blooms On | Ornamental Features |
|---|---|---|---|---|---|
| **Andromeda, Japanese Andromeda** (*Pieris japonica* 'White Cascade') | 5 to 8 | Sun/ part sun | Early spring | Old wood | Broadleaved, flowering; bears small urn-shaped flowers. New foliage is a gleaming rose-bronze. 'Forest Flame' is hardy in Zone 5; *P. floribunda* in Zone 4. |
| **Bayberry** (*Myrica pensylvanica*) | 2 to 7 | Sun | N/A | N/A | Important shore plant; bears small white florets in spring followed by waxy white fruit used to scent candles. Dioecious. |
| **Boxwood, Box** (*Buxus sempervirens* 'Welleri' and hybrids) | 5 to 8 | Sun/ part sun | N/A | N/A | Slow-growing small-leaved shrub for formal uses and topiary. Littleleaf boxwood (*B. microphylla* variety *koreana*), hardy in Zone 4. Protect all boxwoods for winter. |

# Shrubs

| Common Name (Botanical Name) | Hardiness Zones | Light | Bloom Period | Blooms On | Ornamental Features |
|---|---|---|---|---|---|
| Cotoneaster, Rockspray Cotoneaster (*Cotoneaster horizontalis*) | 4 to 8 | Sun/part shade | Spring | Old wood | Spreading flowering semi-evergreen with red fruits in summer. Other species and varieties are taller, bear pink flowers, have showier berries. |
| Dwarf Arborvitae (*Thuja* spp. and cvs.) | 3 to 8 | Sun/part sun | N/A | N/A | Arborvitae dwarfs available in various shapes and sizes from 2 feet to 8 feet. |
| Dwarf Balsam Fir (*Abies balsamea* 'Nana') | 3 to 7 | Sun/part sun | N/A | N/A | Needled globe-shaped shrub 2 to 3 feet tall with horizontal spreading branches. |
| Dwarf Hinoki, False Cypress (*Chamaecyparis obtusa* 'Nana Gracilis') | 4 to 8 | Sun/part sun | N/A | N/A | A graceful dwarf 4 to 6 feet high with deep green, lustrous foliage. *C. obtusa* 'Nana Lutea' is a beautiful lemon-gold color all season and only 2 to 3 feet high. |
| Dwarf Mugo Pine (*Pinus mugo* var. *pumilo*) | 4 to 7 | Sun/part sun | N/A | N/A | A dense rounded dwarf pine with short, dark green needles. |
| Evergreen Azalea (*Rhododendron* cvs.) | 5 to 9 | Part sun | Spring | Old wood | Flowering shrub; not as reliably hardy north of Zone 6 as the deciduous varieties. |
| Firethorn (*Pyracantha coccinea* cvs.) | 5 to 9 | Sun/part sun | Mid-spring | Old wood | Showy, white flowers followed by clusters of bright red fruits. Choose pest- and disease-free 'Mohave' and low-growing 'Rutgers'. Excellent coastal plant. |
| Holly (*Ilex* spp. and cvs.) | 6 to 8 | Sun/part sun | N/A | Old wood | Broad, spiny leaves and colorful berries when near a suitable pollinator. The Meserve hybrids and black-berried inkberry holly (*I. glabra*) are hardy in Zone 4. |
| Juniper (*Juniperus chinensis* cvs.) | 3 to 9 | Sun | N/A | N/A | Shrubby and creeping junipers in every size, exceptionally good shore plants. The male cones are yellow, like catkins, and the female fruit are berries. |
| Mountain Laurel (*Kalmia latifolia*) | 4 to 8 | Part sun | Spring | Old wood | Flowering broadleaved evergreen with shiny leaves and clusters of pale pink cup-shaped florets. |
| Privet (*Ligustrum* spp.) | 3 to 8 | Sun/part sun | Spring | Old wood | Broadleaved; deciduous in northern New York; small oval leaves and clusters of pungent little white flowers and then blue or black fruits. Popular hedge at the shore. |
| Rhododendron (*Rhododendron* spp. and cvs.) | 4 to 8 | Part sun | Spring | Old wood | Broadleaved; bears beautiful flowers. F1 hybrids, including the PJM hybrids and *C. catawbiense* cultivars, are hardy in Zone 4. 'Cheer' often reblooms in the fall. |
| Spruce, Dwarf (*Picea* spp. and cvs.) | 3 to 7 | Sun/part sun | N/A | N/A | Many shrubby slow-growing forms of the stiff-needled tree sold at Christmas. Bird's nest spruce is low and broad; 'Conica' is cone shaped. |
| Siberian Cypress (*Microbiota decussata*) | 2 to 8 | Sun/part sun | N/A | N/A | Wide-spreading and just 18 inches high, good ground cover; foliage resembles juniper. |
| Yew, English, Japanese Yew (*Taxus* x *media*) | 4 to 7 | Sun | N/A | N/A | Slow-growing shrubby needled; tolerant of extensive pruning. 'Hicksii' is a favorite. Some cultivars hardy in Zone 4. |

## PLANNING

**In winter your garden reveals its "bones," the naked woody structures that anchor the landscape.** Take the garden catalogs arriving now to a comfortable chair by a window, and consider what a few new shrubs or a hedge could do for your view. You can start planting new shrubs as early as April, but we recommend waiting to plant a new hedge until fall.

**When is a shrub a shrub?** A forester's definition of a shrub is a multi-trunked woody perennial plant reaching not more than 10 to 20 feet at maturity. Some woody plants can be trained either as trees or shrubs—**shrub althaea, lilacs, witchhazels, shadblow,** and **smokebush** are some examples. Even **common lilac**—though in New York they are trained to a single stalk so often we think of them as small trees.

**Flowering shrubs.** For flowers early to late spring and four-season greenery, consider varieties of flowering broadleaved evergreens—**mountain laurels, rhododendrons, azaleas.** In Zones 6 and 7, **evergreen azalea** foliage adds shades of plum and maroon to the fall scene.

**Shrubs for fragrance.** In their season of bloom, shrubs that bear fragrant flowers become garden destinations. **Winter daphne** (*Daphne odora* 'Aureo-marginata'), the **honeysuckles,** and the perfumed **viburnums** spread their scent far and wide. You can count on **mock oranges** for late spring perfume and **sweet pepperbush** (*Clethra alnifolia)* for summer scent.

**Evergreen shrubs for perennial beds.** If you haven't included shrubby evergreens in your flower beds, plan to tuck in a few this year. The lively green anchors the beds off-season. See October, About Needled Evergreens and Conifers, for descriptions of some of our favorites.

**Deciduous shrubs for seasonal change.** Your shrub border will be more appealing if you include a few plants chosen just for their foliage, color, and texture. In spring the **dwarf cutleaf birch** (*Betula pendula*) is a fresh, vivid green. Yellow **Japanese barberry** (*Berberis thunbergii* 'Aurea') and golden **Scotch heather** (*Calluna vulgaris* varieties) brighten dark corners. In fall, the **dwarf threadleaf Japanese maple** (*Acer palmatum* 'Viride') glows gold, and the **dwarf winged spindle tree** (*Euonymus alata* 'Compacta') is brighter than the sunsets.

**Berried shrubs for winter interest.** The bright berries of both evergreen and leaf-losing **hollies, barberries,** and other berried shrubs cheer winter's gray skies. **Oregon grape** (*Mahonia aquifolium*) and **sweet box** (*Sarcococca hookeriana* var. *humilis*) add dabs of shiny red to the seasonal mix. Bright blue/black or white berries follow the flowers in many species.

**Shrubs for open woodlands.** Garden varieties of native shrubs light up the woods when they come into bloom. In spring, shrubby **redbuds** bloom pink and **shadblow** blooms white. In fall the foliage of **red chokeberry** (*Aronia arbutifolia* 'Brilliantissima') turns scarlet and claret-red, and it has long-lasting, glossy red fruits. The deeply-divided fernlike foliage of the very hardy **staghorn sumac** cultivars (*Rhus typhina* 'Dissecta' and 'Laciniata') turn to intense orange, vermilion, yellow, and purple.

## PLANTING

Give your out-of-bloom gift **azalea** a sunny spot on a sill since it, along with **mums** and **poinsettias,** is among plants that test high as air purifiers. When blooming is over, transplant the **azalea** to a larger pot filled with mixture that is $1/4$ garden soil and $3/4$ peat moss. Keep the soil moist, and when new growth appears, at every watering apply an acid-type fertilizer at ¼ the recommended strength. Increase that over a four-month period until you are fertilizing at the strength recommended on the container. A forced **azalea** is not usually hardy here, but if you summer it outdoors and expose it to several cool, but not freezing, fall nights before bringing it in, it may bloom again.

# CARE

**Free evergreen branches burdened by snow or ice.** Use a broom to brush away accumulations of snow and ice that might harm hedges.

Renew the anti-desiccant spray on **broadleaf evergreen shrubs** growing in exposed positions. If the winter is very bad, wrap them in Reemay for protection.

# PRUNING

Remove branches damaged by heavy snowfall and winter storms.

# WATERING

**Indoors.** Water any shrubs wintering inside as needed.

# FERTILIZING

**Tropical hibiscus,** potted **gardenias,** and other tender shrubs brought indoors last fall are beginning to grow again; add a half-strength dose of soluble fertilizer at every second watering.

# PESTS

**Indoors.** Monitor shrubs growing indoors for signs of spider mite, whitefly, and other problems. See Pests, Diseases, and Controls in the Appendix for controls.

**Outdoors.** Repair or renew deer deterrents and sprays. Check and adjust burlap covers and chicken wire cages protecting shrubs.

# FEBRUARY
## Shrubs

 PLANNING

Keep an eye on shrubs that flower in early spring; when the buds begin to swell, harvest branches to force into bloom indoors.

Place your catalog mail orders for shrubs now.

 PLANTING

Moving very large shrubs is a two-year project. The first step, **root pruning,** also slows growth during the first year by depriving the plant of nutrient intake.

**Year one.** Before growth begins, sever the roots in a circle all around the trunk of the shrub to stimulate root growth within the circle.

**Year two.** The same time next year, tie the branches together at the top. Dig a trench outside the root-pruned circle, dig under the roots, lift the rootball onto a big piece of burlap, and tie the burlap up around the trunk. Very gently transport the plant to its new location. Prepare the soil and plant the shrub as described in Planting in the introduction to this chapter, and then free the branches and prune out damaged twigs.

 CARE

Clear snow, dead branches, and winter debris from the shrubbery.

 PRUNING

If **forsythias, quince,** and other spring-flowering shrubs need thinning, do it well before they bloom, and use the branches for forcing into bloom indoors.

Prune summer- and late-flowering shrubs well before they bloom, too—March or early April. They bloom on new wood, which pruning encourages.

Prune evergreen branches damaged by winter storms any time.

To rejuvenate **hollies,** prune heavily late winter to early spring.

 WATERING

**Indoors.** Water shrubs as needed.

 FERTILIZING

**Indoors.** Fertilize **gardenias** and other tender shrubs brought indoors last fall at every second watering.

 PESTS

**Indoors.** Watch shrubs growing indoors for signs of whitefly, spider mites, and other pests. If you find problems, look up controls in the Pests, Diseases, and Controls section in the Appendix.

**Outdoors.** Check and adjust burlap covers and chicken wire cages protecting shrubs from deer.

As the ground thaws, voles get lively and they can damage young shrub roots. If vole runs appear, bait the main runway with a rodenticide.

Before buds on plants that you suspect of insect infestation break, spray them with horticultural oil. The oil smothers insects and their eggs.

*Moving very large shrubs is a two-year project. Known as root pruning, the process slows growth during the first year by depriving the plant of nutrient intake.*

## Did You Know?

### Flowering Branches Can Be Forced into Bloom

In late winter, branches of spring flowering shrubs (and trees) can be forced into bloom indoors. The time to harvest the branches is just as the buds begin to swell. The warmer your zone, the earlier the forcing date.

Harvest branches two to three feet long and heavily studded with buds. Monitor the water level in the containers—it may need topping twice a week.

**Cold method.** Press the cut ends into snow or icy cold water, and let them rest two days in a cool, dark place. Fill tall vases with cool water, re-cut the branch ends, and arrange the branches in the vases. Set them in the sun next to a window.

**Warm method.** Bring the cut branches indoors, and place them in tall containers in water at bath temperature—90 to 110 degrees Fahrenheit. Tent the containers and the branches with plastic, and set them in a dim, warm room. The warmth and humidity will encourage the scales covering the flower buds to expand, and will ready the dormant buds to open.

The flowers will last longer if kept in a cool room.

**Here are a few of our favorites:**

- **Apple, Crabapple**—cut mid-March; force for two to three weeks; bloom period, seven days.
- **Common Lilac**—cut early March; force for two to four weeks; bloom period, three to seven days.
- **Dogwood**—cut mid-March; force for two to four weeks; bloom period, seven to ten days.
- **Forsythia**—cut February to mid-March; force for one to three weeks; bloom period, seven days.
- **Flowering Peach**—cut early February; force for four to five weeks; bloom period, seven days.
- **Flowering Pear**—cut late January to mid-March; force for two to five weeks; bloom period, seven to fourteen days.
- **Flowering Plum**—cut late January to February; force for three to four weeks; bloom period, ten days.
- **Japanese Flowering Cherry**—cut late January to mid-March; force for two to four weeks; bloom period, seven to fourteen days.
- **Japanese Quince, Flowering Quince**—cut February to mid-March; force for two to five weeks; bloom period, four to seven days.
- **Pussy Willow** (*Salix* species)—cut February; force for one to two weeks; bloom period, indefinitely if allowed to dry. (Remove the bud scales and, when they reach the fuzzy bud stage, remove the branches from the water.)

# PLANNING

Late this month or early next you should be getting ready to plant shrubs you'd like to add to the garden.

Look at your shrub borders and hedges and schedule their pruning.

# PLANTING

As soon as winter wet and cold leaves the ground, you can start planting new shrubs. Use Tree-tone, Holly-tone (for acid-loving plants), or Plant-tone as fertilizers.

For complete instructions on planting a shrub, turn back to Planting, in the introduction to this chapter. Here's how to prepare a shrub for planting:

**Container-grown shrub.** Free the shrub by tipping the pot on its side and rolling it around. If it's too large for that, slit the sides of the container, and peel off the pieces. If roots wrap the rootball, make four shallow vertical cuts equidistant from each other in the sides of the rootball, and slice off the bottom 2 inches.

**B&B shrub.** Handle the rootball gently and as little as possible. Avoid disturbing the burlap, twine, or wire basket as you put the rootball into the planting hole. After the rootball is in the hole, cut the twine around the trunk, and cut off or push the ends of the burlap into the hole. If the cover is plastic, cut away as much as possible, and poke holes in what remains.

**Bare-root shrub.** Keep the shrub in its packaging in a dark, cool place until you are ready to plant. Soak the roots in tepid water for six to twelve hours before planting. Make a firm mound in the center of the hole, and drape the plant roots over and around the mound before filling the hole.

# CARE

**Indoors.** To keep a **gardenia** indoors in good condition, put the pot on a saucer of moist pebbles, or double-pot it and fill the space between pots with moist moss. Grow the plant in a sunny window, and air and mist it daily. When you water, add a half-dose of soluble fertilizer for acid-loving plants.

**Outdoors.** After the last real snowstorm, remove winter covers and winter mulches from protected shrubs.

# PRUNING

To regenerate a multi-stemmed deciduous shrub that is overgrown, before it begins to grow in the spring, take out a third or a quarter of the branches. Make the cut about a foot from the ground.

Prune back flowering shrubs that bloom on this year's new growth now. Cut **butterfly bush** (*Buddleia*) back to 6 to 12 inches from the ground to force new growth. To encourage flowering and maintain a shrubby height and form in **shrub althea** (rose-of-sharon), prune older branches way back to a strong outward facing bud.

# WATERING

Before growth begins, top-dress the soil of **shrubs growing in containers** indoors and outdoors. Tip the containers on their sides, and gently remove the top 2 inches of soil. Replace it with a fertile potting mix that includes Plant-tone. Renew the mulch.

**Indoors.** Water shrubs wintering inside as needed.

# FERTILIZING

**Indoors.** Continue to fertilize **tropical hibiscus, gardenias,** and other tender shrubs at every second watering.

**Outdoors.** Check and adjust the pH, then fertilize.

*Fertilize all shrubs before growth begins. The section on Understanding Fertilizers in the Introduction to the book explains how and when to use the various types of fertilizer.*

**Fertilize all shrubs before growth begins.** The section on Understanding Fertilizers in the Introduction to the book explains how and when to use the various types of fertilizer.

Halve the amount of fertilizer for **mature hedges;** do not overstimulate when you no longer have a lot of room for growth.

Avoid fertilizing flowering shrubs just before blooming. That stimulates growth at a time when you want the plants to direct their energy into flowering. **If you've missed the right moment for fertilizing, wait to fertilize until after they have bloomed.**

We save wood ashes to sprinkle over the ground around the **lilacs** to sweeten the soil and add potassium. Most New York soils are short of potash—potassium. Wood ashes are a valuable source of lime (which sweetens slightly acidic New York soils) and a source of potash.

# PESTS

**Indoors.** Watch shrubs growing indoors for signs of whitefly, spider mites, and other problems. If you find problems, look up controls in the Pests, Diseases, and Controls section in the Appendix.

## Did You Know?

### Pruning Guide for Deciduous Shrubs

**Dead or damaged wood.** Prune any time between late winter and early autumn.

**Flowering shrubs that bloom on new wood.** Prune in late winter or early spring, well before growth begins.

**Flowering plants that bloom on old wood.** Prune right after they bloom to avoid removing next year's flower buds that develop on this year's new growth.

**To encourage dense branching.** Prune during active growth; cut back by half succulent stems beginning to grow lateral shoots.

**To control height.** Prune after new growth has fully developed. Extend the cuts into the old wood.

**To slow or dwarf growth.** Prune after the season's new growth is complete.

**Outdoors.** Before the buds begin to swell, apply a dormant horticultural oil spray to insect-infested shrubs. These dense oils smother the insects and their eggs.

Check the evergreens, especially **euonymus,** for scale, and spray now with ultrafine horticulture oils if it is present.

In deer country, apply a new and different spray to vulnerable shrubs such as **rhododendrons, arborvitae,** and other **broadleaf evergreens,** and replace old deterrents with new ones. (See Pests, Diseases, and Controls in the Appendix to the book.) If deer are very audacious, surround small treasured shrubs with temporary chicken wire screens; for larger plantings, try unobtrusive bird netting.

Voles are active in March. If you see vole runs, bait the main runway with a rodenticide.

# APRIL
## Shrubs

 PLANNING

**Have you tried shrubs with colorful foliage?** Some that brighten the garden all season long are **golden privet** (*Ligustrum* x *vicaryi*), **variegated bigleaf hydrangea** (*Hydrangea macrophylla* 'Variegata') whose handsome leaves are edged white, and *Weigela florida* 'Variegata' whose new leaves are a soft green edged with white.

 PLANTING

You can transplant container-grown and B&B shrubs now and in the months ahead until hard frosts shut everything down in November. Evergreen shrubs will likely do best moved a little earlier, August through October. But right now the new stock at your garden center is likely to be in top condition. Before buying a container-grown shrub, tip it partly out of the pot, and make sure the rootball isn't heavily rootbound.

 CARE

**Indoors.** Repot florist's **azaleas, gardenias, citrus,** and other tender shrubs that are outgrowing their containers. Don't move them outdoors until the thermometer stays above 60 degrees at night, then place them in bright indirect light for summer R&R; they'll be happier for it.

 PRUNING

When flowers fade on the spring-flowering shrubs that **bloom on the last year's wood**, prune back older non-productive wood and the branches that are compromising the natural form of the shrub.

Prune **azaleas** when they finish blooming. Try for a layered "cloud" look; don't just shear off the branch tips.

Shear damaged (and browning or whitened) **boxwood** branches back to live growth.

**Shear hedges.** The pruning guide for deciduous shrubs on this month's pages and the May guide for evergreens will help you to determine when to clip shrubs and hedges.

 WATERING

For a shrub's first season, unless there's a soaking rain, slowly and gently pour two or three 5-gallon buckets of water around the roots once a week throughout spring.

Water shrubs growing in containers as needed.

 FERTILIZING

**Outdoors.** The color of **mophead** and **lacecap hydrangeas** may be cream through rose to pale and dark blue. Which color depends on the variety, and very much on the soil pH. Acidity makes aluminum in the soil more available, and that keeps hydrangeas blue. A pH of 5.0 to 5.5 results in a lovely soft blue. To maintain pink, the soil must be in the pH range of 6.0 to 6.5 or slightly higher. Test the soil now. If the pH needs adjusting, see Soil Preparation and Improvement in the Introduction to the book. The time to adjust the pH is before new growth begins to emerge.

*For a shrub's first season, unless there's a soaking rain, slowly and gently pour two or three 5-gallon buckets of water around the roots once a week throughout spring.*

## Did You Know?

### Growing Shrubs in Containers

You can grow almost any shrub successfully in a container as long as it has good drainage and is big enough to hold the soil needed to protect the roots from our winter weather. Casters on the bottom of the larger containers make moving easier.

**Container.** For a small shrub, a container 14 to 16 inches in height and diameter is enough. Start a youngster of a larger shrub, like **Japanese maple,** in an 18- to 20-inch tub, and plan to move it to a 30-inch tub.

Insulation can keep containers from cracking in winter's cold. Wrap the interior of containers that will remain outdoors with a double row of large bubble wrap or styrofoam before filling them with soil. You can provide added winter protection by packing bags of leaves around the containers in fall.

**Soil.** The ideal container soil is a fertile semi-soil-less mix, 1 part good topsoil, 1 part horticultural perlite, and 2 parts coarse peat moss. For every 7 inches of planter height, add ⅓ cup slow-release organic fertilizer, and 1 cup dehydrated cow manure. Adding a soil polymer, such as SoilMoist™, can reduce watering by as much as 50 percent. Soak the polymer before adding it, and soak the growing medium before you plant. After planting, water until water runs out the bottom. Apply and maintain a 2- or 3-inch layer of mulch.

**Watering.** From late spring to mid-autumn, plan to water weekly or biweekly. The larger the container, the less often you will have to water it. Containers with built-in water reservoirs, or with water rings that let the plant soak up the water from the bottom, help to keep the soil moist.

**Fertilizing.** Once a month during the growing season, add a water-soluble fertilizer, or seaweed or manure tea to the water.

Next season, in late winter before growth begins, top-dress the soil. Tip the container on its side, and gently remove the top two inches of soil. Replace it with fresh fertile potting mix that includes Holly-tone slow-release fertilizer, and renew the mulch.

---

If you are using chemical fertilizers, you should be fertilizing every six weeks or so. Check the section on Understanding Fertilizers in the Introduction to the book for timing.

At every second watering, add a half-dose of a soluble fertilizer to the water for shrubs growing in containers.

 PESTS

**Outdoors.** Continue preventive measures to protect your garden from deer.

Aphids, whiteflies, and spider mites are gearing up to get you down. **Azaleas** growing in full sun are especially susceptible to spider mites and lace bugs. Three applications of permethrin or pyrethrum

at three to four day intervals will help you to control these pests. Be sure to spray the undersides of the leaves.

Scale is often a problem with **hollies.** Spray with summer weight horticultural oils or Neem.

It's not too soon to rake up weeds. Chop off their little green heads to avoid dealing with mature weeds later.

## PLANNING

Spring is in full bloom! **A wonderful time to visit public and private gardens.** When the weather keeps you out of the garden, visit your full-service garden centers looking for must-haves and bargains.

Investigate the many **viburnums.** Some of these big handsome shrubs bear flowers that are spicily perfumed, and in fall many have colorful foliage and fruits. Some bloom as early as the **flowering cherries,** some as late as the end of June. The earlier types bear large rounded flower heads and are called "snowball" or "semi-snowball" varieties. 'Mohawk' and 'Cayuga' are two of several superb fragrant disease-resistant cultivars introduced by the late great plant hybridizer, Dr. Donald R. Egolf of the National Arboretum. **Double-file viburnums** bloom later, with rows of pure white flowers perched all along the tops of their branches; Dr. Egolf's 'Shasta' is considered a rival to the **dogwood.**

 ## PLANTING

May is a fine month for planting new shrubs and transplanting shrubs that have finished blooming.

Fill gaps left by the passing of the spring-flowering bulbs growing among the shrubs by planting big seedlings of **flowering annuals,** along with pots of **tropicals,** like **mandevilla** and dwarf **canna**.

## CARE

**Indoors.** Move shrubs that still are indoors outside to bright indirect light for their summer vacation.

**Outdoors.** To keep summer's downpours from eroding the soil around your shrubs, and to protect their roots from heat and drought, replenish the mulch. Make it 3 inches deep starting 3 inches from the main stem.

 ## PRUNING

Prune shrubs that bloomed on last year's wood when the flowers are finished.

Deadhead **rhododendrons** very carefully; pinch out the dead blossoms, taking care not to damage the tiny emerging leaf buds just behind them.

As **azaleas** finish blooming, clip or prune 2 to 3 inches off the branch tips that have flowered. To reduce the size of an azalea or a **rhododendron** that is getting too tall, take a third of the oldest branches back to 12 inches. Aim at creating a layered look.

After arching forms of **forsythia** have bloomed, prune them by taking older branches right back to the ground. If you leave a piece of the stem, it will branch just behind the cut and likely grow in a direction that crosses other branches to create a massive bramble over time.

Scorched lower branches of **evergreen shrubs** may be from salt damage that occurred when roads or sidewalks were de-iced; drench the soil with water to leach out the remaining salts, and cut out the damaged branches.

Dog urine also can turn the lower branches yellow, especially **boxwoods.** Drench the soil, fence the area, and spray the plants with dog and cat deterrent.

*To keep summer's downpours from eroding the soil around your shrubs, and to protect their roots from heat and drought, replenish the mulch. Make it 3 inches deep starting 3 inches from the main stem.*

 WATERING

If your watering or spring rains have eroded the soil on sloping shrub borders, shovel it back up the slope, and re-establish saucers around the plants to catch and hold the rain.

For a shrub's first season, unless there's a soaking rain every week or ten days, slowly and gently pour two or three 5-gallon buckets of water around the roots every week.

 FERTILIZING

Twice a month add a water-soluble fertilizer, or diluted seaweed or manure tea, to the water for shrubs growing outdoors in containers and to the annuals and tender and tropical shrubs summering in the shrubbery border.

If you are using organic fertilizers, the late winter application is enough until fall.

If you are using granular chemical fertilizers, fertilize every six weeks. If you have fertilized with a six- or eight-month slow-release fertilizer, the early spring application is enough for the year.

## Did You Know?

### Pruning Guide for Evergreens

Winter and snow damage is best pruned before growth begins.

**Dead or damaged wood** on evergreen conifers can be removed at any time.

**Flowering broadleaf evergreens that bloom on new wood,** like **abelia,** should be pruned in late winter or early spring before growth begins.

**Flowering broadleaf evergreens that bloom on old wood—azaleas** and **rhododendrons,** for example—should be pruned immediately after they bloom and before they initiate new growth to avoid cutting off buds being initiated for the following season.

**To slow or dwarf a broadleaf evergreen,** after its main spurt of growth, remove up to a third. You can cut the main stem (leader) back to the first side shoots, but don't take off more than has grown the last year or two.

**To reduce the size** and to encourage dense branching in evergreens whose growth is initiated by candles (new, candle-like growth), **pines,** for example, cut the candles back by half when growth is complete. Prune the tips of **yews, junipers,** and **hemlocks** lightly any time during the growing season.

**To establish a shape,** prune evergreen shrubs and hedges when they are three to five years old.

Save a little pruning of your evergreens for the holidays.

PESTS

Gypsy moths may appear now. Spray with a biological control such as *Bacillus thuringiensis (Bt)*. Other controls are Sevin or malathion insecticide, Pyrethrin, or rotenone.

Apply or change whatever deer deterrents you are using. See the section on Pests in the Appendix to the book.

**Mugho pines** and other **needled evergreen** shrubs that show denuded branches may be under attack by pine sawfly larvae. Spray the affected plants with *Bacillus thuringiensis (Bt)*.

Keep your shrubs free of weeds.

## PLANNING

Study the spring-flowering bulb catalogs, looking for **bulbs** whose peak bloom period matches that of your flowering shrubs. For example, golden **forsythia** and **daffodils** bloom at about the same time and enhance each other.

When the color of a shrub's blossoms matter, buy it from a local garden center at a time when you can see the plant in bloom. Buying locally will also provide an opportunity to:

- Select cultivars that have proven to be winter-hardy in your zone.

- Check the undersides of the leaves and the crotch of the branches for signs of insect infestation.

- Check the condition of the rootball. It's okay if a few roots circle the rootball and there's a thin mat of roots at the bottom; much more will need removal, however, and the plant will need time to recover.

- Get good cultural advice.

 ## PLANTING

If shrubbery borders look bare, fill gaps with potted **flowering maples** (*Abutilon*) and **tropical hibiscus**. In September you can pot them up, and winter them indoors as houseplants.

 ## CARE

If wands of willowy **butterfly bush** get flattened by rain and wind, stake them. They can be pruned and shaped throughout early summer.

Keep the mulch around hedges and shrubbery 3 inches deep to save yourself weeding later.

 ## PRUNING

Finish deadheading **late-blooming rhododendrons** and **azaleas.** Deadhead **tropical hibiscus, flowering maples,** and other tender shrubs.

To let light and air into the interior of old **clipped boxwoods,** remove older inside branches. Prune elongated boxwood shoots after new growth is complete to keep them trim and beautiful.

After the first flush of new growth in **evergreen hedges,** trim the top and sides to keep the height down and the greenery full. Keep the top narrower than the bottom so light can reach the lower branches or they will lose their leaves.

Cut the succulent new shoots on **deciduous hedges** in half.

 ## WATERING

A newly-planted shrub needs a good soaking every week to ten days in summer. If you don't have rain, slowly and gently pour two to three 5-gallon buckets of water around the roots.

Every few days check the soil moisture in shrubs growing in containers, and water as often as necessary to keep them nicely damp.

 ## FERTILIZING

New growth is emerging in the **mophead** and **lacecap hydrangeas**—time to adjust the color toward pink or blue by increasing or decreasing the soil acidity. A pH of 5.0 to 5.5 results in a soft blue color. For pink, keep the soil pH 6.0 to 6.5 or slightly higher. To adjust the pH, see Soil Preparation and Improvement in the Introduction to the book.

If you are using granular chemical fertilizers, continue to make applications every six weeks.

At every second watering, add a half-dose of a soluble fertilizer to the water for **shrubs growing in containers.**

*When the color of a shrub's blossoms matter, buy it from a local garden center at a time when you can see the plant in bloom.*

## Did You Know?

### You Can Multiply Your Shrubs by Rooting Cuttings

**Azaleas, winterberry, coniferous evergreens,** and many other shrubs can be rooted from semi-hardwood cuttings taken June and July. New green growth that is just turning brown and hardening is what is meant by "semi-hardwood." Snap a twig, and if the bark clings to the branch, it's likely semi-hardwood. Here's how it works:

*1* Prepare a rooting box about the size of a seed flat and 5 to 6 inches deep. It must have drainage. Fill the box with 4 inches of a moist mix of $1/2$ peat and $1/2$ perlite or coarse sand. With a pencil, make twelve equidistant planting holes.

*2* Cover the bottom of a saucer with rooting hormone powder.

*3* In early morning, cut a dozen semi-hardened branch ends 4 to 8 inches long at a point about 1 inch below a leaf cluster. Remove the leaves from the bottom 3 inches. Mist the foliage.

*4* Working in shade, remove a strip of bark $1/2$ to 1 inch long on the side of each branch, cutting close to the cut end. Lightly coat the cut ends and the wounds in the rooting powder.

*5* Insert the cut ends 2 to 3 inches in the rooting box, deep enough to fully cover the wounds. Press the soil up around the cuttings.

*6* Water well, and enclose the box in clear plastic. You can use hoops made of wire coat hangers to support the plastic. Punch a few holes in the plastic for ventilation.

*7* Place the box in a shaded, sheltered location. Check the soil moisture every five days; the cuttings mustn't dry out.

*8* In about six weeks, test the cuttings to see if they are rooted. Very gently tug on a couple of the cuttings; when you meet real resistance, they are rooted.

*9* Transplant the rooted cuttings to pots filled with $1/2$ potting soil and $1/2$ peat.

*10* Gradually expose the pots to increasingly strong light while keeping the soil moist. In September, transplant them to the garden, and protect them with a light mulch of hay or open evergreen boughs.

## PESTS

Repair and/or renew deer deterrents and sprays.

Check **rhododendrons** and **azaleas** for lace bug damage. The leaf surfaces will be dull, speckled, and pale, and the undersides will show dark specks of insect excrement. Spray the foliage above and beneath at intervals with horticultural oil or insecticidal soap.

Whitefly and spider mite damage shows up as spotted and blanched leaves. Remove dead or severely infected twigs, and spray with Neem at intervals until the infestation is gone. See Pests, Diseases, and Controls in the Appendix.

Keep your shrubs clear of weeds. If weeds mature and go to seed, there will be an army to rout later.

# JULY
## Shrubs

## PLANNING

Plan for some of your summer reading to be updates on natural controls and improved shrub varieties. Master Gardener programs and state university USDA Extension Agencies put out bulletins, usually free, loaded with nuggets of information valuable to gardeners.

For example, many new superior **viburnums** like the **doublefile** beauty called 'Shasta', and hardy **hibiscus** (shrub althea, rose-of-sharon) selected and introduced by the late great Dr. Donald R. Egolf of the U.S. National Arboretum, are now widely available in New York. The National Arboretum is also growing **euonymus** specimens free of scale insects, a pest that can make growing these beautiful evergreen shrubs a never-ending battle. Scales on the insect's back literally protect them from insecticides, but USDA scientists found predator beetles in Korea that attack and control the pest at the Arboretum without the aid of insecticides.

## PLANTING

When planting shrubs in containers at the seashore, use commercial potting soil rather than the sandy soil in your yard, which lets water drain through so rapidly it leeches the nutrients.

You can continue to plant **container-grown shrubs** this month. **B&B shrubs,** too, but don't buy B&B shrubs whose rootballs have been sitting unmulched and baking at a garden center since they were dug in early spring.

## CARE

After heavy summer storms, check and, if needed, top off the mulch around shrubs and prune out broken branches.

When coastal storms are announced, spray the upper and lower sides of shrub foliage with anti-desiccants to minimize damage from salt spray and salty sea mist.

## PRUNING

Groom and prune the **hedges** and **spring-flowering shrubs.**

Continue to deadhead **tropical hibiscus, flowering maples,** and other shrubs that bloom all summer.

Toward the middle of the month, you can take ¹/₂ inch off the leggy ends of older **azalea** shoots, but do not prune new growth—that's where next year's flowers will be.

## WATERING

Shrubs growing in **big containers** are likely to need watering every four to seven days; the **smaller containers** more often. Containers with built-in water reservoirs, or with water rings that let the plant soak up the water from the bottom, minimize watering chores.

Late July is drought season, and you will probably need to water the garden two or three times before the fall rains arrive in September. If you go a week to ten days without rain, water slowly and deeply, especially newly planted shrubs. Shrubs slow their growth to adapt to high heat unless forced by shallow watering and inappropriate fertilizing to grow when the weather isn't supporting growth.

Before going on vacation, group shrubs growing in containers in light shade, make sure each one has a generous saucer, and water them thoroughly.

## FERTILIZING

At every second watering add a half-dose of a water-soluble fertilizer, liquid seaweed, or a manure tea to the water for shrubs growing in containers.

If you are using granular chemical fertilizers, continue to make applications every six weeks.

If shrubs fertilized with a timed-release chemical fertilizer are failing to bloom as expected or look peaked, supplement with foliar feedings of water-soluble organic or fast-acting liquid fertilizers or manure teas.

 PESTS

Continue preventive measures to protect your garden from deer.

Check **lilac** foliage for the grayish film that is a sign of powdery mildew. Controls are sulfur, ultrafine horticultural oil, copper fungicide, Immunox, or Bayleton.

Spraying with ultrafine horticultural oils helps. A Cornell University control for mildew is to spray with a solution consisting of 1 tablespoon of ultrafine oil and 1 tablespoon of baking soda (soda bicarbonate) dissolved in 1 gallon of water.

Go after the Japanese beetles. Japanese beetle traps are effective, provided they are placed far away from the plantings you are trying to protect, not among them. Do not install pheromone traps that attract beetles from everywhere. Or in the cool of early morning, knock

the beetles off into a jar of sudsy water. Spray serious infestations with pyrethrum.

Whitefly, mealybugs, scale, spider mites, and aphids multiply in hot, airless spots and will spoil the leaves even if they don't do permanent damage. Spray infestations two or three times with some form of Neem, pyrethrum, or horticultural soaps—they won't harm the environment. You can also use horticultural oils. See the section in the Appendix on Pests, Diseases, and Controls.

## Did You Know?

### Shrubs for the Seashore

These plants tolerate salt spray and sandy situations at the shore and inland, too. Most require well-drained soil.

- **Adam's-needle** (*Yucca filamentosa*). Big, dramatic evergreen rosette of sword-like leaves that sends up 6-foot flower spikes.

- **Bayberry** (*Myrica pennsylvanica*). For Zone 6 and north. Beautiful big shrub with gray-green, semi-evergreen leaves that are aromatic when crushed.

- **Beach Plum** (*Prunus maritime*). Round bush that bears clusters of white blooms followed by purplish fruit.

- **Hydrangea** (*Hydrangea* species and varieties). Deciduous shrubs with huge flower heads in mid- and late summer.

- **Inkberry** (*Ilex glabra* 'Compacta'). Black berries, usually evergreen, shrub to 3 feet high.

- **Japanese Rose, Rugosa Rose** (*Rosa rugosa*). Tall rugged bush that bears handsome roses and brilliant fruit.

- **Juniper, Creeping Juniper** (*Juniperus horizontalis*; shore juniper, *J. conferta*). Spreading gray-green evergreen foliage and blue berries.

- **Tamarisk, Salt Cedar** (*Tamarix ramosissima*). Tall shrubs with delicate leaves and feathery clusters of flowers in late summer.

- **Vicary Golden Privet** (*Ligustrum* x *vicaryi*). Small-leaved evergreen for tall hedges.

# AUGUST
## Shrubs

 PLANNING

If you are interested in adding a hedge to your yard, lay it out and order the plants now, so you can start planting when summer heat and drought ends.

**About hedges.** A well-kept hedge adds structure to a garden design. A hedge also makes a handsome frame for a flower bed, a shrubbery border, a garden room, or paths. You can use a hedge to lead the eye to—or from—features in the landscape, dampen noise, and block blown leaves and debris. A prickly hedge can discourage (some) unwelcome visitors. A tall hedge can create a privacy screen, mask neighboring walls, mark distant property boundaries, and break the force of the wind.

To help you decide whether a hedge is for you, here's some advice from seasoned hedge keepers:

- Be sure you will have enough time available to keep your hedge trimmed. Hedges trimmed with hand pruners have a more natural look...and that takes time.

- Don't site a hedge on your property line using shrubs with branches that will reach into the neighbor's space. The neighbor has the legal right to remove branches and roots that invade his/her space.

- Choose species suited to the light and ground space available for the whole length of the hedge.

- Buy young shrubs, 3 feet or less. They are inexpensive and more adaptable.

If the hedge will run through both tall shade and real shade, choose a species that succeeds in either light. There are only a few **hollies** hardy in the cooler areas of New York, but they're good choices. Among them is the small **Japanese holly,** okay in Zone 5, and the big shrubby **Meserve hollies,** okay in Zone 4. **Canadian hemlock** is hardy everywhere and can be sheared to hedge form for decades. In the shadiest area, plant the shrubs closer together.

**For a formal hedge,** use a shrub that can be clipped and sheared. Make it follow symmetrical lines—straight with squared corners, a circle, an oval, or a triangle. Hedges facing each other are more formal. Shearable evergreens, like **boxwood** and **privet,** or naturally columnar evergreens like **dwarf Alberta spruce** (*Picea glauca* 'Conica') are used.

**For an informal hedge,** choose plants with a loose habit and plant them in curves that lead off at an angle. Choose open, asymmetrical shrubs like **forsythia** and *Juniper chinensis* 'Hetzii'. Or plant a mix with compatible needs, for example, **Mugho pines** and **potentillas.**

**Texture.** For a close-up hedge, choose fine-textured *Pyracantha* and **Korean boxwood.** For a distant hedge, choose coarse foliage, like the **Meserve hollies** and **rhododendrons.**

**Pruning.** Be prepared to trim a **clipped hedge** at least twice a year. An **informal hedge** can be trimmed once or twice a year. To trim informal and natural hedges, use hand shears.

 PLANTING

Fall is considered the best planting season in our area. You can plant starting this month, but it can wait until the leaves start to turn in October. **Evergreen shrubs** are best moved August through October.

CARE

If the harvest from your **highbush blueberries** is shrinking, blame birds or bears. Save remaining berries by covering the bushes with bird netting. Console yourself with the thought of the vibrant color highbush blueberry foliage brings to the garden later in the season.

 PRUNING

Give hedges their final trimming for the year.

*You will probably need to water all the shrub beds two or three times before the September rains. The ideal is to apply 1¹/₂ inches of water at each session.*

# WATERING

You will probably need to water all the shrub beds two or three times before the September rains. The ideal is to apply 1¹/₂ inches of water at each session. To find out how long your watering system takes to deliver that much water, mark 1¹/₂ inches on the inside of an empty 1-pound coffee can or other container, and set it where it will catch the water.

Overhead watering is fine as long as you water deeply. There's less waste if you water before the sun reaches the garden in the early morning or late afternoon or evening. In hot, dry periods, daytime overhead watering lowers leaf temperatures and reduces stress. Evening watering is fine since dew naturally wets foliage every clear night anyway.

We don't recommend electrically-timed mechanical watering systems that water too often and shallowly. But we do believe they can do a good job if they are set up with the correct low-pressure nozzles and timed to run long enough and to water gently and deeply every week or ten days in periods of drought.

Continue to water shrubs in containers as needed.

# FERTILIZING

In Zones 3 and 4, if you are using organic fertilizers, make a final application to in-ground shrubs as growth slows—usually about August 15.

If you are using chemical fertilizers, you should be fertilizing every six weeks.

# PESTS

Change deer deterrents and sprays around in the garden.

If your berries are harvested before you can get to them, there may be a bear in the vicinity. In addition, if bear sightings are reported, it's probably not a good idea to put out bird feeders this winter.

Clear the beds of all weeds; don't let them grow up and go to seed!

# SEPTEMBER
## Shrubs

 PLANNING

If you long to do something positive for the environment, plant a "rain garden" this fall to handle flooding from severe storms and to preserve water. Runoff water often carries pesticides, herbicides, heavy metals, and other toxins.

Site the rain garden where the runoff from concrete surfaces goes or where building gutters empty. Make the center slightly lower than the soil level so water can pool there. That way the runoff goes into the soil so the plants get to use it and it doesn't get into the water table, sewers, or streams.

Rain garden plants are bio-remediators—their roots and foliage tie up toxins. Some excellent plants for a rain garden are **birches, ornamental grasses, coneflowers, rudbeckia, weigela, baptisia, coreopsis.** Other plants include **river birch, Northern Lights series azaleas, redosier dogwood, asters, astilbe, campanula, hostas, salvia, Siberian iris, Joe-pye weed, red milkweed, switchgrass.**

 PLANTING

Many consider Labor Day into late October, or even into November in Zones 5, 6, 7, as the best planting and transplanting season for trees and shrubs in New York. It's the perfect time to plant spring-flowering shrubs.

Late plant sales and perfect planting weather combine to make this also a fine time to install a hedge.

**Laying out a hedge bed.** Make the width of the bed equal to the height of the shrubs at maturity. For a 1- to 2-foot high hedge, make the bed 18 inches wide; for a hedge 3 feet tall, make it 3 feet wide; for a hedge 15 feet tall, make it 15 feet wide. Columnar plants need less space. For a double hedge, make the bed wide enough to give the plants on either side plenty of room.

**Planting.** Prepare a trench 12 to 18 inches deep, and improve the soil. Set low-growing shrubs 18 inches apart for a single row. For a double row, set them zig-zag 12 inches apart; to keep out intruders, weave chicken wire between the shrubs. Crowded shrubs can be moved later to replace failed plants. Finish the bed with 3 inches of mulch.

**Fertilizing.** Encourage growth the first two years by fertilizing in late winter, again after the main spurt of growth, and again now as summer ends. As the hedge matures, fertilize at half-strength when you feed other shrubs.

 CARE

When the thermometer hits 60 degrees Fahrenheit, prepare to **move tropical hibiscus, flowering maple,** and **other tender shrubs** indoors. Hose them down, and then spray them with insecticidal soap before the move.

Toward the end of the month or if frosts threaten, move hardy shrubs growing in containers to sheltered locations for the winter.

 PRUNING

Deadhead fall-flowering shrubs.

 WATERING

**Indoors.** Water shrubs moved or stored indoors for the winter as needed.

*When the thermometer hits 60 degrees Fahrenheit, prepare to move tropical hibiscus, flowering maple, and other tender shrubs indoors. Hose them down, and then spray them with insecticidal soap before the move.*

**Outdoors.** Even after cold sets in, the soil stays warm, and roots continue to develop, so water both established and new shrubs sufficiently to keep the soil from drying out.

Pour two or three 5-gallon buckets of water around the roots of **newly planted shrubs** once a week until the ground is frozen unless you have good, soaking rains.

# FERTILIZING

In Zones 5, 6, and 7, if you are using organic blend fertilizers such as Holly-tone or Plant-tone, make a final application now.

If you are using only granular chemical fertilizers, fertilize garden and container plants for the last time just as the growing season ends; depending on your zone that will be some time between early September and early October.

If you are using time-release fertilizers in large containers and the garden, earlier applications should carry the plants through the end of the growing season.

# PESTS

**Indoors.** Check shrubs for whitefly and spider mites. You will find controls in the Pests section in the Appendix.

**Outdoors.** Change whatever deer deterrents you are using. If there are bears in your area, don't stock a bird feeder. See the section on Pests in the Appendix of the book.

Continue to search for and destroy weeds.

PLANNING

Visit nearby public gardens and learn more about the shrubs that blaze into color in the fall. The foliage of some **azaleas** shows streaks of plum, maroon, and gold. Look for dwarfish **witchhazels** like the beautiful 'Diane' and **viburnums** like 'Cayuga' whose fall foliage color is as rich as the perfume of its spring flowers.

The reddest leaves at your garden center are likely to belong to the **euonymus** called the **dwarf winged spindletree**. **Willowleaf cotoneaster 'Autumn Fire'** has purplish leaves and scarlet fruits.

**Large fothergilla** turns brilliant yellow and orange-red; **chokeberry 'Brilliantissima'** has brilliant berries. The **American smoke tree, chittamwood, sweetspire,** and the **sumacs** are others with exceptional autumn color. The **staghorn sumac** cultivar 'Laciniata' turns gold, orange, and scarlet in fall.

The colorful stems of shrubby **red-** and **yellow-twig dogwoods** brighten the scene when there's snow on the ground.

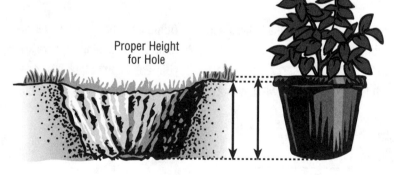

Proper Height for Hole

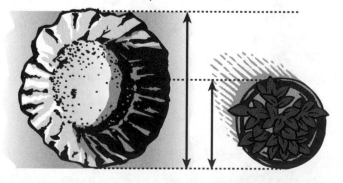

Proper Width of Hole

 PLANTING

When the leaves first start to change color is a good time to dig and transplant, or plant, **deciduous shrubs**—then through November. **Evergreen shrubs** may do better planted this month rather than next.

Plant open spaces in the shrubbery border with spring-flowering bulbs. For ideas, turn to the October pages of Chapter 2, Bulbs, Corms, Rhizomes, and Tubers.

 CARE

In Zones 6 and 7, move container shrubs that are borderline hardy and still out in the open to a frost-free shed or garage.

After the second hard frost, cover low-growing shrubs, like **dwarf evergreen azaleas,** with a light winter mulch of pine boughs; they'll catch blowing leaves and save you a picky clean-up job next spring.

 PRUNING

From now until next spring the only pruning you should do is to remove diseased or dead wood.

*The most important preparation for winter is a deep and thorough watering of all shrubs—new, established, in ground, and in containers—before the soil freezes; if the sky doesn't provide the rain, you will have to.*

 # WATERING

**Indoors.** Water indoor shrubs as needed.

**Outdoors.** Unless you have good soaking rains, pour two or three 5-gallon buckets of water around the roots of newly planted shrubs once every week this fall.

The most important preparation for winter is a deep and thorough watering of all shrubs—new, established, in ground, and in containers—before the soil freezes; if the sky doesn't provide the rain, you will have to.

 # FERTILIZING

**Outdoors.** In Zones 6 and 7, the last application of fertilizer can be made in early October.

 # PESTS

**Indoors.** Watch shrubs moved indoors for signs of whitefly and spider mites. If you find problems, look up controls in the Pests section in the Appendix.

## Did You Know?

### About Needled Evergreens and Conifers

The shrub-size **needled evergreens** and **conifers** are dwarf or slow-growing species and varieties of evergreen trees that grow everywhere in New York. Some are perfect for keeping green all year round in perennial beds and shrubbery borders. Others make fine dense hedges, wind breaks, and edgers for paths and driveways.

Among small evergreens we use to anchor beds of perennials are the dark, chunky little **Mugho pine** and **dwarf blue spruces.** Narrow conical **dwarf Alberta spruce** is a sensational accent in a large flowering border. (Alberta spruce is attacked by spider mites, so make a note to keep it sprayed periodically with horticultural soaps.) Others for perennial beds and shrub borders are pyramidal—for example the **dwarf Colorado blue spruce 'Fat Albert',** shrubby **Hinoki false cypress,** and the **dwarf golden Sawara false cypress.** A cluster of small, clipped, ball-shaped juniper topiaries in a perennial border adds greenery and a smile.

**Evergreen shrubs** that are excellent for hedges and edging include **dwarf spruce** cultivars, the **dwarf junipers,** the **Japanese yew** 'Meyeri' and cultivars, and the **Meserve hybrid hollies** 'Blue Boy' and 'Blue Girl', which are hardy in Zone 4. In Zones 6 and 7 even the handsome **dwarf variegated hollies** can be grown.

To furnish neglected corners, and for low and mid-height screening, consider some of the sprawling **Chinese junipers,** the **Pitzer cultivars, dwarf false cypresses,** and upright little **yews** like 'Pygmaea'. Some of the slow-growing **Japanese pines** are hardy in Zone 5.

**Outdoors.** Apply or change whatever deer deterrents you are using; they love **rhododendrons!**

If vole runs appear around shrubs, bait the main runway with a rodenticide. They are most active October through March.

PLANNING

To see the beauty of a New York garden at this season, train your eye to discern the wonderful structures nature bares when the foliage is gone. The twiggy forms of naked **barberries,** for example, are enormously complex and interesting. Shrubs with berries, such as the brilliant U.S. National Arboretum introduction 'Sparkleberry', a **deciduous holly,** and the **pyracanthas** are charming assets that attract birds.

The **viburnums** do a lot for the garden even after their leaves are gone; the **oak-leaf hydrangea's** towering stems remain after the leaves fall, and the flower heads of the **peegee** and **mophead hydrangeas** furnish the scene. Nature's fall parade rivals spring if you take the time to stop and to really see, feel, smell, breathe in the seasonal changes.

 PLANTING

In Zones 7 and 6, if the weather holds, you can still plant **deciduous shrubs** that are either container grown or balled and burlapped. The air is cold, but the earth still has warmth.

 CARE

It's a good idea to provide winter protection for a **newly planted shrub** to protect the wood from drying in bitter winds and to avoid damage to the crown when alternate thawing and freezing cycles cause the soil to heave it. To protect **rhododendrons** and other broadleaved **evergreen shrubs** growing in exposed positions, apply an anti-desiccant spray to the foliage and/or wrap them in Reemay or burlap.

 PRUNING

**Outdoors.** It's too late to prune shrubs now.

Cold Protection for Shrubs

**Indoors.** You can cut back **flowering maples** if they get leggy, and pinch back ungainly stems of **hibiscus** and other shrubs wintering inside.

 WATERING

**Indoors.** Mist and water shrubs wintering indoors to offset the dryness in the air caused by central heating. **Flowering maples** dry out very quickly indoors: keep an eye on soil moisture in the pots.

**Outdoors.** Shrubs need moisture until the plants are completely dormant. Prepare your in-ground shrubs for winter by giving them a deep and thorough watering just before the ground freezes. If the sky doesn't do it, then you must.

Maintain moderate soil moisture for hardy shrubs outdoors in containers until the ground freezes, and those sheltering in a cold garage or shed.

*It's a good idea to provide winter protection for a newly planted shrub to protect the wood from drying in bitter winds and to avoid damage to the crown when alternate thawing and freezing cycles cause the soil to heave it.*

## FERTILIZING

**Indoors.** At every fourth watering, add a half-dose of soluble fertilizer to the water for tropical **hibiscus, flowering maple,** and other shrubs moved indoors for the cold months.

**Outdoors.** Fertilizing is over for the shrub garden this year.

## PESTS

**Indoors.** Check shrubs moved indoors for signs of whitefly and spider mites. If you find problems, apply the controls recommended in the section on Pests, Diseases, and Controls in the Appendix.

**Outdoors.** If the deer are very bold, wrap **rhododendrons** and other susceptible evergreens in chicken wire cages. Change whatever deer deterrents you are using.

If vole runs appear around shrubs, bait the main runway with a rodenticide.

## Did You Know?

### Some Berry-Making Shrubs Need Pollinators

The shrubs that produce berries are colorful late-season and winter assets. To make sure you will have the show of berries you hope for, before buying a plant for its berries, ask your supplier about the pollinating needs of the species. For some species of berry-producing shrubs, you will need to make sure a male pollinator is nearby in order to guarantee a showy crop of berries.

Most plants have male and female flower parts in the same flower, and they self-pollinate—don't need outside help to produce berries. Other species include both male and female flowers separately on the same plant. These don't require pollinators either; just a little shaking by the wind will do the trick.

But some important berry-producing shrubs are not unisex; they develop as either female or male plants. They're referred to as "dioecious" shrubs. Among popular shrubs that are dioecious are **aucuba, bayberries, fringe tree, hollies, skimmia,** and **yews.** The female of these species must have a suitable male pollinator within pollinating reach to produce a heavy crop of berries. Female plants generally produce the showiest fruit, and they also litter most.

As a rule of thumb, you can provide one male shrub and expect it to cross-pollinate two to ten females or more, depending on species and location. In a neighborhood with many gardens, you may not need to provide a male pollinator. Your garden center or nursery supplier will be able to advise you.

## Shrubs

## PLANNING

Browse your catalogs for holiday gifts—for your loved ones and yourself.

If you worry a lot about pests and diseases, ask Santa for a Brunton Macro-Scope—a microscope that focuses from infinity down to 18 inches and lets you see insects at a distance of 6 feet! (www.closetoinfinity.com)

Gifts that gardeners deeply appreciate—and never have too many of—are superior pruning tools. Inexpensive pruning tools don't cut well and don't last. Good pruning tools cost more, but with care they last a lifetime.

A gardener with lots of shrubbery needs four basic pruning tools:

*1* The tool that goes where the gardener goes is a pair of **bypass pruning shears.** Really good shears snap through twigs and small branches as effortlessly as a hot knife cuts butter.

*2* **Long-handled lopping shears** are invaluable; these are bypass shears with a reach long enough to reach the interior of large shrubs.

*3* To cut through main stems and larger branches, you need a little **pull saw.** Half handle and half short blade with multifaceted teeth, it makes a deep cut as you pull back.

*4* For anyone who owns a hedge, **scissor-like hand-held hedge shears** are essential. If the hedge is a long one and meant to be trimmed, then electric or gas shears are the ones to choose.

A good pruning tool is a treasure, to be cleaned and wiped with an oily rag after each use. After pruning diseased plants, disinfect tools by dipping them in a solution of 1 part bleach to 9 parts water.

## PLANTING

In Zone 7 on a very rare warm year, you can still plant deciduous shrubs the first days of this month.

## CARE

After storms, check and adjust the protective covering on shrubs.

With a broom, as soon as possible after a heavy snowfall, free evergreen shrubs that are weighed down.

Use only snowmelt products that don't harm plants, turf, and concrete.

## PRUNING

Prune overgrown **evergreens** lightly to obtain material for making roping, swags, topiary trees, and wreaths for the holidays.

## WATERING

**Indoors.** Water shrubs indoors as needed.

## FERTILIZING

**Indoors.** Don't fertilize shrubs indoors until you see new growth late next month.

## PESTS

**Indoors.** Watch shrubs growing indoors for signs of whitefly and spider mites. If you find problems, apply the controls recommended in the Pests, Diseases, and Controls section of the Appendix.

**Outdoors.** The scent-carrying oils in evil-smelling deer deterrents don't volatilize in cold air. If you see a lot of deer, wrap **rhododendrons** and other endangered shrubs in chicken wire cages for the winter.

If vole runs appear around shrubs, bait the main runway with a rodenticide.

# CHAPTER NINE

# Trees

*Sweet flowers in spring, cool shade in summer, leaves ablaze in fall, the singing of the winter wind in the pines—trees brighten our lives in every season.*

**Newly planted trees.** A new tree needs a great planting hole and, the first season or two, as much water as you give a young shrub. In its early years, to ensure that it will develop a handsome structure, the tree also will need a little thoughtful but easy pruning. Once established, it will need little fertilizing and watering only in droughts. With a well-grown tree, the living is easy.

**Established trees.** Established trees that aren't doing well usually suffer from crowding, loss of light, compacted soil, and lack of nutrients and water. Pruning the trees to open the crown up to air and light, clearing surrounding vegetation, fertilizing, and watering in times of drought will bring them back. The prompts in the month-by-month pages ahead will help you to get them growing well again.

## CHOOSING NEW TREES

When you are adding a new tree to your property, look for a species whose habit, color, and texture will add variety to existing plantings and the view. Look for trees that have several assets. An example is the **American holly** (*Ilex opaca*). It is hardy in Zone 5, has a handsome silhouette, evergreen foliage with an interesting texture, produces bright red berries, and has few enemies.

**Habit and size.** A tree is the largest plant in the garden, so its silhouette—habit—makes an important difference to your yard and to your neighborhood. Each species has a recognizable volume and sculptural structure—spreading, pyramidal, oval, vase-shaped, round, columnar, clumping, weeping. When adding—or deleting—trees, aim for a variety of silhouettes.

Avoid trees that will grow so big they dwarf your house or garden and rob neighbors of light.

## EVERGREEN OR DECIDUOUS?

**Choose evergreens to keep the yard green and block unwanted views** all year round. Conifers that have flat scale-like leaves—**American arborvitae,** for example—are very dense. The needled evergreens—**hemlock** and **pine**—have an airier presence.

**Choose deciduous trees that bring change** to your garden view with spring's baby leaves, summer's rich green canopy, fall's grand finale—which ranges from buff in the **oaks,** to gold in the **willows,** to the flames of the **sugar and swamp maples.** In winter, a deciduous tree's bare branches and twigs frame the sky and the bark presents arresting textures—think of the silky gray kid of the **American beech,** for example, and the chalky white of **river birch.**

Both evergreen and deciduous trees shade the house and protect it from the sweep of winter wind, thereby saving on the costs of cooling and heating.

**Flowering trees.** A flowering tree in bloom is a sky-high bouquet. Your property, if big enough, can host a flowery parade from early spring when the **ornamental cherries** bloom until mid-fall when the last fragrant blossom falls from the little **Franklin tree** (*Franklinia alatamaha*). Selecting flowering trees that bear colorful fruits will double your pleasure. The **flowering crabapples** and **dogwoods** are two of many whose flowers are followed by plentiful fruits. Some are fragrant—for example, the five-foot **Sargent crab** (*Malus sargentii*), which is truly charming in big perennial beds and shrub borders.

**Make healthy choices.** However perfect a tree is for its site, if it is susceptible to pests and diseases, it's a poor choice.

## PLANTING

**Location.** Site large trees where they will reach full sun as they mature. Many small flowering trees are understory plants that developed in the partial shade of a forest, and they will thrive in partial light. If you are trying a tree that is borderline hardy in your yard, give it a spot sheltered from the north wind. The lovely little **Loebner magnolia** (*Magnolia* x *loebneri*) can make it in some Zone 4 gardens but only with protection.

Don't plant a tree, large or small, in an airless corner, or close to a wall or overhang.

Place trees at distances from each other that allow plenty of space for the lateral development of branches. Columnar trees can be set more closely than pyramidal trees. Large

shade trees are best set 75 feet apart. The absolute minimum for a street tree is 12 feet in every direction and 18 feet is better. Staggered plantings achieve greater density in less space.

Don't plant tall trees near electric or phone lines, and avoid proximity to pipes and septic systems.

Before placing a large tree near a garden, consider the effect on the plants of the shade it will cast at various times of the day and the year. Don't plant so close to a sidewalk or patio that the roots will heave the paving.

**When to plant.** You can plant trees as soon as the ground becomes workable, April for most of us, but the truly ideal planting season begins when the leaves start to change color and ends in November. Choose early spring for planting trees difficult to transplant, **Florida dogwoods** and **magnolias,** for example. Plant trees that bloom in spring in the fall. Plant trees that bloom in summer and early fall in the spring.

**Bare-root trees.** In early spring before growth begins, mail-order suppliers ship young trees bare root. Before placing your order, check on the size and the age of a bargain sapling so you know what to expect. The tree will be shipped when it is time to plant in your area. Follow the shipper's instructions for planting exactly.

**Container-grown and B&B trees.** Container and balled-and-burlapped trees are more costly than bare-root trees. B&B packaging is usually reserved for very large trees. But big trees are also being grown now in 10-, 15-, and even 50-gallon containers. Container and B&B trees may be planted from early spring through summer and into fall. B&B trees dug in spring and protected in the months since by mounds of mulch or soil can stay in good condition.

**Costs.** Buying young trees saves on costs, and they knit into their new environments quickly. Trees 7 to 8 feet tall soon overtake the growth of 15-foot trees set out at the same time. If you are buying a large, expensive specimen, we recommend buying from a full-service nursery or garden center and paying extra to have it planted and for a warranty in case of loss.

**Soil and pH.** Within a year or two, a new tree will send roots out well beyond the amended soil of its planting hole. That means your easiest successes will be with species growing in native soil that has a pH matching their pH needs. However, amending the pH of the planting hole helps, especially with hard-to-transplant specimens like the **American hornbeam** and **sour gum.** You will find information on modifying pH and amending soil in the section on Soil Preparation and

# Trees

Improvement in the Introduction to the book.

**Digging the hole.** If you plant your trees correctly, they will have a much better chance of success. Here's how:

*1* Make the planting hole for a tree three times as wide and twice as deep as the rootball, or five times as wide and as deep as the rootball.

*2* Loosen the sides of the hole, and blend the soil taken from the hole with the organic amendments described in Soil Preparation and Improvement in the Introduction to the book.

*3* Half-fill the bottom of the hole with improved soil, and tamp it down **very firmly** to make a solid base. Instructions for planting bare-root trees usually call for the creation of a cone in the center of the hole over which the roots are to be spread. (See Planting, in the February pages of this chapter.)

*4* Set a container or B&B tree in the hole so the trunk is straight and 2 inches above the level of the surrounding earth. The weight on unsettled soil will cause the tree to sink after planting.

*5* Half-fill the hole once more with improved soil. Tamp it down firmly. Finish filling the hole and tamp the soil down. Shape the soil around the crown into a wide saucer.

*6* Water the area slowly, gently, and thoroughly with a sprinkler, a soaker hose, a bubbler, or by hand. (See Watering, later in this introduction.)

*7* Mulch newly planted trees 3 inches deep, starting 3 inches from the trunk out to the edge of the saucer. Replenish the mulch as needed to keep it 3 to 4 inches deep.

Ground covers such as **pachysandra, ivy, myrtle, hostas,** drought-tolerant **rudbeckias,** and small **flowering bulbs**

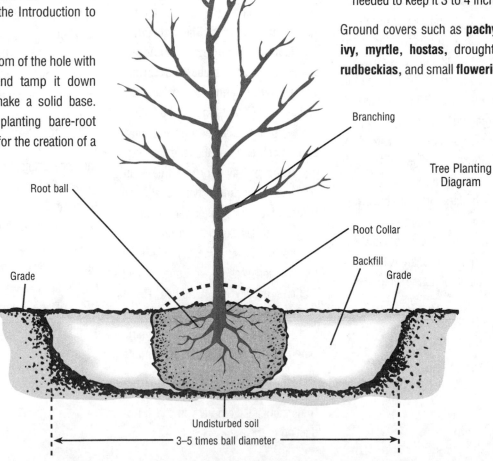

Tree Planting Diagram

Branching

Root ball

Root Collar

Backfill

Grade

Grade

Undisturbed soil

3–5 times ball diameter

# Trees

may be planted outside the water basin (saucer) around a tree when it is first set out. The ground covers will move in around the trunk and become a living mulch that keeps weeds out and spares you hand trimming the lawn grasses.

**Staking and protecting the trunk.** It isn't essential to stake a young tree unless the stem or trunk shows a tendency to lean or to grow at an odd angle. Remove the stake when the tree is growing straight and true.

In Zones 3 through 6, a burlap windbreak helps a young tree through its first few winters. You can either wrap the tree loosely in burlap or place a burlap screen between the tree and the sweep of the wind. Where wildlife is active, wrapping a tree trunk with a protective tape or a plastic casing may keep the critters from chewing through the bark; remove the wrap in spring when growth starts. If your concern is the injury winter sun can inflict on a young trunk, paint it with whitewash, which is calcium carbonate with resins in it, or envelop it in a tree wrap.

## FERTILIZING

**Established trees** surrounded by a lawn or growing in a shrub border receive all the nutrients they need when you fertilize the ground around. Groves of trees benefit from an annual fertilization with an organic lawn food high in nitrogen, for example, Espoma organic lawn food 18-8-6. Woodland trees get their nutrients from the decomposition of their fallen leaves.

**New trees** growing in improved soil rich in organic fertilizers will benefit from fertilization twice a year for the next eight or ten years. **The first annual application of fertilizer should be made before growth begins in spring.** For **flowering and fruit trees,** use Holly-tone or Plant-tone. In the following years, in late winter or early spring, apply fertilizer from the drip line (the outer ring of leaves on the tree) outward to a distance that equals the height of the tree, plus half again its height. The last application should be as growth slows toward the end of the growing season—in Zones 3 and 4, that's usually about August 15; in Zone 5, early September; in Zones 6 and 7, early September to early October. **The number of applications in between depends entirely on the type of fertilizer you are using.** (See Understanding Fertilizers in the Introduction to the book.)

Compost the leaves you rake up in the fall. The nutrients they contain should go to enriching your soil, not clogging a landfill! (See Composting, in the October pages of this chapter.)

## MULCHING AND WEEDING

A 3- to 4-inch-deep mulch spread around newly planted trees keeps weeds out and buffers trees from the weather. For the first two or three seasons, top the mulch off in spring after fertilizing, and once more before winter cold sets in. The last application helps maintain moisture in the ground, which retains its warmth for some time after the air turns freezing cold.

Start the mulch 3 inches from the trunk, and spread it to the outer edge of the tree's saucer. If you pile mulch right up against the trunk, that prevents it from drying out after rain and may harm the bark. Deep mulch right against the trunk also makes a cozy home for field mice or voles that may girdle the tree—eat through the outer layer of the trunk, which can kill a young tree. Keep the mulch free of weeds.

# Trees

If lawn grasses or ground covers move in around to the trunk, they will act as a living mulch, and you can stop mulching.

## WATERING

Newly planted and transplanted trees must have sustained moisture for the first couple of years. After planting and during spring, summer, and fall in weeks where there is no rain, pour two or three 5-gallon buckets of water around the roots. Or use a sprinkler to lay down 1½ inches of water slowly and gently. Set a one-pound coffee can or other container under the sprinkler or the hose, and record how long it took to put 1½ inches in the can—then you'll know.

In summer when the weather isn't supporting growth, young trees adapt by slowing down unless forced to grow by shallow watering and inappropriate fertilizing. In fall, even after cold sets in, roots continue to develop, so water often enough to prevent the soil from drying out even after it gets cold.

After the first year or two, most trees require watering only in times of severe drought.

## PRUNING DECIDUOUS TREES

You prune a tree to encourage its natural structure, to keep the center open, to get rid of suckers, and to remove damaged wood. Never remove more than 25 percent of a tree's growth at one time. "Dehorning," severe lopping off of branches, causes "water sprout" growth. Water sprouts shoot straight up at a 90-degree angle from the branch, and must be removed to maintain the tree's natural shape and keep the center airy and healthy.

**The best time to prune a shade tree is when it is dormant,** after the coldest part of the winter. If sap starts to flow, it will stop when the tree leafs out. Light pruning and thinning in summer will not promote unwanted growth in trees, and you can see what you're doing. However, heavy pruning and dehorning in summer can stimulate new unwelcome growth.

Prune a **spring-flowering tree** that blooms on last year's wood after the flowers fade. Prune a **summer-flowering tree** that blooms on current growth shortly before growth begins.

See March for more information on pruning deciduous trees and May for pruning evergreen trees.

## PESTS AND DISEASES

Choose trees that are disease-resistant, and be willing to accept a normal quota of insect damage. See Integrated Pest Management in the section in the Appendix on Pests, Diseases, and Controls for more information.

You can spray young and small trees, but if full-size trees have problems, we recommend you get professional help from a tree company or a full-service garden center or nursery.

# Trees

## Large Deciduous Trees

| Common Name (*Botanical Name*) | Hardiness Zones | Height (Feet) | Description |
|---|---|---|---|
| **American Beech** (*Fagus grandifolia*) | 3 to 8 | 50 to 70 | Pyramidal native with silver-gray bark and symmetrical branches reaching the ground. |
| **Birch** (*Betula* spp. and cvs.) | 2 to 7 | 30 to 40 | Fast-growing, slender trees known for beautiful bark. Choose a variety resistant to borer. |
| **European Hornbeam** (*Carpinus betulus*) | 4 to 7 | 30 to 40 | Excellent medium to small tree for urban areas. Papery fruit looks like small lanterns. |
| **Ginkgo** (*Ginkgo biloba*) | 4 to 9 | 30 to 50 | Interesting foliage turns golden in fall. Female bears smelly fruits. 'Autumn Gold' is one of the best cultivars and is male. |
| **Honeylocust** (*Gleditsia triacanthos* var. *inermis* 'Shade Master') | 3 to 7 | To 70 | Native, thornless, with fragrant yellow flowers in spring and then long seedpods; yellow in fall. Selected cultivar, rounded shape. |
| **Japanese Pagoda Tree, Chinese Scholar-tree** (*Sophora japonica* 'Regent') | 4 to 7 | 40 to 50 | Airy, exceptionally beautiful tree bearing showy panicles of creamy white, pea-like flowers, then drooping clusters of pale-green, winged pods. |
| **Linden, Littleleaf Linden** (*Tilia cordata*) | 3 to 8 | 40 and up | Native; fragrant, creamy, bee-attracting flowers in late June; yellow fall foliage. Nice shape. |
| **Maple, Swamp or Red Maple** (*Acer rubrum* cvs.) | 4 to 9 | 40 to 50 | Native; small with spectacular fall color. 'October Glory' has brilliant autumn foliage. |
| **Planetree** (*Platanus* x *acerifolia*) | 5 to 8 | 70 to 100 | Shade tree with colorful, peeling, patchy bark. Fuzzy winter seed capsules. |
| **Red Horse Chestnut** (*Aesculus x carnea* 'Briotii') | 4 to 7 | 45 to 60 | Beautiful, pyramidal; bears showy, upright panicles of 8- to 10-inch rosy flowers. |
| **Red Oak** (*Quercus rubra*) | 4 to 7 | 40 to 60 | Long-lived tree with rich, dark-red fall foliage. |
| **Sour Gum, Black Tupelo** (*Nyssa sylvatica*) | 4 to 9 | 30 to 50 | Pyramidal; fall foliage is a mix of fluorescent colors. Good near water. |

# Trees

## Large Deciduous Trees

| Common Name (*Botanical Name*) | Hardiness Zones | Height (Feet) | Description |
|---|---|---|---|
| **Sourwood** (*Oxydendrum arboreum*) | 5 to 9 | 25 to 30 | Native; white flowers in summer; deep red fall foliage. |
| **Sugar Maple** (*Acer saccharum* cvs.) | 3 to 8 | 50 to 70 | Native; big, slow-growing shade tree; rich red, orange, or yellow fall foliage; source of maple syrup. |
| **Tuliptree, Tulip Poplar** (*Liriodendron tulipifera*) | 4 to 9 | 70 to 90 | Native; big, stately; tulip-shaped flowers in May; yellow fall foliage. |
| **Weeping Willow** (*Salix alba* 'Tristis') | 5 to 9 | 50 to 70 | Weeping branches and golden catkins; the most graceful of all trees. |
| **Yellowwood** (*Cladrastris kentukea*) | 4 to 8 | 30 to 50 | Native; fragrant June flowers; yellow fall foliage blooms heavily every other year. Smooth gray bark. |
| **Zelkova, Japanese Zelkova** (*Zelkova serrata* cvs.) | 5 to 8 | 60 to 70 | Elm look-alike. 'Green Vase' and 'Village Green' are resistant to Dutch elm disease. |

## Small Deciduous Flowering Trees

| Common Name (*Botanical Name*) | Hardiness Zones | Height (Feet) | Bloom Time | Blooms On | Description |
|---|---|---|---|---|---|
| **Carolina Silverbell** (*Halesia tetraptera*) | 5 to 8 | 30 to 40 | Early spring | Old wood | Lovely understory tree with white flowers; 'Rosea' is a beautiful pink form. |
| **Eastern Redbud** (*Cercis canadensis* cvs.) | 4 to 9 | 20 to 30 | Early spring | Old wood | Dainty, little, covered with red-purple or magenta buds then rosy pink flowers. New foliage of 'Forest Pansy' is purple. *C. canadensis* 'Alba' is a lovely white. |
| **Florida Dogwood** (*Cornus florida* cvs.) | 5 to 8 | 30 to 40 | Early May | Old wood | Blooms of white or pink, then red berries in fall; reddish leaves. Chinese dogwood (*C. kousa*) blooms later and is more resistant to anthracnose. |

# Trees

## Small Deciduous Flowering Trees

| Common Name (*Botanical Name*) | Hardiness Zones | Height (Feet) | Bloom Time | Blooms On | Description |
|---|---|---|---|---|---|
| **Flowering Cherry Group** (*Prunus* spp. and cvs.) | 4 to 8 | 20 to 40 | Early spring | Old wood | Ornamental plum and cherry trees with pink or white blossoms; beautiful Sargent cherry is hardy. |
| **Flowering Crabapple** (*Malus* and cvs.) | 4 to 8 | 5 to 25 | Spring | Old wood | Wide range of sizes and forms. Red or yellow fruits follow the flowers. 'Sargentii', the dwarf Sargent crab, is scented and exceptionally beautiful. |
| **Flowering/Callery Pear** (*Pyrus calleryana* cvs.) | 4 to 8 | To 30 | Early spring | Old wood | Beautiful, pyramidal; bears clusters of small white blooms; in fall, glossy green leaves turn an attractive orange-wine red lasting into November. |
| **Franklin Tree** (*Franklinia alatamaha*) | 5 to 8 | 20 to 30 | Summer | New wood | Airy, spreading tree with fragrant 3-inch white flowers. Good fall color. |
| **Hawthorn** (*Crataegus viridis*) | 5 to 7 | 25 to 30 | April/ May | Old wood | White flowers and red fall foliage, good bark; orange-red fruits. 'Winter King' is exceptional. |
| **Japanese Snowbell** (*Styrax japonicus*) | 6 to 8 | 15 to 20 | Late spring | Old wood | Lovely, small; white or pink bell-shaped flowers along branch undersides. |
| **Japanese Stewartia** (*Stewartia pseudocamellia*) | 5 to 8 | 20 to 30 | Mid to late summer | New wood | Large shrub or small tree; creamy white flowers; handsome exfoliating bark; colorful fall foliage. |
| **Magnolia** (*Magnolia* spp. and cvs.) | 4 to 8 | 20 to 30 | Blooms same time as forsythia | Old wood | The star magnolia (*M. kobur* var. *stellata*) and Loebner magnolia (*M.* x *loebneri*) are the hardiest. |
| **Mimosa, Silk Tree** (*Albizia julibrissin*) | 6 to 9 | 20 to 35 | Mid-spring | Old wood | Drooping clusters of silky pink stamens perfume the air for weeks. 'E. H. Wilson' and 'Rosea' are hardier than the species. Spray for webworms. |
| **White Fringe Tree** (*Chionanthus virginicus*) | 3 to 9 | 15 to 25 | Late spring | Old wood | In bloom, is misted with fringe-like, lightly scented, greenish-white flowers. |
| **Witchhazel** (*Hamamelis* x *intermedia*) | 3 to 8 | 15 to 20 | Early spring | New wood | Picturesque; bears fragrant yellow or bronzy flowers; colorful fall foliage. |

# Trees

## Evergreen Trees

| Common Name (*Botanical Name*) | Hardiness Zones | Height (Feet) | Description |
|---|---|---|---|
| **American Arborvitae** (*Thuja occidentalis*) | 3 to 7 | 40 to 60 | Beautiful narrow conifer. Green or yellow-green foliage in flat sprays. |
| **Blue Atlas Cedar** (*Cedrus atlantica* var. *glauca*) | 6 to 9 | 40 to 50 | Large, beautiful, bluish needles; Cedar-of-Lebanon (*C. libani*) is hardier and dark green. |
| **Canadian or Eastern Hemlock** (*Tsuga canadensis*) | 3 to 7 | 40 to 70 | Beautiful pyramidal needled native; troubled by hemlock woolly adelgid. |
| **Colorado Blue Spruce** (*Picea pungens* var. *glauca*) | 2 to 8 | 30 to 50 | Aromatic, symmetrical, conical evergreen with soft blue-gray foliage. |
| **Eastern Redcedar** (*Juniperus virginiana*) | 2 to 9 | 40 to 50 | Available in pyramidal and columnar forms. Scalelike leaves. It is one of the hosts for the cedar-apple rust. Plant resistant crabapples and apples. |
| **Hinoki False Cypress** (*Chamaecyparis obtusa*) | 5 to 8 | 8 to 30 | Broadly pyramidal; scale-like, gnarled, twisted, rich green foliage. Tolerates salt spray. |
| **Holly, American Holly** (*Ilex opaca*) | 5 to 9 | 40 to 50 | Pyramidal; glossy, spiny leaves with single red or yellow berries in October. |
| **Japanese Black Pine** (*Pinus thunbergii*) | 5 to 10 | 25 to 35 | Traditional needled evergreen for the shore. Windswept look; tolerant of salt spray. May need spraying for pests and tip blight. |
| **Leyland Cypress** (x *Cupressocyparis leylandii*) | 5 to 10 | 60 to 70 | Fast-growing, graceful, columnar; flat, scale-like, bluish-green leaves and red-brown bark. Tolerates salt spray. |
| **Norway Spruce** (*Picea abies*) | 2 to 7 | 40 to 100 | Fast-growing, pyramidal; often sold as a living Christmas tree. |
| **Pine, Eastern White Pine** (*Pinus strobus*) | 3 to 7 | 50 to 80 | Native; beautiful, graceful, aromatic; can be sheared. |
| **White Fir** (*Abies concolor*) | 3 to 8 | 30 to 50 | Pyramidal; often used as a live Christmas tree. |

# JANUARY
## Trees

 PLANNING

**January winds bring a big sky and the possibility of a new vision for your landscape.** So take your mail-order catalogs to a window overlooking the garden, pull up a comfortable chair, and consider what adding or subtracting a tree or two can do for the scenery.

**Think of your view as a painting.** If your plantings are imbalanced—too much in one spot, too little elsewhere—trees may solve the problem. Balanced plantings impart a sense of security and well-being. Flowering trees paired on either side of a driveway are perfectly balanced and well-suited to a formal dwelling. But you can create a balanced design that is not formal in style by using different trees to create a similar silhouette. For example, one side of the yard could have an **incense cedar,** whose silhouette is pyramidal and narrow, and a wide-spreading **swamp maple,** fronted by shrubs; then balance this on the other side by matching shrubs fronting a clump of **paper birches** and a **Serbian spruce,** which is also narrow and pyramidal but has cascading branches.

 PLANTING

A live **Christmas tree** (see December) can begin to deteriorate after ten days indoors in a heated house. As soon as possible move the tree outdoors. If you have not prepared a planting hole (see Soil Preparation and Improvement in the Introduction to the book), place the tree in a sheltered spot, and cover it with 14 to 18 inches of leaves kept in place by evergreen boughs. As soon as you can, dig a hole, plant the tree, and then mulch the area (see Planting in the introduction to this chapter).

Repotting large **indoor trees** is difficult and necessary only every three or four years. Other years, in late winter as new growth appears, remove the top 2 inches of soil, and replace it with 2 or 3 inches of compost or fertile potting soil.

 CARE

**Established trees.** Use a broom to brush off accumulations of snow and ice on the lower branches of the evergreens.

**New trees.** Renew the anti-desiccant spray—a coating that keeps leaves from losing moisture—on evergreen trees, especially broadleaf evergreens in exposed positions. Check and adjust the burlap protecting trees.

 PRUNING

**Outdoors.** Prune away winter and snow damage any time before growth begins. Cut down old and injured trees. Cut the wood of deciduous trees into logs the size of your fireplace, and stack them to dry. Evergreen wood is soft and bad for your chimney, so compost it or chip it and use it to top paths.

**Indoors.** Remove dead flowers from **flowering maple** and **hibiscus,** as well as yellowing leaves and twigs crowding the crowns of indoors trees such as **ficus.** Thin out some of the tiny lemons developing on a **'Meyer Improved' lemon tree.**

 WATERING

If you have planted a live **Christmas tree,** make sure the ground around it stays moist.

**Indoors.** Maintain the soil moisture of the indoor trees, for example, **citrus, ficus, tropical hibiscus, flowering maples, palms.** Mist and air the room daily or often.

*Prune away winter and snow damage any time before growth begins. Cut down old and injured trees.*

## Did You Know?

### The Basics of Pruning Cuts

When you remove a large limb, follow the three-cut pruning method to avoid stripping bark from the trunk:

*1* About a foot out from the trunk, cut from the bottom of the branch upward about a third of the way through the limb.

*2* A couple of inches out, or beyond the first cut, cut from the top of the branch down. The branch will break away cleanly.

*3* Find the collar or ring at the base of the limb where it springs from the trunk. Taking care not to damage the ring, remove the stub. From the collar an attractive, healthy covering for the wounded area can develop.

Limb Removal

Current wisdom says "no" to painting or tarring these cuts. However, André Viette prefers to paint with orange shellac large wounds caused by removing big branches; the alcohol in the shellac disinfects, and the cuts are sealed.

## FERTILIZING

When you see new growth in indoor trees, begin adding a half-strength dose of fertilizer at every second watering.

## PESTS

Deer go for the tips of reachable branches of **apple trees, arborvitae, cedars, yews,** and other evergreens. Spraying may deter deer, but wrapping trees with burlap or chicken wire is a surer safeguard. Deer also nibble bark; check and adjust the wraps on newly planted trees.

Apply dormant horticultural oils to dormant trees before growth begins to smother insects that have wintered over, such as scale and tent caterpillar egg cases.

## PLANNING

The best time for pruning trees is as winter comes to an end. So, on days when the sun is warm enough to linger outdoors, spend some time studying your trees and making a plan for pruning those that need it.

Place catalog orders for new trees this month.

## PLANTING

Bare-root trees can be planted about a month before the last freeze; mail-order suppliers ship them dormant at your planting time. Your zone determines planting time.

**This is how to plant a bare-root tree:**

*1* Soak the roots as instructed by the supplier, or for six to twelve hours in room temperature water.

*2* Dig a planting hole three times as wide and twice as deep as the roots; keep in mind that the crown of the tree (where trunk meets roots) must end up about an inch above ground level.

*3* Loosen the sides of the hole, and blend the soil from the hole with the organic amendments described in Soil Preparation and Improvement in the Introduction to the book.

*4* Half-fill the bottom of the hole with improved soil, and tamp it down **very firmly** to make a solid base. In the center of the hole build a firm cone. Gently untangle the roots of the tree, and arrange them over and around the cone so the crown of the tree is about 1 inch above the level of the surrounding earth. Make sure the trunk stands perfectly straight before you start to fill the hole.

*5* Half-fill the hole with improved soil, and tamp it down. Make sure the trunk is still perfectly straight. Fill the hole with improved soil, and tamp it down firmly. Shape the soil around the crown into a wide saucer.

*6* Slowly pour on 10 to 15 gallons of water.

*7* Mulch newly planted trees 3 inches deep from 3 inches out from the trunk to the edge of the saucer.

## CARE

**Established trees.** Remove snow weighing down evergreen limbs and prune back damaged and dead branches.

Remember what is done in February in Zone 7 is done in March in Zone 5 and 6.

**Newly planted trees.** Check the stakes and ties. If the ties are damaging the bark, loosen them. If the tree is growing straight and true, you can remove the stakes after the first or second year.

Check whether cycles of thawing and freezing have heaved roots; press heaved roots back into place and replenish the mulch to insulate the soil.

## PRUNING

Keep an eye on flowering trees as the weather warms. The swelling of leaf buds tells you pruning time is coming up. Damaged branches of spring-flowering trees should be pruned first, before growth begins, and well before they bloom. Then prune summer-flowering trees, which will be slower to bud.

In woodlands and groves, clear out underbrush, saplings, and weed trees crowding desirable trees. You can use a string trimmer to level small growth. Use bypass pruning shears—powerful shears with a scissor-like action—to take down saplings. Then remove diseased and dead trees and trees crowding others. Prune out big branches that could fall on driveways and paths in a storm. Remove from deciduous trees any limbs spoiling the symmetry of the structure.

*Check whether cycles of thawing and freezing have heaved roots; press heaved roots back into place and replenish the mulch to insulate the soil.*

Remove dead and damaged limbs from mature deciduous trees, as well as all that cross others or crowd the center of the tree. If the soil beneath appears compacted, loosen it with a hoe—take care not to damage roots near the surface. Then fertilize and water generously.

**Root pruning deciduous and evergreen trees** to check growth and prompt flowering can be undertaken now before growth begins. Use a spade to sever the roots in a circle around the trunk. Go out to where the roots are about the size of your little finger. If your spade encounters roots you need a saw to cut, you are too close; if the roots are web-fine, you are too far out. Water well, and fertilize after root pruning.

 WATERING

**Outdoors.** Check the soil under **broadleaf evergreen** trees; the foliage continues to lose water through transpiration during the winter, and if snow or rain has been scarce, the soil under the tree may need watering.

If you have planted a live **Christmas tree,** maintain the soil moisture.

**Indoors.** Water trees growing indoors, **citrus, ficus, tropical hibiscus, palms.** Mist and air them daily or often.

 FERTILIZING

Add a half-strength dose to the water for trees growing indoors every second time you water.

**Newly planted trees** can benefit from fertilization the first two or three years. Before you fertilize, test the soil pH, and adjust it if needed. When the buds begin to break, scratch in an application of Holly-tone for acid-loving trees and Plant-tone for the others.

**Established trees** in lawns, shrub, and flower borders should be okay with the fertilizer applied to the surrounding lawn and beds.

 PESTS

Voles can damage young tree roots. Bait the main runway with a rodenticide.

To keep rabbits, woodchucks, and other rodents away from new trees, try chemical repellents and fungicide formulations such as Thiram (Arasan) and hot pepper wax.

Deer are hungry. Spray evergreen foliage that is munching-height with deer repellents. Check and adjust burlap covers and chicken wire cages.

Before the buds open on trees suspected of insect infestation, spray them with horticultural oil. The oil smothers insects and their eggs.

# MARCH
## Trees

 PLANNING

**Firm up plans for improving your yard this year.** Consider planting a tree in your yard or a street tree to enhance your neighborhood. If you want to plant a street tree, get municipal permission and their recommendations for trees that tolerate urban conditions. If they say it's up to you, choose trees that won't grow up to block the view—the columnar **flowering pear 'Capital'** is a safe choice.

 PLANTING

You can plant dormant trees when the earth loses its winter wet. Here's how to prepare a tree for planting.

**Container-grown tree.** If the rootball doesn't come out of the container easily, tip the container on its side and roll it around a bit, then try. If the plant is too large for that, slit the sides of the container, and peel the pieces away. If roots wrap the rootball, make four shallow vertical cuts in the sides of the rootball, and slice off the bottom 2 inches.

**B&B tree.** Handle with care! Avoid disturbing the burlap, twine, or wire basket as you put the rootball into the planting hole. Once it is in the hole, cut the twine around the trunk, and cut off or push the ends of the burlap into the hole. If the cover is plastic, cut away as much as possible, and poke holes in what remains.

**Bare-root tree.** Leave the tree in its packaging in a cool dark place until you are ready to plant. Soak the roots in room temperature water as directed by the planting instructions, or for six to twelve hours before planting.

 CARE

Clean up under fruit trees to help prevent diseases.

When winter storms are over, remove trunk covers from protected trees. If a tree that was staked is growing straight and not being heaved, remove the stakes.

**Trees growing in containers.** Before the seasonal growth begins, top-dress the soil. Remove the top 2 inches of soil, and replace it with soil enriched with Holly-tone or Plant-tone.

 PRUNING

**Outdoors.** Before the buds break, prune newly-planted trees lightly the first few years to control the development of the scaffold (the limb structure). Remove branches heading into the center of the tree or crossing others, water sprout growth, and suckers.

Prune **summer-flowering trees before growth begins** this month or in early April. Harvest branches from flowering trees that can be forced into bloom indoors, **flowering cherry trees, crabapples,** and **dogwoods,** for example. (See Flowering Branches Can Be Forced into Bloom in the February pages of Chapter 8, Shrubs ). Prune spring-flowering trees after the blooms fade.

Never take away more than 20 to 25 percent of a tree's growth; this is "dehorning," and it causes "water sprout" growth. The ends of hemlock branches can be lightly pruned throughout the growing season. **Yews** and **junipers** may be pruned at any time during the growth cycle.

**Indoors.** Continue to deadhead and groom trees growing indoors.

 WATERING

**Outdoors.** Maintain soil moisture around a live Christmas tree. Water weekly unless you have a good soaking rain.

Ditto for hardy trees growing outdoors in containers.

**Indoors.** Maintain the soil moisture of the trees growing indoors, **citrus, ficus, tropical hibiscus, palms;** mist the trees, and air the room often.

# FERTILIZING

**Indoors.** Add fertilizer at a half-strength dose to the water every second time you water. Mist often with water at room temperature.

**Outdoors.** If, in its third or fourth season or later, a tree isn't growing well, fertilize.

Stunted growth and leaves that are uncharacteristically red or dark green may signal a shortage of phosphate, and applying a fertilizer with a higher ratio of phosphate should improve matters. Weak stems and a susceptibility to disease might be caused by a shortage of potash; fertilizer with a higher ratio of phosphate and potash would help.

# PESTS

If you see vole activity, bait the main runway with a rodenticide.

If you didn't spray trees susceptible to infestation with a dormant horticultural oil last month, do it now. These botanical oils sprayed on the egg and immature stages of insects smother them.

## Did You Know?

### When and How to Prune Deciduous Trees

New trees may need some shaping, and they will shape up best if you follow the supplier's instructions for pruning after planting and for pruning the next two or three years.

- **Winter damage.** Prune any time.

- **Damaged branches.** Prune them before the leaves fall—they're easier to spot.

- **Flowering trees that bloom on new wood.** Prune in late winter or early spring before growth begins.

- **Flowering trees that bloom on old wood.** Prune immediately after they bloom to avoid cutting off branches where buds are being initiated for the following season.

- **To control height.** Prune after the season's new growth has fully developed.

- **To slow or dwarf growth.** Prune in summer when the plant has stopped growing.

- **Trees that need regular shaping.** Prune while the tree is still dormant, just after the coldest part of the season.

Don't get carried away, but don't be timid. Focus on supporting the tree's natural outline, its growth "habit." Never prune away more than 20 percent at one time.

If you spot the webs of tent caterpillars, in the cool of the evening scoop the tents out with a stick and destroy them. The other way is to spray with a biological control such as *Bacillus thuringiensis (Bt)*. Other controls are Sevin or malathion insecticide, Pyrethrin, or rotenone.

To keep deer away from evergreens and newly planted trees, spray with a repellent they haven't smelled recently. Circle with chicken wire any small trees whose bark the deer are damaging; for larger trees, use unobtrusive bird netting.

PLANNING

**Need more colorful trees?** Check out the yellow and yellow-green evergreens. **Cripp's golden Hinoki cypress** (*Chamaecyperis obtusa* 'Crippsii') is moderate-growing, and the new foliage is rich golden yellow. Some of the new **Japanese maple** cultivars are breathtaking when the sun shines through the leaves. Enter the names of trees that catch your fancy in your garden log, and plan to buy them at a local nursery late in the season when you can see the summer color and maybe buy at a bargain price.

 PLANTING

Spring, right now, is an excellent time to plant trees that bloom in summer and early fall and trees difficult to transplant, like **Florida dogwoods** and **magnolias.**

You can transplant newly-planted container-grown trees the first two years without trauma.

You can move small well-established trees successfully if you root prune first. Here's how:

**Year One.** Now, before growth begins, sever the roots in a circle all around the trunk to stimulate root growth within the circle.

**Year Two.** Next year, about this same time, tie the branches together at the top. Dig a trench outside the root-pruned circle, lift the rootball onto a big piece of burlap, and tie the burlap around the rootball. Drag the plant to its new location. Prepare the soil, and plant the tree as described in the introduction to this chapter. Free the branches, and prune out damaged twigs.

 CARE

**Established and new trees.** Mow with care around the trunks of trees young or old. If the mower consistently gets too close, keep it away by surrounding the trunk with a ring of mulch 3 inches deep.

**Container tree.** Root pruning every two or three years keeps a tree growing well, and dwarfs it without impairing its form. **Do it now, before growth begins.**

If the **tub is small,** tip it onto its side, and slip the rootball out. Disentangle roots binding the bottom of the rootball, and cut away roots growing straight down the outside of the rootball. Remove the bottom 1 to 2 inches of roots. Next, add a layer of fertile soil mix to the bottom of the tub and replant.

If the **tub is too big** for this operation, slide a hand-pruning saw inside the container, and sever an inch of the roots growing around the outside of the rootball. Remove the top inch or two of the soil covering the rootball. Add 2 or 3 inches of soil to the top of the rootball, and then renew the mulch 3 inches deep.

Water the container thoroughly.

Turn your compost pile often.

 PRUNING

Before the trees leaf out, remove "water sprout" growth from tree limbs, and suckers from around the base of the tree and on tree trunks and branches.

The ends of **hemlock** branches can be lightly pruned throughout the growing season. Prune **yews** and **junipers** lightly any time during their growth season.

 WATERING

Maintain the soil moisture in all your container trees.

*Mow with care around the trunks of trees young or old. If the mower consistently gets too close, keep it away by surrounding the trunk with a ring of mulch 3 inches deep.*

For new and transplanted in-ground trees, including a **Christmas tree,** pour two or three 5-gallon buckets of water around the roots once a week throughout spring unless there's a good rain.

# FERTILIZING

**Indoors.** At every second watering, add a half-strength dose of fertilizer to trees growing indoors—**citrus, ficus, palms,** and others.

**Outdoors.** Frequent watering leaches nutrients from the soil in containers, so start monthly applications of a water-soluble organic fertilizer—seaweed or manure tea, for example.

In-ground trees growing in lawns and flower and shrub borders will get all the fertilizer they need when you fertilize the surrounding lawns, borders, and ground covers.

## Did You Know?

### About Growing Trees in Containers

Small hardy trees succeed in containers big enough to allow for growth and insulation. For insulation, wrap the interior with a double row of large bubble wrap or styrofoam before you add soil. Bags of dry leaves placed around the containers for winter add extra protection.

**Soil.** The ideal container soil is a fertile semi-soil-less mix. Mix one part good topsoil, 1 part horticultural perlite (or $1/2$ perlite and $1/2$ PermaTill), and 2 parts coarse peat moss. For every 7 inches of planter height, add $1/3$ cup slow-release fertilizer, and 1 cup dehydrated cow manure. Adding a soil polymer, such as Soil Moist, can reduce watering by as much as 50 percent.

**Containers.** A young tree can withstand most winters if grown in a container 14 to 16 inches in height and circumference. A larger tree would need a 14- or a 16-inch tub and eventually one 30 inches high and 24 inches in circumference. Line the bottom of these large containers with 4 to 5 inches of PermaTill for drainage. It's lighter than gravel.

**Water and mulch.** Before planting, soak the tub until water runs out of the bottom. After planting, top-dress the soil with 2 or 3 inches of mulch.

# PESTS

Continue protecting your trees from the deer.

Scale may turn up on your **hollies.** Spray with summer-weight horticultural oils or Neem.

Rake up weeds.

Late this month, tent caterpillars emerge. Spray trees with signs of infestations with a biological control such as *Bacillus thuringiensis*. Other controls are Sevin or malathion insecticide, Pyrethrin, or rotenone.

Pick off the cone shaped nests of bagworms and destroy them.

# MAY
## Trees

 **PLANNING**

To furnish your yard with song—and to keep insects down—look for places to plant a few trees that meet the needs of birds. They nest in the branches of evergreens like **Canadian hemlock** (*Tsuga canadensis*) and **white pine** (*Pinus strobus*). They eat the fruit of **American holly** (*Ilex opaca*) and **red cedar** (*Juniperus virginiana*). The tiny fruits of the flowering or ornamental fruit trees are staples for birds—beautiful cultivars like the **crabapple** *Malus* 'Narragansett', the **Florida** and **Cornus kousa dogwoods,** and **ornamental** (and real) **cherries.** Many native trees bear fruits birds love—**bird cherry** *Prunus pennsylvanica* cultivars and **American hornbeam** (*Carpinus caroliniana*), a lovely shade tree.

 **PLANTING**

This is a fine month to plant new trees.

**When is a tree a tree?** The forester's definition of a tree is a woody plant having a single main trunk and reaching not less than 10 to 20 feet at maturity. Many tall shrubs can be trained to a tree-like single trunk—examples are the **common lilac** and **shrub althea** (**rose-of-sharon**).

 **CARE**

**Indoors.** When nighttime temperatures stay steady at 60 degrees Fahrenheit and above, start moving your indoor trees—**citrus, ficus, tropical hibiscus, flowering maple, palms**—outdoors for a summer vacation. Summered out in the bright light on a porch or under a tall tree, they'll survive winters indoors under less favorable conditions. Place them in indirect light in a sheltered spot for the first week. Like you, houseplants sunburn when exposed too long too early to direct sun. Don't be alarmed if some drop leaves their first week or two outdoors. The change of light has that effect on some, notably **ficus.**

**Outdoors.** Renew the mulch under newly-planted trees.

Turn your compost pile often.

 **PRUNING**

Prune to encourage dense branching to the ground in **pines, firs, spruces,** and other evergreens whose growth is initiated by candles (new candle-like growths at the ends of branches); cut the candles back by half when they appear at the branch tips. This may be May in Zone 7 but could be June in colder zones. The ends of **hemlock** branches can be lightly pruned throughout the growing season. Prune **yews** and **junipers** any time during their growth season.

When fruits begin to form on **apples, pears,** and **peaches,** thin the tiny fruits so they are no closer than 4 to 6 inches.

 **WATERING**

Keep track of how often the soil in containers of the indoor trees moved outdoors needs watering, and plan a regular watering schedule. Mulching them will help.

Water the outdoor container trees every two weeks, or when the soil seems dry unless they are placed where they get wet when it rains. Mulch the containers.

For newly-planted and transplanted in-ground trees, pour two or three 5-gallon buckets of water around the roots once a week throughout spring unless you have rain.

*For newly-planted and transplanted in-ground trees, pour two or three 5-gallon buckets of water around the roots once a week throughout spring unless you have rain.*

 FERTILIZING

Since frequent watering leaches nutrients from the soil, once a month give all the trees growing in containers a light application of a water-soluble organic fertilizer—seaweed or manure tea, for example.

 PESTS

Get rid of weeds sprouting in the mulch around trees.

Deer sightings may subside now that the woods are full of browsing material. Even so, continue to discourage them from visits to your yard looking for treats.

Woolly adelgid attack **Canadian hemlock** and can do severe damage. Spraying twice a year with horticultural oil is the preferred control. These lightweight botanical oils also control aphids, cankerworms, leafhoppers, leaf rollers, mealybugs, mites, psyllids, scale, tent caterpillars, and webworms.

## Did You Know?

### How to Prune Evergreen Trees

Pruning woody plants stimulates growth, so avoid heavy pruning in summer when the plant is preparing to go dormant.

**Dead or damaged wood** on evergreen conifers can be removed at any time.

**Winter and snow damage** is best pruned before active growth.

To **encourage dense branching** in evergreens with candle-like new growth, cut the candles back by half. Prune the tips of **hemlock** branches lightly any time during the growing season. Prune **yews** and **junipers** lightly or heavily any time during growth.

To **establish a shape,** prune evergreens (sparingly) when they are three to five years old.

To **slow or dwarf a broadleaf evergreen tree—hollies** for example,—when growth ends, cut back no more than 20 percent of the new growth. You can reduce the main stem back to the first side shoots, but don't remove more than has grown the last year or two.

When you are pruning evergreens, remember to save some new growth on **hemlocks, hollies, spruce, pines,** and **cedars** to prune in December for holiday trimmings.

**Caution: Spraying with horticultural oils can temporarily remove the blue in blue hostas and Colorado blue spruce.** Never spray during droughts, and always water the soil deeply before applying.

Rake up weeds.

When you see the first signs of gypsy moths, spray trees showing signs of infestations with a biological control such as *Bacillus thuringiensis (Bt)*. Other controls are Sevin or malathion insecticide, Pyrethrin, or rotenone.

Continue to look for and destroy the nests of bagworms.

# PLANNING

You can grow small ornamental trees in the limited space afforded by a rooftop, a balcony, or a deck by planting them in containers. The best subjects are small flowering trees, and dwarf, semi-dwarf, small, columnar, weeping, and slow-growing forms.

Choose trees well within your cold hardiness range; the soil is more susceptible to freezing in tubs than in the ground. Be aware that containers on rooftops are generally receiving more wind and heat than those on wooden decks or patios and may need watering more often.

Containers on rooftops must be raised three inches from the roofing material. Resting directly on the rooftop, a heavy container full of damp soil can create considerable damage to the ceiling below.

Use lightweight soil mixes to keep down the weight of pots that will require seasonal moving. Use a product such as PermaTill, an aggregate lighter than gravel, to line very large containers. When you have to move a container, do it before watering.

Redwood tubs are good for several years. Plastics hold moisture longer and are okay if they have drainage holes. Glazed clay containers are the most beautiful, but costly, and our winters are hard on them.

# PLANTING

Container-grown and balled-and-burlapped trees transplant well even after they have leafed out.

Many species of trees can be propagated from cuttings taken at certain times of the year. Softwood (new wood, the new green branch tips whose bark has not yet begun to harden) cuttings of some **hollies** and **red maples** taken in June and early July root fairly easily. **Witchhazels** root from softwood cuttings taken from trees three to five years old. **Juniper** cuttings taken during the winter will root.

If you are interested in trying, turn to the section on You Can Multiply Your Shrubs by Root Cuttings in the June pages of Chapter 8, Shrubs.

# CARE

**New trees.** Make sure the mulch around new trees is a full 3 inches deep to avoid weeding.

Turn your compost pile often.

# PRUNING

**Pollarding and pleaching.** Europe's pollarded trees and pleached allées are the result of severe pruning. The process is lengthy, labor intensive, and interesting. The results are elegant and fun to try.

**Pollarding is a form of pruning** where the branches of a tree are cut back every year or so almost to the main trunk. The result is that you get branches that are long, thin, and flexible, and a tree whose crown is ball-shaped. In Europe, **willows** were commonly pollarded to produce whips used in basket-making.

**Pleaching is a system of shearing trees** (or tall shrubs) that are closely planted alongside a broad garden path or walk—**lindens, maples, sycamores** are often used. The trees are closely spaced, and the branches are encouraged to grow together overhead. Shearing trains the top growth into a thin hedge overhead. Because a pleached allée takes forever to achieve and is time-consuming to maintain, you're likely to see this only in public gardens and arboreta. There's a pleached allée in one of the lower garden rooms at Dumbarton Oaks in Washington, D.C.

As the spring burst of growth ends, prune trees you want to keep small or to dwarf.

Reducing the leaf surface reduces the sugar synthesized and translocated to the roots, and that limits next year's growth in the tree.

Remove yellowing leaves and twigs beginning to crowd the crown of indoor

*As the spring burst of growth ends, prune trees you want to keep small or to dwarf.*

## Did You Know?

### These Small Trees Thrive in Containers

- **American Hornbeam** (*Carpinus caroliniana* syn. *americana* 'Fastigiata')
- **American Smoke Tree, Chittamwood** (*Cotinus obovatus*)
- **Amur Maple** (*Acer ginnala* 'Flame')
- **Flowering Autumn Cherry** (*Prunus subhirtella* 'Autumnalis Rosea')
- **Flowering Weeping Cherry** (*P. s.* 'Pendula')
- **Carolina Silverbell Wild Olive** (*Halesia caroliniana*)
- **Chinese Dogwood** (*Cornus kousa* var. *chinensis*)
- **Hawthorn** (*Crataegns viridis* 'Winter King')
- **Foster Hybrid Holly** (*Ilex attenuata* 'Fosteri #2' and others)
- **Flowering Cherry** (*Prunus serrulata* 'Kwanzan', 'Shirotae')
- **Flowering Cherry** (*Prunus yedoensis* 'Akebono')
- **Flowering Weeping Cherry** (*Prunus subhirtella* var. *pendula*)
- **Fragrant Snowbell** (*Styrax obassia*)
- **Japanese Flowering Crabapple** (*Malus floribunda*)
- **Japanese Maple** (*Acer palmatum* cvs.)
- **Japanese Snowbell** (*Styrax japonicus*)
- **Japanese Tree Lilac** (*Syringa reticulata* syn. *amurensis* var. *japonica*)
- **Pink Princess Crabapple** (*Malus* 'Parrsi')
- **Redbud Eastern Redbud** (*Cercis canadensis*)
- **Sargent Cherry** (*Prunus sargentii*)
- **Sourwood Sorrel Tree** (*Oxydendrum arboreum*)
- **Southern Black Haw** (*Viburnum rufidulum*)
- **Trident Maple** (*Acer buergeranum*)
- **Washington Hawthorn** (*Crataegus phaenopyrum*)
- **Varnish Tree, Golden-rain Tree** (*Koelreuteria paniculata*)

trees—**ficus,** for example. Thin out the tiny lemons developing on a **'Meyer Improved' lemon tree** and continue to reduce the amount of fruit on fruit trees.

## WATERING

Maintain the soil moisture of the indoor trees moved outdoors for the season—**citrus, ficus, palms.**

Water trees growing in containers once or twice every week or so, or when the soil seems dry. Since frequent watering leaches nutrients from the soil, once a month during the growing season give the plants a light application of a water-soluble organic fertilizer—seaweed or manure tea, for example.

Pour two or three 5-gallon buckets of water around new trees every week or ten days, unless you have a soaking rain.

## FERTILIZING

Add a half-strength dose to the water for container trees and indoor trees growing outdoors at every second watering.

## PESTS

Get rid of weeds sprouting in the mulch around trees.

June is spray time for bagworms. Use *Bacillus thuringiensis* (*Bt*), Sevin, Neem, or Permethrin, which is also effective against whitefly. If you spot bagworm tents, remove and destroy them now.

Apply fungicidal formulations of copper to control powdery mildew, rusts, and bacterial diseases such as fire blight, bacterial leaf spots, and wilt.

## PLANNING

In seashore gardens so close to the water they are within reach of salt spray, high tides, and brine-laden wind, plant only trees that tolerate salt. In coastal gardens that are out of the reach of salt water or salt spray, you can plant trees that do well in light, sandy soil.

At the shore, evergreens are the best plants for windbreaks. Your choices are varied—broadleaved evergreens such as **American holly** and **privet,** needled evergreens such as **Japanese black pine, hemlock,** and the **junipers.**

## PLANTING

**You can plant container-grown trees even now.** Balled-and-burlapped trees, too, but don't buy them if they've been sitting unmulched and baking at a garden center since they were dug in early spring.

Use commercial potting soil for containers for seashore gardens rather than the sandy soil of the area. The humidity in the air reduces the need to water, but check the soil moisture often anyway.

To prevent plant damage from coastal storms, spray the upper and lower sides of the leaves with anti-desiccant to coat them with a barrier against salt and wind.

## CARE

When a dangerously high tide is expected at a shore property, saturate the soil around trees and shrubs to minimize the amount of seawater it will accept.

To help trees at the seashore recover from exposure to heavy spray and high winds after a storm, spray the foliage thoroughly with a hose to wash off as much salt as possible.

Turn your compost pile often.

## PRUNING

Prune dead wood on evergreen conifers at any time.

Remove water sprouts and suckers from around the base, the trunks, and the branches of flowering fruit trees. The **flowering cherries** usually need repeated attention.

Study the shade enveloping your gardens. Where you are losing too much light to tree branches, mark upper limbs that can be removed to thin the canopy so more light comes through. Consider whether removing a few lower branches will help; late winter is a good time to remove them.

Use a string trimmer to keep down undergrowth in woodlands and groves. Leave the debris in place, and it will decompose and nourish the trees growing there.

## WATERING

Maintain the soil moisture of the indoor trees moved outdoors for the season— **citrus, ficus, palms.**

Water outdoor trees growing in containers when the soil seems dry. Since frequent watering leaches nutrients from the soil, once a month give the plants a light application of a water-soluble organic fertilizer—seaweed or manure tea, for example.

**Established trees.** They need watering in times of severe drought—which is more than two weeks without rain.

**New trees.** Water every week or ten days, unless you have a soaking rain. Slowly and gently lay down $1\frac{1}{2}$ inches of water.

## FERTILIZING

At every second watering, add a half-strength dose of fertilizer to the water for indoor trees growing outdoors for the summer.

*Study the shade enveloping your gardens. Where you are losing too much light to tree branches, mark upper limbs that can be removed to thin the canopy so more light comes through.*

In-ground trees get all the fertilizer they need when you fertilize the surrounding lawns and beds.

#  PESTS

Get rid of weeds sprouting in the mulch around trees.

Troops of Japanese beetles are at full strength right now. The creature is a beautiful metallic green and coppery maroon, and it chews the leaves and stems of many ornamentals. The grub stage is devastating to lawns and gardens, and while grub-proofing reduces the populations in your yard, it does not control the beetles that fly in.

Japanese beetle traps are effective, provided they are placed far away from the plantings you are trying to protect, not among them. If the infestation is minor, beetles can be picked off by hand. Insecticides containing Neem, rotenone, or Sevin insecticide help control this and other bad guy beetles.

## Did You Know?

### How to Handle Surface Roots

When big shade trees mature, roots may surface around the base of the trunk. They're hard on the string trimmer and the mower when you move in close to trim grass and weeds back.

**These roots are important to the trees** so you have to find ways to solve the problem without chopping them off. Here are some don'ts and do's:

**Don't:**

• Don't rototill soil as it will damage roots. If you add a well-prepared and well-drained soil over the roots, you can plant flowers and ground covers. Six inches of soil won't hurt or smother roots.

**Do:**

• Add and maintain a mulch 3 inches deep starting 3 inches from the trunk at least half-way to the drip line.

• Dig planting holes between the roots, amend the soil there with compost or potting soil, and plant ground covers. If there's little room to dig, plant pachysandra; if there's lots of room, plant hostas. Control the weeds that develop for as long as it takes the ground cover to fill in and shade them out.

Neem is an effective control for whitefly, mites, and bagworms. If you spot bagworm tents, remove and destroy them now. Apply fungicidal formulations of copper to control powdery mildew, rusts, and bacterial diseases such as fire blight, bacterial leaf spot, and wilt.

# AUGUST
## Trees

## PLANNING

**For trees, from late this month until December is the best planting season.** So use lazy summer days to consider where you would like to see a tree or trees that are winter assets. In winter, a tree's major assets are its silhouette against the sky and its bark. The symmetrical winter silhouettes of the **incense cedar,** the **white oak,** and the stylish **Serbian spruce** are arresting. The **spruces** are especially beautiful outlined by snow.

The bark of most trees becomes more rugged and interesting with the years, and some species shed their bark in beautiful patterns. The peeling bark of **paperbark maple** (*Acer griseum*) reveals variations on its rich cinnamon color.

Even in a small garden you can find space for at least one deciduous specimen that has beautiful bark—the **river birch 'Heritage',** for example. Planted where it will shelter a big rock, a stand of grass that turns gold in fall, **ferns,** or a few brilliant early **tulips** and **narcissus**, it will be a year-round destination. The chalky white bark of the **lacebark pine** rivals the beauty of the **paper birch,** and it is a smaller tree.

Some other smaller trees with exceptional bark are these:

- **American Sweet Gum** (*Liquidambar styraciflua*)
- **American Yellowwood** (*Cladrastis lutea*)
- **Amur Cherry** (*Prunus maackii*)
- **Japanese White Birch** (*Betula platyphylla* var. *japonica* 'Whitespire')

- **Franklin Tree** (*Franklinia alatamaha*)
- **Hawthorn** (*Crataegus viridis* 'Winter King')
- **Korean Stewartia** (*Stewartia koreana*)
- **Paperbark Cherry** (*Prunus serrula*)
- **Sargent Cherry** (*Prunus sargentii*)
- **Stewartia** (*Stewartia* cvs.)
- **Whitebarked Himalayan Birch** (*Betula utilis jacquemontii*)

## PLANTING

**The best time to plant trees that bloom in spring is in the fall.**

You can still plant container-grown trees this month. B&B trees, too, but don't buy them if they have been sitting unmulched and baking at a garden center since they were dug in early spring.

Evergreen trees do well moved August through October.

Small trees can be transplanted as soon as their leaves color up and fall.

## CARE

**Don't leave orchard fruit lying on the ground.** It attracts raccoons, skunks, possums, and yellow jackets. Not to mention deer.

Turn your compost pile often.

Tree Staking and Guying

*Use lazy summer days to consider where you would like to see a tree or trees that are winter assets. In winter, a tree's major assets are its silhouette against the sky and its bark.*

 PRUNING

Begin to prepare indoor trees summering outdoors for their return to winter quarters—**citrus, tropical hibiscus, flowering maples,** and the others. Deadhead, clear away yellowing foliage, and prune out branches that are crossing or crowding the crown.

 WATERING

Maintain the soil moisture of the indoor trees moved outdoors for the season—**citrus, ficus, palms.**

**New trees.** Continue to water every week or ten days, unless you have a soaking rain.

**Established trees.** They need watering in times of severe drought—more than two weeks without rain. Woodland trees will likely make it through any drought typical of New York.

 FERTILIZING

Mid-month, stop fertilizing established outdoor trees growing in containers. Do continue to fertilize indoor trees summering outdoors at every second watering.

In Zones 3 and 4, the time for the second annual application of fertilizer for new trees, excepting those planted this year, is after August 15 as growth slows. For flowering and fruit trees, use Holly-tone or Plant-tone.

To make room in the compost area for the leaves the trees will begin to shed next month, use up or bag compost in compost piles or bins. (See How to Start a Compost Pile in this chapter's October pages.)

 PESTS

Get rid of weeds sprouting in the mulch around trees.

Bagworms and fall tent caterpillars are usually active right now. If you spot bagworms, physically remove and destroy them now. You can also spray with a biological control such as *Bacillus thuringiensis* (*Bt*). Other controls are Sevin or malathion insecticide, Pyrethrin, or rotenone.

Powdery mildew and rust turn up on susceptible plants. Sulfur controls both, as do fungicidal formulations of copper, which also controls bacterial diseases such as fire blight, bacterial leaf spot, and wilt.

273

## PLANNING

Check out the changing color of the trees in your neighborhood and at public gardens, where the names of those you admire are sure to be available. Then look in your own garden for a spot that would be much more exciting if it had a glow of red, coral, or yellow in the fall.

**When the leaves start to change color is the beginning of an excellent planting season for trees.** Plant sales and pleasant September weather also combine to make this a fine time to install a hedge. You'll find suggestions for planting hedges in the August pages of Chapter 8, Shrubs.

## PLANTING

If you've been wanting a too-expensive tree—a good-sized **Japanese maple,** for example—take advantage of the seasonally discounted prices sometimes offered now. If you are buying a B&B tree, choose one that has just been dug rather than a tree that was dug in spring, unless that tree has been mulched in well

Small trees can be transplanted as soon as their leaves color up and fall.

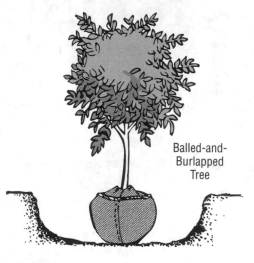

Balled-and-Burlapped Tree

## CARE

In Zone 6 and northward, get ready to move outdoor trees growing in containers from exposed locations to more protected spots for the winter.

**By mid-month move the indoor trees back inside for the winter.** But first, hose them down, let them dry, and then spray the foliage lightly, top and undersides, with a horticultural soap. (See Planning in the September pages of Chapter 4, Houseplants.)

You may need to wrap new trees as a protection from deer rubbing, critter nibbling, and sunscald this fall and winter. Plan to remove wrappings come spring as they eventually constrict the trunks and can cause cracking.

An easy way to prevent winter sun from injuring the bark of young trees is to paint the trunks with white wash—calcium carbonate with resins in it.

As the leaves begin to fall, gather and save them for the compost pile. (See How to Start a Compost Pile in this chapter's October pages.) Dry leaves, along with grass clippings, are a major source of organic material for the compost pile.

If you haven't done so yet, clear finished compost to make room for the leaves coming off the trees.

## PRUNING

Early this month, before preparing the indoor trees vacationing outdoors for their move back inside—**ficus, citrus, palms**—groom them. Remove yellowing foliage and branches that are crossing so that the interior has air and light. Thin some of the tiny lemons developing on a **'Meyer Improved' lemon tree.**

Clear away spent flowers on late blooming flowering trees.

## WATERING

Pour two or three 5-gallon buckets of water around the roots of newly-planted

*Check out the changing color of the trees in your neighborhood and at public gardens, where the names of those you admire are sure to be available.*

trees once every two weeks throughout fall unless you have rain. The earth remains warm even after leaves fall and the air cools, so roots continue to develop.

Check the soil moisture of the indoor trees you move back inside for the winter. Dry air indoors soon sucks the moisture out of the foliage and the soil.

# FERTILIZING

The time for the second annual application of organic fertilizer for newly planted trees is as growth slows toward the end of the growing season: in Zones 3 and 4, about August 15; in Zone 5, early September; in Zones 6 and 7, early September to early October. **Do not fertilize trees planted this year with chemical fertilizer.** For established flowering and fruit trees, use Holly-tone or Plant-tone.

Include mature trees that are doing poorly when you fertilize.

# PESTS

Get rid of weeds sprouting in the mulch around trees.

## Did You Know?

### Trees with Exceptionally Colorful Fall Foliage

- **American Smoke Tree, Chittamwood** (*Cotinus obovatus*)
- **American Sweet Gum** (*Liquidambar styraciflua*)
- **Amur Maple** (*Acer ginnala*)
- **Black Gum, Sour Gum** (*Nyssa sylvatica*)
- **Bradford Pear** (*Pyrus calleryana* 'Chanticleer' 'Aristocrat')
- **Chinese Dogwood** (*Cornus florida* hybrids; *C. kousa C.* x *rutgersensis* Stellar Series)
- **Golden Larch** (*Pseudolarix kaempferi*)
- **Japanese Zelkova** (*Zelkova serrata*)
- **Katsura Tree** (*Cercidiphylium japonicum*)
- **Maidenhair Tree** (*Ginkgo biloba* male cvs.)
- **Mountain Ash, Korean Mountain Ash** (*Sorbus alnifolia*)
- **Northern Red Oak** (*Quercus rubra*)
- **Red Maple, Swamp Maple** (*Acer rubrum* 'October Glory' 'Red Sunset')
- **Sassafras** (*Sassafras albidum*)
- **Scarlet Oak** (*Quercus coccinea*)
- **Sugar Maple** (*Acer saccharum* 'Bonfire' 'Green Mountain')
- **Sweet Gum (** *Liquidambar styraciflua*)
- **Tatarian Maple** (*Acer tataricum*)
- **Tulip Tree** (*Liriodendron tulipifera*)
- **Washington Hawthorn** (*Crataegus phaenopyrum*)
- **Witchhazel** (*Hamamelis* x *intermedia* 'Diane')

Fall tent caterpillars can be controlled by *Bacillus thuringiensis (Bt)*. Other controls are Sevin or malathion insecticide, Pyrethrin, or rotenone.

Treat the indoor trees—**citrus, ficus, palms**—that have been summering outdoors for insects before moving them back inside for the winter.

Change whatever deer deterrents you are using. If bears have been reported in your area, do not put out bird feeders; they attract bears. See the section on Pests, Diseases, and Controls in the Appendix of the book.

Continue to search out and rake up weeds.

If you see signs of vole activity, bait the main runway with a rodenticide.

# PLANNING

**Composting.** If there's no place in your yard for a big open compost pile, consider installing one of the many tidy composters offered at garden centers and by mail order. Or, compost in a black leaf bag; layer in it dry leaves, green weeds, chopped vegetable or fruit peelings, and then poke holes in it. Wet the interior thoroughly, close the bag, and set it outdoors in a sheltered, sunny out-of-sight place to do its thing. Shake the bag, and turn it upside down often to speed the process.

# PLANTING

When the leaves start to change color is the moment many gardeners consider best for transplanting trees. Now through November is also an excellent time for planting trees. The air is cold, but the earth still has warmth.

# CARE

Before adding leaves to an existing compost pile, gather the composted humus collected there, and use it or store it for use next year in plastic leaf bags.

Turn your compost pile often.

Save all of your fallen leaves, and heap them in an out of the way place for composting or for insulation around plants; or grind them to use as mulch and bag them ready for spring. If your leaves are few, suck them up in a vacuum-blower, and blow the residue out over the lawn or the flower borders.

# PRUNING

You can prune out dead or diseased tree limbs, but delay any major pruning until winter.

# WATERING

**Indoors.** Maintain the soil moisture of the indoor trees, mist them often, and air the room daily if you can.

**Outdoors.** Water newly-planted trees and hardy trees in containers every week or ten days if the season runs dry. It is essential for the unchecked growth of newly planted and young trees that they receive a thorough watering shortly before the ground freezes.

# FERTILIZING

Trees benefit from fertilization twice a year for the first eight or nine years of their lives.

However, a tree just planted this year is not likely to need fertilizing until next spring.

In Zones 6, and 7, the time for the last application of fertilizer is between early September and early October. See Understanding Fertilizers in the Introduction to the book.

# PESTS

Check trees for signs of scale, aphids, and mealybug infestations, and control them with ultrafine horticultural oil, horticultural soap, Neem products, or Permethrin.

**Voles are most active October to March.** If you see vole activity, bait the main runway with a rodenticide.

Consider enclosing newly planted trees, especially the evergreens, with chicken wire cages to keep them safe from deer. Or, at the least, change whatever deer deterrents you are using from something new to them and obnoxious. Deer disregard deterrents they become accustomed to. See the section on Pests, Diseases, and Controls in the Appendix of the book. If bears have been reported in your area, do not put out—or do remove—bird feeders.

*Save all of your fallen leaves, and heap them in an out of the way place for composting or for insulation around plants; or grind them to use as mulch and bag them ready for spring.*

## Did You Know?

### How to Start a Compost Pile

Dead leaves become an asset when you use them to make compost, the soil-like substance remaining when nature reduces organic material to humus.

Compost is called "black gold" because a 1-inch layer mixed into the soil releases its nutrients as the plants grow. Compost also replaces the organic content lost to healthy plant growth. It improves drainage, soil structure, and aeration; sustains the microbial activity essential to healthy soil; encourages big root systems; buffers soil temperatures; and reduces the need for watering—100 pounds of humus holds 195 pounds of water.

Along with dry leaves, the other materials used in building a compost pile are grass clippings, chopped vegetable and fruit peels, healthy weeds, and plant debris. **Never compost disease- and insect-infested plant materials.**

Your compost pile will deliver finished (ready to use) compost sooner if you break up the leaves with a blower/vacuum or a leaf shredder before putting them on the pile. Or, run a mulching mower over them. Or pile them into a garbage can, and churn them with a string trimmer.

Here's the basic approach to building a compost pile:

*1* Heap dry leaves in an out-of-sight place with access to a hose. Outline a base for the compost pile that is about 4 feet wide by 4 feet long. As the ingredients become available, build onto this base a 4-foot-high pile of layers of any of the following four combinations of organic materials:

A. 3 parts dry leaves (Carbon)
   3 parts fresh grass clippings (Nitrogen)

B. 2 parts dry leaves (Carbon)
   2 parts straw or wood shavings (Carbon)
   1 part manure (Nitrogen)
   1 part fresh grass clippings (Nitrogen)
   1 part fresh garden weeds/harvested
     plants (Nitrogen)
   1 part kitchen food scraps (Nitrogen)

C. 6 parts dry leaves (Carbon)
   3 parts kitchen scraps (no meat or fish) (Nitrogen)
   3 parts fresh grass clippings (Nitrogen)

D. 3 parts dry leaves (Carbon)
   1 part fresh garden weeds/harvested
     plants (Nitrogen)
   1 part fresh grass clippings (Nitrogen)
   1 part kitchen food scraps (Nitrogen)

*2* As you build the pile, sprinkle over each layer about an inch of garden soil and/or compost to encourage microbial activity. Or sprinkle on a microbial activator to speed up decomposition. Compost starter, activators, and/or inoculants hasten the composting. To make a compost rich in nitrogen, add dustings of bone meal for the phosphorous and calcium it contains; blood meal; or a high nitrogen garden fertilizer. To make it high in potassium, calcium, and carbon and to reduce acidity, dust fireplace ashes onto the layers. If you wish to help reduce soil compaction and enhance aeration, dust on gypsum, which also adds calcium and sulfur.

*3* Keep the pile moist, and turn it weekly, or as often as you can, with a pitchfork to hasten decomposition. Depending on the season, your climate, and how often you turn it, the pile will become compost in a few months (warm regions), or In year or two (cooler areas).

## PLANNING

If you would enjoy harvesting branches of red-berried **holly** branches to make traditional swags and ornaments for the holidays, grow your own. But choose with care. Hollies are dioecious (see Some Berry-Making Shrubs Need Pollinators in the November pages of Chapter 8, Shrubs). That means that most females require a male pollinator to fruit well.

And, if you garden in Zones 4 and northward, buy only from a nursery you know will stand behind its plants.

The beautiful **English holly** (*Ilex aquifolium*) and many other lovely species are not winter hardy north of our Zones 6 and 7. One handsome tree that is hardy in Zone 5 is the 40- to 50-foot pyramidal **American holly** (*Ilex opaca*). It matures single bright red berries in October that persist through winter. The cultivar 'Croonenburg' is self-pollinating, which means you only need one plant to have berries. 'Greenleaf', which does need a pollinator, sets bright red berries sooner and is a smaller tree.

 ## PLANTING

As long as the ground isn't frozen, you can plant trees in November.

**If you are planning to buy a live Christmas tree for the holidays, choose a permanent home for it now, one suited to the tree's mature width and height,** and dig the planting hole while the weather is pleasant and the ground easy to work. Improve the soil from the hole (see Soil Preparation and Improvement in the Introduction to the book), and put it back in the hole. Cover the area with 12 to 18 inches of leaves held down by evergreen boughs to keep them from blowing away.

 ## CARE

Apply an anti-desiccant spray to the foliage of newly-planted evergreens growing in exposed positions, or wrap them in Reemay or burlap.

In Zones 3 to 5, move hardy trees growing in containers to a sheltered corner out of the wind for the winter, or store them in a garage or shed.

 ## PRUNING

Don't be concerned for their health when evergreens show some yellow in the interior of the branches—**pines, arborvitae, juniper,** and **yews** among them. When it happens we find hard to predict, but the good news is it's most likely normal.

The plants we call evergreens lose some of their older leaves at more or less regular intervals, but they look green all year because they don't drop them all at the same time. (The exception is the **golden larches,** which turn a vibrant deep gold and look quite exceptionally beautiful, then they drop their leaves all at once, like the **maple** trees.) A plant must renew its foliage as part of its life cycle. Some **pine** species lose needles every fifteen to eighteen months, while some **hollies** drop their leaves at four-year intervals. So when yellow shows up in an evergreen, chances are that it is a normal part of a cycle and not a problem.

## WATERING

**Outdoors.** The earth remains warm even after leaves fall and the air cools, so roots continue to develop. That's why watering is recommended when fall is

*If you are planning to buy a live Christmas tree for the holidays, choose a permanent home for it now, one suited to the tree's mature width and height, and dig the planting hole while the weather is pleasant and the ground easy to work.*

dry. Be sure to water newly planted trees thoroughly before the ground freezes.

Water outdoor trees growing in containers every two weeks or when the soil seems dry. Water these trees thoroughly too, before the ground freezes so the plants don't go into winter dry.

**Indoors.** Maintain the soil moisture of the indoor trees—**citrus, ficus, palms**—mist them often, and air the room daily if you can.

# FERTILIZING

**Do not fertilize trees at this season, indoors or out.**

# PESTS

Deer will even eat **holly** leaves when they are hungry, and young trees are especially susceptible. So if deer nibble your plantings regularly, cage your new trees and especially evergreens, with chicken wire to keep them safe. See the section on Pests, Diseases, and Controls in the Appendix of the book.

Bait vole runs approaching trees with a rodenticide.

## Did You Know?

### How to Care for Indoor Trees

For trees that live indoors in winter, a bright, airy, cool room is best. Daytime temperatures should be between 68 and 75 degrees Fahrenheit with a drop of 7 to 10 degrees at night, and humidity between 30 and 60 percent. Temperatures higher than 68 degrees take the humidity from the air.

• Air the room daily for about ten minutes unless it's freezing outside, and mist the plants with water at room temperature.

• If the room is warm, run a humidifier, keep wet sponges around, and/or grow the plants on saucers filled with wet pebbles.

• Keep the soil evenly damp, not soaking wet.

• When there's new growth, include a half-strength dose of houseplant fertilizer at every second watering.

• Supplement inadequate window light with grow lights.

• Check for insects often. For controls, see Pests, Diseases, and Controls in the Appendix.

• Every few weeks remove yellowing or damaged foliage, dead flowers, branches that cross, and those that are becoming ungainly.

• When repotting, use the houseplant soils recommended under Soil in the introduction of Chapter 4, Houseplants.

# DECEMBER
## Trees

 PLANNING

**About cut Christmas trees.** The **Douglas fir** and the **balsam fir** (*Abies balsamea*) stay fresh longest and are popular. Fraser fir (*Abies fraseri*) is fast becoming the most popular Christmas tree.

**Live Christmas trees.** Choose a **Colorado blue spruce** (*Picea pungens glauca*) 'Hoopsii' and 'Thompsonii'. An 8-foot ceiling can't take a tree taller than 7 feet. Before buying, give the plant a health check. Is the rootball moist? Do needles drop when you shake it?

 PLANTING

If you're planning on a **live Christmas tree,** prepare a planting hole for it (see November, Planting).

 CARE

**Cut tree.** Remove the lower branches to fit the tree holder, and cut at least ½ inch off the bottom for easy water intake. Keep it in a shaded location.

Before bringing the tree indoors, to keep the needles fresh longer, spray the tree with an anti-transpirant like biodegradable Wilt-Pruf. One application before you decorate the tree should last.

After the holidays, take the branches for winter mulch, and move the tree to be recycled as mulch or wood chips.

**Live tree.** Keep it indoors no more than two weeks. Before it comes in, keep it outdoors in a sheltered spot with good light; spray needles with an anti-desiccant to help prevent drying out, water the soil well, and let it drain. If it's a B&B tree, place it in a leak-proof tub.

Stand the tree far from heat sources. Keep the temperature under 65 degrees Fahrenheit if or when possible. Don't fertilize, and water only if the soil feels dry. Air the room. Place a plastic film down under the tree to protect the floor from leaks.

If you cannot plant your live tree when you move it outdoors, place it in a sheltered spot with good light, and heap leaves or bags filled with leaves 14 to 18 inches deep all around the rootball.

**New trees outdoors.** Spray an anti-desiccant on young evergreens in exposed positions. Protect them from bitter winds by erecting a burlap screen.

 PRUNING

Lightly harvest mature evergreens with cones and berries to use in holiday decorations—**pines, fir, hollies.**

 WATERING

**Cut Christmas tree.** Keep the stand filled with water containing tree preservative; fresh fir trees drink lots; **pine trees** drink some; **spruce** don't take up much water at all.

Maintain the soil moisture of the indoors trees—**citrus, ficus, palms**—and mist them and air the room often. If there's no snow or rain, water all new outdoor plantings thoroughly.

 FERTILIZING

Make a New Year's resolution to stick to non-polluting fertilizers and biodegradable controls. Decades of nursery experience have shown that trees that are inherently healthy, planted in a suitable climate, in soil properly prepared (see Understanding Fertilizers in the Introduction to the book), and given all the water they need the first years are strengthened by normal stresses.

 PESTS

Trees growing indoors come under attack from mealybugs and spider mites. Frequent showers and spraying with horticultural soaps discourages those pests.

# CHAPTER TEN

# Vines, Ground Covers, & Ornamental Grasses

*What these three types of plants have in common is speed. The full, vigorous growth of the ground covers and most vines and ornamental grasses solves loads of landscape problems—provided you keep them in check!*

## VINES

Vines are probably the most versatile of all garden plants. Nearly all can be trained to grow in whatever direction suits your pleasure—downhill to act like a waterfall, up a drain pipe to soften a naked corner, sideways to green a fence or hide a tree stump. Many open exquisite blossoms, and some scent the air.

**Caution: Even cultivated vines can be as invasive as weed vines—so plant even the vines we recommend only where they won't escape and invade native plants.**

**Perennial vines.** Generally deep-rooted, the perennial vines grow vigorously and thrive for years rooted in a modest planting hole or a large planter or tub. Cold-hardiness in your area has to be there in a perennial vine. The top of it will be up in the wind, so you want to make sure it will withstand the coldest winters your region can throw at it. If a vine's cold-hardiness is doubtful, place it where it will have the protection of a north-facing wall at its back. Most are heavy when mature and need a strong support.

An evergreen vine is a good choice when you want year-round greening and screening. A deciduous vine is a better choice when you want summer screening coupled with access to sun in winter. While a perennial vine's major contribution is its foliage, some maximize your investment. **Wisteria** and **sweet autumn clematis** produce masses of blooms and add a sweet fragrance to the garden. **Climbing hydrangea** produces flowers, and the foliage takes on a nice color in fall. (One of the most beautiful of all vines, the climbing hydrangea takes its time growing, unlike most vines.)

**Annual vines.** The annual vines grow at the speed of light—instant effect. That gives you an opportunity to see whether a vine is the right answer to a given situation. Annual vines are useful for summer screening, and they're also good choices to clothe walls and fences that will need repainting periodically. Most annual vines need only light support. Many are easily grown from seed planted in spring. Where the growing season is short, the annual vines are usually started indoors early or purchased as seedlings. Some have

fragrance, such as **sweet peas,** for example; the lovely **hyacinth bean** is somewhat scented, and its handsome purple pods are edible when boiled to a mush.

**Tropical and semi-tropical vines.** In late spring, tropical vines like **passion flower, mandevilla,** and **bougainvillea** are sold in big pots already blooming. They're great accent plants for patios and porches. Perennial in warm climates, they can live through winter in a greenhouse or a bright window as houseplants, or in a frost-free attached garage or root cellar.

## TRAINING, PLANTING, AND MAINTENANCE

**Training.** Vines need supports. How a vine climbs—the plant parts it uses to hold itself to advancing positions—dictates the type of support it needs. When you are choosing a vine, that's an important consideration. **Cross vine** climbs by twining itself around its support. **Climbing hydrangea** uses aerial rootlets to cling to its next position. **Clematis** holds on with twisting leaf-stalks (petioles).

Perennial vines also require pruning in spring, summer, autumn, and winter. You prune a new vine lightly the first year or two to direct its growth and develop a graceful framework. Then you prune it annually to control growth and encourage flowering. So another important consideration when you are choosing a vine is how you will prune it when it gets up on whatever you want it to climb.

**Caution: Don't plant a vine where it can get into shutters, gutters, windows, attic, or other areas of your house.** Vines get into things. It's their nature. They grow over things. That's their nature. Don't plant a vine near trees or large shrubs; if you fail to keep a vine pruned, it will smother everything within reach.

**Planting and maintenance.** Vines, like shrubs, are sold bare root and also as container-grown plants and are planted and maintained as for shrubs.

Because a vine makes considerable growth in a single season, the best time to plant one is early spring before growth gets underway. A perennial vine can be planted in fall after it has been dormant and cut back.

**Transplanting vines.** You can transplant a perennial vine planted a year or two ago fairly easily. Before you dig it up, cut the stems back to within 2 or 3 feet from the crown, and tie them together. Then proceed as described for moving established shrubs under Planting, in the February pages of Shrubs, Chapter 8. If the vine is a flowering plant, move it shortly after it blooms to avoid cutting off next year's blooms.

**Pruning.** Perennial vines need a regular schedule of pruning to lead the branches in the direction you want them to grow and to contain their growth. Those vines that flower on last year's growth—spring bloomers usually—should be pruned as soon as they finish blooming in late spring or early summer. Flowering vines that bloom on new wood are pruned before they begin to grow, and that means pruning in late winter or early spring; they usually bloom late in the season. See About Pruning Vines in the February pages.

## GROUND COVERS

Ground covers are low-maintenance plants used to carpet the earth where lawn turf and ornamental plants are impractical or undesirable. Any fast-growing plant that spreads and grows without much attention can be used as ground cover—**daylilies** in the sun, **hostas** in shade. Many vines also fit the job description. But the plants specifically designated as ground covers spread rapidly and grow so thickly they keep out weeds even when they die down in winter; an example is that the foliage of **lily-of-the-valley** vanishes in the fall, but the rhizomes remain so densely packed few weeds can get in.

If you like a garden that has a serene look, use just one type of plant as ground cover. Like a turf lawn, it will unify the various elements in view—shrub borders, flower beds, specimen plantings, and trees. On the other hand, combining several compatible ground covers adds extra texture to the area, makes it more interesting. Using several also is a safeguard should one type of plant fail. For a richly varied carpet, plant drifts of small winter-flowering bulbs in sunny places here and there over-planted with aromatic **Greek oregano, thyme,** and **ajuga.** In areas that have part sun, plant **myrtle** (*Vinca minor*) or **pachysandra.** In the dappled shade under trees, the luminous foliage of **lamium** is lovely.

**Caution: The plants designated as ground covers, like weeds, spread rapidly.**

The toughest evergreen ground covers are **ajuga, pachysandra, myrtle,** and **ivy.** All four can be walked on some and can be used as replacement for a lawn. Ajuga and myrtle bear sweet little flowers in early spring. Ivy can take a few years to get going, but once started it spreads irresistibly. All four are seen by environmentalists as a potential threat to native plants, so use them responsibly. Don't plant a ground cover where it might invade stands of native plants or woodlands.

## PLANTING AND MAINTENANCE

The easy way to carpet an area with a ground cover is by planting rooted cuttings. Starting with seed is economical and generally successful if you start the plants indoors in flats and grow them to a size that fills a 3-inch pot before putting them outdoors. (See starting seeds indoors, in January In the Annuals chapter.) Often enough you will find you have friends willing to share, provided you do the work!

Planting a Ground Cover is the April sidebar. To get a ground cover off to a fast, successful start, provide a well-prepared bed with humusy fertile soil. Dig the whole area to be planted, and improve the soil just as completely and carefully as you do a bed for perennials. If you are installing an invasive ground cover such as **ivy, vinca,** or **ajuga,** plan to edge it with a 6-inch metal barrier to prevent it from overrunning neighboring plantings.

Planting through a mulch cover will minimize weeding chores, which can be burdensome in the year or two it will take for the ground cover to thicken enough to keep invaders out.

**Watering.** The first season of growth, a newly installed ground cover will need watering any time the perennial bed needs watering, which is weekly or every ten days unless you have a soaking rain. Water the soil slowly, gently, and thoroughly with a sprinkler, a soaker hose, a bubbler, or by hand. In the following years it should need watering only if the leaf tips are wilting; then water thoroughly as you would a perennial bed.

**Pruning.** An occasional pruning keeps a ground cover neater and stimulates branching and new growth. **Pachysandra, plumbago** (*Ceratostigma plumbaginoides*), and **Ivy** when fully mature will benefit from shearing every few years.

**Fertilizing.** You fertilize a bed of ground covers when you fertilize the perennials. (See Fertilizing and Fertilizers in the introduction to Chapter 6, Perennials.)

In fall, clear ground cover(s) of fallen leaves only if they have matted down. Leaves that slip through the foliage decompose on the ground, and that nourishes the soil.

Like perennials, ground covers don't fill out until the second or third season, but once they are flourishing, you can divide them to make new plants to fill gaps or enlarge the beds.

## ORNAMENTAL GRASSES

Ornamental grasses are lovely in perennial beds, and since many grow aggressively, they also make excellent ground covers. On hot summer days the foliage sways and whispers in the slightest breeze, and late summer when most flowers have peaked, the airy, dancing flowerheads (inflorescences) are a delight. The seedheads and drying foliage remain beautiful fall and winter, anchoring the garden's fourth season.

The ornamental grasses have another great virtue: deer don't eat them.

## DESIGNING WITH GRASSES

You can learn much about the use of grasses from a visit to the two-acre Friendship Garden at the U.S. National Arboretum in Washington, D.C. They, and other botanic gardens, are showing us how to use grasses in low-maintenance naturalized plantings that include a healthy diversity of flowering perennials, bulbs, small trees, and shrubs. There are no straight paths. The heights, mixtures, and widths of the flower beds vary to avoid any formal sense. Medium-size grasses are islands with curved borders. Fruiting and berry-producing plants promote a healthy ecological balance by encour-

# Vines, Ground Covers, & Ornamental Grasses

aging birds and beneficial insects. (See the October pages of this chapter.)

**Size.** When you are choosing a grass, the first consideration is its size. Sizes are judged by the end-of-season height and width of the foliage. The large landscaping grasses are used boldly, in big spaces. They're excellent plants for transitional areas and screening. Some thrive in moist situations. Massed, medium-tall grasses make good bank-holders and ground covers. A few patches of medium-tall grasses woven through a perennial border add beauty and interest. Some we like are **maiden** and **silver grasses** (*Miscanthus* species and varieties), bold plants with broad, grassy, gracefully arching leaves. We also favor **switchgrass** (*Panicum virgatum*) and beautiful 3- to 4-foot (but, alas, cold tender) **fountain grass** (*Pennisetum alopecuroides*), with arching foliage that ends summer topped by flower spikelets.

The little grasses, those under 2 feet, are generally used as ground cover for small areas and to add variety to the front of a flower border. Our favorites are the little **sedges** (*Carex* species), **mosquito grass** (*Bouteloua gracilis*), and **blue sheep's fescue** (*Festuca amethystina* variety *superba*).

**Form and texture.** Once you have decided on a size, consider the plant's structure and textural effect. **Chinese silver grass** is very erect, and **maiden grass** arches, while the foliage of the fountain grasses, well . . . fountains. The texture of the leaves and their color impact the garden design—fine, coarse, bold, bluish, greenish, reddish, gold, striped, variegated. We like contrast, so we recommend combining both upright and fountain-like forms, fine and coarse-textured grasses, green and variegated forms.

Think all this through before you fall in love with the seedheads, the "flowers" of the ornamental grasses. They are almost all irresistible!

Finally, when planning a grass garden, we recommend grouping several plants of a few varieties rather than setting out a few plants of many varieties.

## Planting and Maintenance

Like the perennial flowers, newly-planted ornamental grasses begin to fill out the second year. Starting them indoors from seed saves money, but the seedlings will take two years to gain any size. Planting root divisions is more satisfactory unless you need lots and lots.

Like perennials, ornamental grasses are available as seed, container grown, and bare root. They are best started in spring, not fall. Follow the planting procedures for perennials, and provide improved soil and generous planting holes. Set the crowns 1/2 to 1 inch higher than the soil surface. Don't "drown" the grasses in mulch—2 to 3 inches of mulch is enough.

**Maintenance.** Ornamental grasses develop throughout the year without pruning, staking, spraying, or dead-heading. Let the seedheads ripen and stand through fall and winter. In late winter or early spring, just before new foliage emerges, give them their annual haircut. Cool-season grasses begin to grow in cool weather and need their haircut earlier than warm-season grasses. Our plant list tells you which is which and the January sidebar explains the difference between them.

Most ornamental grasses need annual fertilization. The time for it is when signs of new growth appear. With grasses, be sure to use a slow-release organic fertilizer such as Holly-tone or Espoma Organic Lawn Food. In prolonged droughts, water slowly and deeply.

Once installed, ornamental grasses are not expected to require division for at least five to ten years.

## Pests and Diseases

The vines, ground covers, and grasses we recommend are vigorous plants with few problems.

# Vines, Ground Covers, & Ornamental Grasses

## Annual Vines

| Common Name (*Botanical Name*) | Zones Light | Height (Feet) | Climbing Method | Description |
|---|---|---|---|---|
| Black-eyed Susan Vine (*Thunbergia alata*) | Tender perennial Morning sun, afternoon shade | 6 to 8 | Twining | Dark-eyed flowers in gold, orange, and creamy white. |
| Cypress Vine (*Ipomoea quamoclit*) | Annual Sun to shade | 10 to 20 | Twining | Lacy. Red, fern-like leaves. |
| Hyacinth Bean (*Dolichos lablab*) | 9 to 11 Sun | 15 to 20 | Twining | Decorative pea-like flowers, and purple pods that are edible when boiled to a mush. |
| Mandevilla (*Mandevilla* x *amabalis*) | Tender perennial Sun to part shade | 8 to 10 | Twining | Large pretty pink blooms. |
| Moon Vine (*Ipomoea alba*) | 8 to 10 Sun | 10 | Twining | Large, fragrant white flowers in late afternoon, fade next morning. |
| Morning Glory (*Ipomoea purpurea*) | 7 to 10 Sun | 10 | Twining | Funnel-shaped flowers, summer until frost. 'Heavenly Blue' is an excellent cultivar. |
| Sweet Pea (*Lathyrus odoratus*) | 6 to 8 Sun to part shade | To 6 | Clinging | Sweet fragrant pea flowers in lovely shades. A cool weather plant. |

## Perennial Vines

| Common Name (*Botanical Name*) | Zones Light | Height (Feet) | Climbing Method | Description |
|---|---|---|---|---|
| Boston Ivy (*Parthenocissus tricuspidata*) | 4 to 8 Sun | 50 plus | Clinging | Deciduous. Three-lobed shiny leaves turn scarlet in fall. |
| Chinese Trumpet Creeper (*Campsis grandiflora*) | 6 to 9 Sun | 15 to 20 | Clinging | Deciduous. Trumpet-shaped coral or yellow flowers on new growth in summer. |
| Clematis (*Clematis* spp. and cvs.) | 3 to 9 Sun, bright shade; shade for roots | 5 to 20 | Twisting petioles | Deciduous. The most beautiful flowers borne by vines are the large-flowered summer-flowering clematis hybrids. Sweet autumn clematis (*C. terniflora*) is covered with small sweetly fragrant flowers in fall. |
| Climbing Hydrangea (*Hydrangea petiolaris*) | 5 to 9 Part shade to shade | Over 60 feet | Clinging | Deciduous. Magnificent massive vine when mature. Flat, scented, white florets in late May. |
| Coral Honeysuckle (*Lonicera sempervirens*) | 6 to 9 Sun to shade | 30 to 50 | Clinging | Semi-evergreen. Trumpet-shaped flowers, red with yellow throats. |

# Vines, Ground Covers, & Ornamental Grasses

## Perennial Vines

| Common Name (*Botanical Name*) | Zones Light | Height (Feet) | Climbing Method | Description |
|---|---|---|---|---|
| **Cross Vine** (*Bignonia capreolata*) | 5 to 9 Sun or shade | 8 to 12 feet | Twining | Evergreen. Clusters of narrow tubular red and yellow flowers. |
| **English Ivy** (*Hedera helix*) | 5 to 9 Sun, part shade, shade | To 90 feet | Clinging | Evergreen. Glossy dark green foliage with three lobes. Invasive; keep it in check. |
| **'Goldflame' Honeysuckle** (*Lonicera x heckrottii*) | 4 to 8 Sun to part shade | 10 to 20 feet | Twining | Deciduous. 'Goldflame' buds, carmine, then yellow, and then pink, bloom late spring into fall. Few seeds produced. |
| **Hardy Kiwi** (*Actinidia kolomikta*) | 4 to 8 Sun to part sun | To 30 feet | Twining | Deciduous. An ornamental variety. Foliage is blotched with pink and white. May flowers yield fruits in fall. |
| **Japanese Hydrangea Vine** (*Schizophragma hydrangeoides*) | 5 to 8 Sun to part shade | 20 to 30 feet | Clinging | Deciduous. It resembles climbing hydrangea and bears large flattened flower heads in summer. |
| **Silver Lace Vine** (*Polygonatum aubertii*) | 4 to 9 Sun to part sun | Unlimited | | Rampant vine with fragrant florets late summer and early fall. Good shore plant. |
| **Virginia Creeper** (*Parthenocissus quinquefolia*) | 3 to 9 Sun to part shade | 30 plus | Clinging | Deciduous. Glossy dark-green leaves turn a brilliant red and purple in autumn. |
| **Wisteria** (*Wisteria* spp. and cvs.) | 5 to 8 Sun | 25 to 30 | Twining | Deciduous. Vigorous rampant vines; 1- to 2-foot hanging clusters of fragrant pea-like flowers. |

## Perennial Ground Covers

| Common Name (*Botanical Name*) | Zones Light | Height (Inches) | Type | Ornamental Qualities |
|---|---|---|---|---|
| **Astilbe** (*Astilbe chinensis* 'Pumila') | 4 to 8 Part sun | 12 | Deciduous | Fern-like foliage; feathery flower spires in summer. Best in moist soil. |
| **Barrenwort** (*Epimedium* spp.) | 5 to 9 Takes dry shade | 6 to 12 | Deciduous | Small, heart-shaped foliage turns reddish or gold in fall. Yellow, pink, white, red florets in spring. |
| **Cotoneaster** (*Cotoneaster dammeri*) | 5 to 8 Sun to part sun | To 12 | Evergreen | Low shrubby; dainty leaves; white flowers followed by red berries. |
| **Bearberry, Kinnikinick** (*Arctostaphylos uva-ursi*) | 2 to 8 Sun to part shade | 6 to 12 | Broadleaved evergreen | Low, trailing. In spring, clusters of tiny pink flowers, then red berries. 'Massachusetts' tolerates wet conditions. |

## Perennial Ground Covers

| Common Name (Botanical Name) | Zones Light | Height (Inches) | Type | Ornamental Qualities |
|---|---|---|---|---|
| Beach Grass (*Amophila breviligulata*) | 4 to 7 Sun | 24 to 36 | | Not ornamental but an excellent sand binder for oceanside dunes and bays. Invasive in flower beds. |
| Beech Fern (*Thelypteris hexagonoptera*) | 3 to 9 Shade | 10 to 24 | Deciduous fern | Broadly triangular fronds for shade and acid soils. Spreads quickly. |
| Bergenia (*Bergenia cordifolia* cvs.) | 3 to 8 Part shade | 8 to 12 | Evergreen | Beautiful heart-shaped, glossy, leathery, reddish-tinted leaves. Rose-pink flowers in late winter, early spring. |
| Bouncing Bet (*Saponaria officinalis* 'Rosea Plena') | 2 to 8 Sun | 24 to 36 | Deciduous | Fragrant double pink flowers in summer; spreads rapidly and does best in sandy soil. |
| Bugleweed (*Ajuga reptans* cvs.) | 4 to 9 Part sun to part shade | 4 to 8 | Semi-evergreen | Rosettes topped in spring with blue, white, or pink flower spires. 'Burgundy Glow' foliage is colorful. |
| Christmas Fern (*Polystichum acrostichoides*) | 3 to 8 Part shade | 24 | Evergreen | Good for cool woodlands; deep-green leathery fronds. Shield fern (*P. braunii*) is semi-evergreen with arching fronds. |
| Cinnamon Fern (*Osmunda cinnamomea*) | 3 to 8 Bright shade | To 60 | Deciduous | Tall, dramatic; arching green outer fronds and fertile inner fronds that turn cinnamon-colored and then wither. |
| Creeping Juniper (*Juniperus horizontalis* spp. and cvs.) | 3 to 9 Sun | 4 to 6 | Evergreen | Needled, wide-spreading, drought-resistant. Shore Juniper (*J. conferta*) thrives in sandy soils, stands salt spray. |
| Creeping Phlox (*Phlox stolonifera*) | 3 to 8 Part shade to part sun | 5 to 12 | Deciduous | Excellent for stone walls and rock gardens. Lavender-blue, pink, or white flowers on 12-inch spikes in spring. |
| Deer Fern (*Blechnum spicant*) | 5 to 8 Shade | 6 to 8 | Evergreen | Glossy dark green fronds resembling Boston fern. The hardiest evergreen fern. |
| Foamflower (*Tiarella cordifolia* and cvs.) | 3 to 8 Bright shade | 6 to 12 | Semi-evergreen | Charming as underplanting for perennial garden. In spring, pink or/and white bottlebrush flowers top attractive foliage. |
| Ginger (*Asarum europaeum*) | 4 to 7 Part shade | 6 to 8 | Evergreen | Excellent once established. Glossy, kidney-shaped evergreen leaves. |
| Golden Moneywort (*Lysimachia nummularia* 'Aurea') | 3 to 8 Sun to shade | 1 to 2 | Deciduous | For moist situations. 'Aurea' turns lime-gold and green. Bears masses of small cup-shaped yellow flowers. |
| Japanese Painted Fern (*Athyrium nipponicum* 'Pictum') | 3 to 8 Dappled light | 12 to 18 | Deciduous | Handsome fronds are multicolored reddish, silver, and silvery-green. Slow-growing; brightens shaded places. |

## Perennial Ground Covers

| Common Name (Botanical Name) | Zones Light | Height (Inches) | Type | Ornamental Qualities |
|---|---|---|---|---|
| Japanese Spurge (*Pachysandra terminalis*) | 4 to 8 Bright shade | 8 to 10 | Evergreen | Low, wide-spreading, rather formal. Green-white, barely visible flower spikes in early spring. Relentless but not rapid spread. |
| Lady Fern (*Athyrium filix-femina*) | 3 to 8 Part shade to shade | 16 to 36 | Deciduous | Very hardy. Thick clumps of graceful arching fronds with pointed leaves; spreads in time. |
| Lamb's Ears (*Stachys byzantina*) | 5 to 7 Sun to part sun | 6 to 12 | Deciduous | Woolly, silvery foliage; remove flower spikes. Named varieties are the best choice. |
| Leadwort (*Ceratostigma plumbaginoides*) | 5 to 9 Part sun | 6 to 12 | Deciduous | Sprawling mats of glossy leaves topped in late summer by the bluest of flowers that set off the rusty-red bracts. Decorative and a good choice for a small area. |
| Lenten Rose (*Helleborus orientalis*) | 4 to 8 Sun to part sun | 12 to 18 | Evergreen | Dense stands of shiny deeply divided leathery leaves; late winter's nodding flowers look like small roses. |
| Lily-of-the-Valley (*Convallaria majalis*) | 2 to 7 Part shade | 6 to 8 | Deciduous | Foliage is like tiny furled umbrellas. Exquisitely scented white nodding "bells" in May. Hard to get rid of once established. |
| Ostrich Fern (*Matteuccia pennsylvanica*) | 3 to 8 Sun to part shade | 36 to 60 | Deciduous | Grand "fiddlehead" fern. Emerging fronds are edible. One of the tallest native ferns, it grows wild on moist wooded slopes. |
| Rock Polypody, American Wall Fern (*Polypodium virginianum*) | 3 to 8 Part shade | 12 | Evergreen | A neat little fern that thrives in rocky situations and can spread to 5 feet. |
| Snow-in-Summer (*Cerastium tomentosum*) | 3 to 10 Sun | 6 to 12 | Evergreen | Grayish-green foliage covered with soft hairs. A profusion of small white flowers in mid- and late spring. |
| Spotted Deadnettle (*Lamium maculatum*) | 4 to 8 Part shade | 8 to 12 | Semi-evergreen | Beautiful silver-white-green foliage. Pink or white florets in May/June. 'White Nancy' flowers are white. |
| Stonecrop (*Sedum* spp. and cvs.) | 3 to 8 Sun | 2 to 6 | Evergreen | Low-growing ones make excellent fillers. 'John Creech' is very attractive. |
| Vinca, Periwinkle (*Vinca minor*) | 4 to 9 Sun, part shade, shade | 3 to 6 | Evergreen | Small, dainty, shiny dark green leaves on trailing stems 2 to 3 feet long. In early spring, has pretty lavender-blue flowers. Now on the "invasive" list. |
| Wintergreen, Checkerberry (*Gaultheria procumbens*) | 4 to 7 Part shade | 3 to 5 | Evergreen | Semi-herbaceous, semi-shrubby native; aromatic foliage once used for flavoring. Edible fruit. Flowers are small, nodding, pinkish-white urns. |

# Vines, Ground Covers, & Ornamental Grasses

## Ornamental Grasses

| Common Name (Botanical Name) | Zones Light | Height | Growth Season | Description |
|---|---|---|---|---|
| **Blue Fescue** (*Festuca* spp. and cvs.) | 4 to 8 Full sun | 8 to 12 inches | Cool | Powdery blue leaves; flower stalks change from blue-green to buff color. |
| **Blue Oat Grass, Avena Grass** (*Helictotrichon sempervirens*) | 4 to 8 Full sun | 2 to 3 feet | Cool | Semi-evergreen blue-green foliage. Delicate oat-like seedheads sway above foliage. Tolerates clay soil. |
| **Blue Switchgrass** (*Panicum virgatum* 'Dallas Blues') | 5 to 9 Full sun | 4 feet | Warm | Excellent for borders. Powder-blue leaves turn bright yellow in the fall. |
| **Blue Wild Ryegrass** (*Elymus racemosus*) | 5 to 9 Sun | 30 | Warm | Dune stabilizer; intense blue topped by inflorescenses in July and August. Invasive. |
| **Feather Reed Grass** (*Calamagrostis* x *acutiflora* cvs.) | 4 to 9 Full sun | 4 to 5 feet | Warm | Arching leaves; early summer flowers dry to golden spikes in fall. 'Karl Foerster' is outstanding. |
| **Fountain Grass** (*Pennisetum alopecuroides* 'Hameln') | 4 to 9 Sun | 3 feet | Warm | Graceful foliage; soft bottlebrush spikes in summer. |
| **Hakonechloa, Golden Variegated Hakonechloa** (*Hakonechloa macra* 'Aureola') | 4 to 9 Part shade | 2 feet | Cool | Small mound of cascading foliage striped green and gold. Combines well with hostas. |
| **Little Bluestem** (*Schizachyrium scoparium*) | 3 to 9 Full sun | 2 to 3 feet | Warm | Native. Narrow, strong blue foliage turns copper-orange in fall. Late summer blooms. |
| **Moor Grass** (*Molinia caerulea* cvs.) | 4 to 9 Sun, part sun | 3 to 8 feet | Warm | Foliage topped in mid-summer by airy, luminous 5- to 8-foot plumes. |
| **Morning Star Sedge** (*Carex grayi*) | 3 to 8 Shade | 1 to 3 feet | Cool | Arching, drooping; masses of flower spikes in spring. Excellent near water. Other species are hardy in Zone 4. |
| **Northern Sea Oats** (*Chasmanthium latifolium*) | 5 to 9 Sun, part sun | 3 to 5 feet | Warm | Beautiful oat-like seedheads in summer. Self-sows. Beautiful into winter, and great for cutting. Invasive soil-binder. |
| **Red Baron Blood Grass** (*Imperata cylindrica* 'Red Baron') | 4 to 9 Sun, part shade | 1 foot | Warm | Turns red as the season progresses. Prettiest when back-lit by the sun. |
| **Ribbon Grass** (*Phalaris arundinacea* 'Feesey's Form') | 6 to 9 Sun, part shade | 2 feet | Cool | Handsome but invasive. Green and white, spreading, tolerant of moisture. |
| **Silver Grass, Eulalia** (*Miscanthus sinensis* spp. and cvs.) | 5 to 9 Sun | 6 to 8 feet | Warm | Showy and beautiful. Silky tassels mature into fluffy plumes that last well into winter. |
| **Tufted Hair Grass** (*Deschampsia caespitosa*) | 4 to 9 Sun, part shade | 2 to 3 feet | Warm | Fresh green foliage and golden inflorescences that top a tufted mound. Naturalizes in moist areas. |

 PLANNING

Take your garden catalogs to a window with a view of the garden—and consider whether plantings of vines, ground covers, and ornamental grasses can solve problems or make some tired old things new.

**Vines.** Imagine a vine blooming on a garage corner, the garden shed, hiding a tree stump, covering an unsightly structure. Try out the idea by plant a fast-growing annual climber. The three best are the purple-podded, scented **hyacinth bean,** whose beautiful beans are edible; white-flowered **moonvine;** and **morning glory** 'Heavenly Blue'.

**Ground covers.** If drought plagues your lawn—or your lawn plagues you—consider replacing portions of the grass with one of the ground covers on the plant list for this chapter.

**Ornamental grasses.** Dream a grass garden. Low-growing species add texture and movement to the front of flower beds. Mid-height grasses are the natural transition plant to a woodland or water and, in combination with native wildflowers, make a beautiful flowering meadow. You can use grasses 6 feet and up to replace a high-maintenance espalier fronting a masonry wall; the tall grasses also make excellent summer screening.

The recommended ratio for a sunny meadow garden is one-third flowers to two-thirds ornamental grasses for sunny places; one-third grasses and two-thirds flowers for shade.

 PLANTING

**Outdoors.** Late this month or in February, you could sow seeds in a cold frame or hot bed for vines, ground covers, and ornamental grasses that need to be stratified (chilled) in order to germinate. You can multiply **trumpet vine** this way.

The Planting section of the November pages of Chapter 6, Perennials, describes stratification.

CARE

Winter winds are going to keep blowing for weeks, so check and adjust the ties and supports of mature vines. Tie down branches whipping in the wind. Free branchlets burdened by snow or ice, particularly lower branches buried in snow.

Snow cover protects low ground covers, such as **pachysandra,** from winter cold and wind, so let it be.

 PRUNING

If your ornamental grasses lose their looks, cut them back.

Prune away broken vine branches.

 WATERING

Water cold-tender vines wintering in containers in a shed or garage often enough to keep the soil slightly damp.

FERTILIZING

It's too early to fertilize.

PESTS

Repair or renew deer deterrents on vines. Check and adjust burlap covers and chicken wire cages.

If vole runs appear near vines, bait the main runway with a rodenticide.

*Winter winds are going to keep blowing for weeks, so check and adjust the ties and supports of mature vines. Tie down branches whipping in the wind.*

## Did You Know?

### Barbering Ornamental Grasses

Ornamental grasses peak in summer and early fall. Allowing the grasses to stand through winter adds to your pleasure in the view, but you can cut them down any time they lose their looks. Late in the season the stalks flop over, providing some winter protection for the new shoots—nice. But you must give them an annual haircut **before** those new shoots get much growth, or you will be in danger of trimming the newbies with the golden oldies.

The low-growing grasses and new plantings of the big grasses can be trimmed with hand shears. When a big grass matures, simplify the annual haircut by roping the leaves together with sisal twine. Tie them all the way to the top so they end up looking like a telephone pole. Then saw the top off a few inches above the crown. If you use a chain saw, take care not to catch the twine in the teeth!

The best time to barber a grass plant is just as new growth begins, so knowing when to check for growth is helpful. Our grass table divides grasses into **cool-season** and **warm-season grasses**.

**Cool season.** In New York the cool-season grasses begin to grow in late February or in March when winters are mild. If that's your area, when winter relents check to see if they are ready for a haircut.

These grasses are a good choice when you are looking for plants that will be highly visible—the main show—starting early in the growing season.

**Warm season.** The warm-season grasses begin to grow later—late March, April, or even May in the north and in cold years. In mid-spring check their progress, shears in hand.

A warm-season grass is a good choice when you are combining grasses and flowers.

The spring-flowering bulbs come into bloom before and after the grass starts to grow and make the garden pretty while the grass is getting itself together. As the grass grows, it will hide the ripening of the bulb foliage.

# FEBRUARY
## Vines, Ground Covers, & Ornamental Grasses

 ## PLANNING

Place your order for mail-order catalog plants this month.

The ground may be ready to start planting as early as late March or early April in warm Zone 7. Zone 6 gardeners should plan to be ready to plant toward the end of April. In colder zones, planting is often not safe until May.

 ## PLANTING

**Indoors.** Start seeds of **annual vines** late this month or next. **Morning glory, moonflower,** and **hyacinth bean** can be started eight to ten weeks before the outdoor air warms to 60 degrees Fahrenheit. They and many of the perennial vines grow readily from seed.

If you plan to plant lots of ornamental grasses, consider starting your own from seed. See Starting Seeds Indoors under Planting in the January pages of Chapter 1, Annuals.

If you plan to move a vine, root prune it when the ground becomes workable to prepare it for the change. A vine that has been in the ground a year or two can be moved any time before growth begins. Moving a mature vine is a two-year project. See the February pages of Chapter 8, Shrubs, under Planting.

 ## CARE

If there's a thaw in February, you can start cleaning up the ground covers; a light raking will do, just enough to get rid of soggy patches of leaves, twigs, and such.

After warm spells, check new plantings of ground covers, vines, and ornamental grasses for signs of heaving. Gently press the crowns back into the ground. Replenish the mulch, or add a winter mulch of pine boughs to stabilize the temperature of the soil.

 ## PRUNING

When the weather permits, prune weak stems of big-flowered **clematis** like 'Dutchess of Edinburgh', and the Jackmanii group back to a healthy stem. Take dead stems back to the ground. Prune the remaining stems back to a pair of strong buds.

 ## WATERING

**Indoors.** Maintain moisture for seedlings started indoors or in a cold frame or hot bed, and also for vines wintering in containers in a shed or garage.

**Outdoors.** When the ground thaws, check the soil moisture of vines growing under overhanging structures. If the soil is not frozen and dry, water the plants.

 ## FERTILIZING

**Indoors.** Fertilize transplanted seedlings when the appearance of two or three new leaves indicates the root system is growing again.

Every two weeks, fertilize all the seedlings that will remain indoors another six weeks or more with a soluble houseplant fertilizer at half strength.

## PESTS

**Indoors.** Seedlings started indoors that are crowded and lack good drainage and air may show symptoms of damping off, which rots stems near the soil surface. Discard affected plants, reduce watering, and increase light and fresh air. If the problem reappears, mist the seedlings with a fungicide such as Thiram (Arasan).

**Outdoors.** Before buds on vines suspected of, or susceptible to, insect infestation swell, spray them with a dormant horticultural oil. The oil smothers insects and their eggs.

To keep away rabbits, woodchucks, and other rodents attacking vines, try applications of chemical fungicide formulations such as Thiram (Arasan) or hot pepper wax.

## Did You Know?

### About Pruning Vines

All vines need pruning to develop a strong beautiful framework and to enhance production. But the rules vary with the vine. **Wisteria** needs pruning two or three times a year; **clematis** varieties have individual pruning requirements.

Here are some of general guidelines:

• Prune a newly-planted vine lightly the first year or two to direct its growth so that it develops a graceful framework.

• Prune all vines to remove dead, extraneous, or weak wood now and then throughout the growing season.

• Prune large, fast-growing rampant vines like **trumpetcreeper** and **sweet autumn clematis** severely in spring and again as needed. When depends on the plant.

• In late winter and spring, prune **flowering vines that bloom on new wood.** These typically bloom late in the season. Any time just after the coldest part of the season and before growth begins is good. Cut back shoots that bloomed last year to a strong bud(s) near the base of the shoot, leaving the framework of the vine intact.

• In late spring and early summer, right after the flowers fade, prune **flowering vines that bloom on wood produced last year.** These bloom in spring. Cut branchlets that have flowered back to strong replacement shoots or buds; they will carry the next year's flowers. That gives the plant time to mature the wood that will flower the following year.

• In summer, prune **vines grown for their foliage**—like **ivy**—right after the major thrust of seasonal growth. It's best to avoid pruning vines in fall. The wounds heal more slowly, and pruning may stimulate growth, which could come too late to harden off before the first frosts.

## PLANNING

Vines hold moisture, so make sure the lumber you acquire to make a support for a vine is pressure-treated; untreated wood rots in the presence of constant moisture.

When the snow goes, the ground around the ornamental grasses is bare until the grasses get their growth but it doesn't have to be. Plan next fall to plant the area with spring-flowering bulbs and some of the big showy flowers recommended in Companion Plants for Ornamental Grasses on the September pages of this chapter.

## PLANTING

**Sweet peas** are cool-weather plants. When the weather permits, string supports for them and start seeds indoors in individual peat pots.

**Planting vines.** A vine is just a shrub with a boarding-house reach—so for basic how-to information think "shrub," and look in Chapter 8, Shrubs.

• Site the planting hole within reach of the support it will climb, leaving room for the roots to mature without crowding the support.

• Keep 3 inches or more between vine foliage and a house wall. Moisture can cause damage to and through even masonry walls.

• Train a vine destined to climb a wall that will need maintenance on a hinged trellis (that can be lowered for access to the wall) or a framework of wires attached to nails driven into the wall.

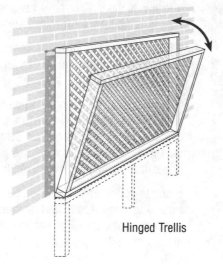

Hinged Trellis

• For walls and fences that need regular painting, choose annual vines. **Dutchman's-pipe** has big, heart-shaped leaves that create a dense screen in a single season.

• Avoid planting vines within reach of trees, large shrubs, windows, or shutters.

• After planting, lead or tie the longest stems to the support with a soft, unobtrusive twine.

## CARE

**Indoors.** Pinch out the growing tips of seedlings that are becoming leggy.

**Outdoors.** After the late winter fertilization described below, top the mulch off to maintain a 2- to 3-inch layer.

## PRUNING

**Ornamental grasses.** Cut cool-season grasses to a few inches above the crown.

**Ground covers.** Shear overgrown ground covers before growth begins, among them **pachysandra** and **myrtle.**

**Vines.** Before growth begins, prune back vines that will bear flowers on shoots that develop this year. Remove wandering and crowded shoots of **sweet autumn clematis** and **trumpet vine** (*Campsis radicans*); they bloom on new wood late in the growing season.

## WATERING

**Indoors.** Continue watering seedlings started indoors. Water vines wintering in containers in a shed or garage often enough to keep the soil slightly damp.

**Outdoors.** Make sure the soil of vines growing under overhangs and pergolas has sufficient moisture.

# FERTILIZING

**Indoors.** Fertilize transplanted seedlings when two or three new leaves signal that growth has begun. Every two weeks, fertilize seedlings that will remain indoors another six weeks with a water-soluble houseplant fertilizer at half strength.

**Outdoors.** Spring clean ground covers, vines, and ornamental grasses; dig in the remains of last year's mulch; and prepare for this year's growth.

*1* Check and adjust the soil pH.

*2* Fertilize:

• If you are using organic fertilizers, apply them four to six weeks before growth begins.

• If you are using chemical fertilizers, apply them just before growth begins.

• If you are using time-release fertilizers, just before growth begins apply an eight-month formulation.

# PESTS

**Indoors.** If damping off rots stems of young seedlings near the soil surface, discard affected plants, reduce watering, and increase light and fresh air circulation. If the problem persists, mist the seedlings with a fungicide, such as Thiram (Arasan).

Apply a new and different spray to vines that deer come to browse on. See Pests, Diseases, and Controls in the Appendix.

Voles are very active eating plants October to March. If you see vole runs, bait the main runway with a rodenticide. See Pests, Diseases, and Controls in the Appendix.

## Did You Know?

### All About Clematis

Clematis species and hybrids have a lot to give. The vines are deciduous and climb by attaching leaf petioles (stalks) to their supports. Once established, clematis species expand at a rate of 5 to 10 feet in a single season and will cover other vegetation, walls, trellises, posts, fences, and arbors. The big beautiful flowers of the clematis hybrids are especially lovely planted with **climbing roses.**

**Site.** Clematis vines need to have their heads in the sun, but the roots need to be in cool, moist earth. If the roots aren't in shade, mulch heavily. A site with protection from strong winds is best; avoid hot, dry, airless sites.

**Soils.** A pH between 6.5 and 7.5 is best, but clematis tolerates somewhat acid soils.

**Support.** Provide a structure of twine or wire for support; use twine or wire to lead the vines to a fence, a tree, or other support.

**Pruning.** Pruning affects the way clematis blooms, and the timing is important. When you buy a clematis, ask for pruning instructions.

Prune clematis that blooms in spring on old wood—for example, **anemone clematis** (*C. montana*) hybrids rosy-red 'Rubens' and white 'Alba'—immediately after flowering to control rampant growth.

In late winter or early spring, prune back large-flowered hybrids like 'Duchess of Edinburgh', a double white; 'Henryi', a large single white; 'Jackmanii Superba', dark purple; and 'Nellie Moser', a mauve pink. These bloom on old and new wood. Take dead stems back to the ground. Prune weak stems back to a healthy stem and the remaining stems back to a pair of strong buds.

To keep its growth in check, in early spring remove congested shoots of **sweet autumn clematis** (*C. terniflora* {formerly *C. maximowicziana*}), a rampant vine that bears a froth of tiny, fragrant, whitish flowers on new wood.

## PLANNING

As the flowering vines come into bloom, record those dates in your garden log as prompts for next year's pruning dates.

**Buying ornamental grasses.** Before you buy ornamental grasses, here are a few things to consider:

- Height and width at maturity.

- Form—upright or fountaining.

- Texture—fine or coarse.

- Color—solid green, variegated, or striped.

- Drainage—most need a well-drained site, but a few do well in moist spots.

- Light—full sun for nearly all.

- Cold hardiness—not all the popular ornamental grasses survive winters in Zones 3, 4, and 5. Quite a few are just fine in Zones 6 and 7. One beautiful grass not likely to winter over even in Zones 6 and 7 is tall **pampas grass,** whose plume-panicles are luminous. The compact variety, *Cortaderia selloana* 'Pumila', does survive most winters there.

## PLANTING

The ground is usually ready for planting in early April in warm Zone 7, toward the end of April in Zone 6, and in May in cooler gardens.

**Indoors.** Transplant seedlings outgrowing their containers to larger pots.

**Outdoors.** Now and through May are excellent planting times for vines, ground covers, and ornamental grasses.

## CARE

Check and repair supports for vines. Provide training wires or strings for annual vines.

When you have prepared the soil for this year's growth, replenish the mulch.

## PRUNING

**Indoors.** Pinch out the tips of leggy seedlings, and transplant the bigger ones to larger pots if the weather is still too cold for transplanting out to the garden.

Give the warm-season grasses an annual haircut.

Remove winter-damaged **pachysandra, barrenwort** (*Epimedium*), and invasive **lamium.** Cut back wandering strands of **vinca.**

## WATERING

**Indoors.** Maintain the soil moisture of seedlings started indoors and of vines wintering in containers in a shed or garage.

## FERTILIZING

If you have not yet prepared the soil for the year's growth, do so now. See Fertilizing, in March.

## PESTS

Apply dormant horticultural oils to vines that had problems last year with whiteflies, spider mites, and scale. See Pests, Diseases, and Controls in the Appendix.

Continue preventive measures to protect your garden from deer.

*Ground covers are vulnerable to curious pets. To keep cats out, apply diatomaceous earth. It doesn't bother dogs, but some of the animal deterrents offered by garden centers do.*

## Did You Know?

### Planting a Ground Cover

A new ground cover takes off and fills out most rapidly when you start with rooted cuttings and plant in fertile, improved soil.

*1* If you will be replacing turf, in early spring or in fall when the soil is dry, spray the bed with Round-Up®, or remove the top layer of turf.

*2* Cover the area with the amendments recommended in the Introduction to the book under Soil Preparation and Improvement, including 2 or 3 inches of compost, decomposed leaves, or peat moss.

*3* Rototill three times over a two-week period, each time 8 inches deep. If you are installing an invasive ground cover such as **ivy** or **ajuga,** bury a 6-inch metal barrier along the border.

*4* To keep weeds out, plant through a cover of 3 inches of mulch. If even minimum weeding will be difficult, plant through a porous landscape fabric; push the edges of the fabric sheet into the ground, and weight them with rocks or heel them in. Make rows of X-shaped slits in the fabric, and insert the plants through the slits with a trowel. Landscape fabric slows the rooting of the above-ground branches, so plant densely.

*5* Working in even rows and starting at the widest end, scoop out a row of evenly spaced planting pockets 8 to 14 inches apart. If you are planting on a slope, dig the holes so the uphill side is lower to keep water from escaping down the slope. Set the cuttings in the hole, and firm them into place.

*6* Position the second row of plants zig-zag between those of the row above. Row three repeats row one; row four repeats row two.

*7* Put down 1½ inches of water right after planting. Newly-planted ground covers need 1½ inches of gentle rain or watering every ten days to two weeks.

*8* Weed faithfully, and keep the mulch topped up until the ground cover has grown dense—at least two years.

*9* Fertilize the bed as and when you do perennials.

Ground covers are vulnerable to curious pets. To keep cats out, apply diatomaceous earth. It doesn't bother dogs, but some of the animal deterrents offered by garden centers do. Train dogs to stay away because their urine will burn plants.

Squirrels dig up new plantings because they are sure you have hidden nuts in the holes. Try cat and dog deterrents to keep them away.

# MAY

 ## PLANNING

Record the date you planted ornamental grasses. Plan to thin or divide the plants every five to ten years.

Check out your garden centers' offerings of tropical and semi-tropical vines. They're great accent plants for patio or porch—like **mandevilla** and **bougainvillea.**

 ## PLANTING

When the weather warms, move seedlings started indoors to a protected shaded spot outdoors to harden off for a week or so, and then transplant them to the garden.

 ## CARE

When the vines start to grow vigorously, carry twine with you when you go to the garden, and tie new shoots to training strings or wires headed in the direction you want them to follow.

Early this month move tropical and semi-tropical vines that have wintered in a shed or garage back to their spot outdoors. Remove the top 2 inches of soil in the pot, and replace it with compost and a slow-release fertilizer in an eight-month formulation.

 ## PRUNING

Prune **anemone clematis,** the *Clematis montana* hybrids, immediately after flowering to reduce its bulk and to control its direction.

Check the new shoots on all vines; cut back to the main framework all shoots not headed in the direction you intend.

Root out seedlings of ground covers that are stepping out of bounds. If you need new plants, pot up the rogues and coddle them until they are growing lustily, then transplant them to bare spots.

Prune—deadhead and pinch back—vines that have finished blooming.

Keep **sweet pea** flowers picked to keep the plants producing.

 ## WATERING

Keep track of the moisture in the soil for seedlings and newly-planted ground covers. Unchecked growth is the name of the growing game, and that requires sustained moisture. If May has little rain, water the garden slowly and deeply every week to ten days.

Check the moisture level in the soil of vines growing in containers even if it rains; their foliage may be keeping the rain from the soil beneath.

 ## FERTILIZING

If you are using granular chemical fertilizers, fertilize every six weeks.

## PESTS

Weeds are flourishing; get them gone.

Apply or change whatever deer deterrents you are using. See the section on Pests, Diseases, and Controls in the Appendix to the book.

*Root out seedlings of ground covers that are stepping out of bounds. If you need new plants, pot up the rogues and coddle them until they are growing lustily, then transplant them to bare spots.*

Early spraying with fungicidal formulations of copper will help to save susceptible plants from blackspot, powdery mildew, rusts, and bacterial diseases such as bacterial leaf spots and wilt.

Depending on your zone, gypsy moths may begin to appear. The Pests section in the May pages of the Trees chapter describes controls.

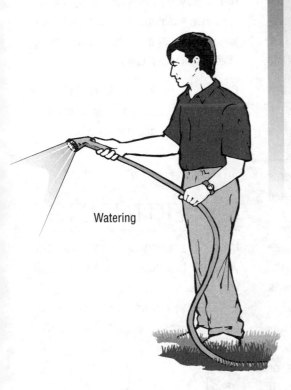

Watering

## Did You Know?

### About Vines and Their Supports

The plant part each vine uses to attach itself to its support tells you what type of support it will need. The support it will need tells you whether a vine is suited to the job you have planned for it. The table of plants in the introduction to this chapter indicates which uses which. There are variations, but here's the general idea:

**Twining stems.** For vines that climb by twining stems, **cross vine** and **wisteria,** for example, suitable supports are narrow—a slim but strong post, a pipe, or wires.

**Tendrils (twisting petioles).** Vines that climb by twisting tendrils—**clematis,** for example—require a structure of wires or wire mesh to climb on.

**Clinging aerial rootlets.** Vines that climb by aerial rootlets that secrete an adhesive glue, like **English ivy,** need only a rugged surface, such as a brick or stucco wall or a rough, unpainted fence for support.

However they climb, vines that eventually will be very heavy—like **climbing hydrangea, bittersweet, trumpet vine,** and **wisteria**—need very strong supports to hold them up.

Vines hold a lot of moisture. It is essential that the lumber you buy to create their support be pressure-treated.

 PLANNING

Good sized container-grown vines, ornamental grasses, and ground covers may be on sale this month, so if you are in the market for new plants, make a point of visiting the garden centers.

 PLANTING

If you are thinking of planting a large transitional area in **ornamental grasses,** consider starting seeds now for transplanting in September or early October. If the grasses you are interested in are named varieties—**blue switchgrass** (*Panicum virgatum*) 'Heavy Metal', for example, not just the original blue switchgrass species—then it's best to plant divisions, as cultivars do not reliably come true from seeds.

Coddling the seeds and monitoring their germination will be easy if you start them in trays or flats kept indoors or in a cold frame. When the seedlings are 2 or 3 inches high, transplant them to an empty row in your kitchen garden or to a sheltered spot in the flower beds. When the rains return in September, transplant the seedlings to permanent homes in the garden.

 CARE

As the vines grow, check the new shoots and adjust them to their supports.

Top up the mulch around your vines. Make sure the roots of the **clematis** vines have enough mulch to stay cool. The heads can be in sun, but the roots need to be cool. We like fine grade hammermill bark, pine and hardwood bark, West Coast fir bark, cedar bark, and cypress. Compost and leafmold (decomposed leaves) are beneficial mulches, but weeds and roots grow into them and they decompose quickly in summer.

PRUNING

As the blooms fade, lightly prune stems and shoots of vines that have finished blooming.

**Annual sweet pea** vines are likely to yellow when summer comes—pull the roots up and compost them. The vines add nitrogen to the soil—as do all legumes. A leafy annual vine, **Dutchman's pipe,** for example, would be a good follow-on plant for **sweet peas,** or plant seedlings of large **marigolds.** If you grow **sweet peas** in the kitchen garden, a good follow-on crop would be a big leafy vegetable such as **kale.**

Run control patrol on established ground covers, and root out and pot up or discard stragglers headed for forbidden pastures.

 WATERING

Keep track of the moisture in the soil for seedlings and newly-planted ground covers. Unchecked growth is the name of the growing game, and that requires sustained moisture. If June has little rain, water the garden slowly and deeply every week to ten days.

Check the moisture level in vines growing in containers even if it rains; their foliage keeps the rain from the soil beneath.

FERTILIZING

If you are using chemical fertilizers, you need to fertilize every six weeks. If you have already applied an organic fertilizer, you won't need to repeat until September.

 PESTS

Keep the beds clear of weeds. Weeds that mature and go to seed will be followed by an army of offspring.

Renew deer deterrents and sprays.

Check vines for lacebug damage. The leaf surfaces will be dull, speckled, and pale, and the undersides will show specks of insect excrement. Spray the foliage with horticultural oil or insecticidal soap as directed on the package.

Whitefly and spider mite damage shows up as spotted and blanched leaves. Remove dead or severely infected shoots, and spray with Neem at the intervals indicated on the package until the infestation is gone. See Pests, Diseases, and Controls in the Appendix.

Watch out for aphids and mites.

Handpick Japanese beetles—they're sluggish in the cool of early morning. Drop them into soapy water, and flush them down a drain. If they multiply, spray the plants with Neem, which will discourage feeding by adults. Try placing Japanese beetle traps far from the plantings you wish to protect, not among them. Insecticides containing Neem, rotenone, or Sevin insecticide are controls. Milky Spore applied this year will help keep populations down next year.

Slugs and snails are good climbers. Diatomaceous earth, a natural control, works in dry soil but isn't effective on moist soil. If June is wet, do them in with iron phosphate (Sluggo), slug and snail bait, and traps. You can make your own slug trap by pouring a little beer into shallow aluminum plates or empty tuna fish cans.

## Did You Know?

### About Pruning Ground Covers

It isn't necessary to prune ground covers every year. But when a ground cover like **pachysandra** matures, it gets straggly. When that happens, prune it before growth begins in order to encourage compact new growth. Do not remove more than a third of the top growth at one time.

- Use hand shears to thin low ground covers like **pachysandra, ivy, vinca.**

- Use hand shears to deadhead **ajuga, myrtle,** and other spring-blooming ground covers immediately after they have bloomed.

- Use head shears to shear **euonymus, juniper, liriope, ophiopogon.**

- Use a string trimmer to cut back **tall meadow plants.**

- Use a hedge trimmer to trim **ferns** when they brown in fall.

- Use a lawn mower (if you can raise it sufficiently—at least 4 inches off the ground) to trim and renew low-growing ground covers such as **ivy** and **myrtle.**

# JULY
## Vines, Ground Covers, & Ornamental Grasses

 ## PLANNING

Assess the summer condition of your ground covers, vines, and ornamental grasses, and make a memo in your garden log suggesting care and improvements to make this fall.

Check garden centers for bargain plants to fill gaps and replace plants lost to winter weather. For ideas, get out your garden catalogs and books, and look up plants suggested in our July sidebar, Spring-Flowering Bulbs Are Great Companion Plants, and the September sidebar, Companion Plants for Ornamental Grasses.

 ## PLANTING

Set tall containers planted in summer-flowering bulbs—**dahlias** and red and yellow **canna,** for example—among beds of ornamental grasses to color the view while waiting for the grasses to rise to their summer or fall glory period.

 ## CARE

Prune and retie new shoots of **clematis, Chinese trumpet creeper,** and other vigorous vines to keep the plants growing in directions that will improve the framework.

 ## PRUNING

**Wisteria** needs pruning two or three times a year to keep its exuberant growth in bounds and to make it produce a sumptuous show of flowers. **Trumpet creeper** can use an extra trim when it gets unruly. The time to do it is soon after the blooms begin to fade. Prune both to establish the framework of the vine and to encourage flowering. Cut the long lateral (side) branches back to two or three buds. You will need to prune again in fall.

Many vines, including **wisteria** and **trumpet creeper,** can be multiplied by rooting cuttings taken now. Rooting cuttings is described in the June pages of Chapter 8, Shrubs.

 ## WATERING

**Vines** that are sheltered from rain benefit from being hosed down now and then in summer—but don't hose a vine when it is coming into, or already in, bloom as that may bruise flowers that are open or make them soggy.

Check the moisture level in vines growing in containers even if it rains; their foliage may be keeping the rain from the soil beneath.

**Ornamental grasses** once established are pretty well drought-tolerant. They only need watering in prolonged droughts. You can tell they need water because the edges of the leaves curl up. Water slowly and deeply, making sure you're laying down at least an $1\frac{1}{2}$ inches of water.

 ## FERTILIZING

If you are using only chemical fertilizers, you will need to fertilize every six weeks.

If you have already applied an organic fertilizer, you won't need to repeat until fall.

 PESTS

Continue preventive measures to protect your garden from deer.

Continue Japanese beetle patrol and control.

Whitefly, mealybugs, scale, spider mites, and aphids multiply in hot, airless spots and will spoil the leaves even if they don't do permanent damage. Spray infestations two or three times with some form of Neem, pyrethrum, or horticultural soaps—they won't harm the environment. You can also use horticultural oils. See the section in the Appendix of the book on Pests, Diseases, and Controls.

Rust loves **lily-of-the-valley** and **ferns.** Control rust by avoiding overhead watering and by cutting out and disposing of infected foliage. Twice a month spray with a horticultural oil, Mancozeb, manzate, or a sulfur- or copper-based fungicide.

Continue weed patrol and control of too-eager ground covers.

## Did You Know?

### Spring-Flowering Bulbs Are Great Companion Plants

Many of the spring-flowering bulbs that catalogs offer at good prices if you order early are excellent companion plants for **ornamental grasses** and low-growing **ground covers.** The bulbs carpet the earth with color while the grasses are waking up. The larger bulbs bloom above ground covers such as **pachysandra, myrtle, ivy,** and **ajuga.** They also show up well against the emerging growth of the grasses, which later masks their ripening foliage.

These **small spring bulb flowers** are very effective planted in front of the taller ornamental grasses—they bloom in about this order in full sun, later in part shade.

- **Early Crocus** (*Crocus* spp. and cvs.)
- **Snowdrops** (*Galanthus*)
- **Winter Aconite** (*Eranthis*)
- **Squill** (*Scilla tubergeniana*)
- **Daffodils** (*Narcissus* Miniatures and Early cvs.)
- **Glory-of-the-Snow** (*Chinodoxa luciliae*)
- **Bluebell** (*Hyacinthoides non-scripta*)
- **Grape Hyacinth** (*Muscari* spp. and cvs.)
- **Botanical/Species Tulips** (*Tulipa* spp.)
- **Giant Snowflake, Summer Snowflake** (*Leucojum aestivum*)

These **large-flowering bulbs** are attractive planted here and there among ground covers, and they add early color to beds of ornamental grasses.

- **Yellow Daffodils**
- **Lily-flowered Tulips**
- **Red Parrot Tulips**
- **Fosteriana Tulips,** 'White Emperor', 'Orange Emperor', 'Red Emperor'
- *Tulipa greigii,* 'Sweet Lady', 'Goldwest', 'Oriental Splendour'
- **Foxtail Lily** (*Eremurus stenophyllus*)
- **Giant Onion** (*Allium giganteum*)
- **Indian Lily** (*Camassia quamash*)

# AUGUST
## Vines, Ground Covers, & Ornamental Grasses

 PLANNING

Spend some time in the early morning or late afternoon asking your plants for progress reports.

Summer heat and drought reveal the vulnerabilities of plants, sites, and your annual soil maintenance program. Young **vines** whose leaves are showing crisped edges here and there may need more consistent watering. Patches of **ground cover** that are wilting when others do not may need you to add more mulch or more humus when you fertilize and refurbish the soil early next year.

 PLANTING

In spite of the heat and drought, container-grown **vines, ground covers,** and the smaller **ornamental grasses** can be planted successfully this month as long as you water them every week or so and hose them down with a gentle spray if they wilt on hot days.

 CARE

After summer thunderstorms, check the **vines** and make sure they are securely fastened to their supports.

 PRUNING

By now, aggressive vines like **sweet autumn clematis, trumpet creeper,** and **wisteria** will have made a lot of new growth; prune to thin excess growth and to keep the main stems developing a desirable framework.

 WATERING

Now and then, hose down and water **vines** that are sheltered from rain. Check the moisture level in vines growing in containers even if it rains; their foliage keeps the rain from the soil beneath.

This month is usually dry, so expect to compensate for the missing rain by watering **ground covers, vines,** and **ornamental grasses** two or three times this month, every week to ten days. The ideal is to put down 1½ inches of water at each session.

Overhead watering is fine as long as you water deeply. There's less waste if you water before the sun reaches the garden in the early morning or late afternoon or evening. In hot dry periods, daytime overhead watering lowers leaf temperatures and reduces stress.

 FERTILIZING

If you are using chemical fertilizers, you should be fertilizing every six weeks or so.

If you have already applied an organic fertilizer, you won't need to repeat until fall.

If **vines** fertilized with a time-release chemical fertilizer are failing to grow as expected, supplement with a foliar feeding of water-soluble organic or fast-acting liquid fertilizers.

Patches of **pachysandra** that are browning, wilting, and dying may be getting too much sun in winter when the leaves fall, or they may be suffering from volutella leaf and stem blight. Spraying with a copper-based fungicide helps the blight. Scale and mites can also be a problem; the control is to spray with an ultrafine horticultural oil.

*Spend some time in the early morning or late afternoon asking your plants for progress reports. Summer heat and drought reveal the vulnerabilities of plants, sites, and your annual soil maintenance program.*

## PESTS

Change deer deterrents and sprays around in the garden.

Clear the **ground covers** and other beds of all weeds; don't let them grow up and go to seed!

High humidity and heat encourages powdery mildew. Avoid overhead watering, and apply sulfur, ultrafine horticultural oil, copper fungicide, Immunox, or Bayleton.

Check for fungal leaf spot, and apply a fungicide if needed. If you see continuing signs of mites, hose the plant down regularly and spray with insecticidal soaps or ultrafine horticultural oils.

## Did You Know?

### How to Calculate the Amount of Ground Cover Needed

To know how many plants you will need to fill an area with a ground cover, divide the square footage of the bed by the amount of space each plant will need. Here's the drill:

Start by measuring the area to be planted. Outline the bed with shrub and tree marking paint or a hose, and then measure the length and the width. Multiply the length by the width, and that gives you the square footage. To get the approximate size of a free-form shape, outline the area with a hose, and then shape the hose into a square or a rectangle that encompasses the area, measure, and multiply the length by the width.

Next, divide the spacing required for the plant you have chosen into the square footage of the area to be planted. The answer is the number of plants you will need. Most plant tags recommend spacing between or around plants. Typical spacing for crowns of **Japanese painted fern** is 24 inches apart; for **'Munstead' lavender,** 15 inches; for **dusty miller,** 8 inches apart. The number of inches "apart" means "all around." To get the square inches needed for one dusty miller plant, multiply 8 times 8, which gives you 64 square inches. Divide 64 into the square footage of the area multiplied by 12, the number of inches in a foot. That tells you how many plants you will need.

Some growers' tags indicate how many plants to set out per square yard; Blooms of Bressingham tags recommend for the **barren strawberry** (*Waldsteinea ternate*) 'Red Ruby Strawberry' three to four plants per square yard. A square yard is 9 square feet. Dividing 9 (square feet) by four (plants) yields 2.2—one plant for every 2.2 square feet.

Small ground covers that spread are planted one to four per square foot—four for upright plants like **pachysandra;** one to two for vining plants like **vinca**—two plants if it is rooted in a small pot, one if it is rooted in a large pot.

The more closely spaced these ground covers are, the sooner they fill in the area. Widely spaced plants will need two or three years to fill in.

# SEPTEMBER

##  PLANNING

If you would like to reduce the need to hand trim grasses around deciduous trees, plan to under-plant them with low-maintenance all-season **ground covers** like **ajuga, lamium,** or **vinca**—plants that can take shade in summer and sun in winter. Indian summer is a good time for the project. Here's what's involved:

*1* To avoid disturbing tree and shrub feeder roots located in the top 12 inches of the soil, remove the turf by hand.

*2* Starting 4 or 5 inches from the trunk, add 4 to 5 inches of topsoil, and top that with 2 to 3 inches of humus—compost, partially decomposed leaves or seaweed, or other decomposed organic material.

*3* Over every 100 square feet (an area 10 by 10 feet) spread the following—available at any garden center.

Holly-tone: 4 to 7 pounds
Superphosphate: 3 to 5 pounds
Green sand: 5 to 10 pounds
Clay soils only: gypsum 5 to
  10 pounds
Osmocote® four-month: 2 pounds

*4* Work all this into the bed by hand.

*5* Rake the bed smooth, and plant your ground cover. Mulch 2 to 3 inches deep.

*6* Water slowly and gently to put down about 1½ inches of water.

*7* Water every week to ten days if you run into a dry spell.

*8* In the following years, fertilize an evergreen ground cover with lawn fertilizer when you fertilize the lawn. Fertilize a flowering ground cover twice annually with Holly-tone.

## PLANTING

Now and as the first leaves begin to fall is an excellent planting season for **vines, ground covers, ornamental grasses,** and their companion plants. Warm Zone 7 gardeners can plant into October and even November some years.

## CARE

When temperatures head below 60 degrees Fahrenheit, move **cold tender** and **tropical vines** to a greenhouse or try them as houseplants. Or move them to a frost-free shed, attached garage, or root cellar.

##  PRUNING

You can divide-to-multiply established stands of **blue fescue, blue oat grass, feather reed grass,** and many other grasses and **ground covers** early this month.

**Wisteria** benefits from pruning two or three times a year. Give it its second trim now or in October. Cut the laterals back again leaving only two or three buds to each shoot.

## WATERING

If your vines are sheltered from rain, even when rainfall is plentiful, make sure the soil doesn't dry out.

## FERTILIZING

If you are using organic blends, such as Holly-tone or Plant-tone, then you will need to fertilize the last time this month.

If you are using chemical fertilizers, the last fertilization for garden and container plants can be a little later—by the end of this month or early next month.

*When temperatures head below 60 degrees Fahrenheit, move
cold tender and tropical vines to a greenhouse or try them as houseplants.
Or move them to a frost-free shed, attached garage, or root cellar.*

If you are using time-release fertilizers, the spring applications of an eight-month formulation should carry the plants through the end of the growing season.

 PESTS

Change the deer deterrents you are using to keep them deterred!

Give new **ground covers** a radical weeding. Check and remove ground covers creeping outside their boundaries.

Weed around **vines** and **ornamental grasses,** scratching up the soil so that fall rains can give the plants a deep watering.

## Did You Know?

### Companion Plants for Ornamental Grasses

Ornamental grasses can stand alone as specimen plants. But to achieve a naturalistic effect, plan to include foliage, bark, and stem plants—that's the way nature designs her wild gardens.

For structure and contrast, include small and medium-sized deciduous trees such as:

- **Chinese dogwood** (*Cornus kousa* var. *chinensis*)
- **Franklin tree** (*Franklinia alatamaha*)
- **Fringe tree** (*Chionanthus retusus*)
- **Serviceberry, Shadblow** (*Amelanchier* spp.)
- **Witchhazel** (*Hamamelis* x *intermedia* cvs.)

For change and as foils to the dramatic effects of the dried seedheads and foliage in the winter landscape, include shrubs and some evergreens:

- **Azaleas and Rhododendrons**
- **Cotoneaster**(*Cotoneaster* cvs.)
- **Fountain Buddleia** (*Buddleia alternifolia*)
- **Rugosa rose** (*Rosa rugosa* 'Sir Thomas Lipton')
- **Siebold Viburnum** (*Viburnum sieboldii*)
- **Winterberry** (*Ilex verticillata* 'Sparkleberry')

For contrast with the grasses' buff and tan, sea green and green, gold and pale gold colors, plant colorful, carefree perennials:

- **Asters** (*Aster* spp. and cvs.)
- **Astilbe** (*Astilbe* x *arendsii*)
- **Black-eyed Susan** (*Rudbeckia fulgida* var. *sullivantii* 'Goldsturm')
- **Catmint** (*Nepeta faassenii*)
- **Daylilies** (*Hemerocallis* cvs.)
- **Joe-pye Weed** (*Eupatorium purpureum*)
- **Purple Coneflower** (*Echinacea purpurea* and cvs.)
- **Russian Sage** (*Perovskia atriplicifolia*)
- **Sedum, Stonecrop** (*Sedum spectabile* 'Autumn Joy' and cvs.)
- **Tickseed** (*Coreopsis verticillata* 'Golden Showers')'
- **Yellow Loosestrife** (*Lisimachia punctata*)
- **Fern-leaved Yarrow** (*Achillea filipendula* 'Coronation Gold')

# PLANNING

**Ornamental grass** gardens peak this month. Plan to visit nearby public and botanic gardens to learn more about keeping the garden beautiful in fall.

The Friendship Garden at the U.S. National Arboretum in Washington, D.C. is a brilliant example of a grass garden designed for the average ranch home. It covers a one-third acre front yard, and its seasonal progression offers examples for us all.

The plants develop throughout the year without pruning, staking, spraying, or deadheading. In late winter, the grasses are cut back to the ground, mulched, and fertilized as growth begins. Watering is by underground or surface irrigation system. Seedheads ripen and stand through fall and winter. Fruiting and berry-producing plants promote a healthy ecological balance that encourages birds and does not exclude insects. A majority of insects are beneficial, as we explain in Pests, Diseases, and Controls in the Appendix to the book.

Color, texture, and unfolding growth are present in all four seasons. In spring, naturalized flowering bulbs carpet spaces between the cut-back ornamental grasses. **Lily-flowered tulips** and other exotic forms bloom with **narcissus** and **species iris.** In summer, easy-care flowering perennials like **black-eyed Susan** and **Russian sage** bloom along the walks and among the half-grown grasses.

From early summer to fall, the dominant grasses lift tall, light-catching inflorescences to the wind. The tallest grasses and a few **hollies** shield the gift shop from the road. Smaller species grow closer to the building. A few small, well-placed native trees and flowering or fruiting shrubs mimic a meadow's variety. Additional seasonal color comes from big tubs of annuals, vegetables, and herbs.

In late summer and early fall, sweeps of **sedum** turn russet-pink-coral, then fade to brown, and the trees color red and orange. With cold weather, **ornamental grasses** stand tall—rustling, tossing in the wind, and eventually binding snow at their feet.

Through all its seasons, the broad paths and comfortable stopping places invite meditation. For the birds and other small creatures, there are banquets of seeds, insects, worms, as well as nesting spaces and materials in this garden where chemical controls are never needed.

# PLANTING

Continue to divide, move, and transplant vines, ground covers, and ornamental grasses, and to set out spring-flowering bulbs and other suitable companion plants.

# CARE

In fall, clear your ground cover of fallen leaves with a leaf blower.

# PRUNING

Limit pruning to dead or diseased material.

# WATERING

Check the soil around **vines** sheltered from rain, and make sure it's moderately damp. The roots are still growing even if the air is cold, and water is essential.

# FERTILIZING

If you are using fertilizers that are organic blends, such as Holly-tone or Plant-tone, fertilize now if you didn't do it last month.

*Continue to divide, move, and transplant vines, ground covers, and ornamental grasses, and to set out spring-flowering bulbs and other suitable companion plants.*

If you are using only chemical fertilizers, the last fertilization should be before the final weeks of Indian summer.

If you are using time-release fertilizers, a spring application of an eight-month formulation should carry the plants through the end of the growing season—no fertilizer need be added at this time.

 PESTS

Apply or change whatever deer deterrents you are using. See the section on Pests, Diseases, and Controls in the Appendix.

Voles get active again in October. If their runs appear around vines, bait the main runway with a rodenticide. André Viette's winter baiting station is a pair of paper cups scented with apple juice, with a dose of the bait in the bottom, set under a half-tire. Another way is to nestle the baited cups in straw held down by plywood and topped with a brick or a big stone. Be sure pets cannot get to the bait.

## Did You Know?

### Ground Covers for Problem Sites

If you find turf grass high-maintenance or have a problem with growing it under trees, consider these solutions:

**Lawn substitute.** Four ground covers are commonly used as substitutes for turf lawns. They are evergreen and can be walked on occasionally without being damaged.

- **English Ivy** (*Hedera helix*). An evergreen with tough glossy dark green leaves on woody vines. There are lovely small-leaved and also variegated forms.
- **Pachysandra, Japanese Spurge** (*Pachysandra terminalis*). Low-growing, wide-spreading, formal ground cover. Short green-white flower spikes in early spring.
- **Vinca, Periwinkle** (*Vinca minor*). Small, dainty, shiny dark green leaves on slim trailing stems 2 to 3 feet long. Lavender-blue flowers in early spring.
- **Wintergreen, Checkerberry** (*Gaultheria procumbens*). Evergreen shrubby ground-hugging mat with aromatic foliage and bright berries.

**Under trees.** Tree shade and root competition are hard on turf grass. These ground covers do well under trees.

- **Bugleweed** (*Ajuga reptans*). Semi-evergreen rosettes of leaves and flowering spikes in blue or white in spring.
- **Hosta.** Small colorful hostas like 8-inch 'Gold Edger'; 3-inch 'Venusta'; 7-inch *H. helemoides*.
- **Golden Moneywort** (*Lysimachia nummularia*) 'Aurea'. Deciduous, lime-green, low-growing, and spreads rapidly in moist soil. In early summer, it bears masses of small cup-shaped yellow flowers.
- **Lilyturf** (*Liriope muscari*). Grass-like, and 12 to 18 inches high. Flowering spikes in blue, purple, lavender, or white in late summer.
- **Lily-of-the-valley** (*Convallaria majalis*). Deciduous, lovely 6- to 8-inch high ground cover ideal for open woodlands. The flowers are exquisitely fragrant.
- **Spotted Deadnettle** (*Lamium maculatum*). Semi-evergreen, low-growing, silver-white-green variegated foliage lightens the shadows. Pink or white florets in May and June.

# NOVEMBER
## Vines, Ground Covers, & Ornamental Grasses

 PLANNING

Plan to bring the garden indoors for winter.

Gather armfuls of the most beautiful grasses and their seedheads, tie them loosely in bunches, and hang them to dry upside down in a dark, dry, warm place. Keep them from shedding by spraying them with hair spray or a spray varnish. When they are dry turn the bundles right side up and display them in tall vases. Seedheads bound together make attractive table decorations and ornaments for the Christmas tree.

Harvest strands of **clematis** several feet long while they still are pliant, prune away small shoots, and twine the stems into a circle to make a wreath. Tie the circle with raffia and let the wreath dry, and then you can use it as is or use raffia to tie on dried herbs, flowers, or seedheads of the grasses.

 PLANTING

If you have unplanted containers of **vines, ground covers,** or **ornamental grasses,** water them thoroughly, and sink the pots up over the container rims in empty spaces in the kitchen garden or elsewhere. With a winter mulch of evergreen boughs, they should still be good to go in late winter when the ground dries enough for planting.

 CARE

Rake away leaves creating mats over patches of **ground covers.**

 PRUNING

Use an edger to control ground covers like **ajuga** and **vinca.** Pot offsets and plantlets, and store them in a frost-free place or sink them in the ground to fill empty spots later.

 WATERING

Before the first anticipated hard freeze, water all your **vines, ground covers,** and **ornamental grasses** slowly, deeply, and thoroughly.

 FERTILIZING

There is no fertilization this month.

 PESTS

In deer country, wrap susceptible **evergreen vines** with Reemay, or if they have been attacked in the past, circle them with bird netting or chicken wire cages. Change whatever deer deterrents you are using. See the section on Pests, Diseases, and Controls in the Appendix of the book.

If vole runs appear around shrubs, bait the main runway with a rodenticide. See Pests, Diseases, and Controls in the Appendix.

## Did You Know?

### Multiply by Dividing

You can fill gaps, empty spots, or start new beds by dividing to multiply.

### Vines

Many vines, including **wisteria** and **trumpet vine,** are easily multiplied by rooting cuttings of parent plants. The process is described in the June pages of Chapter 8, Shrubs.

Annual vines and some perennial vines will grow from seed. Some need stratification (chilling) to germinate. Seeds of **trumpet vine** sown in the fall will germinate some months later. Planting in the November pages in Chapter 6, Perennials, describes the process of stratification. Seeds to be stratified this time of year are sown out in the garden.

### Ground Covers

Some ground covers can be started from seed, including common **myrtle** (*Vinca minor*). When seeds are available, starting the plants yourself from seed is the most cost-efficient way, but remember that named varieties may not come true from seed gathered in your garden.

Most ground covers root easily from cuttings or root division. Those that multiply by means of above-ground runners, like **ajuga** and **vinca,** you can divide by simply cutting the plantlet from the parent and digging it up and transplanting.

**Ivy** is easy. You can divide a densely-rooted clump in spring, but cuttings taken in late summer or early fall root more quickly. **Lamium** cuttings root easily in spring; divisions of the plant root easily in spring or early fall. Rampant growers like **creeping Jenny** (*Lysimachia nummularia*) can be grown from cuttings taken in spring or divisions planted in fall. **Pachysandra** will root from cuttings almost all year round, but we find the easiest is to dig clumps in very early spring before the plants start to grow or in early fall. Dig the clumps by shovel and include as much of the roots and the soil clump as you can get.

**Ferns** are usually propagated by root division in spring. Plants that clump, like **liriope,** are multiplied by dividing a mature crown; use a spading fork to lift and gently break the clump apart, or use a spade to cut the clump apart.

### Ornamental Grasses

You can buy seeds to start some ornamental grass species (but not so many hybrids or cultivars), including **blue fescue** (*Miscanthus sinnensis*) and the **fountain grasses.** To get a head start, sow the seeds indoors early next year. Starting Seeds Indoors under Planting in the January pages of Chapter 1, Annuals explains the process.

**Grasses** are not likely to need division for at least five to ten years. However, once a grass has filled out, you can divide the crown every year. Use a spading fork to lift and gently break the clump apart, or use a spade to cut the clump apart. The important thing is to be sure that each division has at least one growing point.

Most grasses are best divided in spring, before new growth begins, including **fountain grass, Chinese silver grass,** and **switch grass.** The smaller grasses can be divided in spring but also in fall, including **blue fescue, blue oat grass,** and **feather reed grass.**

# DECEMBER
## Vines, Ground Covers, & Ornamental Grasses

 PLANNING

If you are considering planting a slope with a **ground cover,** think outside the box. Consider, for example, **forsythia.** Most species and varieties are upright or/and fountaining, but low-growing *Forsythia* x *intermedia* 'Arnold Dwarf' roots where it touches, can withstand drought, and needs only periodic trimming. Deer don't munch forsythia, which is an added advantage. To bloom at the same time as your forsythia hill, naturalize bulbs—**daffodils, narcissus,** and **lemon yellow daylilies**—between the shrubs. They'll help cover the slope and maintain the soil there.

Another idea is low-growing **roses.** A new series of ground cover roses won Gold Medals in 1996 from rose societies in Australia, Britain, and America. These bloom continuously, are immune to pests and diseases, and do not need deadheading. The plants are 2 to 2½ feet tall by 4 feet across. The star is 'Flower Carpet', whose blooms are lavender pink and spicily perfumed. 'Jeeper's Creepers' is a white variety, and 'Baby Blanket' is a light pink. Any of them would add to the beauty of your garden and can help cover bare spots.

 PLANTING

Planting is over for this year. Take the time to assess what did and did not grow well last year, and consider whether to move or replace vines, ground covers, and ornamental grasses.

 CARE

Use evergreen boughs to provide winter protection for **ginger, Lenten rose,** and other evergreen ground covers that suffer in cold weather. A discarded Christmas tree provides greens to cover them.

 PRUNING

Prune **wisteria** laterals back again if you haven't done it a second or third time; leave only two or three buds to each shoot.

Peruse garden catalogs to see if there are any new pruning tools that would make your job easier next year. Family and friends would probably appreciate knowing your holiday gift wishes.

 WATERING

**Indoors.** Keep the soil for tropical and semi-tropical **vines** wintering indoors moderately damp.

 FERTILIZING

Nothing to fertilize this month. Be sure any leftover fertilizers are tightly sealed and stored away from children and pets.

 PESTS

The scent-carrying oils in deer deterrents don't volatilize in cold air. If you are concerned, wrap **hydrangea** and other still-green vines in Reemay for the winter.

If vole runs appear around shrubs, bait the main runway with a rodenticide.

# CHAPTER ELEVEN

# Water and Bog Plants

*Water cradling aquatic flowers in bloom, the sound of water rushing over stones,
the glow of a fountain splashing in the moonlight—to have it all is surprisingly easy.
Space, dollars, and even maintenance are not issues.*

You can install, plant, and maintain a water garden more easily than you can install a flowering border of comparable size. You don't even need a yard to have a water garden—all you need is enough space for whatever container you have in mind. In our climate, even in warm Zone 7, a small water garden freezes, but the hardy water garden plants can handle that. You can ready the pond at any season, but the best time for planting a water garden is mid-spring.

**Water garden containers**. A water garden consists of a container, water, plants, and fish. It can be as small as a wall fountain or as simple as a Chinese water pot or a half-barrel out on your patio. Preformed plexiglass liners in sizes up to about 10 by 10 feet are used to contain smaller in-ground ponds. Larger, free-form, in-ground ponds are waterproofed by relatively inexpensive flexible rubber liners or some form of cement or gunnite.

**Fountains, streams, and waterfalls**. To enjoy sparkle and splash, you will need to add a pump that pushes the water through a bubbler or a fountainhead. The electrical installation should

be made by a qualified electrician and should include a ground-fault circuit interrupter. Upgrading to a pump and adding a filter to the system improves aeration. To return the water to the pond via a stream or waterfall, you will need a pump able to lift the water and move it the distance involved; pump manufacturers' packaging usually provides this information.

**Recirculating bog gardens.** An interesting and environmentally friendly way to filter the water and return it to the pond is via a garden (recirculating and water-proofed by a liner) of **bog plants** and a pebble-lined stream.

You can have a beautiful pond without pump or filter. The magic formula given in the April pages is a combination of plants, fish, and critters that does a pretty good job of keeping the pond components in balance. In addition, Richard Koogle, director of

operations at the Lilypons Water Gardens nursery, recommends the use of a supplemental bacterial product that controls algae by speeding the decomposition of waste from fish and plants. This is especially important if you are not using a pump or filter.

An in-ground water garden comes together in four basic steps:

*1* Prepare the physical container and complete the excavation for the pond and other features on which you have decided—recirculating bog garden, streambed, or waterfall. You waterproof the system and add water.

*2* If you are using a recirculating pump and a filter, they go in next.

*3* Set containers of water garden plants under the water. Some may need to be raised on platforms,

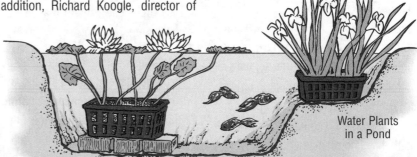

Water Plants
in a Pond

## Did You Know?

### About Bog Gardens

A recirculating bog garden will improve your water garden's filtering system. It's a shallow pond waterproofed with a flexible liner and planted with **bog plants.** A streambed that leads the water back to the pond is part of it. The plants rooted in gravelly muck at the bottom take up nutrients that feed on undesirable algae; this helps to keep the water clear and fresh.

Typically, a bog garden and streambed are about 12 inches deep. The bottom is a planting bed consisting of about 4 inches of coarse gravel topped by 4 inches of pea gravel or sand. You plant the roots and ball of soil around the **bog plants** directly in the gravel at a depth that gives them about $1/2$ to 1 inch of water overhead.

Avoid invasive bog plants like **saggitaria,** which takes over unless diligently weeded. Instead use **irises, papyrus,** and **dwarf bamboo** (*Dulichium arundinaceum*), a low-growing, feathery bamboo-like plant that stays less than 15 to 18 inches tall and is not overly invasive.

which can be pots, bricks, or stones. Plants for a recirculating bog garden are rooted in the gravelly mix at the bottom of the bog.

*4* Release fish, snails, and other livestock to help control pests and unwanted algae—and for the pleasure of learning more about them.

## PLANTING

Like land plants, water garden plants respond to fertilizing and have active and dormant seasons. Some are hardy, surviving our **frost-belt** winters; others are tropical and need winter protection in our region. The containers for pond plants have no drainage holes.

There are three groups: **submerged or oxygenating** plants; **aquatics;** and the usually upright, or marginal, **bog plants** that edge a pond and/or live in a connected bog garden.

*1* **Submerged plants.** Also called oxygenating plants, these are leafy stems that grow up from containers at the bottom of the pond. They are there to add oxygen to the water and to take up nutrients that otherwise fuel algae growth that makes water murky.

*2* **Aquatics.** These are floaters. Some are **large-leaved floating plants,** and some are **small-leaved floating plants.** The stars are the **water lilies** and the **lotus.** They bear exotic blossoms and spread big beautiful leaves that provide fish with cool shade and a refuge from predators.

The **small-leaved floating plants** are mainly for contrast. They trace delicate green patterns between the lily pads and the **lotus** leaves. Some bear tiny flowers. The prettiest are species of *Nymphoides* whose flowers are $3/4$ of an inch across and centered by yellow stamens. They flower abundantly spring through fall. Another popular little floater is **Australian water clover** (*Marsilea mutica*), a dainty little plant that looks just like its nickname, **four-leaf clover.**

*3* **Bog plants.** Also known as marginal plants because they are placed at the margins of a water garden, these upright forms thrive in partially-submerged containers, at the pond's edge, or in a bog's mucky soil or gravel. Some are narrow-leaved, like water-loving varieties of **irises,** and others are broad-leaved, like **elephant's ear.** These linear forms provide contrast with the flat, floating forms of the aquatics, adding to the beauty of the water garden.

**Bog plants** can also be planted in a naturally wet spot. But before planting in any area big enough to be considered a wetland, consult the local environmental authorities.

# Water and Bog Plants

## CARE

Here's a look at year-round maintenance for an established water garden:

**Spring.** Clear organic debris and leaves from the pond, the bog area, stream, or waterfall. If the pond is small, empty and clean it, and then refill it. Groom and fertilize the perennial plants. Start the pump (which has to be shut off for winter). Add a supplemental bacterial product to speed the decomposition of waste from fish and plants, especially if you are not using a pump and filter. Resume feeding the fish. Clean the filter as needed. Maintain the water level.

**Spring/summer.** Clean the filter. Remove fading foliage and blooms. Feed the fish. Every thirty days add a pellet to kill mosquito larvae. Anytime plants and or livestock are in the pond, it is necessary to keep up the water level. Wind, sun, and dry weather can evaporate so much pond water that you might think the liner is leaking, especially if it is running over a waterfall and over a bog garden or streambed.

**Fall.** Keep the pond as clear of leaves as you can. If it is small, cover it with deer fence or some other mesh to keep the leaves out. Lift the pump, clean it, and bring it indoors. We've had bad luck with pumps left in the pond for winter. Shut the pond down for winter. If the pond is small and less than 30 inches deep, fish may be safer indoors

in a fish tank for the winter. In Zone 5 we bring ours in despite the fact we've seen goldfish survive brutal winters in ponds smaller and shallower than ours. Maintain the water level.

Bring indoors for the winter **hardy lilies** not so hardy in your zone and all the **tropical lilies** and tender **bog plants.**

**Winter.** Where fish and plants will winter in the pond, put a de-icer to work.

## Did You Know?

### About Water Lilies

Water lilies are the stars of the water garden. They come into bloom and fade away over a period of three to four days. There are two types:

**Hardy water lilies** that we mention are perennial in New York's Zone 4 and southward. The choice for Zone 3 is more limited. Some water lilies that are naturally hardy in Zone 3 may not survive winters in small, shallow ponds under 30 inches deep. When in doubt, winter your hardy lilies indoors as suggested for tropical lilies. Planted after the chill of early spring but before growth gets underway, hardy water lilies may produce blooms the first summer, but most need two to three years to reach their peak. The flowers are open only during the day.

**Tropical water lilies** can be planted when temperatures average 75 degrees Fahrenheit or above—May-June in Zone 7; June in Zone 4. They aren't recommended for planting in Zone 3. They open the year they are planted. To keep them for another year, collect and store the tubers in a frost-free location for the winter. There are day- and night-blooming varieties. Day bloomers are sweetly fragrant; night bloomers are headily scented, open as the stars come out, and stay open until late morning. In warmer regions, these tropical lilies sometimes continue to bloom after the hardy water lilies have shut down for the season.

**One of a pond owner's few chores is removing yellowing foliage.** A lily pruner makes the job easy. Removing closed, four-day-old blossoms seems to speed the rate at which water lilies present new flower buds.

## PESTS

If predators are plentiful in your area, make the sides of the pond excavation vertical. That makes fishing harder. You might also place a few cinder blocks in the pond to give the fish extra hiding places.

# Water and Bog Plants

## Aquatic Plants

| Common Name (Botanical Name) | Hardiness Zones | Light | Type |
| --- | --- | --- | --- |
| Anacharis (Egeria densa) | 5 to 10 | Sun | Submerged/oxygenating plant. |
| Australian Water Clover (Marsilea mutica) | 6 to 11 | Sun to part sun | Small aquatic with floating leaves. |
| Coontail (Ceratophyllum demersum) | 4 to 10 | Sun to part sun | Submerged/oxygenating plant. |
| Dwarf Saggitaria (Sagittaria subulata) | 5 to 11 | Sun to part shade | Submerged/oxygenating plant. |
| Lotus (Nelumbo spp. and cvs.) | 4 to 11 | Sun | Large flowering aquatic. |
| Myriophyllum (Myriophyllum spp.) | 4 to 11, according to species | Sun to part sun | Submerged/oxygenating plant. |
| Parrot's-feather (Myriophyllum aquaticum) | 6 to 10 | Sun to part shade | Small aquatic with floating leaves. |
| Snowflake, Floating-heart (Nymphoides spp.) | 5 to 11 | Sun to part sun | Small flowering aquatic with floating leaves. |
| Water Lilies, Hardy (Nymphaea cvs.) | 3 to 10 | Sun | Large flowering aquatic. |
| Water Lilies, Tropical Nymphaea spp. and cvs.) | 10 to 11 | Sun to part shade | Large flowering aquatic. |
| Wild Celery (Valisneria americana) | 4 to 11 | Sun to part sun | Submerged/oxygenating plant. |

# Water and Bog Plants

## Marginal Plants

| Common Name (*Botanical Name*) | Hardiness Zones | Light | Height |
| --- | --- | --- | --- |
| **Arrowhead** (*Sagittaria* spp. and cvs.) | Varies with species | Sun to part sun | 2 to 4 feet |
| **Sweet Flag, Calamus** (*Acorus calamus*) | 4 to 11 | Sun to part sun | 30 to 36 inches |
| **Canna** (*Canna* spp. and cvs.) | 7 to 10 | Sun | 6 feet plus |
| **Dwarf Bamboo** (*Dulichium arundinaceum*) | 6 to 11 | Sun to part sun | 15 to 18 inches |
| **Dwarf Papyrus** (*Cyperus haspan*) | Tropical | Sun to part shade | 30 inches |
| **Elephant's Ear** (*Colocasia* spp. and cvs.) | Tender perennial | Any light | 5 feet |
| **Golden Club** (*Orontium aquaticum*) | 6 to 10 | Sun to shade | 18 inches |
| **Horsetail** (*Equisetum hyemale*) | 3 to 11 | Sun to shade | Up to 4 feet |
| **Iris** (*Iris* spp. and cvs.) | 4 to 9 | Sun to part shade | Up to 4 feet |
| **Lizard's Tail** (*Saururus cernuus*) | 4 to 9 | Sun to part shade | Up to 2 feet |
| **Narrow-leaved Cattail** (*Typha angustifolia*) | 2 to 11 | Sun to part sun | To 4 feet |
| **Pickerel Rush** (*Pontederia cordata*) | 3 to 11 | Sun | 2 to 3 feet |
| **Spike Rush** (*Eleocharis montevidensis*) | 6 to 9 | Sun to part sun | To 12 inches |
| **Water Arum** (*Peltandra virginica*) | 5 to 9 | Sun to part sun | 2 to 3 feet |
| **White Bullrush** (*Scirpus albescens*) | 5 to 11 | Sun to part sun | 4 to 6 feet |

## PLANNING

**January is a fine time to plan a water garden.** Study your grounds from indoors to determine where you'd like to see a pond, keeping in mind a water garden's need for light, good drainage, and so on.

**Potential locations.** On flat land, a pond in the curve of a flower border is quite lovely. A stone wall or a fence can be an appealing backdrop. A sloping yard invites an installation of small ponds spilling into each other, a good spot to establish a recirculating bog garden and stream. If you are home mostly in the evening, or wish to grow the fragrant night-blooming **tropical water lilies,** look for a spot where you can see the pond surface reflecting sunsets and moonrises.

If the yard is tiny, you might pave it and install a fountain splashing water back into a basin. For a deck, the water garden could be a Chinese water pot with a **miniature water lily** surrounded by potted plants or a wall fountain planted with a single small **floating-leaved plant.**

**Light, power, water, maintenance.** Light influences blooming. For **water lilies** and **lotus** to bloom fully, they must receive at least six hours of direct sun daily. If your pond is to be aerated by a sun-powered fountain, the site must be in full sun.

If you plan to have an electrically run pump to move water, the pond must have access to a power source and include a ground fault circuit interrupter. It also must be within reach of a hose. For low maintenance, try to avoid sites that collect blown debris and leaves.

If your pond is to be an in-ground installation, make sure the site isn't home to buried electrical, gas, or water lines.

**Drainage.** Good drainage is necessary. Do not site a pond where puddles collect during wet periods because it may be heaved when the water table rises—with spring thaw and after big storms.

Where a site is lower than the surrounding land, be prepared to grade the area. This avoids run-off water that will bring mud, grass, and weeds into the pond and contaminate it with residues from chemically treated trees and grounds, roofing, spouting (fresh copper in particular), and petroleum from driveways.

Alternatively, be prepared to create diversion channels to conduct the runoff away from the pond.

**Land level matters.** Site your pond on ground that is or can be leveled. A rock ledge can be a problem, but if it juts well above ground, you may be able to use it in creating a waterfall.

**Protection from predators.** When choosing a site, try to avoid places popular with predators, notably raccoons. Scrambling for fish, they'll upset the plantings, not to mention the fish. Devoted to snails (*escargots nature),* they pick the meat out, and leave the shells in a row on the ledge.

You have time now to study water garden catalogs. An **album of aquatic plants and materials**—liners, pumps, bubblers, fountains, and other accessories—comes in handy when choosing plantings for the pond. Make one up from catalog pages and take it when you are shopping for pond materials at local garden centers.

*Study your grounds from indoors to determine where you'd like to see a pond, keeping in mind a water garden's need for light, good drainage, and so on.*

## Did You Know?

### About Filters

Your pump needs a filter if you are returning water to the pond via a fine spray nozzle, and for larger ponds. How frequently the filter will need cleaning should be a consideration when you are choosing one. There are three main types:

*1* **Mechanical filters.** For a small pond (under 5 by 8 feet and holding 300 gallons of water), a small, inexpensive combination pump-and-filter is sufficient. These filters slip off and on easily for cleaning, likely to be a daily occurrence in hot weather. For ponds twice that size, a popular filtering system consists of a small pump connected by tubing to a velcro-fastened filter. This type likely needs cleaning every one to five days.

Pumps for large ponds (say 16 by 26 feet and holding 4,000 gallons of water) usually push the water through large filters outside the pond and may return it via a waterfall, a streambed, or a recirculating bog garden. These filters are likely to need maintenance every two to seven days.

*2* **Biological filters.** A biological filter needs cleaning only a few times a month. The filter is a large or small gravel-filled cylinder installed outside the pond and screened by a waterfall, plantings, or decorative fencing. Filtering is done by bacteria that colonize layers of gravel. Though not inexpensive, costs balance out, as biological filters are powered by inexpensive pumps and use less electricity.

*3* **Recirculating bog garden.** An effective filtering system for a large pond is one that includes a biological filter outside the pond and returns the water via a shallow recirculating bog garden and streambed or waterfall.

 PLANTING

It's too early to plant.

 PRUNING

**Indoors.** Discard aquatics and bog plants wintering indoors that are rotting.

 FERTILIZING

There is no fertilizing to do during this season.

 CARE

**Break ice** forming on the surface of the pond if fish are wintering there. Gases from the pond must have an escape route.

 WATERING

**Indoors.** Check on and maintain the moisture of the **tropical water lilies** and **bog plants** wintering indoors.

PESTS

Check plants wintering indoors for rot and rinse stems and foliage at weekly intervals if signs of rot appear until the condition clears.

## PLANNING

When the weather permits, visit sites on your grounds that you like for a water garden and try to visualize a shape that will be just right.

If your architecture and landscaping are formal, consider a symmetrical shape—an oval, a circle, a triangle, a square, or a rectangle. Plan to return the water to the pond through classical statuary—the human form or stylized metal frogs, for example. A tall jet of water also makes a formal statement.

If your architecture is casual and the landscaping naturalized, then consider an asymmetrical or a free-form design. In nature there's hardly a perfect curve or a straight line anywhere. Returning the water via a pump tumbling over piled-up rocks, a stream, or a bog garden enhances the natural look.

**In-ground ponds.** The surface area and depth govern the number of gallons a pond will hold. This capacity influences the required size of the pump and filter and the number of plants and fish you can have. Calculate the size and depth of your pond and the gallons it will hold, and your supplier can help you choose suitable equipment.

**Calculating the size of the pond.** A popular pond size is between 10 by 10 feet and 10 by 15 feet. To buy suitable equipment, you need to know the size and water holding capacity of the pond you plan. To calculate the size, outline the shape with a hose or a string. Then measure the length and the width. Multiply the length by the width; that gives you the square footage of the surface. With that number plus the depth you plan on, figure out how many gallons it will hold (see Calculating Pond Measurements): that number dictates many other choices.

To get the approximate size of the surface of a kidney-shaped or a free-form pond, outline it with a hose, then shape the hose into a square, a rectangle, or a combination of these shapes that encompasses the area, and multiply the length by the width.

The usual pond depth is between 18 and 30 inches. Anything deeper may be classified as a pool, and local regulations may require that you fence it. Bog gardens and streambeds are about a foot deep.

In Zone 6, fish are considered safe to winter over in a small pond 24 inches deep. In a large pond, the depth can be as little as 18 inches. In Zone 7, fish are okay for winter in a pond 18 inches deep.

Farther north in ponds under 36 inches deep, the fish are safer indoors for the winter.

Most pumps for in-ground ponds push or pull the water through a cleansing filtering system (see January). The number of gallons of water in the pond dictates the size of the filtering system and the power of the pump, and the number of gallons is determined by surface size. The farther and higher the water has to be pushed by the pump, the more powerful the pump needs to be. And, the more powerful the pump, the more it costs to buy and to operate.

## PLANTING

No planting this month.

## CARE

If fish are wintering in the pond and the surface is frozen, break it to allow gases to escape.

## PRUNING

Keep an eye on the health of water garden plants wintering indoors, and remove any with signs of rot or disease.

*The surface area and depth govern the number of gallons a pond will hold. This capacity influences the required size of the pump and filter and the number of plants and fish you can have.*

# WATERING

**Indoors.** Continue to monitor the moisture in pond plants stored indoors last fall, and replenish if needed.

# FERTILIZING

**Indoors.** Begin to watch marginal plants wintering indoors for signs of growth; if they do start to grow, fertilize them at half strength.

# PESTS

**Indoors.** Check tender **aquatics** wintering indoors for signs of scale or whitefly. The remedy is to rinse the stems and foliage at weekly intervals until the condition clears.

## Did You Know?

### About Recirculating Pumps

The sound and movement of a water garden are created by a pump. The pump returns (and aerates) the water via a bubbler or a fountain, or the pump returns the water via a filter, waterfall, streambed, or a recirculating bog garden.

The larger the pond and the farther the water has to be pushed, the more powerful the pump needs to be and the costlier it will be to buy and to operate.

Small floating fountains powered by the sun are the easiest to install and maintain and are ideal for small water features like wall fountains and tubs. They rest on islands of wiring encased in watertight containers. Sun power turns them on and sends up sprays or showers 8 to 24 inches high, depending on the strength of the unit. The largest solar fountains can move 60 gallons an hour!

The downside to this free energy and beauty is that when the sun doesn't shine, sun-powered pumps don't perform. You can't count on a sun-powered floating fountain to make magic in the moonlight unless it includes a storage unit for sun power.

### Calculating Pond Measurements

**To Calculate the Square Footage of the Pond Surface**

**Rectangle:** length x width = square feet of surface

**Circle:** 3.14 x {$\frac{1}{2}$ the diameter x $\frac{1}{2}$ the diameter} = square feet of surface

**To Calculate the Cubic Feet of Water in a Pond**

**Rectangle:** length x width x depth = cubic feet

**Circle:** 3.14 x {$\frac{1}{2}$ the diameter x $\frac{1}{2}$ the diameter} x depth = cubic feet

**To Calculate the Capacity of a Pond**

There are 7.5 gallons of water per cubic foot, so the number of cubic feet multiplied by 7.5 gallons = the number of gallons in the pond

# MARCH
## Water and Bog Plants

 PLANNING

You can install a good-sized, in-ground pond in one weekend with just one helper. And if you have four or five strong backs and pairs of willing hands, you can do it in one day. **This month invite likely helpers to a mid-May pond installation picnic.** That will give you time to decide on equipment, to locate it, and to have the equipment delivered before the date chosen.

If you are planning to enhance your pond with a stream, a waterfall, or a flowing bog garden, it is a good idea to have these elements dug and shaped before your pond installation party.

**Electrical source.** To accommodate the line from the pump to its source of electricity, you will need to dig a trench 12 inches deep from the pond edge to the outlet. It must be at least 6 feet from the edge of the pond.

To get ready for the pond installation day, have a licensed electrician install a weatherproof outlet for the pump. Any standard three-prong household electrical outlet will do, but it must have a ground-fault circuit interrupter.

The electrical circuit must have reserve amp capacity beyond what is needed for the operation of the pump. This is especially important with pumps using more than 8 amps. Overload can cause the circuit breaker to turn off the current.

**Equipment.** A water garden kit will simplify everything. Otherwise, plan ahead for the day of the installation and have assembled the pond liner, pump, filter, and tubing to take the water from the pump to its point of return—bubbler, fountain, bog garden, waterfall, or stream. If the liner is flexible rubber, it will need an underlay (old carpeting will do) and coarse builder's sand to level the liner. If you plan to edge the pond with flat coping stones, provide the stones and mortar to cement them in place; in the frost belt, you may want to consider metal reinforcing strips or wire for the cement. Before you buy, check the measurements.

**Preformed pond.** With a string and stakes, outline the pond, **adding 2 inches all around** to allow for the sand that will buffer the liner. At either end, dig deep enough to be sure there are no hidden obstructions. New York is "ledgy."

**Flexible liner.** Outline the pond. For a rectangular or a square pond, use a carpenter's square to get the angles just right; for a circular pond, use a string tied to a central stake to outline the circle.

**To determine the width of the liner:** measure the outline at the widest point, then add twice the depth to allow for the sides, **plus** 2 feet more to cover the edges of the ground around the pond. To determine the length, measure the maximum length, then add twice the depth, **plus** 2 feet more.

 PLANTING

As the weather permits, clean up flower beds that are part of the pond setting.

**Indoors.** Start seeds indoors for slow-growing and hardy annuals and perennials you plan to plant around the pond.

# CARE

If you left your pump in the pond, take it out, clean it, and turn it on to see if it is working well. Things go wrong with small pumps that winter in the water, and a small adjustment may fix the problem.

 # PRUNING

If you are not using a pump and filter, as soon as the weather warms **add a supplemental bacterial product to speed the decomposition of waste** from fish and plants and prevent the growth of detrimental algae. Read the container directions and make a mental note about the timing of additional doses.

 # WATERING

**Indoors.** Continue to monitor moisture in **bog plants** wintering indoors and the water levels over the **tropical water lily** tubers.

## Did You Know?

### About Waterproofing a Water Garden

You can create a water garden in any almost container that is watertight and non-toxic, from a wall fountain to a half-barrel to as large as you please.

The smallest container that is a suitable home for plants and fish is a round or oval kettle about 3 feet in diameter by 18 inches deep. That's enough to accommodate a couple of snails, two or three goldfish, one pretty little **water lily**—such as 'Dauben' or the white pygmy 'Ermine'—and the lovely bog plant we call **sweet flag.** A small electric pump and a bubbler would add a musical dimension and aerate the water.

Next in size are in-ground ponds waterproofed by preformed fiberglass pond liners that start at about 4 by 6 feet. They accommodate enough livestock and vegetation to keep a pond in balance: the snails, the fish, **submerged plants,** and a pair of **water lilies** like white 'Gonnere' and 'Albida', along with a small floating-leaved plant, and one or two **marginal** or **bog plants.**

The most popular water garden is an in-ground pond waterproofed by a sheet of flexible rubber about 10 by 10 feet. It accommodates snails, fish, five **water lilies,** one space-eating **lotus,** a few small-leaved floaters, and a few marginals.

Larger ponds, free-form ponds, bog gardens, and streams are all waterproofed with flexible rubber liners or fish grade PVC (polyvinyl chloride) rubber. Black pond liners give the pond a natural look; black reflects the sky and shows off the flowers and the fish.

 # FERTILIZING

The fish in the pond are not likely to become active until the water temperature exceeds 44 degrees Fahrenheit. **Don't throw fish food in the pond water until the fish are visibly frisky.**

 # PESTS

Wild creatures are getting restless; keep an eye out for raccoons in a fishy mood.

Continue to monitor the health of water garden plants wintering indoors.

# PLANNING

If mail-order suppliers deliver **aquatics** too soon to plant, store them in a cool shady place, and keep them wet. Most except **lotus** will hold for at least two weeks.

The formula in the sidebar gives the proportions of living elements needed to keep a pond in balance. A 10-by-10-foot pond with 100 square feet of surface (see February) can have 60 to 70 percent floating cover and be attractive. A 20-by-50-foot pond is more beautiful with only a third of its surface covered.

This "magic formula" for stocking a pond and keeping it in balance was developed by Charles Thomas, former President of Lilypons Water Gardens, Buckeystown, Maryland. You can substitute a **lotus** for one large **water lily.**

# PLANTING

Water garden plants will be in the garden centers late this month or next, depending on the zone. You can plant **hardy lilies** and **lotus** when the pond water has warmed up enough to feel comfortable, about 60 degrees Fahrenheit—April-May for Zone 7. Wait to plant **tropical lilies** until the pond water averages 75 degrees Fahrenheit—mid- to late May in Zone 7.

Plant the rhizomes and tubers in pans 6 to 8 inches deep that hold 9 to 20 or more quarts of soil. Extra growing room encourages multiple crowns and more flowers. Heavy garden soil, which garden centers sell bagged, is good for **aquatic plants.** Avoid planting mixes including peat, manures, vermiculite, and other light materials that float. Test the soil pH and amend the soil so that it is between pH 6.5 and 7.5. Push a fertilizer tablet for aquatics into the soil of each container.

Set tubers and rhizomes so the growing tips are just above the soil; set plants with crowns so the crown is an inch below the soil level. To keep the soil in place, cover it completely with $1/2$ inch of rinsed gravel $1/2$ to $3/4$ inches in diameter. Soak the planted containers and keep them in bright shade, and wet, until you are ready to place them in the pond. Be sure to pack the garden soil tightly into the container so that, once the potting is completed and the container has been topped with gravel, it is brim full. Otherwise, when you submerge the container and the air in it is displaced with water, you'll end up with a pot half full of soil, which isn't enough for the plants to perform to their greatest potential.

# CARE

**Established pond.** Check the pH of the water before the season gets underway and, if needed, adjust it to between pH 6.5 and 7.5, as recommended in the introduction to this chapter.

If you removed the pump for winter, clean it and return it to the pond. Reposition **bog plants** that are askew, and clear away dead or damaged stems and foliage.

Don't be alarmed if the pond water gets murky as air temperatures rise during April warm spells. Pond plants and critters will soon become active, and the water will clear.

Keep fertilizer carts and lawn mowers far from the pond rim to avoid getting chemicals and grass clippings into the water.

# PRUNING

**Established pond.** When the water becomes comfortable enough to work in, groom the **hardy perennials.**

Check **aquatics** and **bog plants** that have been in their containers for two or three years, and if they are crowded, divide them. Plants growing in large tubs can wait twice as long to be divided.

Prune and groom the **submerged plants,** repot them, and return them to the pond.

# WATERING

**Established pond.** As the pond gets active, begin to keep an eye on the water level. It can drop surprisingly quickly on hot, windy days, especially when the water is running over rocks and through a bog garden. When the water level falls below normal, **top the pond.** When adding tap water that includes chlorine, chloramine, or chlorine dioxide, follow label directions on a neutralizing agent to get rid of these elements.

# FERTILIZING

**Established pond.** Push a bar of aquatic fertilizer into the soil in each container. Use a nitrogen-phosphate-potash formulation (NPK) of 10-14-8.

When the fish become active, resume feeding them: apply moderate amounts in the beginning and increase the dose as the weather warms and they become more active. If your water garden does not have a pump and filter, add a supplemental bacterial product to speed the decomposition of waste from fish and plants.

## Did You Know?

### How to Stock Your Pond

**Aquatics** and **bog plants** for a water garden (but not those for a flowing bog recirculating system) grow in soil in pans, pails, and tubs placed in the pond. The container sizes are measured in inches and quarts. Containers for aquatics have no drainage. When you are planting bog plants in containers for aquatics, make one or two nail holes in the bottoms.

**Formula for Stocking Every 1 to 2 Square Feet of Pond Surface**

- 1 bunch (6 stems) **submerged/oxygenating plants**
- 1 black Japanese snail
- 2 inches of fish for fish up to 6 inches long
- $1/10$ of a small or medium-sized **water lily** (that is, 1 lily per 10 to 20 sq. ft.)
- $1/3$ of a **marginal** or a small, **floating-leaved plant** (that is, 1 bog or marginal plant or 1 small-leaved floater for every 3 to 6 sq. ft.)

Here's a "for instance" for planting and stocking a pond about 10 by 10 feet, that is, 100 square feet of surface:

- 50 to 100 bunches of **submerged/oxygenating** plants
- 50 to 100 **black Japanese snails**
- 100 to 200 inches of **fish in assorted sizes up to 6 inches long**
- 5 to 10 **water lilies**
- 18 to 33 **marginal and/or floating-leaved plants**, 3 each of each variety chosen.

# PESTS

**Established pond.** With spring warmth, insects become active. Moving water and hungry fish discourage insect development, and so do frogs. Add tadpoles if you foresee insect problems.

## PLANNING

Before your pond installation party, review the pond equipment you have ordered and lay out digging tools, a crowbar for rocks, shears, a tarp for the excavated soil, a 2-by-4-inch board the width of the pond, a carpenter's level, a tape measure, and cement blocks, bricks, slate, or treated wood to help level the edges.

**Installation**. The installation procedure goes about like this:

### 1 Digging the pond

**Preformed pond.** Following the outline created earlier (see March), excavate a hole that will fit the preformed liner but is about 1 inch deeper.

**Flexible liner.** Following the outline created earlier (see March), dig a hole 15 to 30 inches deep and in the center create a trough 1 inch deep and 18 inches across. If the soil is firm, slope the sides at a 75-degree angle; if it crumbles, slope the sides at a 45-degree angle.

### 2 Leveling the excavation

**Preformed pond and flexible liner.** Center a 2-by-4-inch board across the hole and check the level of the rims; then make them even. Flatten high spots. Use sand to raise spots that are lower by fewer than 2 inches. To raise areas more than 2 inches low, use cement blocks, bricks, slate, or treated wood covered with sand.

### 3 Creating a pond rim

**Preformed pond and flexible liner.** To prepare for the edging that will be installed later, cut the sod around the pond into strips 10 inches wide and 12 to 15 inches long. Without detaching the strips from the lawn, roll them up gently away from the pond.

### 4 Placing the liner

**Preformed pond.** Line the bottom of the excavation with an inch of sand. Place the pond so the rim is just above ground level. Check and adjust the level of the rim to within 1/4 inch.

**Flexible liner.** Line the bottom of the excavation with an inch of sand. Then cover the sand with the underlayment. Open the liner, and gently spread it over the underlayment. If you find the liner heavy, fold it in fourths and unfold it from inside the excavation. Smooth the liner, pushing the excess up over the rim of pond.

### 5 Filling the pond

**Preformed pond.** Begin filling the pond, and as the water level rises, pack sand (or soil) behind the sides of the form. Keep the pressure inside and outside similar by adding sand or soil at a rate matching the rise of the water level so the form doesn't buckle.

**Flexible liner.** Fill the pond to within 1 inch of the top. Cut the surplus liner off leaving an overlap of 6 to 12 extra inches all around. Smooth the overlap over the dirt around the pond, and nail it firmly in place using 4- to 6-inch spike nails (no other kind).

### 6 Edging the pond

If you plan to edge the pond with sod, scratch up and fertilize the soil you stripped of sod in Step 3, then roll the grass strips back, and firm them in place.

If you plan to edge the pond with coping stones (stones used for the flat, topmost layer of a stone wall or walk), cut off and discard the sod strips. To protect the liner, place the coping stones so they extend 1 to 2 inches over the rim of the pond. You can use mortar to keep them in place, and metal reinforcing-rods or wire inside a 2- to 3-inch mortar base. Use as little mortar as possible so the stone looks natural. Check the level of the stones often as you work.

After the mortar has dried, clean the stones with a stiff brush and a mixture of 1 part ordinary vinegar to 1 part water, or muriatic acid and water, and

*If you do not have a pump and filter, ask your supplier for a reliable bacterial product to speed the decomposition of waste from fish and plants. Use it as often as called for in the directions.*

## Did You Know?

### Submerged/Oxygenating Plants Help Keep the Water Clear

**Submerged plants** are included among pond plantings to gobble the nutrients feeding undesirable algae and to add oxygen. Four available from most suppliers are: **Anacharis** (*Elodea canadensis* var. *gigantea*); **dwarf saggitaria** (*Sagittaria subulata*); *Myriophyllum* species; **Washington grass** (*Cabomba caroliniana*).

These plants are usually sold in bunches of 6 stems about 6 inches long. Growing in sand-filled pans set on the pond bottom, they quickly develop stems 2 to 3 feet long. Allow 6 square inches of container surface for every bunch of submerged plants; use a separate container for each variety. To plant, take off the rubber bands, and gently press the ends of each bunch 2 inches into the sand. Add sand to within an inch of the rim, and top that with rinsed gravel. Water the containers to displace trapped air. Never fertilize—their job is to take nutrients from the water.

Koi and goldfish over 6 inches sometimes browse the **submerged plants** to death. If that is happening, cover the pans with plastic mesh domes; the plants grow through the mesh and the fish graze without harming the roots. You can make your own dome using a plastic mesh sold by aquatics suppliers.

rinse thoroughly. Drain the pond, and then refill it with fresh water.

 PLANTING

Get the **hardy water garden plants** in this month. Late this month, Zone 7 can begin planting **tropical lilies.** Instructions for planting and stocking the pond are given in June.

 CARE

**Outdoors. Hardy water lilies** in a pond can come into bloom about mid-May in Zone 6, later farther north. Once the weather is warm, the pump should be on and the pond in full gear. Clear the filter as often as suggested by the manufacturer.

 PRUNING

To keep the pond healthy, **promptly remove yellowing and dying vegetation**.

 WATERING

Restore the level of the pond water any time it shows a measurable dip.

 FERTILIZING

As long as the water temperature remains under 75 degrees Fahrenheit, fertilize **lotus** and **water lilies** monthly.

Take care not to get lawn chemicals and clippings into the pond when you are fertilizing and mowing.

 PESTS

If you do not have a pump and filter, ask your supplier for a reliable bacterial product to speed the decomposition of waste from fish and plants. Use it as often as called for in the directions.

If the fish aren't keeping up with the insects, add tadpoles. **Avoid pesticides and herbicides in the vicinity of the pond.** Control grass and weeds growing into the pond from the edging. Add a pellet to kill mosquito larvae.

PLANNING

The beauty of your water garden depends in part on its setting. Here are some suggestions:

**Pot, tub, or barrel water garden.** Surround the container with potted plants of different heights.

**Formal pond.** Plant **boxwood, roses,** or **Japanese maples** in the background of a pond that is symmetrical—oval, circle, triangle, square, or a long narrow rectangle. Repeat the dominant color of the pond flowers in the plantings around it.

**Naturalized pond.** Use native plants found near water in the setting—**reeds, native shrubs, dogwoods,** and in shaded areas **ferns, green mosses, Solomon's seal.**

**Free-form pond.** Use Japanese-style garden plants with a kidney-shaped or free-form water garden—a **dwarf ornamental cherry, dwarf azaleas, Siberian irises, quilted hostas, ferns, mosses,** and **forest flowers.**

 PLANTING

**Established pond.** Complete the planting of **hardy** and **tropical water garden plants.**

**Planting and stocking a new pond.** Before placing fish and other wildlife in a brand new pond, allow the water a couple of weeks to de-chlorinate and warm.

The plants can go into the pond any time after it is filled. **Aquatic plants** need a specific amount of water overhead. The amount is indicated in mail-order catalogs and on plant tags. Some can rest on the bottom of the pond, while others will need to be raised on platforms that can be made of stones, clean bricks, and weathered cement blocks. **Avoid new cement blocks because they raise the water pH.** When wet, plant containers can be heavy, so slide and float them to their destinations.

When planting a new pond, put the **submerged plants** in first, at a depth of 1 to 2 feet. Next, set out the **large floating-leaved plants**—allow several feet between **water lily** and **lotus** containers. Place the **small floaters** next.

Group the pond's **marginal** or **bog plants** on the far side of the pond 1 to 2 feet apart at the depth recommended on the plant tag. If they are going into a recirculating bog garden, set the rootballs (with a good ball of earth all around) into the gravel on the bottom, with about $1/2$ to 1 inch of water overhead.

 CARE

**Established pond. Clear the filter as often as necessary** to keep the pump free. If the filter becomes clogged, the water flowing back to the pond will slow or stop.

If you do not have a pump and filter, add a supplemental bacterial product to speed the decomposition of waste from fish and plants.

Keep fertilizer carts and lawn mowers far from the pond rim to avoid getting chemicals and grass clippings into the water.

**New pond.** If you have mortared the coping stones around the pond rim, check the pH of the water, which may be affected by runoff from the mortar. If the pH is way up, particularly after the first couple of rains, adjust it as directed in the December pages.

## PRUNING

Remove yellowing leaves and dead flowers, leaving nothing to decay.

If strands of the **submerged plants** elongate and become puny, raise the containers to positions where they receive more direct sunlight. When they're 8 inches tall and growing well, you can cut them back or divide them and make more plants. Just break off the top 5 or 6 inches, press the ends into a container filled with sand, and place it in the pond.

 WATERING

Continue to monitor and maintain the water level of the pond.

 FERTILIZING

When the water temperature is over 75 degrees Fahrenheit, fertilize **lotus** and **water lilies** twice monthly. Fertilize the **marginal plants** monthly but only if they are not growing well. Do not fertilize the **bog plants** in a recirculating bog system, nor the **submerged plants.** Their job is to use up the nutrients that feed unwanted algae.

## Did You Know?

### Submerged/Oxygenating Plants Can Be Invasive

Two beautiful but **extremely invasive plants,** sometimes recommended as **submerged plants,** are illegal where they survive winters—the lovely **water hyacinth** and **water lettuce.** Water hyacinths are sold here in Zone 5, and I plant them every year, knowing it's okay because they die when cold weather comes.

But they multiply rapidly in climates where they live through the winter; they get into the waterways and clog them. Federal statute forbids the shipment of water hyacinth in interstate commerce.

### Harvesting Water Lilies

**Water lilies** last three or four days as cut flowers if they're picked early the first day they open. To harvest a **water lily,** plunge your arm down the stem and pinch off a foot of the plant.

Arrange the stems of **hardy water lilies** in water that reaches within an inch of the base of the flower; set **tropical water lilies** so the water is within 3 inches of the base of the flower.

To stop the **water lilies** from closing at night, drop hot wax onto the base of each flower petal. The wax will keep the petals from closing when bedtime comes.

 PESTS

Weed around the coping stones. If needed, add a pellet that kills mosquito larvae. Avoid pesticides and herbicides around the pond.

## PLANNING

If you are troubled by water that turns a murky green or green-brown, ask your aquatics supplier to recommend a biological or microbial product to suppress the **algae** that is making it happen. These products control algae by speeding up the decomposition of the fish and plant waste on which unwanted algae feed.

Algae can be beneficial, but some are not. **The three main algae** are a good-guy, moss-like **clinging alga,** and two other not-good guys—a **floating surface alga,** and a **drifting alga.** The good-guy, clinging algae produces beautiful deep-green filaments on the stones and the sides of the pond and fuzzes over plant stems and snail shells. Welcome it. You can control the unwanted floating and drifting types by raising the water level and pushing them off the surface with a broom. Biological products keep them all in check.

You can solve the problem by replacing sun-lovers with water lilies that bloom with only four to six hours of direct sun. Among them are the very popular **hardy water lilies** 'Charlene Strawn' which is yellow; 'Virginia', a white; and red 'James Brydon'.

A few tropical water lilies also bloom with less sun. Among them are 'Albert Greenberg', a rose-tinged gold that does well in any pond over 4 feet and blooms longer than other tropicals; 'Director George Moore', a compact tropical with magnificent deep-blue flowers; and 'Panama Pacific', blue tinged with red, which grows small or large according to the space available.

Several tropical **bog plants** also succeed in partial sun, including **elephant's ear** and **taro,** species of *Colocasia,* and several species of **papyrus** (*Cyperus*), including the charming dwarf **umbrella plant.** These all need to winter indoors or be replaced annually.

**When thunderstorms come close, turn off the pond pump** to avoid attracting lightning.

**Black water is beautiful.** A black dye sold by water garden suppliers is the magic that gives a velvety black look to the water gardens in many public gardens, including the National Aquatic Gardens at the U.S. National Arboretum in Washington, D.C. The inky surfaces mirror the sky, mask the algae, and the **water lilies** stand out beautifully while the fish seem to float in and out of a mysterious deep.

The vegetable-based dye doesn't kill the algae, but it does hide it. The label on the dye container tells how much to use. The proportions don't change with regional temperature or the contents of the water. After you've used the dye a few times, you'll know how much you want to put in. It's safe for pets and wild life that may come there to drink.

## PLANTING

The sun changes positions throughout the year and trees expand: your pond can end up with more shade at certain times than you anticipated. **Shade may be the culprit if water lilies and lotus are failing to bloom up to expectation.**

## CARE

**Clear the filter.** If you do not have a pump and filter, add a supplemental bacterial product to speed the decomposition of waste from fish and plants.

## PRUNING

Pinch off yellowing leaves and dead flowers as they occur. **Water lilies** are continually putting out new leaves and stretching them outward as more arise. As they fade, get rid of them.

# WATERING

Now that the high heat of summer is here, **check and adjust the water level** of your pond daily, especially when the day is hot, dry, and windy.

**If your water is heavily chlorinated** and you are adding as much as 10 percent to the volume of the pond—if it's down as much as 2 inches, for instance—add a 10 percent solution of a de-chlorinator when you top it.

If your water is filtered, keep lawn sprinklers away from the pond, especially if the spray drips into the pond from foliage that's been treated with herbicides or pesticides.

 # FERTILIZING

As long as the water temperature is above 75 degrees Fahrenheit, continue to fertilize the **water lilies** and the **lotus** twice monthly.

## Did You Know?

### The Magnificent Lotus

The lotus is an extraordinary plant. The large, pointed flower bud rises above the water on a stem 2 to 6 feet tall and unfolds an enormous perfumed blossom. Colors are lush shades and combinations of white, pink, red, yellow, and cream. For three days the lotus blossom opens in the morning before the **water lilies** and closes at tea time. The third day the petals fall, leaving the seedpod that is sought after for dried arrangements. It looks like the spout of a watering can, or ET, the extraterrestrial movie character.

Mail-order suppliers ship lotus tubers bare root the few weeks in spring when the rootstock is in tuber form. Later the tubers send out runners and atrophy, which makes planting impossible. They can be planted April to May in Zones 5, 6, 7; May in Zone 4.

Use pans 16 to 24 inches in diameter, 9 to 10 inches deep, for **standard lotus; miniatures** make do with half to two-thirds this size. Set the tubers 2 inches under the soil with the top half-inch of the growing tip above the soil (see April, Planting). Place the pans in the pond with 2 to 3 inches of water overhead; they bloom sooner in shallow water.

Two or three weeks after being planted, a lotus sends up a first set of floating leaves. They look like lily pads without the notch. A second set of leaves rises and opens high above the water. The leaves of **miniature lotus** are 6 to 16 inches across, and the stems are 2 to 3 feet tall; **standard lotus** leaves can be 2 feet wide, and the stem the height of a tall person—6 feet.

 # PESTS

Add a pellet that kills mosquito larvae. Get rid of grass and weeds growing into the pond from the edging, but keep pesticides and herbicides away from the pond.

# AUGUST
## Water and Bog Plants

 PLANNING

**Goldfish** usually live ten to fifteen years unless they encounter a predator. When you go on vacation, you won't have to plan to have the fish and other pond creatures fed in your absence. In a balanced pond (see the April sidebar) the fish feed on the **submerged plants,** on the moss-like **algae** on the sides of the pond, and on the insects and larvae you do want to be rid of. In fact, your pond might be clearer when you come back because you haven't been feeding the fish.

 PLANTING

As your pond plants mature, keep an eye out for those that can or need to be divided.

You can plant or transplant container-grown and rooted hardy **water lilies** and many **bog plants,** from early spring until a few weeks prior to the first killing frost. Water lilies that are moved while blooming just sulk a bit.

Water lilies need dividing when they become crowded. The blossoms of water lilies like 'Virginia' and 'Charlene Strawn' usually stand an inch or two above the water; when their pads also are held high (and the rhizomes are 12 or more inches under water), that's a sign the plants will need dividing next spring before growth begins.

**Lotus** tubers are shipped bare root in spring in plastic bags containing moist materials. They're almost as easy to grow as water lilies, but they can be transplanted only during the few weeks in spring when the rootstock is in tuber form. When the rootstock puts out runners, the tubers atrophy, and transplanting is virtually impossible.

**Irises** can be divided any time after they bloom, including **Japanese irises,** such as *Iris kaempferi*, *I. laevigata* 'Variegata' (the big yellow flag), *I. Pseudacorus,* and the **Louisiana hybrid irises.**

 CARE

When thunderstorms threaten, turn off the pump.

Clear the filter consistently. It's apt to clog more often this time of the year.

If you do not have a pump and filter, add a supplemental bacterial product to speed the decomposition of waste from fish and plants.

Monitor the pond as the trees begin to shed their first leaves, and remove leaves and debris from the pond daily.

 PRUNING

The **submerged plants** may need pruning and division. If you are losing the open water to the summer growth of **small- and large-leaved floating plants,** cut them back enough to keep about a third of the water surface clear.

Deadhead consistently and remove yellowing and decaying foliage.

 WATERING

When the water level of the pond falls below its normal height, top up the pond. If you are adding more than an inch of tap water to the pond—water that includes chlorine, chloramine, or chlorine dioxide—also **add a dechlorinating chemical** according to the label directions for neutralizing these elements.

 FERTILIZING

Do not fertilize **water lilies** and **lotus** after August 1.

*If you are adding more than an inch of tap water to the pond—water that includes chlorine, chloramine, or chlorine dioxide—also add a de-chlorinating chemical according to the label directions for neutralizing these elements.*

## Did You Know?

### About Attracting Wildlife

In a city, a pond 2 feet by 3 feet is enough to attract songbirds, butterflies, and dragonflies, though it's minimal space for frogs.

In less urban settings, a secluded pond, 10 feet by 10 feet and up, attracts small animals such as deer, fox, raccoons, possums, and uplands game birds. In wild mountain terrain, a large pond will draw in all sorts of native animals.

Site your pond where you can watch nervous visitors and not be seen. Stock the pond with native minnows and small goldfish rather than showy koi, which attract predators, especially raccoons. If you want showy fish, do without a filter that keeps the water clear. Or add a black dye (see July) to limit visibility and make the water look deep and inviting; there are no bad side effects.

Make the area safe for birds. If there are cats around, provide a high observation post 6 to 8 feet from the pond for the birds. It can be a tree or shrubbery that screens them from hawks. Birds like a clear path to the water—a high-up branch far away, then one closer and lower, then a landing site at the pond, a broad stone for example. Plant berried shrubs and let pines and hemlocks grow tall to provide nesting places, materials, and safe perches.

Hardy plants rooted in a recirculating bog should be taking all the nutrients they can use from the water. However, some may be more aggressive than others; cut these back and push a half-strength dose of fertilizer into the soil of the containers of less successful plants.

 PESTS

Add a pellet that kills mosquito larvae.

**If your aquatic plants begin to have a chewed look** at the edges, look for little brown snails, and remove them by hand.

Pull out grass and weeds growing into the coping or the pond from the edging.

**If night raiders are visiting your pond, cover it** with screens at night. Or below the water level, install broad mesh fencing that fish can dive through to evade marauders. Less colorful fish attract fewer predators.

# SEPTEMBER
## Water and Bog Plants

 PLANNING

When nights are below 65 degrees Fahrenheit, it is time to **bring the most valuable cold-tender pond bog plants indoors if you wish to save them** for next year. They thrive when set in pans filled with an inch of wet pea gravel in a big south-facing window. Keep the soil moist. During the darkest months of the year, supplement the daylight with fluorescent light.

When the **tropical water lilies** stop blooming, many owners discard them and plan to start fresh next year. But it's possible to collect and save the tubers. Here's how:

*1* A week or so after a killing frost, lift the rootstock, and gently wash off as much soil as you can.

*2* Pick off one or more tubers, air dry them for two days, and then remove the remaining soil.

*3* Store them in jars of distilled water, in a cool closet at about 55 degrees Fahrenheit.

*4* In late winter, two months before the pond water temperature will warm to 75 degrees Fahrenheit, bring the tubers out and set them to sprout in a pan of water in a sunny window.

*5* When the pond temperature reaches a constant 75 degrees Fahrenheit, replant the tubers and return them to the pond. They should bloom two to three months later.

 PLANTING

You can divide spring-blooming **hardy bog perennials** successfully the early days of this month.

In the beds that create the setting around your pond, **hardy perennials** can be divided up to a month before the ground is expected to freeze and also in early spring before new growth begins. The rule of thumb for **autumn-flowering perennials** is to divide them in early spring, before any sign of growth appears.

**Most perennials benefit from division.** If you want more plants to fill out or enlarge the beds, check out those that have been in the ground two years—if they are growing well, it's okay to divide them.

 CARE

**Continue to keep the pond filter clear.** If you do not have a pump and filter, add a supplemental bacterial product to speed the decomposition of waste from fish and plants.

**Remove leaves that fall into the water at once.** If there are deciduous trees near the pond, when the first leaves begin to fall, cover the surface with bird netting and clear it of leaves now and then. Keep the netting in place until all the leaves have fallen and been cleared away. This will make cleaning the pond much easier.

When the water temperature falls below 55 degrees Fahrenheit, any tubs, half-barrels, and water gardens less than 30 inches deep are likely to become too cold for the fish. You have two solutions: set the fish free to start a new life in a large pond, stream, or lake; or bring them indoors to a fish tank for the winter. In any case, stop feeding them (see October).

## PRUNING

Continue to deadhead flowering pond plants, and clear away yellowing and dead foliage as soon as you spot it. Rotting foliage may incubate pests and diseases over the winter months.

Keep an eye on the annuals or tender perennials and discard them when they are played out.

*Continue to deadhead flowering pond plants, and clear away yellowing and dead foliage as soon as you spot it. Rotting foliage may incubate pests and diseases over the winter months.*

 WATERING

Keep track of the water level in your pond, and bring it back to normal as often as it falls.

 FERTILIZING

The water is surely below 75 degrees Fahrenheit by now, so stop fertilizing the plants.

 PESTS

If Indian summer lingers and mosquitoes are a concern, add a mosquito larvae control pellet.

As the foliage in the pond collapses with the cold, colorful fish become more obvious to predators. The bird netting recommended in the Care section of this month to keep leaves out of the pond also affords some protection for the fish and snails.

## Did You Know?

### How to Attract Butterflies and Hummingbirds

It takes just a few nectar-bearing plants in the pond area to attract butterflies and hummingbirds, and this is a good time to plant those that are hardy perennials.

**Butterflies** fly down to showy plantings of brilliant blooms—purple, yellow, orange, and red. They hover over flowers that have flat-topped or short, open-mouthed tubular blossoms that make landing platforms. Single rather than double-flowered types make gathering nectar easier for them.

The number one attraction for butterflies is the **butterfly bush** (*Buddleia davidii*). It bears graceful flower spikes on new wood, so if it doesn't die to the ground in your zone, before growth begins in early spring, cut it back. Other butterfly magnets are **butterfly weed** (*Asclepias tuberosa*), a sweetly scented perennial, and *Lantana camara*, which is grown as an annual here. **Passion flower** (*Passiflora*), a flowering tropical vine, is popular with these beautiful flying acrobats.

**Hummingbirds** spend their days looking for the food necessary to fuel their amazing energy output. Their primary diet is nectar, rounded out with tiny insects. They rely on sight, not scent, to locate nectar and go to many of the flowers that attract butterflies. Some of these flowers that do well in part sun are **pentas, impatiens, red cardinal flower,** and **beebalm.**

# OCTOBER
## Water and Bog Plants

## PLANNING

As the temperature plummets, the foliage and flowers of the pond plants begin to subside, a signal the season is over. Now you must evaluate what to discard and what to keep. If the growth of the **small floating-leaved plants** is invasive, discard a few. At the end of the season, many pond owners discard the less costly **cold-tender bog plants,** saving limited indoor winter storage space for the most valuable.

If your **tropical water lilies** grew from tubers you saved last year, decide now whether their performance this year makes saving them worth the effort. (See September.)

 PLANTING

In our region, **fall is an important planting season in the garden.** Make time now to evaluate the effect of the plants in your water garden and around the pond. Consider additions that will increase your pleasure in your pond. For inspiration, study the album of aquatic plants you made from the pages of mail-order catalogs back in January.

Consider adding an evergreen to the setting for your pond. The **weeping hemlock** is a dark evergreen that stays low for years, as does the very hardy **mugho pine.** For fun add a trio of **boxwoods** pruned to globe shape.

Deciduous trees and shrubs add structure and are airier than evergreens. A **Sargent crabapple** (6 to 10 feet high) in bloom, reflected in a pond, is lovely. For summer bloom, plant a **hardy hibiscus.** We love 'White Chiffon'. You can keep hardy hibiscus, which is also known as **shrub althea,** at shrub height by trimming it back before growth begins in early spring, or you can train it up as a small tree.

## CARE

To keep falling leaves from getting into the pond, cover it with bird netting or deer fencing. They're dark and not intrusive.

A biological filter (see January) needs a thorough cleaning at the end of the growing season.

**Discard played-out annuals.** Cut back the **submerged/oxygenating** plants. Clear away fading vegetation. Dying organic matter in the pond will decay, producing toxic levels of methane gases that harm the fish and the **hardy perennials** staying on for winter.

Slide the containers of the cold-hardy **water lilies** and the pond **bog plants** to the deepest spot in the pond for the winter. The water will be warmest there.

 PRUNING

Keep any plants still in the pond clear of decaying foliage and spent flowers.

 WATERING

Maintain the water level of the pond for the sake of the fish and the plants wintering over in the pond.

## FERTILIZING

There is no fertilizing to do at this season.

*As the temperature plummets, the foliage and flowers of the pond plants begin to subside, a signal the season is over. Now you must evaluate what to discard and what to keep.*

If fish are going to winter in your pond, stop feeding them when the thermometer drops below 55 degrees Fahrenheit. They will go dormant and can winter safely in the deepest part of ponds 30 inches and deeper. If they are disturbed, they'll swim a bit, then go back to their rest.

 PESTS

When raccoons and other little mammals are getting ready to nap for winter, they become very interested in food. **With the vegetation fading or gone from the pond, the fish are more visible.** If you see a lot of critter activity, cover the pond with bird netting to discourage fishing expeditions.

## Did You Know?

### About Feeding the Fish

**Fish gobble larvae and insects and nibble plants, so it's not necessary to feed them. But they're fun to feed.** Once they know you, they will come as you approach and make their interest in food obvious. Fish that aren't fed remain wild and hide when you are there. Feeding creates a relationship fairly rapidly with the goldfish and koi; golden orfe are less responsive.

To make friends with your fish, the first days they are in a pond, let them find their own food. Then, at a time of day you can come regularly to the pond, sit next to the water and lean over the pond for a minute or so. Then gently drop a pinch of fish flakes onto the water. The first few times you drop in food they'll wait until you are gone to come up for it. But eventually they'll come when you are there and even be at the surface before you feed them.

Feed fish only as much as they eat in five minutes. Extra fish food and waste loads the water with more nutrients than the plants can absorb. The result is a green growth called algae bloom that uses up nitrogen and then dies, consuming oxygen faster than the water can absorb it from the air. Lacking oxygen, the fish die. The bigger fish die first. Smaller fish tolerate water with low oxygen content longer.

Fish eat more in hot weather and again in the fall as they stoke up for winter dormancy. When the water temperature drops to 55 degrees Fahrenheit, their body processes slow as they become dormant and can no longer digest the food. So stop feeding at that point or you will be polluting the water.

# NOVEMBER
## Water and Bog Plants

## PLANNING

**Adding a waterfall.** If you're considering changing the configuration of the pond, perhaps by adding a waterfall, this is a good time to start the project.

Take advantage of warm spells to prepare the pond for the winter ahead. If the pump is not hard-wired into its electrical source, unplug it and lift it. Clean it and store it indoors. If it can't be unplugged, take the pump out of the pond, flush it with clean water, and return it to the pond.

Even in the unlikely event the pond water doesn't freeze, the pump must not go on in winter. Here's why: in summer the coolest water is at the bottom of the pond but in winter the warmest water is in the bottom and that's where fish gather. If the pump goes on, the bottom will get cooler and the fish will suffer.

A large pond **benefits from cleaning** every two or three years. Small pond and water features need annual cleaning. Plan to begin after the pond plants have subsided and all the tree leaves have been cleared away.

*1* Prepare a temporary home for the pond livestock by filling a container with pond water. Use the pump and a hose to spill the pond water out over nearby garden plants; it is rich in nutrients.

*2* When the water is almost gone, net the fish, snails, and other livestock and place them in their temporary home. Cover it to keep the fish from jumping out.

*3* Slide the plant containers out of the water and cover them with moist newspaper.

*4* Use a plastic scoop to remove the organic waste from the bottom of the pond. Use a hose and sponges to clear algae and clean the sides.

*5* Refill the pond. If the water includes chlorine, use a de-chlorinating agent to prepare the water for the return of the critters.

*6* Gradually blend enough of the fresh pond water into the fish container to bring its temperature down; that way the fish will have acclimated to the new temperature in the pond before you return them to it. Then return them to the pond.

*7* Clean and groom the winter hardy plants that will remain in the water. Slide them to the deepest spot in the pond and submerge them.

## PLANTING

**Hardy water lilies** stored in water deep enough to be below the ice level can live through winter in the pond. If your winters are hard and the pond isn't deep enough to escape ice even at its lowest point, move the hardy water lilies in their pans to a frost-free garage or a root cellar. Cover each with damp newspaper and wrap in a plastic bag. Check the rhizomes now and then—don't let them dry out.

**Indoor water garden.** You can bring the sound and movement of water indoors for the winter (and help add to the moisture in the air during the heating season) by creating a small water garden powered by a push-button hydroponic unit. Indoor water garden kits are available, but any large shallow container lined with pebbles will do. A young **umbrella plant** (*Cyperus alternifolius*) is very pretty in an indoor water garden. Add one or two small bunches of cuttings of **coleus** (*Tradescantia* species), **philodendron,** or **pothos** bunched together and anchored in the pebbles. Add a **baby fern** resting on an upside-down water glass tall enough to keep the pot bottom above water level.

*If you have covered the pond with bird netting to keep falling leaves out, you can remove it as soon as the leaves have all fallen. But keep the netting on if the pond has fish and is attracting the attention of wild visitors like raccoons and herons.*

Filtered light is best. Check the water level and keep it above the roots and cuttings.

 CARE

If you have covered the pond with bird netting to keep falling leaves out, you can remove it as soon as the leaves have all fallen. But keep the netting on if the pond has fish and is attracting the attention of wild visitors like raccoons and herons.

 PRUNING

There's no pruning to be done at this time.

 WATERING

Do not allow the plants brought indoors for the winter to dry out.

### Frogs in the Pond

Frogs are a water garden's very good friend and charming ornament. In the tadpole stage, they do a fine job of clearing up leftover fish food and undesirable algae. Those that make it to froghood are a huge help with mosquito control.

Frogs sleep winter away buried in mud around the edges of your pond. If your water garden includes a recirculating bog garden, they likely will winter in the gravelly muck at the bottom.

The only trouble with frogs is you get fond of them, and they are independent creatures that may not stay, especially when rainy weather invites them to venture abroad. But if they are happy in your pond, they will make babies and in time may provide a frog chorus that will add greatly to your evening pleasure.

As long as the pond isn't frozen, maintain the water level if there are fish and plants wintering in the pond.

 FERTILIZING

There's no fertilizing to do at this season.

 PESTS

Raccoons spend winter in a den, sleeping but not hibernating. Be aware that in warm periods they're up and about, and they're good fishermen.

## Water and Bog Plants

# PLANNING

With the gift-giving season near, it is a fine time to plan ways to make your water garden more interesting next year.

If you put together an album of catalog pages showing garden equipment such as liners, pumps, bubblers, fountains, and other accessories, look through it for inspiration. Santa may be pleased to know of your interest.

# PLANTING

Planting is over for the year.

# CARE

**Where it is likely ice will cover the pond surface** for more than three or four consecutive days (most everywhere in Zone 5 and north), if you are keeping fish and plants in the pond, it is a good idea to install a floating de-icer. A thin film of ice is likely to thaw under noon sun, but ice that covers the surface for days keeps the pond from breathing. When the water isn't frozen, the surface of the water takes from the atmosphere the oxygen your pond creatures need; and it disperses gases released by organic decay and carbon dioxide wastes built up by animal life. When ice covers the surface, the exchange can't take place, and the living things down in the water suffer.

A de-icer is a simple heating element attached to a flotation device. The best de-icers are equipped with thermostats so they turn themselves on only when warmth is needed. The most popular are rated at 1500 watts. Float the de-icer only during the weeks or months it is needed and always in conjunction with a ground fault circuit interrupter.

# PRUNING

No pruning needs to be done at this season.

## Did You Know?

### Adjusting the Water pH

Livestock will do best in water with a pH between 6.5 and 7.5. Before putting fish or livestock into a new or recently de-chlorinated pond, use a pH tester to take the pH readings for three days running. Mornings, the water is nearest neutral. If the pH is too high, use a pH reducer such as AlkaMinus to lower it. If it is too low, use AlkaPlus to raise it. You also can raise pH with baking soda; for each 100 gallons of water add one teaspoonful of soda each day until the water pH test is satisfactory.

Most water gardeners don't have pH problems, but to be on the safe side check it now and then. An excess of fish and fish food creates more ammonia than plants absorb, which can raise the pH of the water up to and over 8.0. The solution is to correct the pH and cut back on fish and fish food. If the fish become lethargic but show no signs of disease, it can be a sign the pH is off.

# WATERING

As long as the water isn't frozen, maintain the level if there are fish wintering in the pond.

# FERTILIZING

There's no fertilizing to do at this season.

# PESTS

Even raccoons and other intrepid fishermen are not likely to be a bother this time of the year.

New York gardens, like gardens everywhere, can host problems. In this section, we give you an overview of some of the problems you might encounter and how to control them. This section includes the sound environmental approach to handling pests, which is known as Integrated Pest Management. That is followed by sections describing common problems and controls that are considered acceptable now. **Always follow label instructions.**

## Integrated Pest Management

Known as IPM, integrated pest management is an environmentally friendly approach to dealing with the pests that bug your plants.

The goal of IPM is to try to handle problems by taking into account the environment in which the problem occurs. To disrupt the environment as little as possible, we try to encourage and sometimes even release certain predatory "beneficial" insects that are natural enemies of the destructive insects. We also employ some physical barriers, such as row covers, to keep plants safe.

**Beneficial insects.** The first line of defense in IPM is to encourage beneficial insects and to use biological controls, rather than poisons—pesticides—to control the others.

There are two groups of beneficials, the predators and the parasites. The most familiar predators are praying mantids, ladybugs, green lacewings, and spiders. They hunt and feed on the others. The parasites are primarily various tiny wasps that hatch inside other insects and . . . you can imagine!

Several mail-order houses (see Plant Sources in the Appendix) offer batches of the beneficial insects with instructions on releasing them. Successfully established in your garden, the beneficials help control the bad guys. To keep beneficials with you season after season, you must not use broad-spectrum insecticides.

**Horticultural oil sprays.** If you need more control than the beneficials provide, look into horticultural oils. Sprayed on infected plants, these dense oils smother insects and their eggs. Some are based on petroleum and others on vegetables such as cottonseed and soybeans. They're environmentally okay. Applied in early spring before plant buds break, they control the undesirables and have a limited effect on the beneficials. Sprayed on in summer, they control whiteflies, mealybugs, scale, spider mites, and aphids.

**Botanical pesticides and insecticidal soaps.** Safer as far as the beneficials are concerned, some of these are derived from plants. From pyrethrum, a daisy-like flower, manufacturers extract an insecticidal chemical. The tropical Neem tree provides a very effective insecticide that is also a fungicide; it even can help with Japanese beetles. (The main control for Japanese beetles is to treat the soil with Milky Spores in late summer. The spores infest the larvae. To be effective the treatment must be repeated the following year.) Insecticidal soaps are milder than the sprays—they are effective when they come into contact with the insects.

## Common Insect Pests and Controls

Many factors play a role in how light or heavy your insect problems will be.

*1* The presence of natural parasites and predators cuts down on pests and diseases, as explained under Integrated Pest Management (IPM).

*2* Dry or wet seasons encourage certain problems.

*3* Very cold winters can reduce insect populations.

By choosing pest- and disease-resistant plants that thrive in our climate and by being faithful to the healthy garden practices we recommend, you can avoid many of the most common problems—spider mites, whitefly, Japanese beetles, blackspot, mildew, rust, and nematodes.

# Pests, Diseases, & Controls

**What you can't avoid, try to control.** Identify the problem and apply controls early in the developmental cycle, not late. The development stage of each species is affected greatly by warm early seasons and cool late seasons. Just as the growth of the plant on which an insect or disease preys is delayed or stimulated by the weather, so is the insect affected.

**Keep an eye on plants that hosted problems in previous years.** The colder the zone and the season, the later the infestation will come. Blackspot, mildew, mites, whitefly, and Japanese beetles will appear earlier in gardens in Zone 6 and 7 than in yards in Zones 3 and 4. Warm climates may face more broods of insects per year.

**Here are various controls that are appropriate for certain stages in the development of pests and diseases:**

• With aphids, leafhoppers, earwigs, thrips, crickets, grasshoppers, scale, and similar insects, the metamorphosis to adulthood is simple. All stages of larvae and adults are similar to each other and all feed on the host plant. The egg hatches, and there is a series of nymphs, which shed their skin (molting), getting larger each time until the final adult stage. A little cricket molts and molts and becomes a large adult cricket. You use the same control from beginning to end of the cycle.

• For other creatures, metamorphosis requires an egg stage, a larval stage, a pupal stage (resting stage), and then there is a miraculous transformation into a very different adult.

• With some insects such as beetles, the grub stage feeds on the roots of plants, and the adult beetle feeds on the leaves, stems, and flowers of the host plant.

• In the case of butterflies and moths, the adult feeds only on nectar. For the larval stage—the caterpillar—most butterfly species must locate a specific host plant because the caterpillar would die rather than eat anything else. After mating, a female butterfly flutters slowly near plants, touching down and tasting them through sensory organs on her front legs. When she finds a plant acceptable for her kind, she will deposit one or more eggs, and then wander off looking for other host plants . . . or die.

**Here is a list of pests and their controls:**

**Aphids.** Small, pear-shaped insects, they have piercing, sucking mouthparts and, in some cases, can transmit diseases. Aphids stunt and deform leaves and stems and produce a sugary, sticky substance called honeydew. A black fungus quickly spreads on the honeydew and slows down photosynthesis. This fungus is called sooty mold. *Controls: Aphids usually can be sprayed off with a strong jet of water from a hose. Repeat if they return. If they persist, try a soap-based insecticide or products with malathion or Pyrethrin. Some biological controls are green lacewings, lady beetles, and aphid lions. Some natural controls are applying rubbing alcohol with cotton swabs, horticultural soap, and ultrafine horticultural oil.*

**Beetles.** Beetles and weevils belong to a group called *Coleoptera*. Weevils, or curculios, are beetles that have jaws at the end of long snouts. Some have a larval stage that feeds on plants. An example is the black vine weevil, which is most destructive to garden plants. Many other species of beetles, including the June beetle and the rose chafer, affect garden plants. The **Japanese beetle,** a metallic green and coppery maroon insect, is one of the most destructive pests east of the Mississippi. They chew the leaves and stems of some 200 species of perennials, ruin roses, basil, and other favorites, completely devouring those they like. If there are wild grape vines on your property, root them out; they are an attractive host plant for the Japanese beetle. The grub stage is devastating to lawns and gardens. Apply Milky Spore control or a grub control product to the lawn and gardens now and again next year, and there should be fewer Japanese beetles in the future. But that won't stop them from flying in. *Controls: Japanese beetle traps are effective, providing they are placed far away from the plantings you are trying to protect rather than among them. If the infestation is minor, beetles can be picked off by hand. Insecticides containing Neem, rotenone, or Sevin insecticide control many of the negative beetles.*

**Bugs.** True bugs belong to the *Hemiptera* family and do their damage by piercing and sucking. Examples are squash bugs, stink bugs, and the tarnished plant bug. *Controls: Products containing Sevin insecticide are best, along with Pyrethrin or malathion. These are most effective when the bugs are in an early stage of development.*

**Caterpillars.** Caterpillars are the immature stage of moths and butterflies. Their mouthparts chew holes in the leaves, stems, and flowers of most everything. Caterpillars may be smooth or fuzzy and range in size from very small to the huge tomato hornworm. They include leaf rollers and tent makers. Among them are other destructive pests such as the gypsy moth and tent caterpillar. *Controls: One of the best ways to get rid of a minor infestation is to pick the critters off by hand. The other way is to spray with a biological control such as Bacillus*

*thuringiensis. Other controls are Sevin or malathion insecticide, Pyrethrin, or rotenone, or Permethrin.*

**Leafminers.** Leafminers can be the larval stage of small flies, moths, and beetles. Over seven hundred kinds of leafminers affect plants in North America. Leafminers burrow between the upper and lower epidermis of the leaf, making irregular serpentine tunnels. *Controls: Spray with a product containing malathion or Pyrethrin. Sprays must be applied before the larvae hatch out and enter the leaf. Once inside, the only effective control is a leaf systemic insecticide. An alternative is to cut off the affected foliage; columbine and some plants affected by leafminers generally grow back healthy.*

**Mealybugs.** Mealybugs are one-eighth of an inch long and have a mealy, waxy covering. They lay eggs on the undersides of leaves and affect stems, roots, and foliage. Like aphids, they exude honeydew. The presence of sooty mold is an indicator that mealybugs, aphids, or soft scale is present. Mealybugs affect a wide range of hosts, including ferns, ficus, and African violets. *Controls: Lady beetles are a predator control and are available from biological companies. Spraying with horticultural soaps and ultrafine horticultural oils controls mealybugs.*

**Scales.** Soft and hard scales have piercing, sucking mouthparts. The crawler stage is mobile. After that, the insect becomes stationary. Hard scales resemble tiny oyster shells and occur in great numbers. Soft scales are larger, more cup-shaped, and are especially destructive to houseplants. *Controls: Ultra-fine horticulture oils and horticultural soaps are effective controls.*

**Whiteflies.** These tiny whiteflies erupt into clouds of insects when the plant is touched, and then settle back. Their piercing, sucking mouthparts stunt and yellow the host plant. Sooty mold may follow. *Controls: The most effective control is to spray four times with an insecticide, five to seven days apart. Ultrafine horticultural oil or insecticidal soaps may be used. Pyrethrin and malathion are also effective. The undersides are where whiteflies cling, so be sure to spray there most thoroughly. Insecticidal soap can handle small infestations. For persistent infestations, use insecticides based on seeds of the Neem tree or Permethrin.*

## Botanical and Natural Controls for Common Insect Pests and Diseases

**Copper.** Use fungicidal formulations. *Use to control: Blackspot, peach leaf curl, powdery mildew, rusts, and bacterial diseases such as fire blight, bacterial leaf spots, and wilt.*

# Pests, Diseases, & Controls

**Crab shells.** Crab shells are the crushed shells of crabs, crab meal, currently sold only by wholesalers. A source of nitrogen must be provided, such as dried blood or cottonseed meal. *Use to control: Harmful nematodes. Apply crab meal at the rate of 5 pounds per 100 square feet.*

**Diatomaceous earth.** This is a powdery substance mined from fossilized silica shells that are the remains of an algae. Physical contact destroys soft-bodied insects. Rain and high humidity may render it less ineffective. *Use to control: Ants, aphids, caterpillars, cockroaches, leafhoppers, slugs, snails, and thrips.*

**Horticultural oils.** These are botanical oils sprayed on the egg and immature stages of insects to smother them. *Use to control: Woolly adelgids (which do so much damage to Canadian hemlocks), aphids, cankerworms, leafhoppers, leaf rollers, mealybugs, mites, psyllids, scale, tent caterpillars, webworms.* Note: *Spraying with horticultural oils can temporarily remove the blue in blue hostas and Colorado blue spruce. Never spray during droughts, and always water deeply before applying.*

**Horticultural soaps.** This control dates back to the late 1800s. *Use to control: Soft-bodied insects such as aphids, fruit flies, fungus gnats, lacebugs, leafhoppers, mealybugs, psyllids, scale, scale crawlers, spittle bug, thrips, whiteflies.* Note: *Water deeply before using. Do not use on plants under stress, especially drought. Do not use on plants you have just set out, or on delicate plants such as ferns and lantana.*

**Neem.** These products are derivatives of various parts of the Neem tree (*Azadirachta indica*). Neem is a broad-spectrum repellent, growth regulator, feeding inhibitor, and contact insect poison. It is partially systemic. The most effective formulation is made from the extract of the Neem seed. It also controls certain diseases. *Use to control: Aphids, leafminers, gypsy moths, loopers, mealybugs, thrips, mites, crickets, mosquitoes, lace flies, flea beetles.*

**Pyrethrin.** This is an extract of the flowers of *Chrysanthemum cinerariifolium*. *Use to control: Many piercing, sucking, and chewing insects such as ants, aphids, beetles, cockroaches, coddling moths, grasshoppers, leafhoppers, Japanese beetles, leafminers, loopers, Mexican bean and potato beetles, spider mites, stink bugs, ticks, thrips, weevils, whiteflies.*

**Rotenone.** Rotenone is a very old botanical pesticide, first used in the mid-1800s. It is prepared from the roots of the tropical plant *Lonchocarpus*. *Use to control: Aphids, beetles, caterpillars, Colorado potato beetle, thrips.*

**Ryania.** This is a powdered extract from the roots and stems of the South American shrub, *Ryania speciosa*. *Use to control: Caterpillars, corn earworms, European corn borer, leaf beetles, thrip.*

**Sabadilla.** Sabadilla is made from the grinding of the seeds of the Sabadilla plant. *Use to control: True bugs, caterpillars, Mexican bean beetle, thrips.*

**Ultrafine horticultural oils.** These are dense refined oils, some based on petroleum and others on vegetables such as cottonseed and soybeans. When sprayed on plants, they smother insects in the egg and immature stages, and they control certain diseases. *Use to control: Blackspot, mildew, and certain insects including adelgids, aphids, leafhoppers, mealybugs, mites, scale.* Note: *A Cornell University control for mildew is to spray with a solution consisting of 1 tablespoon of ultrafine oil and 1 tablespoon of baking soda dissolved in 1 gallon of water.*

**Wettable sulfur.** This is a mined mineral. *Use to control: Blackspot, leaf spot, mites, powdery mildew, rusts, and other plant diseases.*

## Chemical Controls for Common Insect Pests and Diseases

**Carbaryl** (Sevin). *Use to control: Beetles, caterpillars, Japanese beetles, mealybug, thrip.*

# Pests, Diseases, & Controls

**Mancozeb, manzate.** *Use to control: Fungal diseases (especially rust on asters and hollyhocks), anthracnose, and botrytis blight.*

**Sevin** (see Carbaryl).

**Malathion.** *Use to control: Aphids, beetles, leafhopper, leafminer, mealybug, spider mites, thrips, and whitefly.*

**Parzate** (see Mancozeb, Manzate).

**Permethrin.** *Use to control: A wide range of insects, including whitefly.*

## Common Non-Insect Pests and Controls

**Nematodes.** Nematodes are microscopic worm-like creatures. Some feed on roots, others feed on foliage. Endoparasitic nematodes enter the root, causing galls. An example is root-knot nematode. Others are cyst nematodes, such as the golden nematode of potatoes. There are ectoparasitic forms that feed on the outside of the roots. Symptoms are a yellowing and stunting of the plant, lack of vigor, and wilting during hot weather. *Controls: Growing orange French marigolds for three months and tilling them into the soil before planting has been effective. Also effective is the application of ground crab shells. Scatter on the ground and dig into the soil. A source is Neptone's Harvest Organics, 88 Commerical Street, Gloucester, MA 01930, phone 1-800-259-4769.*

**Spider mites.** Spider mites are so tiny you need a magnifying glass to see them. They can attack all parts of a plant but are most prevalent under the leaf. These piercing, sucking pests cause a yellowing of the plant, and finally result in a rusty and sometimes silvery look to the leaf. For a positive identification, shake the perennial over a white pad, and if little dots move on the paper, you have spider mites. Roses, indoor plants in hot dry conditions, and evergreens in dry airless corners are especially susceptible. *Controls: Hosing the plant down regularly discourages spider mite activity. Insecticidal soaps, ultrafine horticultural oils, and miticides can be used.*

**Slugs and snails.** These plant pests feed on lush foliage, leaving holes in the leaf. Irregular, shiny, slimy trails are a telltale sign. Complete defoliation can occur on some lush-leaved annuals and perennials, hostas, for example. *Controls: Diatomaceous earth, iron phosphate (Sluggo), slug and snail bait, beer in shallow aluminum plates or tuna fish cans, or commercially available traps.*

## Common Diseases and Controls

**Bacterial disease.** Bacteria is not a fungus, and although the symptoms may be similar, in order to control the causative agent, you must use a bacteriacide such as copper fungicide. *Controls: Copper fungicide, Kocide 101, Agri-Strep or sulfur.*

**Botrytis grey mold (Botrytis blight).** Symptoms are a grayish-to-brown powdery covering on buds, leaves, and stems. This disease affects many perennials, including peonies. *Controls: Sulfur, Daconil 2728, Immunox.*

**Foliar diseases.** Symptoms on perennials are leaf spots and blight that can be bacterial or fungal in origin. *Controls: Sulfur, copper fungicides, Daconil, Mancozeb, Immunox.*

**Leaf spots.** Most gardeners encounter this as "blackspot." Leaf spots can be caused by a bacterial or fungal agent. Examples are blackspot of roses and leaf spot on tall bearded iris. *Controls: Copper fungicide, Daconil, horticultural oil, Immunox, sulfur.*

**Powdery mildew.** This fungus covers buds, stems, and leaves with a white-gray powdery substance. High humidity increases the severity of powdery mildew. If you water often with underground sprinkling systems, you may find this disease difficult to control. Powdery mildew is commonly found on asters, monarda, and phlox. *Controls: If it appears in your garden, when buying new plants, go for those advertised as mildew resistant. Roses, lilacs, and many other garden favorites are also* susceptible. Wide spacing for good air circulation and air movement helps. Apply sulfur, ultrafine horticultural oil, copper fungicide, Immunox, Bayleton.

**Root and stem rot.** Symptoms are the wilting and rapid death of the plant. The crown or rhizome of the plant may be wet or slimy. The cause may be bacterial or fungal. *Controls: For fungal causes, use Terrachlor or Mancozeb. For bacterial causes, use copper fungicides, Kocide 101, Agri-Strep.*

**Rust disease.** This form of fungus may be a single or double host disease. The first indication is yellow or pale spots on the upper surface of the leaf, with powdery orange spores visible on the bottom of the leaf. Asters, chrysanthemums, lily-of-the-valley, and hollyhocks are common hosts. *Controls: Any fungicidal control labeled for rust. Also, sulfur, copper fungicide, Daconil, Immunox, Mancozeb.*

**Viral diseases.** These diseases are not fungal or bacterial in origin but in fact are particles of protein and genetic material so small that an electron microscope is needed to see the virus. Piercing, sucking insects commonly spread viral diseases. Viral diseases may be difficult to diagnose. Symptoms are a mottling or mosaic discoloration of the leaf or ring spots. *Control: No known control except removing the infected plant.*

## Common Animal Pests and Controls

**Bears.** Where bears are a problem, they may come to bird and hummingbird feeders. They harvest berries and sometimes take your pets. If there are bear sightings near you, take in bird feeders and other attractions.

**Birds.** Our feathered friends are beautiful, lovable, inspiring, and useful in that they eat insects, some good and some bad. They also eat berries and fruit, your kind as well as theirs; seeds you give them and seeds you don't; and sunflowers.

- A bird mesh cover is almost the only way to protect fruit that birds want to eat.

- Cover ponds with bird netting to keep the fish safe from herons and other expert fishermen.

**Deer.** The most destructive of all the wild creatures that visit our gardens is the deer. New repellents come on the market every season, but at this writing we know of none that has proven to be a **permanent** deterrent.

When deer really want what you've got, they come on in and get it in spite of flashing lights, jets of water, ultra sound devices, evil smelling egg and protein sprays, predator odors, bitter Bitrex, hot pepper wax, garlic, and systemic repellants. Deer-Off® can be used on fruits and vegetables as well as flowers, trees, and shrubs; when tested by Rutgers University, it lasted for up to three months. Some nurseries successfully protect clients' plants with their own deterrent sprays and may sell you their version. Some gardeners have luck discouraging deer by hanging old pantyhose containing human or canine hair around the property. However, most deterrents of this type fail to keep deer away once they get used to it.

Here are approaches that have some effect:

- **Don't invite deer by planting Class A fatal attractions: Apple or pear trees.** If you have fruit trees, be sure to harvest the fruits daily before the deer get to them. Arborvitae, rhododendrons, and broadleaved evergreens are winter favorites, along with shrub althea and hydrangeas. Hostas and other big, lush-leaved plants, phlox, 'Autumn Joy' and other *Sedum spectabile* varieties, tomatoes, peas, beans, and other leafy vegetables are summer favorites. Roses, raspberries, and other members of the *Rosa* family—deer relish them all.

• **Protect small endangered plantings,** beds of hostas and daylilies for example, by screening them with enclosures of deer fencing or chicken wire supported by wooden or metal stakes. Deer generally avoid small, enclosed spaces that could be traps. Protect large plantings with bird netting.

• **Enclose your property or gardens. A single strand of electric wire 30 inches high** with a stake every 20 feet and baited with peanut butter can be effective. Close the peanut butter into a square of aluminum foil, and crimp it on to the wire every 20 feet. The deer nibble the peanut butter and, without being really hurt, learn to avoid the fence.

• **Enclose your property with a deer fence 8 to 10 feet high** supported by a post every 40 feet. This high, tensile steel fencing can be unobtrusive.

• **Train a dog** to run deer off your property without leaving it.

• **Discourage visits by positioning a variety of alarming and distasteful smells** where deer customarily enter your grounds, and change the smells often. For example, hang at the height of a deer's nose tubes of crushed garlic, or dog urine, or Irish Spring or lavender soap, or human hair dampened with odorous lotions. Place a different scent at each entry point. And, **this is crucial,** change each deterrent every four to six weeks while the weather is warm enough to volatilize scents.

• **For winter, wrap rhododendrons, arborvitae, and other species that deer love in burlap or chicken wire.**

• **Try new plants from those on the list of deer-resistant plants** at André and Mark Viette's site, www.inthe-gardenradio.com.

**Moles and Voles.** You think "moles" when you see tunnels heaving the lawn and blame them when perennials disappear and bulbs move around. But they are innocent. Moles eat bugs, grubs, and worms only. The culprits are voles, *Microtus* species. Often called pine and meadow mice, these small rodents are reddish-brown to gray, 2 to 4 inches long, and have short tails, blunt faces, and tiny eyes and ears. They live in extensive tunnel systems usually less than a foot deep with entrances an inch or two across.

Protecting the plant is easier than getting rid of voles. They dislike tunneling through coarse material. Keep them away by planting with VoleBloc or PermaTill, which are bits of non-toxic, light, long-lasting aggregates like pea gravel with jagged edges. The stuff promotes rooting. Here's how to apply it:

**Established plantings.** Dig a 4-inch wide, 12-inch deep moat around the drip line of perennials under attack, and fill it with VoleBloc, and mulch with VoleBloc.

**New plantings.** Prepare a planting hole 2 inches deeper than the rootball(s), and layer in 2 inches of VoleBloc. Set the rootball in place, and backfill with VoleBloc. Mulch with more VoleBloc.

**If vole damage appears in winter,** bait the main area around the plants with a rodenticide, pull the mulch apart, spray the crown lightly with a repellent, and put the mulch back in place.

**Tunnels heaved in the lawn between March and October** are apt to be moles hunting for grubs. Apply a grub control such as Merit or Marathon to kill off the grubs, and the moles will find another supermarket.

**Rabbits, woodchucks, raccoons, and other rodents.** Try chemical fungicide formulations such as Thiram (Arasan) and hot pepper wax. Or fence gardens with 6 foot high chicken wire that starts 24 inches underground. If you have woodchucks to deal with, leave the chicken wire loose and floppy, not stiff enough to climb. Keeping raccoons out of the vegetable garden requires enclosing your garden overhead as well; keeping them from fishing in your water garden may require covering the pond with netting.

# Public Gardens

You can learn so much about plants and garden design by wandering the paths of public gardens! We love visiting gardens close to home where we know that the trees, shrubs, and perennials make it through our own winters. And we love seeing what the public gardens in other parts of New York can grow that we haven't dared try. The best time to visit is when the gardens are peaking—in most New York public gardens May and June are sure to offer lavish displays. The other best time to visit public gardens is when you can see what plants the pros use to keep color in the garden in fall and winter.

**Bailey Arboretum**
Bayville Road and Leeks Lane
Locust Valley, NY 11560
516-676-4497

**Boscobel**
RD 2, NY 9D
Garrison-on-Hudson, NY 10524
914-265-3638

**Brooklyn Botanic Garden**
1000 Washington Avenue
Brooklyn, NY 11225
718-622-4433

**Buffalo and Erie County Botanical Gardens**
South Park Avenue and McKinley Parkway
Buffalo, NY 14218
716-828-1040

**Clark Garden of the Brooklyn Botanic Garden**
193 I.U. Billets Road
Albertson, NY 11507
516-621-7568

**Conservatory Garden**
Central Park Conservatory
839 Fifth Avenue
New York, NY 10021
212-860-1330

**Cornell Plantations**
One Plantations Road
Ithaca, NY 14850
607-255-3020

**Cutler Botanic Garden**
840 Front Street
Binghamton, NY 13905
607-772-8953

**Demonstration Garden**
Cornell Cooperative Extension, Suffolk County
246 Griffin Avenue
Riverhead, NY 11901
516-727-7850

**Donald M. Kendall Sculpture Gardens at Pepsico**
700 Anderson Hill Road
Purchase, NY 10577
914-253-2000

**Dr. E. M. Mills Memorial Rose Garden**
Thorndon Park
Syracuse, NY 13204
315-473-4333

**Gardens at George Eastman House**
900 East Avenue
Rochester, NY 14607
716-271-3361

**George Landis Arboretum**
Lape Road
Esperance, NY 12066
518-875-6935

**Highland Park**
Monroe County Parks
375 Westfall Road
Rochester, NY 14620
716-244-8079

**Innesfree Garden**
Tyrell Road off US 44
Millbrook, NY 12545
914-677-8000

**Italian Gardens, Vanderbilt Historic Site**
US 9
Hyde Park, NY
914-229-6432

# Public Gardens

**International Bonsai Arboretum**
1070 Marrin Road
West Henrietta, NY 14596-9623
716-334-2595

**Kykuit**
The Rockefeller Estate
Pocantico Hills, NY 10591
Open by reservation only
914-631-9491

**Liberty Hyde Bailey Hortorium**
467 Mann Library
Cornell University
Ithaca, NY 14853
607-256-2131

**Lyndhurst**
635 South Broadway
Tarrytown, NY 10591
914-631-4481

**Maplewood Rose Garden**
County of Monroe Department of Parks
39 West Main Street
Rochester, NY 14614
716-428-5301

**Mary Flagler Cary Arboretum/**
**Institute of Ecosystem Studies**
Route 44A
Millbrook, NY 12545
914-677-5359

**Mohonk Mountain House Gardens**
100 Mountain Rest Road
New Paltz, NY 12561
914-255-1000

**Nassau County Bailey Arboretum**
Bayville Road
Locust Valley, NY 11560
516-676-4497

**New York Botanical Garden**
200 Street and Southern Boulevard
Bronx, NY 10458
212-220-8700

**Old Westbury Gardens**
71 Old Westbury Road
Old Westbury, NY 11568
516-333-0048

**Planting Fields Arboretum**
Planting Fields Road
Oyster Bay, NY 11771
516-922-9201

**Queens Botanical Garden**
43-50 Main Street
Flushing, NY 11355
718-886-3800

**Staten Island Botanical Garden**
1000 Richmond Terrace
Staten Island, NY 10301
718-273-8200

**Stonecrop Gardens**
Cold Spring, NY 10516
914-265-2000

**S.U.N.Y. Agricultural Technical College**
Department Ornamental Horticulture
Farmingdale, NY 11735

**Vassar College Arboretum**
Vassar College
Raymond Avenue
Poughkeepsie, NY 12601
914-452-7000

**Wave Hill**
The Bronx
675 West 252nd Street
Bronx, NY 10471
212-549-2055

# Resources

## Mail-Order Nurseries with a Wide Selection

**André Viette Farm & Nursery**
994 Long Headow Road
P. O. Box 1109
Fishersville, VA 22939
*Perennials, daylilies, grasses*

**Arborvillage Farm Nursery**
P.O. Box 227
Holt, MO 64048
*Trees and shrubs*

**Arrowhead Alpines**
P.O. Box 857
Fowlerville, MI 48836
*Alpine plants*

**B & D Lilies**
P.O. Box 2007
Port Townsend, WA 98368
*Lilies*

**W. Atlee Burpee & Co.**
300 Park Avenue
Warminster, PA 18991
*Wide selection*

**Bluestone Perennials, Inc.**
7211 Middle Ridge Road
Madison, OH 44057-3096
*Perennials, shrubs*

**Borbeleta Gardens**
15974 Canby Avenue
Faribault, MN 55021
Phone: 507 334-2807
*Perennials, etc.*

**Brent and Becky's Bulbs**
7463 Heath Trail
Gloucester, VA 23601
*Specialists in bulbs*

**Carroll Gardens**
444 E. Main Street
Westminster, MD 21157
*Perennials, roses, shrubs, trees*

**Chiltern Seeds**
Bortree Stile
Ulverston
Cumbria LA12 7PB, England
*Seeds*

**Crownsville Nursery**
P.O. Box 797
Crownsville, MD 21032
*Perennials, grasses*

**Eastern Plant Specialties**
P.O. Box 226W
Georgetown, ME 04548
*Trees, shrubs, perennials, wildflowers*

**Ferry-Morse Seeds**
P.O. Box 1620
Fulton, KY 42041-0488
*Seeds, plants, bulbs*

**Forestfarm**
990 Temerow Road
Williams, OR 97544-9599
*Trees, shrubs, perennials*

**Heronswood Nursery**
7530 NE 288th Street
Kingston, WA 98346
*Perennials, trees, shrubs*

**High Country Gardens**
2902 Rufina Street
Santa Fe, NM 87505
*Perennials, roses, grasses*

**Jackson & Perkins**
1 Rose Lane
Medford, OR 97501-0702
*Roses, perennials, bulbs*

**Johnny's Selected Seeds**
184 Foss Hill Road
Albion, MN 04910
*Vegetables, herbs, flowers*

**John Scheepers, Inc.**
23 Tulip Drive
Bantam, CT 06750
*Bulbs, kitchen garden seeds*

**Klehm's Song Sparrow Perennial Farm**
13101 E. Rye Road
Avalon, WI 53505
*Peonies, perennials, shrubs,
    trees, roses*

**Kurt Bluemel, Inc.**
22740 Greene Lane
Baldwin, MD 21013
*Grasses, perennials*

**Oikos Tree Crops**
P.O. Box 19425
Kalamazoo, MI 49019-0425
*Trees, shrubs*

**Old House Gardens**
536 Third Street
Ann Arbor, MI 48103
*Heirloom bulbs*

**George W. Park Seed Co.**
1 Parkton Avenue
Greenwood, SC 29647-0001
*Vegetable and flower seeds,
    bulbs, plants*

**Plant Delights Nursery, Inc.**
9241 Sauls Road
Raleigh, NC 27603
*Perennials, grasses*

**Prairie Nursery, Inc.**
P.O. Box 306
Westfield, WI 53964
*Native wildflowers, native grasses*

# Resources

**Roslyn Nursery**
211 Burrs Lane
Dix Hills, NY 11746
Phone: 631-643-9347
*Trees, shrubs, perennials*

**Seed Savers Exchange**
3076 North Winn Road
Decorah, IA 52101
*Vegetable and flower seeds*

**Seeds of Change**
P.O. Box 15700
Santa Fe, NM 87506-5700
*Organically grown vegetable and flower
    seeds*

**Select Seeds**
180 Srickney Road
Union, CT 06076-4617
*Heirloom flower seeds, annuals,
    perennials*

**Shepherd's Garden Seeds**
30 Irene Street
Torrington, CT 06790
Tel: (800) 482 3638

**Siskiyou Rare Plant Nursery**
2825 Cummings Road
Medford, OR 97501
*Perennials, trees, shrubs, grasses*

**Stokes Seeds, Inc.**
P O Box 548, Buffalo, NY 14240
*Perennials*

**Thompson &. Morgan, Inc.**
P.O. Box 1308
Jackson, NJ 08527-0308
*Seeds, plants, bulbs*

**Wavecrest Nursery**
2509 Lakeshore Drive
Fennville, MI 49408
*Trees, shrubs, perennials*

**Wayside Gardens**
1 Garden Lane
Hodges, SC 29695-0001
*Everything —Perennials, shrubs,
    roses, bulbs*

**We-Du Nurseries**
Route 5, Box 724
Marion, NC 28752-9338
*Perennials, wildflowers*

**White Flower Farm**
P. O. Box 50
Litchfield, CT 06759-0050
*Perennials, shrubs, roses, bulbs*

**Wildseed Farms**
P. O. Box 3000
Fredericksburg, TX 78624
*Wildflower seeds*

## Mail-Order Catalogs
**(Tender Perennials, Annuals, Tropicals, Houseplants, Bromeliads, Bougainvilleas, Cactus, Orchids, Pineapples, Begonias, Gesneriads, and African Violets)**

**Banana Tree, Inc.**
715 Northampton Street
Easton, PA 18042

**Davidson-Wilson Greenhouse, Inc.**
R.R. 2, Box 168
Crawfordsville, IN 47933

**Glasshouse Works**
Church Street
Stewart, OH 45778

**Going Bananas**
24401 SW 197 Avenue
Homestead, FL 33031

**Good Scents**
R.R. 2, P O Box 168
Crawfordsville, IN 47933

**Kartuz Greenhouse**
P. O. Box 790
Vista, CA 92085

**Lauray of Salisbury**
493 Undermountain Road, RT 41
Salisbury, CT 06068

**Logee's Greenhouse, Ltd.**
141 North Street
Danielson, CT 06239

**Lyndon Lyon Greenhouse, Inc.**
P. O. Box 249
Dolgeville, NY 13329

**Stokes Tropicals**
P. O. Box 9868
New Iberia, LA 70562

**Sunshine State Tropicals**
6329 Alaska Avenue
New Port Richey, FL 34653

## Mail-Order Catalogs for Roses

**Chamblee's Rose Nursery**
10926 US Highway 69 North
Tyler, TX 75706-8742
Phone: 800 256-7673

**David Austin Roses, Ltd.**
15059 Highway 64 West
Tyler, TX 75704
Phone: 800 328-8893

# Resources

**Edmund's Roses**
6235 SW Kahle Road
Wilsonville, OR 97070-9727
Phone: 888 481-7673

**Hardy Roses for the North**
Box 2048
Grand Forks, BC Canada VOH 1HO
Phone: 604 442-8442

**Heirloom Old Garden Roses**
24062 NE Riverside drive
St Paul, OR 97137
PHone: 503 538-1576

**High Country Roses**
P. O. Box 148
Jensen, UT 84035-0148
Phone: 800 552-2082

**Historical Roses**
1657 W Jackson Street
Painesville, OH 44077
Phone: 216 357-7270

**Jackson & Perkins Co.**
1 Rose Lane
Medford, OR 97501-0702
Phone: 800 292-4769

**Lowe's Own-Root Roses**
6 Sheffield Road
Nashua, NH 03062
Phone: 603 888-2214

**Meilland Star Roses**
P. O. Box 249
Cutler, CA 93615
Phone: 800 457-1859

**Nor'East Minature Roses, Inc.**
P. O. Box 307
Rowley, MA 01969-0607
Phone: 800 426-6485

**The Antique Roses Emporium**
9300 Lueckemeyer Road
Brenham, TX 77833
Phone: 800 441-0002

## Mail-Order Catalogs Water Plants, Ponds, and Pools

**Lilypons Water Gardens**
6800 Lilypons Road
Buckeystown, MD 21717
Phone: 800 999-5459

**Gilberg Farms**
2172 Highway O
Robertsville, MO 63072
Phone: 636 451-2530

**Springdale Water Gardens**
P. O. Box 546
Greenville, VA 24440-0546
Phone: 800 420-5459

## Nurseries with Good Plant Selection

**Atlantic Nurseries**
691 Deer Park Avenue
Dix Hills, NY 11746
Phone: 631 586-6242

**Brookville Nurseries**
5300 Northern Boulevard
Glen Head, NY 11545

**Helderledge Farm**
435 Picard Road
Altamont, NY 12009
Phone: 518 765-4702

**Hickory Hollow Nursery
and Garden Center**
713 Route 17 South
Tuxedo, NY 10987
Phone: (845-351-7226)

**Hicks Nurseries**
100 Jericho Turnpike
Westbury, NY 11590
Phone: 516 334-0066

**Martin Viette Nurseries**
6050 Route 25 A
East Norwich, NY 11732
Phone: 516 922-5530

**Matterhorn Nurseries**
227 Summit Park Road
Spring Valley, NY 10977
Phone: 845 354-5986

**Nabels Nurseries**
1485 Mamaroneck Avenue
White Plains, NY 10605
Phone: 914 949-3963

**Palmiters Garden Nursery**
2675 Geneseo Road
Avon, NY 14414
Phone: 585 226-3073

**Rosedale Nurseries**
51 Saw Mill River Road
Hawthorne, NY 10532
Phone: 914 769-1300

# Glossary

**Alkaline soil:** soil whose pH greater is than 7.0. It lacks acidity, often because it has limestone in it.

**Acid soil:** soil whose pH is less than 7.0. A pH of 6.0 to 6.9 is mildly acid. The pH in which the widest range of flowers thrive is slightly acid, in the pH 5.5 to 6.5 range. Except for areas where limestone is prevalent, as it is in the northwest corner of Connecticut, most garden soil in America is in this range. A pH of 5.5 to 6.5 is also suited to many plants described as acid-loving.

**All-purpose fertilizer:** available in 3 forms: powdered, liquid, or granular. It contains balanced proportions of the three important nutrients—nitrogen (N), phosphorus (P), and potassium (K). It is suitable for most plants.

**Annual:** a plant that lives its entire life in one season. It germinates, produces flower, sets seed, and dies the same year.

**Balled and burlapped:** a tree or shrub grown in the field and dug, whose root- and soil ball is wrapped with protective burlap or other covering tied with twine. Abbreviated B&B.

**Bare root:** describes plants without any soil around their roots, often packaged by mail-order suppliers. The rule of thumb is to soak the roots 10 to 12 hours before planting them.

**Bedding plants:** usually annuals that are massed (planted in large groups) in a bed for maximum show.

**Beneficial insects:** insects and their larvae that prey on pest organisms and their eggs. Some that are well-known include ladybugs and praying mantis.

**Botanical names:** plant names given in Latin accurately identifying the genus, species, subspecies, variety, and form. Here's an example: *Picea abies* forma *pendula* is the 1) genus, 2) species, and 3) form; it is the botanical name for Weeping Norway Spruce. *Picea abies* 'Nidiformis' is the a) genus, 2) species, and 3) variety. When the varietal name is between single quotes, it's what we call a "cultivar"—a cultivated variety, which means a variety that has been cultivated and given a name of its own.

**Bract:** a modified leaf structure resembling a petal that appears close behind the flower. In some flowers, those of flowering dogwoods, for example, the bract may be more colorful than the flower itself.

**Bud union:** a thickened area above the crown on the main stem of a woody plant. This is the point at which a desirable plant has been grafted, or budded, onto a strong but less ornamental rootstock.

**Canopy:** the overhead branching area of a tree, including its foliage.

**Cold hardiness:** the ability of a plant to survive the winter cold in a particular area or Zone.

**Cold frame:** In cold regions where the soil is slow to warm in spring, a cold frame is a great place to start seedlings for the vegetable garden and the flower beds. It is also a great place to store dormant plants over winter—for example, tender perennials that can stand some chill, like geraniums, begonias, and caladium corms.

**Common names:** there is no such thing as an accurate "common name" for a plant. Many are British antiques included for their charm—for example, love-in-a-mist, and wild fennel. Names commonly used for plants are rarely common the world over, or even in a single country or state. Because they can vary from region to region, they are not as much help in locating plants as the scientific botanical names. Botanical names find their way into common gardener language. Examples are: impatiens, begonia, petunia, salvia, zinnia, aster, astilbe, phlox, iris. In time, you will find yourself remembering many of the botanical names of the plants that interest you most, rather than their common names.

**Compost:** organic matter, such as leaves, weeds, grass clippings, and seaweed, that has undergone progressive decomposition until it is reduced to a soft, fluffy texture. Soil that has been amended with compost holds air and water better and also has improved drainage.

# Glossary

**Corm:** a thick energy-storing modified stem, similar to a bulb, which is found at the base of a plant such as a caladium.

**Crown:** the point on a plant where the roots meet the stems.

**Cultivar:** the word stands for "cultivated variety." Cultivars are varieties named by growers. They are developed, or selected, from natural variations and hybrids. Always given in single quotes.

**Deadhead:** the process of removing faded flower heads from plants in order to improve their appearance, stop unwanted seed production, and most often to encourage more flowering.

**Deciduous:** trees and shrubs that lose their leaves in fall, a sign the plant is going into dormancy for the period of weather ahead.

**Division:** the splitting apart of perennial plants in order to create several smaller plants. Division is a way to control the size of a plant, multiply your holdings, and also to renovate crowded plants that are losing their vitality.

**Dormancy:** the period, usually the winter, when perennial plants temporarily cease above-ground growth and rest. However, heat and drought can throw plants into summer dormancy. Certain plants, for example, oriental poppies and certain bulbs, can have their dormancy period in summer.

**Drought tolerant:** describes plants that tolerate dry soil for varying periods of time. They are often succulent and/or have tap roots.

**Exfoliate/exfoliating:** peel off in layers, as with bark.

**Established:** the point at which a new planting begins to show new growth and is well rooted in the soil, indicating the plant has recovered from transplant shock.

**Evergreen:** herbaceous woody plants that do not lose all their foliage annually with the onset of winter.

**Fertility/fertile:** refers to the soil's content of the nutrients needed for sturdy plant growth. Nutrient availability is affected by pH levels.

**Foliar feeding:** refers to the practice of making applications of dissolved fertilizer and some insecticides to just the plant's foliage. Leaf tissue absorbs liquid quickly.

**Floret:** a tiny, single flower, usually one of many forming a cluster.

**Germinate/germination:** refers to the sprouting of a seed, a plant's first stage of development.

**Graft (union):** the point on the stem of a strong, woody plant where a stem (scion) from another plant (usually one that is more ornamental) has been inserted into understock so they will join together. That point is called the bud union.

**Hardscape:** the permanent, structural, non-plant part of a landscape, such as walls, sheds, pools, patios, arbors, and walkways.

**Hardy:** able to withstand cold.

**Herbaceous:** plants with soft stems that die back with frost.

**Hot bed:** A hot bed is essentially a cold frame that has some insulation, and is equipped with an underground heating cable regulated by a thermostat. It allows you to start seeds and to grow seedlings earlier in spring than a cold frame and is used as a cold frame at other seasons.

**Humus:** almost completely decomposed organic materials such as leaves, plant foliage, and manures.

**Hybrid:** a plant that is the product of deliberate or natural cross-pollination between two or more plants of the different species or genera.

**Inflorescence:** the method of bearing flowers, often used in reference to the flower heads of ornamental grasses.

**Leader:** the main stem of a tree.

**Loam:** a mix of sand, clay, and humus. A loam is the best soil for gardening.

# Glossary

**Microclimate:** pockets on a property that are warmer or cooler than the listed climatic zone. Hilly spots, valleys, nearness to reflective surfaces or wind-breaks, and proximity to large bodies of water can all contribute to altering the surrounding temperature.

**Mulch:** a layer of material (natural or man-made) used to cover soil to protect it from rain or wind erosion and to help maintain the soil temperature and moisture. Mulches also discourage weeds.

**Naturalize:** a plant that adapts and spreads in a landscape habitat. Some plants we think of as "native" are imports that have "naturalized"; for example, *Phlox drummondii*, the annual phlox, self-sows and has naturalized in sand in the Outer Banks of North Carolina.

**Nectar:** the sweet fluid produced by glands on flowers that attract pollinators such as bees and hummingbirds.

**Organic material, organic matter:** any substance that is derived from decomposed plants or animals.

**Organic fertilizer:** a fertilizer that is derived from anything that was living, such as bonemeal, fish emulsion, manure, plants.

**Peat moss:** acid organic matter from decomposed sphagnum mosses, often mixed into soil to raise its organic content and sometimes as a mild acidifier.

**Perennial:** a flowering plant that lives for more than one season; the foliage dies back to the crown with frost, but the roots survive the winter and generate new growth in the spring.

**Perennialize:** sometimes confused with "naturalize." The two words are not synonymous. Tulips may perennialize, that is come back for four years or more, but they don't become wild plants. "Naturalize" applies to a garden plant that becomes a wildflower of a region that is not its native habitat.

**pH:** pH is a measurement of the relative acidity (low pH) or alkalinity (high pH) of soil or water and is based on a scale of 1 to 14, pH 7.0 being neutral.

**Pinch:** to remove tender stems and/or leaves by pressing them between thumb and forefinger. The purpose is usually to deadhead or to encourage branching and compactness. Hand shearing achieves the same purpose on plants whose blooms are too small to pinch out one at a time, pinks, for example.

**Planting season:** refers to the best time to set out certain plants. The most vigorous growth occurs in spring. Early spring is the preferred planting time, particularly for woody plants and for some, but not all, species that react poorly to transplanting. Early fall, after summer's heat has gone by and before cold comes, is an excellent time for planting, provided your climate allows the roots two months or so to tie into the soil before cold shuts the plants down. Traditional planting seasons are spring and fall—plants growing in containers have added a new and valuable season to plant, the summer.

**Pollen:** the powdery grains on the anthers of a flower that are the plant's male sex cells. Pollen is transferred by wind and insects, and to a lesser extent by animals, to the female plants where they fertilize them.

**Polymer (water-holding polymers):** Gelatin-like organic molecules that absorb many times their size in water and are added to container soils to increase their water-holding capacity and reduce watering chores. An example is Soil Moist.

**Raceme:** describes a flower stalk where the blossoms are an arrangement of single-stalked florets along a tall stem, a spike.

**Rhizome:** an energy-storing modified stem, similar to a bulb, usually growing horizontally near the soil surface. The roots emerge from the bottom, and growth shoots up from the upper portion of the rhizome. Irises grow from rhizomes.

**Rootbound (or potbound):** the condition of a plant that has been confined in a container too long. Without space for expansion, the roots wrap around the rootball, mat at the bottom of the container, and grow through the drainage holes.

# Glossary

**Root division/rooted divisions:** sections of the crown of a plant, usually a perennial, that has been divided. This is often the source of containerized perennial plants. A root division will perform exactly like the parent plant.

**Rooted cuttings:** stem sections taken from perennials usually, or from woody plants, that have been handled so as to grow roots. Rooted cuttings will perform exactly like the parent plant.

**Seedling:** plantlets started from seed; flats and containers of annuals are usually seedlings. Seeds of hybrids can't be counted on to perform exactly as the parent did, although they may. This is why growers of quality plants sell root divisions or rooted cuttings of cultivars rather than seedlings.

**Self-sow:** some plants ripen their seeds, sow them freely, and the offspring appear as volunteers the following season.

**Semi-evergreen:** tending to be evergreen in a mild climate but behaving like a deciduous plant in a colder climate.

**Shearing:** the pruning technique where plant stems and branches are cut uniformly with long-bladed pruning shears or hedge trimmers. Shearing is also a fast and easy way to deadhead plants with many tiny blooms, e.g. pinks.

**Slow-release fertilizer:** fertilizer that does not dissolve in water and therefore releases its nutrients gradually. It is often granular and can be either organic or synthetic.

**Soil amendment:** anything added to change the composition of the soil. Most often the element called for is humus—compost.

**Starter solution:** a solution of organic or chemical fertilizer in which a rootball is dipped before planting to get it off to a quick start; used primarily with annuals, vegetables, and perennials.

**Sterile:** unable to bear seed.

**Succulent growth:** the production of (often unwanted) soft, fleshy leaves or stems; it can result from the over-use of fertilizers or severe pruning.

**Suckers:** shoots that form new stems that can be useful, or not, depending on the plant. Removing basal suckers, for exampled, keeps the parent plant strong and attractive.

**Summer dormancy:** in excessive heat some plants, including roses, slow or stop productivity. Fertilizing or pruning a somewhat dormant plant will stimulate it into growth.

**Tuber:** the end of an underground stem, a tuber generates roots below while the upper portion puts up succulent stems. Example: potatoes.

**Variegated:** foliage that is streaked, edged, or blotched with various colors—often green with yellow, cream, or white.

**Variety:** the only accurate names for plants are the scientific botanical names, and these are given in Latin—genus, species, subspecies, variety, and form. In botany, "variety" is reserved for variants of a species that occurs in the wild or natural habitat. It should not be used instead of, or confused with, "cultivated variety"—which has been shortened to "cultivar." Cultivars are horticulural selections.

**Wings:** the tissue that forms edges along the twigs of some woody plants, such as winged euonymus, or the flat, dried extension on some seeds, such as maple, that catch the wind and enable the seeds to fly away to land and grow in another place.

**Winter mulch:** light mulch applied usually after the ground freezes; pine boughs, straw, and ground leaves are typical.

**Zone, climate zone:** The USDA has divided the country according to winter low temperatures into Zones 1 to 11. Growers label plants with the number of the USDA Zones in which they are known to survive winter. New York goes from Zone 3 to Zone 6/7. A city garden often is five to ten degrees warmer than a nearby country garden, enough to change the climate zone.

# Bibliography

*The American Horticultural Society Flower Finder*, Jacqueline Hériteau and André Viette
*André Viette Gardening Guide*, Viette Staff
*Armitage's Manual of Annuals, Biennials, and Half-Hardy Perennials*, Allan M. Armitage

*Cathy Wilkinson Barash's Edible Flowers*, Cathy Wilkinson Barash
*Check List of Pyracantha Cultivars*, Donald R. Egolf and Ann O. Andrick
*Conifers for Your Garden*, Adrian Bloom

*Designing with Perennials*, Pamela J. Harper
*Discovering Annuals*, Graham Rice

*Eastern Butterflies*, Peterson Field Guides

*Fern Growers Manual*, Barbara Hoshizaki

*A Garden of Herbs*, Eleanor Sinclair Rohde
*The Gardener's Guide to Growing Hellebores*, Graham Rice and Elizabeth Strangman
*Gardening with Climbers*, Christopher Grey-Wilson and Victoria Matthews
*Gardening with Grasses*, Michael King and Piet Oudolf
*Garlic, Onions & Other Alliums*, Ellen Spector Platt
*Genus Hosta*, W. George Schmid
*Glorious Gardens*, Jacqueline Hériteau
*Good Housekeeping's Illustrated Encyclopedia of Gardening*, Hearst Publishing

*Hardy Geraniums*, Peter F. Yeo
*Heirloom Flowers*, Tovah Martin and Diane Whealy
*The Herb Society of America Encyclopedia of Herbs and Their Uses*, Deni Brown
*Herbaceous Perennial Plants*, Allan M. Armitage
*Herbaceous Perennials: Diseases and Insect Pests*, Margery L. Daughtrey and Morey Semel
*Herbs, Their Culture, and Uses*, Rosetta E. Clarkson
*Hollies: The Genus Index*, Fred C. Galle
*Hortus Third*, Staff of L. H. Bailey Hortorium, Cornell University
*The Hosta Book*, Paul Aden
*Houseplants*, Better Homes & Gardens

*Index of Common Garden Plants*, Mark Griffiths, RHS

*Jackson & Perkins Beautiful Roses Made Easy*, Terri Dunn, André Viette, & Mark Viette, Cool Springs Press
*Japanese Iris*, Currier McEwen

*Lawns: Your Guide to a Beautiful Lawn*, Nick Christians with Ashton Ritchie

*Manual of Cultivated Conifers*, P. Den Ouden and Dr. B. K. Boom
*The Manual of Woody Landscape Plants*, Michael A. Dirr
*Mid-Atlantic Gardener's Guide*, André and Mark Viette with Jacqueline Hériteau
*Morning Glories and Moonflowers*, Anne Halpin

*The National Arboretum Book of Outstanding Garden Plants*, Jacqueline Hériteau, H. M. Cathey, and the Staff of the National Arboretum

*Ornamental Grass Gardening*, Reinardt, Reinardt, and Moskowitz
*Ornamental Grasses: The Amber Wave*, Carol Ottesen
*Ortho's Complete Guide to Vegetables*, Jacqueline Hériteau

*Peonies*, Allan Rogers
*Perennial Garden Plants*, Graham Stuart Thomas
*Perennial Ground Covers*, David S. MacKenzie
*Perennials for American Gardens*, Ruth Rogers Clausen and Nicolas Ekstrom
*Plants That Merit Attention, Volume 1, Trees*, Janet M. Poor
*Pruning Made Easy*, Lewis Hill

*Rhododendrons of the World*, David G. Leach
*Rodale's All-New Encyclopedia of Organic Gardening*, Rodale Press
*Rose Gardening*, Elvin McDonald

*Shrubs and Vines for American Gardens*, Donald Wyman
*Siberian Iris*, Currier McEwen

*The Time-Life Complete Gardener: Perennials*, André Viette and Stephen Still

*The Vegetable Gardener's Bible*, Edward C. Smith

*Water Gardens*, Charles Thomas and Jacqueline Hériteau
*The Well-Tended Perennial Garden, Planting & Pruning Techniques*, Tracy DiSabato-Aust
*Wyman's Gardening Encyclopedia*, Donald Wyman

*The Year in Trees*, Timber Press

# Index

# Index

# Index

# Index

# Meet the Authors

*André Viette*

Radio host of the weekly three-hour live nationwide call-in radio program "In the Garden with André Viette," aired every Saturday from 8 to 11 am, a distinguished horticulturist, author, and lecturer, André owns the Viette Farm and Nursery in Fishersville, Virginia, (website: inthegardenradio.com) and is the former owner of the famous Martin Viette Nursery in Long Island, New York. A graduate of the Floriculture School of Cornell University, New York, instructor in horticulture at the Blue Ridge Community College, noted breeder of daylilies, and Past President of the Perennial Plant Association of America, André was honored in 2001 with the PPA Award of Merit for his contribution to the perennial plant industry. He holds the Garden Club of America 1999 Medal of Honor for his outstanding contribution to horticulture, and numerous other awards including Conservation Farmer of the Year. He has served on the Advisory Council of the National Arboretum, the Board of the American Horticultural Society, and is presently on the Board of the Lewis Ginter Botanical Garden and the Edith J. Carrier Arboretum. André is the recipient of the 2004 Liberty Hyde Bailey Award, the highest honor given by the American Horticultural Society.

*Mark Viette*

Nurseryman, lecturer, contributor to horticultural journals, and horticultural instructor at the Blue Ridge Community College, Mark Viette is alternate host as well as president and general manager of Viette Communications, which produces and distributes the national weekly radio call show, "In the Garden with André Viette." Mark is also director of marketing and sales for the André Viette Farm and Nursery. He holds a BS degree in horticulture from Virginia Tech and has completed five plant-finding trips to Europe and South America in search of exotic perennials to introduce to American home gardens.

*Jacqueline Hériteau*

Jacqueline (Jacqui) is the author of many noteworthy garden books, including *The National Arboretum Book of Outstanding Garden Plants* and the *Virginia Gardener's Guide*. With André, she co-authored *The American Horticultural Society Flower Finder* and the *Mid-Atlantic Gardener's Guide*. She is a Fellow of the Garden Writers Association of America, and her contribution to gardening literature won her the 1990 Communicator of the Year Award from the American Nursery & Landscape Association. Jacqui's most recent book is the *New England Gardener's Guide*, (Cool Springs Press, 2003) co-authored with her daughter, Holly Hunter Stonehill.

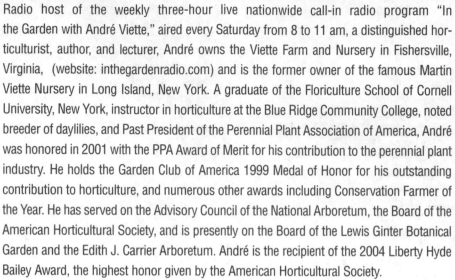

# NOTES

# NOTES

# NOTES

# NOTES

# NOTES

# NOTES

# NOTES

# NOTES

# NOTES